Actors and Icons
of the Ancient Theater

For Helga Rogers

ERIC CSAPO

Actors and Icons
of the Ancient Theater

WILEY-BLACKWELL

A John Wiley & Sons, Ltd., Publication

This edition first published 2010
© 2010 Eric Csapo

Blackwell Publishing was acquired by John Wiley & Sons in February 2007. Blackwell's publishing program has been merged with Wiley's global Scientific, Technical, and Medical business to form Wiley-Blackwell.

Registered Office
John Wiley & Sons Ltd, The Atrium, Southern Gate, Chichester, West Sussex, PO19 8SQ, United Kingdom

Editorial Offices
350 Main Street, Malden, MA 02148-5020, USA
9600 Garsington Road, Oxford, OX4 2DQ, UK
The Atrium, Southern Gate, Chichester, West Sussex, PO19 8SQ, UK

For details of our global editorial offices, for customer services, and for information about how to apply for permission to reuse the copyright material in this book please see our website at www.wiley.com/wiley-blackwell.

The right of Eric Csapo to be identified as the author of this work has been asserted in accordance with the UK Copyright, Designs and Patents Act 1988.

Wiley also publishes its books in a variety of electronic formats. Some content that appears in print may not be available in electronic books.

Library of Congress Cataloging-in-Publication Data

Csapo, Eric.
    Actors and icons of the ancient theater / Eric Csapo.
        p. cm.
    Includes bibliographical references and index.
    ISBN 978-1-4051-3536-8 (hardcover : alk. paper) 1. Acting–History–To 500.
2. Theater–Greece–History–To 500. 3. Theater–History–To 500. 4. Theater–Rome.
5. Actors–Greece. 6. Actors–Rome. I. Title.
    PA3203.C78 2010
    792.02′80938–dc22
                                                                    2009027227

A catalogue record for this book is available from the British Library.

Set in 10.5/13pt Minion by SPi Publisher Services, Pondicherry, India
Printed and bound in Malaysia by Vivar Printing Sdn Bhd

I   2010

A
263
78
610

Contents

List of illustrations   vi
Preface   viii
List of abbreviations   xiii

1   A Portrait of the Artist I: Theater-Realistic Art
     in Athens, 500–330 BC   1

2   A Portrait of the Artist II: Theater-Realistic Art
     in the Greek West, 400–300 BC   38

3   The Spread of Theater and the Rise of the Actor   83

4   Kallippides on the Floor Sweepings: The Limits of Realism
     in Classical Acting   117

5   Cooking with Menander: Slices from the Ancient
     Home Entertainment Industry?   140

6   The Politics of Privatization: A Short History
     of the Privatization of Drama from Classical Athens
     to Early Imperial Rome   168

Bibliography   205
Index   227

Illustrations

1.1   Attic red-figured calyx krater, *c*.400–375 BC   4

1.2   Attic red-figured column krater, Mannerist style, 500–490 BC   7

1.3   Attic red-figured column krater fragment, 430–420 BC   8

1.4   Attic red-figured calyx krater, *c*.425 BC   9

1.5   Attic red-figured pelike, *c*.425 BC   10

1.6   Attic marble relief fragments, *c*.340 BC   13

1.7   Marble relief from Peiraeus, *c*.400 BC   15

1.8   Attic red-figured hydria, Pan Painter, 490–480 BC   16

1.9   Attic red-figured volute krater, Pronomos Painter, *c*.400 BC   18

1.10   Attic red-figured chous, Painter of the Perseus Dance, *c*.420 BC   25

1.11   Attic polychrome oinochoe, *c*.400 BC   29

2.1   Apulian red-figured calyx krater, Tarporley Painter, *c*.400 BC   46

2.2   Apulian red-figured bell krater, McDaniel Painter, *c*.370 BC   50

2.3   Apulian red-figured bell krater, Schiller Painter, *c*.370 BC   54

2.4   Apulian red-figured bell krater, 375–350 BC   59

2.5   Paestan red-figured bell krater, Asteas, *c*.350 BC   62

2.6   Apulian relief guttus, *c*.330 BC   64

2.7   Sicilian red-figured calyx krater, Gibil Gabib Group, probably Capodarso Painter, 340–330 BC   68

5.1   Reconstruction of the mosaic floor of the triclinium of the House of Menander in Mytilene   141

5.2   Reconstruction of the mosaic floor of the portico
        of the House of Menander in Mytilene   142

5.3   Mosaic emblema from House of Menander, Daphne,
        250–275 AD   145

5.4   Marble relief, first century AD copy of a Hellenistic original   145

5.5   Marble relief, Roman copy of a Hellenistic original   149

5.6   Mosaic scene from Menander's *Synaristosai*,
        Dioskourides, 125–100 BC   150

5.7   Mosaic scene from Menander's *Theophoroumene*,
        Dioskourides, 125–100 BC   151

5.8   Marble relief, first century AD copy of Early Hellenistic original   152

5.9   Cameo, *c*.100 BC   152

5.10   Detail of an ivory consular diptych of Flavius Anastasius
        Probus, 517 AD   159

5.11   Detail of left leaf of an ivory consular diptych
        of Flavius Anastasius Probus, 517 AD   160

5.12   K. Weitzmann, *Illustrations in Roll and Codex*, 2nd ed., pl. 44   162

Preface

This book pursues several recent developments in the history of the ancient theater. In some cases new evidence urges new perspectives, in others new perspectives permit a more positive appraisal of old evidence that residual habits of thought once ignored, marginalized, denied, or otherwise sought to contain. The result is a series of investigations of topics conspicuously absent or under-developed in such standard historical surveys as Margarete Bieber's *History of the Greek and Roman Theater* (2nd ed. Princeton 1961) or Arthur Pickard-Cambridge's *Dramatic Festivals of Athens* (2nd ed. Oxford 1968, reissued with supplement 1988). My aim is to explore what new or newly vindicated bodies of evidence might yield to the theater historian. I hope to show that the margin-alization of this evidence was never merited. On the contrary, it directly related to topics that just about anyone would consider central to the history of ancient theatre: the growth of realism in art and acting; the spread of theater through-out the ancient world; the role of theater in the development of the cultural koine of the Greek world; the history of the canonization of its authors; the rise of the acting profession; the consequences of this rise upon acting, drama and popular consciousness; the role of Macedon in transforming Greek theatre; the use of theater and theater imagery in later antiquity; and the development and use of private drama. All of these topics have some connection – often a very direct connection – to the central theme advertised by my title: the changing image of actors in antiquity. By "image" I mean to imply both the way actors presented themselves and the way others represented them.

Though it does in some sense bridge the full millennial span of ancient theater history, this book is not a full, continuous, or consistent survey of ancient actors and their reception. I doubt whether any such history is yet possible. The book is rather prolegomena to such a history where the focus is sometimes more on the raw materials of history than on the finished product. Our evidence comes in disparate clumps unevenly spread across time and different media. I try to make something out of these clumps. In each chapter I am primarily concerned with potential bodies of evidence, whether new or old, that seem undervalued and underexploited for the purpose of theater history. I am not in all cases the first to treat this material in recent times. Ancient theater iconography, in particular, has been exceptionally well-treated in the last fifteen years – to mention only the chief monographs – by J. R. Green's *Theatre in Ancient Greek Society* (London and New York 1994) and Oliver Taplin's *Comic Angels and Other Approaches to Greek Drama through Vase-Paintings* (Oxford 1994) and *Pots & Plays* (Malibu 2007). My approach and my questions are for the most part different from these works and so, often, are my conclusions.

Part of the reason for the shape and content of this book has to do with its origins. Four of the six chapters are the revised and annotated Nellie Wallace Lectures that I delivered at Oxford during Trinity Term 2004. A fifth derives from a lecture delivered at the same time and place to the Archive of Performances of Greek and Roman Drama. Beyond limiting myself to the history of the ancient theater, I chose topics that stood the best chance of seeming both new and interesting to an audience containing some of the best and most broadly read classical scholars in the world. I had little concern for continuity of subject or unity of theme until Al Bertrand, then commissioning editor of Blackwell, kindly invited me to publish the lectures together in a single volume. No amount of further work could erase the pluriformity of my initial purpose, but it did at least permit me to develop the common themes and contents of the various chapters. As it turned out, my topics interact in surprisingly many ways.

Three chapters deal quite literally with the image of the actor: in Attic art (Chapter 1), in West Greek art (Chapter 2) and in Hellenistic and Imperial art (Chapter 5). Some have tried to warn theater scholars away from the artifacts by demonstrating that the artists' selectivity and distortions render them uncertain and less than perfect documents for reconstructing an ancient performance. I (among others) would argue that the very unstraightforwardness of the relationship between image and dramatic production greatly enhances the iconography's value as a source of evidence for theater history. Selection and distortion have a great deal to tell us about the way ancient artists saw or liked to see or, better still, thought their customers liked to see drama in the ancient world. Because what is or is not present in a picture is due not to the mechanical reproduction but the imaginative reconstruction of a performance, the artifacts can reveal what caught the fancy of theater viewers and how this changed with time, place, usage, social class, or political orientation. In Attica, for example (Chapter 1), we find a marked increase in the realism of theater art around the 420s BC together, with a radical shift in its preferred subject matter. Before this date theater-realistic art is choral and restricted to large and expensive vessels used in the symposium. After this date there is a rapid growth of images that show actors, but they are restricted, almost exclusively, to small, inexpensive media intended for a much broader market. Within a decade or two of this development

(Chapter 2), we find highly realistic theater images on West Greek pottery of a wide variety of shapes and sizes, but this time almost exclusively focussed on actors. The imagery confirms evidence, studied in Chapter 3, for the early and very broad spread of theater across the Greek world by the end of the fifth century and the beginning of the fourth. But it also gives evidence of a decidedly actor-centered concept of drama in the Greek West. Most surprisingly the imagery reveals a preference for subjects drawn from a restricted corpus of old dramas. This, in turn, seems to indicate that the process of the canonization of the tragic and comic "greats" had already begun by this time. We pick up this topic later in Chapters 5 and 6 which study, among other themes, "classicism" in Hellenistic and Imperial art and culture. But the continuity in the process of canonization also reveals a growing difference in the degree of detail that each art shares with dramatic performance. In the fourth century BC, some painterly selections and distortions, as we will see in Chapter 2, actually bring us closer to the details of performance than we can get by reading our dramatic texts. In Chapter 5, on the contrary, we will see that artisanal selections and distortions can demonstrate that we are moving ever farther from the influence of contemporary performance.

Chapter 1, we noted, shows a heightened realism in theater art after 420 BC and a simultaneous shift in focus from choral music and dance to the actor and acting. Chapter 4 provides evidence for a radical shift in the style of acting from about 420 BC toward mimetic realism. This is no coincidence. In Athens visual artists traded ideas freely among themselves, among whom we must include mask makers, costume designers, set painters, and indeed also actors. In the same period we know that dramatic poetry and dramaturgy became more realistic; and theater music – a medium to which a term like realism is less easy to apply – became markedly more mimetic. While it would be wrong to say that artistic realism somehow began in the theater, it is certainly true that theater was at its experimental hub. Consistently with this trend, Chapters 1 and 2 show that artifacts with theatrical subjects are among the earliest to reveal the traits and tendencies normally covered by the term realism in the visual arts. Chapters 1 and 3 explore some of the external socio-economic motives that might have encouraged the development of realism in both theater art and acting: from the commemorative function of votive choregic reliefs and paintings to the star system that began to shape the acting profession from as early as the last two decades of the fifth century BC.

The rise of the actor had not just artistic and theatrical effects but social and political consequences as well. These are explored in Chapter 6. From the very beginning dramatic production always combined public with private money, and public with private interests. If Greek drama flourished in Athenian democracy, it also flourished under Syracusan autocracy – both tragedy and comedy, and both genres probably from the very start. Drama is a medium, not a message, and it is (at least primarily) a medium of mass communication that can be adapted to almost any message or purpose. The nature and function of drama were, however, affected by the different political regimes that drama served in antiquity. Macedon seems to have had as profound an influence as Athens in determining drama's form, function, and venues for later antiquity. Among more immediate effects, Macedon's adaptation of theater contributed significantly to the growth in the status and power of actors. The greater and longer term effect, however, was the "privatization" of theater, a term that covers many types of dramatic performance, but all of them adapted to suit the personal ambitions of Hellenistic autocrats and Roman Republican élites.

There are several people that deserve to be singled out for thanks. Thanks are due first to the staff at Wiley-Blackwell, but for whom this book would not exist: Al Bertrand who encouraged me to write this book, Haze Humbert who for many years put up with my excuses for not getting on with it, and Galen Smith who nudged me with patient and gentle persistence until I actually finished the job. Secondly, to the Classics Faculty at Oxford for inviting me to give the Nellie Wallace Lectures that are at this book's core, and especially to Robert Parker, Robin Lane Fox, Jane Lightfoot, and the Fellows of New College who offered a Fellowship and fellowship in Trinity Term 2004, three months that I consider the high point of my academic career. Thanks to Oliver Taplin, Amanda Wrigley, and Fiona Macintosh for incorporating one of these lectures into the APGRD program, and to Oliver, Beaty, and Charis for the use of their magnificent sixteenth-century house in the tranquil idyll of Great Haseley.

The final push, like the first, began back in Oxford four years later, and that was largely thanks to the support of the Faculty of Art, University of Sydney, and the friendship and generosity of Scott Scullion and Worcester College. The work was continued in Paris, at the École Normale Supérieure, where as Visiting Professor I enjoyed the hospitality of Monique Trédé. For a delightful and profitable stay I thank, in addition to Monique, Brigitte Le Guen, Alexa Piqueux, Sylvain Perrot, and all who attended Monique's Friday seminars. Thanks also to Glenn Most, Chiara Martinelli, and Rolando Ferri for invitations to try out my ideas in Pisa. The Australian Research Council provided the research time that permitted completion and funds to cover the sometimes prohibitive costs of plates and copyrights.

Writing the acknowledgment paragraphs of this book makes me realize just how much others have contributed to the contribution that the world is (perhaps luckily for them) destined to receive as my own. A great deal of the material in this book was discussed with my colleagues at the University of Sydney, Richard Green, Andrew Hartwig, and Peter Wilson, both in and out of our semi-spontaneous Friday-morning theater-history seminars at CCANESA. One should at least suspect that good ideas, if any, were generated at this forum. Richard Green, Sebastinana Nervegna, Jeff Tatum, and Peter Wilson also read large swathes of this manuscript and offered many corrections and suggestions. For his unfailing support and indefatigable proof reading I thank Ben Zaporozan. William Slater was, as always, most generous in sharing his encyclopedic knowledge, more often now over the internet than over dinner. My greatest intellectual debt is to my wife Margaret Miller, who has guided and corrected my thoughts on almost everything that appears in this book (and an awful lot that has been left out).

I am grateful to Pat Easterling, Edith Hall, Svetlana Shadrina, and the Syndics of Cambridge University Press for permission to reproduce most of Chapter 4, and to C. Hugoniot, F. Hurlet, S. Milanezi, Samuel Leturcq, and the Presses Universitaires François-Rabelais for permission to reproduce extended passages in Chapter 3. I would like to acknowledge the rare generosity of those individuals and institutions who continue to support the ideals of collegiality and the commonwealth of scholarship by providing, as in days of yore, images and copyrights without asking anything in return: Jeff Rusten; Jacklyn Burns and the J. Paul Getty Museum; Daniel Berger and the Department of Archaeology of the Italian Ministero peri Beni e le Attività Culturali; Pietro Giovanni Guzzo and the Soprintendenza Archeologica Napoli e Pompei; Jasper Gaunt and the Carlos Museum of Emory University; Joachim Heiden and the Deutsches Archäologisches Institut in Athens; Annemarie Kaufmann-Heinimann and the editors of *Antike Kunst*; Elena Obuhovich, Vladimir Matveyev and the State Hermitage Museum; Vera Slehofer and the Antikenmuseum Basel; Craig Mauzy and Agora Excavations; Irma Wehgartner and the Martin von Wagner Museum in Würzburg; Jennifer Marsh and the Museum of Fine Arts, Boston; Matilde Romito and Salerno's Settore Beni Culturali, Musei-Biblioteche; Karen Richter and the Princeton University Art Museum; Sandra Laplace-Claverie and the Bibliothèque nationale de France; and Céline Rebière –Plé and the Musée du Louvre. Special accolades are reserved for William Knight Zewadski for his general support of classical scholarship and in particular, in the present instance, of my own.

This volume such as it is, is dedicated to the kindness and selfless generosity of my sister Helga who looked after the children while we were trying to function as scholars on research leave, both when the book was started and when it was finished.

Eric Csapo

Abbreviations

Add	T. H. Carpenter, *Beazley Addenda: Additional Reverences to* ABV, ARV² *and* Paralipomena, 2nd ed. Oxford, 1989.
ARV	J. D. Beazley, Attic Red-Figure Vase-Painters, 2nd ed. 3 vols. Oxford, 1963.
LIMC	*Lexicon Iconographicum Mythologiae Classicae*, 8 vols. Zurich and Munich, 1981–1999.
MTS	T. B. L. Webster, *Monuments Illustrating Tragedy and Satyr Play*, 2nd ed. London, 1967.
MMC	T. B. L. Webster, *Monuments Illustrating Old and Middle Comedy*, 3rd ed. by J. R. Green. London, 1978.
MNC	T. B. L. Webster, *Monuments Illustrating New Comedy*, 3rd ed. by J. R. Green and A. Seeberg, 2 vols. London, 1995.
P&P	O. Taplin, *Pots and Plays: Interactions between Tragedy and Greek Vase-painting of the Fourth Century* BC. Los Angeles, 2007.
Para	J. D. Beazley, *Paralipomena*. Oxford, 1971.
PCG	R. Kassel and C. Austin, *Poetae Comici Graeci*, currently 8 vols. Berlin / New York, 1983–.
PhV	A. D. Trendall, *Phlyax Vases*, 2nd ed. London, 1967.
PP	A. D. Trendall, *Paestan Pottery*. London, 1936.
RVAp	A. D. Trendall and A. Cambitoglou, *Red-Figure Vases of Apulia*, 2 vols. Oxford, 1978–82.
RVP	A. D. Trendall, *The Red-Figured Vases of Paestum*. Rome, 1987.
RVSIS	A. D. Trendall, *Red Figure Vases of South Italy and Sicily*. London, 1989.
TrGF	*Tragicorum graecorum fragmenta*, 5 vols. Göttingen, 1971–2004.

Papyri are cited with P + abbreviated collection name (*POxy, PMich,* etc.). Plays by Aristophanes (Ar.) and the one work of Plato (Pl.), that is, *Laws,* capable of being rendered with a monosyllabic English title are cited by the English title. Plato's *Republic* is abbreviated *Rep.* Otherwise ancient authors and works and modern collections of literary fragments are abbreviated according to the lists found in the *Oxford Classical Dictionary,* 3rd ed. by S. Hornblower and A. Spawforth (Oxford 1996) xxix–liv. Journals are abbreviated according to the lists found in the *American Journal of Archaeology* 104 (2000) 10–24.

A Portrait of the Artist I
Theater-Realistic Art in Athens, 500–330 BC

This chapter aims to demonstrate the existence of an iconography of theater and actors in fifth-century BC Athens. The claim would not have surprised anyone thirty years ago, but many archaeologists and art historians, nourished on the binarist theories fashionable in the Cold War Era, are directing reductive methods and exclusionist rhetoric to the construction of boundaries between art and its "Other" (variously identified as "texts," "history," or "reality"). In 2003, for example, Jocelyn Penny Small published a book called *The Parallel Worlds of Classical Art and Text* where, in constructing a vision of two solitudes that live side by side but never mix, she states categorically "that contemporary Attic vase painters did not base their representations on ... plays."[1] Yet she omits mention of nearly all of the material I consider important to this discussion. The book offers a kind of blunderbuss deconstruction of every possible link between the plastic arts and other forms of cultural expression. Its premise that art is a fully self-contained and autonomous activity has a certain appeal for classical archaeologists who teach in departments of Archaeology or Fine Arts and do not want to oblige their students to learn Greek or read ancient literature. But this is only the hard end of a vision I wish to render more supple. Even Oliver Taplin, who has not the least sympathy with this kind of intellectual isolationism, tends in his *Comic Angels* to underestimate the importance of theatrical subjects in Attic (as opposed to West Greek) vasepainting.

Some other contemporary historians of ancient art dismiss both the possibility that an object of art could reflect the influence of the theater and the possibility that, if such an influence did exist, it might be useful to any who might wish to learn something about performance or about the ancient reception of theater. I refer to the tendency on the part of historians of Greek art to insist upon the absence or near-total absence of subjects with historical or realistic content as opposed to mythological or mythologized content. It was not all that long ago that art historians like E. H. Gombrich contrasted the mythically oriented images and narratives of the Near East with the "antimythical" vision of the Greeks.[2] Greek art served as the foundation of Western realism. This was progressivist and orientalist, it is true. But the reaction on the part of scholars like Gloria Ferrari is no less categoric. She maintains that all Greek vasepainting is essentially mythical.[3] For many vasepaintings this is largely true. Even scenes of everyday and apparently contemporary life ("genre scenes") are usually still linked in some way with the mythical imagination. For example, scenes of hoplite battle generally show heroic nudity or military tactics more suited to the world of Homer than to the world of the artist; scenes showing women preening or spinning might have inscriptions that label the principal figure "Helen." Many apparently realistic scenes can thus gesture compulsively toward the archetypal world of myth. But the reductive claim that attempts to take all vasepainting out of the reach of history can only be maintained by distorting the meanings of "myth" and "history" well beyond recognition. "Myth" must be extended to include the decidedly more ambiguous category of "ritual" to embrace scenes of sport, sacrifice, or choral dance, and even "social rituals" like scenes of the symposium or the hunt. "History" must be contracted to exclude all of the above. But even if "myth" remains a universal norm in the representational arts (and I am far from being convinced that it is), there are exceptions. Indeed the majority of art historians would, I think, balk at the notion that all ancients painted with the same brush. Himmelmann in particular has studied the development of realism in the treatment of several subjects, comic scenes among them (by realism I mean the choice of specific, historic or everyday life scenes that are familiar to the artists and their patrons and treated in such a way as to offer the impression of the familiarity of lived experience).[4] But even Himmelmann excluded much of the evidence relating to theater and largely ignored tragedy. More recently Steinhart has explored with admirable subtlety the interraction between art and mimetic performances, although with a primary focus on non-theatrical mimesis.[5] In this chapter we take a close look at the phenomenon of theater-realism: it is a very minor theme in Attic art, but even if it is exceptional, it is important, and deserves a place both in art history and in theater history. In doing this I claim no originality except in the details of my presentation: many scholars have discussed this theme, both great archaeologists such as Erika Simon and Richard Green, and great theater historians such as T. B. L. Webster and Oliver Taplin (all of them notable and successful transgressors of the boundaries of their discipline).

Depicting Myth

Over the course of the fifth century tragedy became "the most familiar and popular way in which hundreds of thousands of Greeks came to know the great myths."[6] The validity of this claim (the words are Oliver Taplin's) is supported by the way tragedy influenced the choice and treatment of mythical scenes in (fifth-century) Attic and (fourth-century) West Greek vasepainting. For Athens it is (in the fourth century) richly confirmed by the frequency of distinctly tragic elements in literary allusions to myth.[7] Yet despite the huge popularity of tragedy and despite its impact upon the way myths are represented, very few Attic vasepaintings depict (or even evoke) tragic performance, so few in fact that the paradox has become a celebrated mystery.[8]

The paradox is all the greater considering that the fifth century was the great age of both Athenian drama and Athenian red figure. Indeed both tragedy and vasepainting are uniquely well-preserved – far better than any other genres of art in this period – with thirty-three complete plays and nearly a hundred thousand vases. Moreover, even those who insist that Attic red figure pottery renders its subjects in an essentially mythical form cannot deny that it draws them from nearly every facet of social life. There are at best five surviving Attic pots or fragments that can be said to depict tragedy in performance. Tragic performance is even harder to find in West Greek pottery. Of some twenty thousand known vasepaintings, as many as 450 can be reasonably argued to show influence of tragedy – but of these no more than two could be said unambiguously to "show tragedy."[9]

An early fourth-century Attic vase may serve us as an example of the general practice (see FIGURE 1.1).[10] The subject is an incident in the life of the mythological hero Telephus. Not yet the practiced sailors that they would one day become, the Greeks messed up their first expedition to Troy. They landed in Mysia by mistake and, without bothering to check their position, immediately began to lay waste to the territory. The king of Mysia, Telephus, drove them out again but was wounded by Achilles. Realizing their mistake, the Greeks returned home. Telephus' wound began to fester and the oracle of Apollo told him that "the wounder would heal." So Telephus went to Argos, where the Greek chiefs were meeting to plan a second attempt on Troy. They interpreted the oracle to mean that rust from Achilles' spear would heal Telephus and in return Telephus agreed to guide the expedition to Troy. This was the general outline of the myth before Euripides sensationalized it in a tragedy of 438 BC. Euripides turned Telephus' encounter with the Greek chiefs into a hostage-taking incident: Telephus infiltrated the war council disguised as a beggar, but when he was exposed as an enemy infiltrator, he grabbed Agamemnon's infant son, jumped on an altar, and threatened the baby with his sword. The Greek chiefs were in this way forced to negotiate with Telephus, but the outcome was the generally the same as the pre-Euripidean version of the myth. The Greeks arranged for the healing of Telephus' wound and Telephus in turn agreed to act as navigator for the second expedition to Troy (which did end up in the right place). It is the climactic hostage-taking incident invented by Euripides that we see in FIGURE 1.1: Telephus, center, kneels on

Figure 1.1   Attic red-figured calyx krater, *c*.400–375 BC, Berlin Antikensammlung 3974.
©bpk Berlin 2009.

the altar threatening the baby; Agamemnon in the upper right reacts at first with ill-considered aggression.

Euripides' tragedy not only invented the hostage scene and turned it into the climactic moment in the story of Telephus, but it also created the visual archetype that would emblematize the play for all later antiquity. There can be no doubt that the climax of Euripides' *Telephus* was staged in precisely this way: it is parodied through precisely these visual clues (with a little, but not much verbal reinforcement) in the *Acharnians* and the *Thesmophoriazusae* of Aristophanes.[11] The precise configuration that we find at the center of this scene – a man kneeling on an altar and threatening a baby with a sword – reappears on no less than fifteen fourth-century West Greek pots (not to mention Etruscan art), to the near exclusion of all other episodes from Telephus' life, precisely because of the impact of Euripides' tragedy.[12] A man kneeling on an altar and threatening a baby with a sword could only signal the story of Telephus in both comedy and in art because thousands of Greeks had seen the same combination of visual signals in a theatrical performance of the play.

There are perhaps other minor *theatrical* features in the composition. For example, it could be argued that the women who register an emotional reaction by running to the left and right on the margins of the scene are at least functionally reminiscent of a chorus, or that the contrastingly placid presence of Apollo, hovering above the action (upper left), recalls a fragment of the play in which Telephus calls upon Apollo, or indeed recalls the generally placid and benign indifference of the gods, as expressed in tragedy's more anthropocentric universe. Yet despite all this and despite the scene's total dependence upon the plot of Euripides' tragedy, this is no illustration of tragedy, but of *myth*.

Depicting Choruses

By contrast with the mythologizing norm of theater-influenced vasepaintings, for which the Telephus vase might serve as an example, four Attic vases reveal varying degrees of the opposite of the mythologizing vision, namely realistic details of tragic performance that intrude upon and undermine any merely mytholgical conception of a scene. All are choral and thereby perhaps susceptible to being categorized as ritual and hence quasi-mythical in the broad and dilute sense urged by those who insist that all vasepainting is cut from mythical cloth. But this would not do justice to the details of our vases, of which two at least are decidedly more focussed upon a theatrical performance than upon any possible myth or myth-like subject.

Before we examine the tragic paintings, however, something must be said to excuse my reluctance to look at vasepaintings depicting satyrs in pursuit of the question of theater-realism. Many vases are (I think rightly) suspected of being in some way connected with satyrplay.[13] The problem is in proving a connection with theater. Satyrs have too strong a connection with music and dance in the Greek mythic imagination, on the one hand, and with choruses of men performing as satyrs in Dionysian processions, on the other, to allow us to insist upon the usual indices of dramatic performance, namely pipers, choral groupings or suggestions of mask and costume. Even if all these markers were present they would not suffice to prove any specific connection with satyrplay as opposed to mythic and cultic forms of satyr performance. And yet, it is necessary to say, if only in passing, that satyr vases can nevertheless reveal a realism that is inconsistent with purely mythical imagery. For example, a vase by the Leningrad Painter is for good reasons, frequently related to satyrplay.[14] Signs of performance include the presence of a human piper, the use of loincloths with erect phalloi, called *perizomata*, lines at the wrist and ankles indicating the body-tights worn by all ancient actors, as well as mask-like features (bug-eyes, double-lines marking the hair-line at the back of the three-quarter mask), and even a certain amount of co-ordination in the satyrs' movements. Nevertheless nothing permits us to insist that it shows a dramatic performance. At best we can insist that, if these are in some sense mythical satyrs, they are satyrs drawn after the manner and appearance of men who perform as satyrs.

The case for iconographic theater-realism must be made on the strength of tragic and comic performance, which have no existence apart from theater. From the first half of the fifth century we have two vases that may depict tragic choruses. Although they offer no hints at masks, they declare their theatricality through such details as the presence of pipers and identically dressed chorusmen in a narrative context.[15] One of these is a pelike in Berlin that shows, on each side, a dancing maenad accompanied by a piper.[16] Even if the piper signals a performance, there is nonetheless nothing to distinguish this maenad from any other. One could say that the painter bypasses the performer and refers us directly to the mythic maenad he represents.

The second is an Attic hydria surviving in only six fragments.[17] The vase originally showed a piper and at least seven to nine members of a chorus, dressed as Persians, dancing around a pyre upon which sits a man who is usually thought to be Croesus. The pot was made a few years after the battle of Plataea, a brief period in which tragedians, notably Aeschylus (*Persians*) and Phrynichus (*The Capture of Miletus, Phoenician Women*), flirted with historical rather than mythological subjects. For a few decades, when Athens believed it had experienced events of mythic proportions, there was a vogue, paradoxically, for something approaching history in the theater. Cyrus sacked Sardis in 546 BC and so the story of Croesus being nearly burned on the pyre is in some sense "historical," though the history is to our eyes heavily mythologized. Its treatment in art might also have been mythologized. Interestingly it was not – or at least not fully. The piper is a clear allusion to performance and the fact that the costumes of the dancing Persians are nearly identical signals a chorus. The two preserved faces, however, have no attributes that suggest a mask and their mouths are closed. Here again the artist seems to focus on the characters that the masks represent and not on the performers. But for all that, the theater-realism of the vase is no more compromised than the integrity of any possible mythical conceptualization of the image. We are betwixt and between.

The case for realism is decidedly better on a column krater in Basel (see FIGURE 1.2).[18] It dates to the first decade of the fifth century and is probably our earliest evidence of tragedy. On it three ranks and two files of young men dance in rectangular formation. This is surely a synecdoche for three files and four ranks, the distinctive and possibly normal formation of the tragic chorus.[19] The depiction of a full tragic chorus of twelve would have been visually confusing and awkward on the limited space provided by the pot's surface. The choreuts are costumed as soldiers but are not really soldiers: they wear diadems rather

Figure 1.2   Attic red-figured column krater, Mannerist style, 500–490 BC, Basel BS 415. Courtesy, Antikenmuseum Basel und Sammlung Ludwig. Photo: Claire Niggli.

than helmets, dance rather than march, and carry no weapons. A series of Os emerge from their mouths in added red paint (not visible in FIGURE 1.2) to show that they are singing. They approach the *orchestra's* central altar, behind which rises a smaller figure who is presumably an actor. This may be one of the many "ghost-raising" scenes which were especially popular in early tragedy.[20]

Masks are richly suggested. The faces of the choreuts (and to some extent the actor) are all alike: they have wide eyes, gaping mouths, jutting chins, and chin-lines that extend, unusually, right up to the hair-line. And since ancient masks covered the entire head as well as the face, we should also notice the unnatural hair-line position of the diadems, and the highly unusual strand by strand rendering of the hair.[21] The painter seems to have taken pains to suggest that there is something unnatural, something artificial, about these heads. Even the breast-plates, on closer examination, appear not to be breastplates, but frilled, sleeveless tops (not part of the normal Greek vestimentary repertoire) with patterns that are similar enough to suggest the near-uniformity of dramatic choral costume. No detail could justify the relegation of this image to mythic fantasy, unless

Figure 1.3   Attic red-figured column krater fragment, 430–420 BC, Kiev, Museum of the Academy of Sciences.

(and this is perhaps the fatal admission) it is the absence of lines at the wrists and ankles of the choreuts to mark the body-tights that appear normally to have been worn by both actors and choreuts, at least in drama later in the century.

In 2002 the publication of a fragment of a vasepainting from Olbia gave us the first image that renders tragic performers with unambiguous realism (see FIGURE 1.3).[22] The fragment belongs to an Attic bell krater produced in about 425 BC. On either side of a piper and his boy assistant dances a tragic choreut whose mask and costume are depicted with scrupulous realism. The faces of the masks are overpainted with added white in an effort to contrast the (conventionally white) female flesh of the characters with the darker skin of the nape and neck of the male performer under the female mask. The reproduction is unfortunately of poor quality, but it appears to me also that the lines of the sleeves of the choreuts' body-tights are also visible. The piper too appears in all his theater paraphernalia. The piper's harness (*phorbeia*) is rendered in detail and, rarer still, his assistant, who stands by holding his pipe case (*sybene*) to which is attached at the top the reedcase (*glottokomeion*) containing the extra mouthpieces and reeds required for modulating the music. One can see the top of one of the mouthpieces held in the assistant's hand above the break. Froning in her publication mistakes this for the boy's thumb(s) and concludes that he is clapping to keep time (whence Revermann takes the notion that this may be a rehearsal).[23] But this is not a

Figure 1.4   Attic red-figured calyx krater, *c.*425 BC, formerly Malibu 82.AE.83. Courtesy, Ministero per i Beni e le Attività Culturali, Department of Archaeology, Italy. All rights reserved.

natural way to clap (it is both ineffectual as it deadens the sound and quite painful – try it!). But it is no thumb. Compare the detail with the detail of the small piper's assistant in Dioskourides' mosaic of the *Theophoroumene* who also holds the same equipment (below, FIGURE 5.7). This is unprecedented theater-realism in Attic art, and it is not just the manner of rendering details of costume that has changed. The fragment also reveals a significantly different conception of its subject matter. The earlier mythological vases gave us at least small hints about what story was being told. Here we know only that the tragedy had a chorus of young women, but this was true of the majority of tragedies at this date. I suspect that we would know nothing more specific even if the whole scene were preserved. It is precisely the lack of anything that could be linked to narrative, either mythical or dramatic, that is astonishing. For the first time the art shows us a performance, pure and simple, without even a hint at the story behind the performance, let alone the myth behind the story.

The earliest vasepaintings to show scenes of comedy are probably also choral. Two extraordinary vasepaintings depict what appears to be a comic chorus dressed as fighting cocks (FIGURES 1.4 and 1.5).[24] There can be no serious doubt

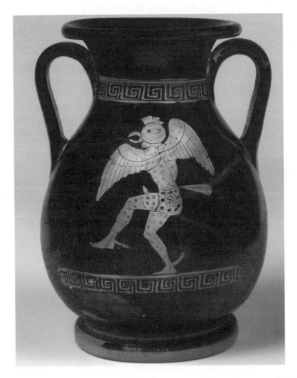

Figure 1.5 Attic red-figured pelike, *c.*425 BC, Atlanta 2008.4.1. Courtesy, Michael C. Carlos Museum of Emory University.

that their subject is a costumed performance of some kind. Pipers appear on both vases (there is one on the reverse of FIGURE 1.5), and the posture of the birdmen clearly indicates some form of dance. That the artist saw costumed figures and not some mythological birdmen is clear from the detailing of the costume. One can, for example, see the lines demarcating the "shorts" which hold the tail and phallus, or the details of the strings which tie on the phallic spurs (note in particular the left cock's left ankle on FIGURE 1.4). But what genre of performance is it?

The calyx krater (FIGURE 1.4) has been known since 1985, but the pelike (FIGURE 1.5) was unknown before 2008, and so the controversies that have raged over the identity of the performers has not until now had the benefit of what is obviously a second artistic rendition of the same performance. The calyx krater has been said to represent a comic chorus, comic actors, a non-dramatic procession, and a satyrplay. Of all these explanations, the suggestion that it represents a satyrplay is, though most persistent, the easiest to dismiss. The hypothesis is based entirely upon a comparison of the "shorts" worn by the actors, with erect phallus and tail attached, including the typical decorative motif of the eyespot and "wagonwheel," that are otherwise known from representations of satyrs (compare below, FIGURE 1.9).[25] But this hypothesis must be rejected for the simple reason that there exists no satyrplay without a satyrchorus and indeed satyrs are the one constant and indispensable feature of satyrplay. A satyrplay without real satyrs is unthinkable. The "shorts" must be regarded as the standard costume-designer's response to the requirement of supporting an erect phallus and a tail: it does occasionally appear on creatures other than satyrs.[26] A further hypothesis argues that our scene is from a comedy in which a chorus of satyrs is transformed (during the course of the drama) into cocks.[27] But this rather messy hypothesis is also without foundation: though we do have comedies with choruses of satyrs, we have no play, comedy, or satyrplay in which satyrs are transformed into beasts of any other species.[28]

Another line of investigation suggests that these vases are not dramatic at all, but represent costumed figures from a Dionysian procession. Attic vasepainting from 560 to 480 BC preserves about twenty choruses of men costumed as animals or costumed men riding animals, most often accompanied by a piper.[29] This group of vasepaintings cannot be directly related to drama and certainly not comedy "as we know it," since they come to an end at about the time of the first productions of comedy in Athens, traditionally (though not securely) dated to 486 BC. The human characters are also for the most part unmasked and few of them show any sign of the usual comic costume. What they do seem to show is processional movement (interspersed with occasional round dances) and though many scholars refer to this group of vasepaintings as "comic," "pre-comic" or "protocomic" vases, they are more safely classified as "*komos* vases" (a *komos*, in literature of the Classical period, is a usually drunken choral procession, frequently involving costumes and musicians, and closely, though not exclusively, associated with Dionysus).[30] The preponderance of dolphin riders among the *komos* vases helps confirm that these vases are related to Dionysus: dolphins are closely associated with cultic dithyramb, a Dionysian processional song that before the end of the sixth century took the form of a *komos*. One of the dolphin-rider vases indeed shows ostrich riders on the obverse led by a man in a satyr mask (in Attic art of this period satyrs are unambiguously creatures of Dionysus and one must conclude that the procession is Dionysian).[31] At first sight FIGURES 1.4 and 1.5 might seem to belong to this *komos* series (which does include two examples of men dressed as cocks).[32]

There are, however, serious obstacles to viewing FIGURES 1.4 and 1.5 as part of this series. First there is a gap of about half a century between the end of the series of processions of animals and animal riders. The closest parallels after 480 BC are with the depiction of dramatic choruses. Secondly, the *komos* vase's style of presentation is different: in that genre the dancers move in the same direction with identical movements; but here the cocks on the calyx krater (FIGURE 1.4) face each other and assume different postures (they appear to be facing off for a fight). A much nearer comparison is offered by the tragic chorus on FIGURE 1.3, where the choreuts on either side of the piper adopt different postures (perhaps phases of the same dance). The pipers accompanying the cock dancers are also more conspicuous and more elaborately dressed than we find on the komos vases. The dress of the piper on FIGURE 1.4 is comparable in its elaboration to the costume worn by Pronomos (FIGURE 1.9, below), while the costume of the piper on the reverse of FIGURE 1.5, though the standard eye-spot decoration of theatrical pipers (cf. FIGURES 1.2 and 1.3), is considerably more ornate and formal than that worn by pipers on the *komos* vases.[33] We might add that the fact that two vases, certainly by different hands (note the differences in the rendering of minor details of the costume on FIGURES 1.4 and 1.5), produce dancers in identical costume (but very different poses) suggests that the performance was something more memorable and conspicuous than one among many choruses from a Dionysian Parade.

The Kiev fragment (FIGURE 1.3) is the nearest parallel in time and style of presentation for our cock-men, though in this case the subject matter is obviously comic in some sense. If the vases do commemorate a comic performance, it is probably not a comedy we can identify. Richard Green first identified this scene on the calyx krater as a depiction of the chorus of Aristophanes' *Birds* (the pelike was not known until 2008). But there is a growing consensus that the calyx krater is too early for *Birds,* and this seems to be confirmed by the style of the pelike as well.[34] Moreover, the fact that these birds are fighting cocks and that cocks (or any other domesticated bird) do not appear in the chorus of *Birds* is an insuperable obstacle.[35] It has been suggested that they are not choreuts but actors on the strength of an ancient scholiast that tells us that the Just and Unjust Arguments in Aristophanes' *Clouds* (first produced in 424 BC) appeared as fighting cocks.[36] But both the dating and the very recently discovered pelike tell against such a connection with *Clouds*. While the calyx krater (FIGURE 1.4) seemed to focus on an aggressive interaction between the cocks, as would suit the debate in *Clouds,* the pelike (FIGURE 1.5) presents only a single figure, making it clear that the painter did not feel a focus upon a confrontation was necessary to evoke the performance to which the vase alludes. A single figure better represents the notional unity of a chorus than the division between antagonists of a comic agon. The pelike (and hence also the calyx krater) should therefore refer to a chorus and most probably a comic chorus.

Choregic Art

The earliest vases to depict theatrical performance in a realistic style all take the chorus for their subject. It is not until about 430 BC that Attic painters take any

Figure 1.6   Attic marble relief fragments, *c.*340 BC, Athens, Agora Museum S1025 + S1586. Courtesy, Agora Excavations, The American School of Classical Studies

interest in actors. But before we examine vasepaintings with actors, it will be helpful to contextualize this choral art.

Scenes of dramatic choruses appear in other media besides vasepainting. Two fourth-century marble reliefs survive that take for their subject the entry (*parodos*) or perhaps the exit (*exodos*) of a comic chorus.[37] The reliefs, found in the Athenian agora, served as bases for monuments erected to celebrate victories in the dramatic competitions in Athens somewhere around 340 BC (FIGURE 1.6). These monuments were erected by the choregoi, wealthy Athenian citizens, who were appointed to sponsor the training and equipping of a chorus for a festival competition. It was the choregos, as representative of the chorus, who actually received the prize awarded to the best production in each genre category on behalf of the chorus and the trainer of the chorus (in the fifth century usually the poet). The choregos is thereby obliged to memorialize the victory by erecting a monument on behalf of his chorus and, to be sure, himself, in or near the sanctuary of the god at whose festival the chorus performed. When one evokes the image of a choregic monument, one normally thinks of the grand monuments, like the Lysikrates monument that still stands in Athens, built to carry the tripods that served as prizes for victory in the dithyrambic competitions of the City Dionysia. The monuments erected to commemorate a victory in drama at the City Dionysia were much simpler.[38] Most commonly they took a form shared by several other types of victory monuments (for some types of athletic victories, for example): a base which held a pillar or column which in turn supported a relief or painting. The base as well as the relief or painting of such monuments could be decorated with imagery relevant to the commemoration. This is the case with the reliefs from the Agora. Both reliefs show highly realistic details, including mask and the belly-and-buttock padding typical of comic costume. In both, the comic chorus dances in formation. And in one case (FIGURE 1.6), we have the remains of pipers (the same or

similar scenes were replicated on the four sides of the monument base). A fragmentary chous, produced a little earlier than the Agora reliefs, offers a very
similar scene and exemplifies the Athenian vasepainter's habit of copying or
adapting imagery from choregic monuments (other examples are discussed
below).[39]

We also have surviving examples of the principal reliefs held by such choregic
monuments (and we may safely assume that the imagery of choregic paintings
was much the same as the imagery of choregic reliefs). The surprising thing is
that, unlike the two base fragments that survive, none of these principal reliefs
shows a scene of drama in performance. Is this by chance?

What the principal reliefs do show is no less interesting for our purposes.
There are four main varieties of images. One variety, which is not strictly relevant to our purposes, is a relief that simply shows masks and alludes to an alternative type of choregic dedication, which is the dedication of the masks used by
the chorus (and the actors?) in the sanctuary of Dionysus.[40] A second type of
image shows choreuts approaching, often with sacrifice, the altar of Dionysus,
or Dionysus himself, who in any case stands behind his altar to receive the offering. Scenes of this type are commonly referred to as "adoration scenes" after an
analogous schema in Christian art. A third variety shows Dionysus reclining on
a dining couch often with a woman at his feet and, beside the couch, a wine
steward who draws wine from a large jar. The woman may hold a mask or there
might be masks affixed to the wall. This schema is traditionally and still frequently mislabelled as "Totenmahl" but would better be called a monoposiast
scene (after its main feature, a man or god on a couch drinking alone). The most
common type of choregic relief, beginning, it appears, in the last decade of the
fifth century, is a combination of the adoration and monoposiast scheme in
which a group of choreuts, usually holding their masks, approaches the couch
where Dionysus lies drinking, usually beside a female companion.

A relief from Peiraeus, dating to about 400 BC is a fine example of the mixed
adoration-monoposiast variety (FIGURE 1.7).[41] It shows three figures in costume, one wearing a mask and two carrying their mask in their hands as they
approach a couch upon which reclines Dionysus. The female figure at Dionysus'
feet wears a fawnskin, like a maenad, and is labeled with a name ending in –IA,
evidently an abstract noun for a personified abstraction. Playfulness (Paidia)
and Tragedy (Tragoidia) have been suggested, but there are many other possibilities. She does not, like many others, hold a mask. The wine steward has also
been omitted.

The relief is commonly referred to as the "Actors' Relief," but there should
be no doubt that the three figures carrying masks are choreuts: the costumes
are nearly identical (the condition of the masks does not allow any judgement
about their similarity) and they carry large tambourine-like instruments, called

Figure 1.7   Marble relief from Peiraeus, *c.*400 BC, Athens NM 1500. Courtesy, German Archaeological Institute. DAI-Neg.-No. D-DAI-ATH-NM 610.

tympana, to show that they are involved in the production of music. The length of their costumes and the belt high above the waist shows that they play female roles. The *tympana* show that they are a Dionysiac chorus, probably bacchants. The choreut on the left wears his mask (it is all but obliterated, but traces remain) and also postures and shakes his *tympanon* as if merging with his role.[42]

Just as vasepainters might imitate the imagery of the reliefs on the base of choregic monuments (as in the case of the fragmentary chous, mentioned above), so we have many that seem to develop or extract from the imagery of the principal reliefs of such monuments. The adoration schema is, for example, played with by one of our earliest vases depicting tragic choreuts.

From about 490 BC we have a hydria by the Pan Painter showing, on the left, two chorusmen (FIGURE 1.8). Their faces are identical, suggesting masks, and their costumes nearly so. We can tell that they are not real soldiers, because, although they wear clothing suggestive of military corselets, they have wreaths in their hair and no other armour, just as on the Basel krater (FIGURE 1.2).[43] The choreuts, apparently awestruck and shy, are firmly led by Hermes. The reason for their timid awe is the imposing presence of Dionysus to whom Hermes is about to introduce them. Dionysus "makes an expressive gesture of greeting and welcome as he steps forward to meet them, right arm outstretched."[44] Green interprets the scene as a subtle commentary on drama and early literacy. In my view, however, Hermes is here, not for any connection he may have with education or

Figure 1.8   Attic red-figured hydria, Pan Painter, 490–480 BC, Hermitage B 201 (St. 1538). Courtesy, The State Hermitage Museum, St. Petersburg. Photograph © The State Hermitage Museum.

writing, but as the bringer of luck and success in competitions, Hermes *Enagonios* (= "Hermes Who Manifests Himself In Competition"), a manifestation of Herme who is mentioned in several Athenian victory dedications.[45] Moreover, the tablets Hermes carries are not, I think, the script of the tragedy, as Green argues, but the wax tablets judges used to register their votes at musical and dramatic competitions.[46] If this is right, the Pan Painter is giving creative expression to an idea implicit in many votive reliefs celebrating victories in choral music: mortal worshippers, elevated by victory, approach the god who is most frequently engaged in sympotic activity.[47] The image on the Pan Painter's hydria, through the shyness of the choreuts and the expansively welcoming gesture of the god, gives a more purely epinician touch to the usual "adoration" type.

"Adoration" votives focussed upon the victory sacrifice. The sacrifice of the victorious choregos and his chorus was conceived differently from ordinary sacrifice. Though dramatic choruses, unlike dithyrambic or "circular" choruses, won no prize, like a tripod, destined to serve as a dedication, they did, like circular choruses, win animals for sacrifice to Dionysus.[48] These animals were sacrificed by the choregos and the chorus in the sanctuary of Dionysus adjacent the theater immediately after the victory at a celebration technically designated by the term *epinikia*.[49] Victory was thus imagined as conferring the right to enter the sanctuary of Dionysus to sacrifice and feast with the god.[50] In Aristophanic comedy the *epinikia* are conceived as an invitation to dine at the premises of the priest of Dionysus and in the presence of the god.[51] The Pan Painter seems to share a similar conception of dramatic choral victory, as not merely a sacrifice in which the god makes an epiphany, but a celebratory banquet at which the god receives the victorious chorus, choregos and poets as his personal guests.

The Pan Painter adds a motif from the iconography of the Introduction of Heracles. Heracles in Greek myth, poetry and art is the archetypal victor.[52] From the victory rituals of athletes at the Panhellenic games, Attic art developed a distinct iconography for the portrayal of Heracles' ascent to Olympus. Its symbolic structure borrowed two moments from the ritual of *eiselasis,* the homecoming parade of the victorious athlete riding home in a chariot to be received by his family and friends.[53] Over a hundred Archaic and Classical Attic vasepaintings show Heracles, upon completion of a life assimilated to athletic struggle in a prize competition – upon the successful completion of many *athloi* (which in Greek means "contests," not "labors") – making his final ascent to Olympus in a chariot driven by Victory (*Nike*) or Athena to the house of his father. Often we see Olympian gods emerging to receive him. Other artifacts show the final stage in the journey where the hero is "introduced" (literally for the first time), usually by Hermes or Athena, to his father Zeus and other members of his divine family.[54] On a typical example of the type we see Athena leading Heracles, hand on wrist, towards Zeus who extends his hand to greet his son.[55] The Pan Painter here (FIGURE 1.8) seems to make a relatively small but significant adjustment to the "adoration" pattern of choregic iconography by deploying the "introduction" schema in order to suggest the victorious chorus' transport to the immortal glory and godlike state of Dionysian victory. In the Pan Painter's "Introduction" Dionysus makes the same welcoming gesture to the victorious choreuts as Zeus to Heracles, while Hermes retains his characteristic role as guide and go-between.

Adoration reliefs in choregic art are proabably the ultimate inspiration for the many "genre scenes" that typically show choreuts in costume, but holding their masks, or showing other signs of being "off-stage." Although the Peiraeus relief (FIGURE 1.7), of around 400 BC, is the earliest actual relief on which we find the motif, Scholl has conjectured that a mid fifth-century BC monument served as the original for an Early Imperial marble showing the remains of a hand and arm holding a satyr-mask.[56] The relaxed pose and the appearance of conversation that we find on the left, "adoration," side of the Peiraeus relief, where the second choreut has turned back away from the god and towards the last choreut in line, is closely paralleled in other adoration reliefs of fourth-century BC date.[57] But this type of scene must have appeared in choregic art much earlier, as Scholl suggests, because there survive eleven whole or fragmentary Attic vases with so-called "genre scenes" in which choreuts hold masks in their hands and sometimes face another choreut as if in conversation: seven depict tragic choreuts, three depict satyric choreuts, and one comic choreuts.[58]

Figure 1.9 Attic red-figured volute krater, Pronomos Painter (name vase), c.400 BC, Naples NM 81673. Drawing by E. Malyon.

All have at least one unmasked choreut, but several also contain a masked choreut, who, like the last choreut in the Peiraeus relief, wears a mask and dances or at least adopts a stance appropriate to the role he played in the drama. Minor variations exist, as in a comic scene in Heidelberg where the dancing choreut is just beginning to take off his mask, or as in a tragic scene in Boston where the unmasked choreut is seen dressing (suggesting a "before," rather than an "after" picture). The important point is that when a figure puts on a mask he also puts on the mythical or narrative illusion that the mask creates. In all of these scenes the masks and costumes are depicted in highly realistic detail. The artists play with the contrast between realism and illusion: the juxtaposition of a masked choreut who appears to be possessed by his mask to an unmasked choreut who appears to be very much part of our world is sufficiently common and deliberate that we must regard it as a major theme in choregic art. Unlike choreuts, actors in Attic art are never seen unmasked and are also never so free of the mythical or narrative illusion.

The most inspired adaptation of choregic art appears in the vasepainting of the end of the fifth century, just shortly after the mixed adoration-monoposiast imagery begins to appear on reliefs. The Pronomos vase (FIGURE 1.9), the most famous theatrical vase of antiquity, is a notable example of creative play with the imagery of mixed adoration-monoposiast reliefs.[59] Produced around 400 BC, it depicts the cast of a satyrplay celebrating victory in the sanctuary of Dionysus. On the upper band the god Dionysus reclines on a couch in the monoposiast pose, accompanied by two females, one who (as on a monoposiast relief in Cagaliari) sits at the foot of the god's couch and holds a mask in her hand.[60] But as on the relief from Peiraeus (FIGURE 1.7) choreuts stand, for the most part, mask in hand in the presence of the god. Also present are the choregos, the chorus trainer, the piper and three figures dressed in the costume of actors, all (but the dancing satyr and the piper) adopting the stance of performers relaxing in the sanctuary after a hard-won victory. The sanctuary is indicated by the choregic monuments with tripods depicted underneath the handles which also serve to reinforce the theme of victory in a musical contest.

The combination of compositional types makes for a rather strange-looking scene: the cast of a satyrplay lounge lazily about the sanctuary of Dionysus while the god, who pays them no attention (nor indeed they him), drinks all alone with his girlfriend on his couch. Its paradoxical appearance is the result of the painter's sticking rather close to two different choregic models while adapting them to his own ends. The god as monoposiast appears here with the same divine insouciance that we find in scenes of the monoposiast type. But the choreuts of the adoration-type motif, who were normally depicted as a train of worshippers approaching the god, now invade the god's space, dispersed as they are throughout the sanctuary. The artist has converted the standard imagery of victory into a compostion that focuses more decidedly upon the theme of repose after a difficult struggle. The choreuts are no longer there, as in the adoration scenes, to perform sacrifice. There is no longer any suggestion of sacrifice. The choreuts are there because they have won the right to share the god's joyful tranquility. And yet it is important that the choreuts appear more or less as they do in adoration scenes, standing for the most part, and in conversation with one another, because choreuts holding masks standing beside one another in relaxed conversation recalls the established imagery of choral victory and because the idea of victory is thematically very important to this composition. The point might have been lost if the world of the god and the dramatists were fully merged into one great symposium scene.

The major motifs of the adoration type scenes are all present. The choreuts wear their costumes and carry their masks. They are grouped in pairs facing one another as if in conversation, many of them seeming to turn back, in the direction opposed to that of their gait, to face their conversation partner, as if they were still in a line (as they would be if the adoration format were strictly followed). As in the Peiraeus relief and many of the genre scenes, there is one choreut (and only one) who escapes the realistic style in which his fellows are depicted. Here it is the choreut labeled Nikoleos just to the left of the centrally seated piper. He does not hold, but wears his mask and, consequently, like the other masked choreuts in choregic art, he does not stand conversing with his fellow choreuts, but dances like a satyr and for all appearances becomes one. Perhaps by yielding to the mythical illusion in one case the artists mean to underscore the theatrical realism of the others: beside what appears to be a satyr or a bacchant we have performers who only sometimes pretend to be satyrs or maenads.

There are other mythical as well as illusionistic details on the vase that contrast sharply with its general theater-realism. The most obvious mythical detail is the presence, top center, of Dionysus (labeled) embracing a female figure (unlabeled) and a winged "Desire" (labeled) to her right. A still more effective contrast between the real world of Dionysus' theatrical choreuts and the mythical world of Dionysus' choruses of satyrs and maenads emerges when one looks at the other side of the vase.[61] There Dionysus, his female companion (surely Ariadne) and Desire move briskly accompanied by four real satyrs and two maenads: these satyrs are distinguished from the satyrplay choreuts by their dance and the absence of any trace of costume, namely the satyr-shorts (*perizomata)* with the phalloi and tails that are the typical costume of satyrplay satyrs.

The Pronomos vase shows all the people who contributed to the victory of the performance: the chorus, the choregos, the piper, the poet in his capacity of chorus trainer, and even the actors. The presence of actors is particularly interesting, but the subject of the vasepainting is nonetheless principally choral and choregic in conception. The choregos was almost exclusively concerned with the chorus and the personnel hired to instruct the chorus. He probably had little, if any, contact with the actors before the competition. (Selected and paid by the archon, a city official who organized the festival, the actors in drama competed for a prize entirely separate from the prize for the best production for which the chorus and choregos competed.) It is sometimes said that the actors have a privileged place on the Pronomos vase, immediately beside (or in one case on) the couch of the god. But this is not so much a "privileged" as a "mythical space." Almost all the human figures on the vase have names inscribed beside them, and these are real personal names. The choreuts, the chorus trainer (a.k.a. poet), the choregos, and the piper all have the names of performers. But the actors have no such inscribed names, with the exception of the actor in the Heracles costume, who is labeled "Heracles." Of all the labeled characters on the vase he is the only one labeled with the name of his mask and not with the name of the man who carries the mask. Indeed, all three actors lack not only their own names but even their own faces. The facial features of all three actors simply reproduce those of their masks. Furthermore, in the case of the actor at the end of Dionysus' couch, the actor not only lacks his own name and face, but his gender as well. As the mask is female, so the "actor" appears as a female. The only masculine trait he retains is the dark color of his skin, which is dark like the skin of the other male characters, but it contrasts with the color of his mask, with the color of the flesh of the real woman in Dionysus' embrace, and with the color of the Desire beside him, which are all rendered in white paint as female and childish flesh were conventionally depicted. In contrast to the choreuts and all those involved with the chorus, the actors are, as real individuals, insignificant, but as mythical characters, fully present. At this level too, realism is played off against illusionism, and theatrical performance against its mythical narrative. But significantly, the performance-realistic style is reserved for the chorus and its supporting personnel.

The Pronomos vase is not the only vase of this period to make free play with choregic motifs. Several vasepaintings datable between 410 and 380 BC, most of them by painters closely associated with the Pronomos Painter, include Dionysus, usually reclining, in his sanctuary and accompanied by female figures or other members of his thiasos. They develop the implied comparison and contrast we find on the Peiraeus relief (FIGURE 1.7) between the dramatic chorus, evidently costumed as bacchants, and the mythical thiasos of Dionysus, represented by the god himself and the female at the end of his couch wearing a fawnskin and dressed as a maenad. On the Pronomos vase, for example, we have satyr choreuts in the sanctuary of Dionysus on what is traditionally recognized as the "front" of the vase (FIGURE 1.9) and mythical satyrs running and dancing in the wild with Dionysus on the "back." On three other vases, all close to the Pronomos Painter, and all of about 400 BC, we have scenes of real satyrs and choreuts mixing freely in the sanctuary of Dionysus, while the god himself reclines, twice on a couch, and in one case embracing a female figure.[62] By placing mythical Dionysian dancers beside victorious dramatic choreuts choregic art implied the choreuts' elevation to membership in the Dionysian thiasos. The Pronomos Painter plays with this figure of choregic art: he puts Dionysus' mythical and theatrical choruses in juxtaposed but clearly separated spaces on front and back of the vase. The associates of the Pronomos Painter, through indiscriminately mixing mythical and real dancers, develop the metaphor into a dull equation that loses its poignancy because it also flattens the pointed contrast between mythical and real, divine and mortal.

The image of choreuts relaxing after a dramatic victory is an appropriate subject for choregic art. It is certainly present in the Peiraeus relief (FIGURE 1.7). We saw that the motif was adapted by eleven vasepaintings dating from 470 to 350 BC, and this allowed us to conjecture the existence of the motif on choregic paintings or sculptures.[63] A series of sculptures, the first earlier or contemporary with the Peiraeus relief and the Pronomos vase, also extracts the figure holding the mask. These are not, however, from victory monuments, but from tombstones. Four Attic funerary monuments present the image of a young (beardless) man who is reasonably taken to symbolize the person buried in the tomb. Three of these show the youth holding a female mask and in two cases (not enough of the third is preserved to tell) also wearing female costume.[64] As in the case of the Peiraeus relief, scholarship has traditionally regarded these figures as actors or poets. The artistic context we have been examining makes it far more likely that these figures, albeit solitary, are to be taken as choreuts. Statistical probability, indeed, urges us to read them this way. The numbers of Classical Attic tombstones that remain is relatively small and their survival random. It is far more likely that indications of theatrical connections refer to choreutic service than service as an actor or poet. It is, in fact, almost impossible to imagine that any healthy Athenian male ever managed to escape choreutic service at least once in his life.[65] Much more important than the fact of chorus duty, however, are the symbolic values associated with chorus duty: cultivation, civic responsibility, and piety.

There is also an eschatological link between participation in the chorus of the god of theater and participation in the chorus of the god of the mysteries and the afterlife.[66] This explains the use of choral vases as grave goods (that is how most of them survived) as well as the use of choreutic imagery on funerary stelae. Images of actors and poets would soon acquire some of this eschatological symbolism (as we will see), but in Athens in the fifth century the eschatological symbolism of theatrical performance is concentrated on the image of the choreut. It is not until early Hellenistic times that we can say with assurance that scenes of figures holding masks (always seated and usually surrounded by others, or by papyrus rolls) were used to mark the graves of poets.[67] The earliest possible rendering of the type of the dramatic poet with a mask is the seated and bearded figure accompanied by two masks on the Lyme Park relief of about 360 BC.[68] But the identification of this figure with a poet is far from certain. He is associated with a plurality of masks (here two), as poets often are in the Hellenistic sculptures. Though this may seem to indicate a poet rather than a choreut (who needs only one mask) it is hardly reassuring that both masks (to my eyes at least) appear to represent the same character.[69] In Hellenistic sculptures and paintings the poets always have different masks, representing the different characters who interact in their compositions.

Depicting Actors

Attic art does have a few scenes of performing actors. They are, however, very different from the art in the choregic style that we have just examined. First, Classical Attic artifacts that take actors as their subjects are much less numerous than artifacts that focus upon the chorus or choreuts. Secondly, if we can trust the available remains, actors first appear in Attic art around 430 BC, a good deal later (by sixty years) than the first dramatic choruses. Thirdly – a most curious fact – all remaining scenes focussed on actors (i.e. excluding actors incidental to choral scenes) appear only on vases, and all of these vases, with a single exception, are a form of winejug called a *chous* (plural *choes*). Choes are normally small and simply decorated: a demotic art in contrast with the art of the large sympotic vases upon which the choral scenes appear.

The chous is a ritual vase associated with drinking contests that took place on the second day (notably called *Choes)* of the Anthesteria (a festival lasting three days in the winter month of Anthesterion, roughly February). The subjects of choes are often Dionysian, doubtless a reflection of the fact that Dionysus is the sovereign deity of the Anthesteria. But the subjects are not limited to activities that take place at this festival. They notoriously include illustrations of competitions performed at other festivals.[70] To take an example close to our present investigation, there are many examples of choes (and related forms of winejug) that reproduce the image of a winged Victory or an Eros who carries ribbons toward a prize tripod to decorate it (a common practice in celebration of a dithyrambic victory), perhaps the most common motif of reliefs on choregic monuments constructed to hold prize tripods.[71] And yet there was no dithyrambic competition at the Anthesteria. So, though we have the isolated testimony of a biographical work falsely ascribed to Plutarch that Lycurgus some time between 338 and 326 BC revived a comic competition that had fallen into neglect at the Anthesteria, it is probably wrong to assume that comic actors on our choes refer to the comic competitions that Lycurgus later "revived."⁷² There is evidence to suggest that the original "choruses" that were notionally revived at the Anthesteria belong to a period long before comedy became a recognisable genre.⁷³ Noteworthy, however, is the fact that almost all the images related to drama on choes are comic. This may have something to do with another intriguing fact about the imagery on choes. It also frequently relates to childhood and childish play and typically show children performing ritual or festive roles, possibly because important rites of passage for young children also took place on the day called Choes.⁷⁴ Children are especially common on a group of miniature choes produced between 420 and 390 BC.

Comic actors appear to provide a linkage between the realm of Dionysian ritual and childsplay, but so, often, do grotesque figures, and it is sometimes very difficult to say if a subject is comic or not. How, for example, does one measure the importance for our question of a late fifth-century chous fragment from the Athenian agora that shows a grotesquely ugly aulete and most of the trunk of a naked male body with a large paunch and a large penis?⁷⁵ Between the figures is an apparently ritual object that resembles a long pole with a cross bar near the top fixed in a base which is shrouded in ivy. The same object appears once in a choral scene and once in a processional scene.⁷⁶ Here the fact that the aulete's features are distorted shows that we have a ritual scene produced in a grotesque style and no representation of comedy. The decisive criterion is that the painter, even if he does show us something laughable, does not in fact show us anything artificial.

In other cases the presence of comic costume is not in doubt. On a miniature chous of about 400 BC we see, along with two children, a figure who wears a padded comic bodysuit (*somation*) fitted with a very large phallus and clearly wearing a mask, though the mask type is not easily recognizable.⁷⁷ A somewhat earlier chous shows, from right to left, a dog, a boy (?) masked and dressed in comic costume running with a stick, and a boy running with a cake.⁷⁸ But even if the costumes are those of actors, these scenes are almost certainly not images of actors. The figures have the same dimensions as the other children on the vases, and one would more confidently claim that we have here the images of children who play the role of actors playing the role of comic characters. The same applies to a miniature chous found on the shore of the Black Sea.⁷⁹ The chous shows five children, all unmasked, but each either carrying a comic mask or at least juxtaposed to one. They are dressed as adults in the service of Dionysus: from left to right we have a figure who might be dressed as a choregos (?), a figure whose dress and phallus stick suggest he impersonates an entertainer from the Dionysian Parade (or *Pompe*), two figures who wear the *somation* and phallus of comic actors, and a fifth figure whose dress is much like the first figure, but who carries a single stick, which is often taken to be an aulos (musical pipe).⁸⁰ All the masks

Figure 1.10 Attic red-figured chous, Painter of the Perseus Dance (name vase), *c*.420 BC, Athens BΣ 518. Drawing by E. Malyon.

are masks of comic actors (not choreuts).[81] If there is any trace of a choregic formula here, it is limited to the fact that each of the figures (except the last) holds his mask in his hand so that one can see the performer beneath, but these performers are neither choreuts nor actors but clearly children.

Images of children playing the part of actors would seem to presuppose an iconography of the actor. Four vasepaintings make this supposition a certainty. The oldest is from a fragmentary cup.[82] One fragment shows the right side of a torso wearing a comic body suit (*somation*). Moore dates it to 450–440 BC, but *MMC* to 430 BC, which is more in line with the iconographic comparanda. It is not impossible that the figure is intended to be a comic choreut, possibly of the sort with mask in hand, but this is unlikely. Though choreuts did, apparently, wear the comic *somation* under their costumes, we have no example of a chorus that danced naked and, as the *somation* with no further overlay represents "stage-nakedness," this figure is very likely to be an actor. Moreover, as the figure is not on a chous but on a cup, we have pretty certainly the actor himself (our very first) and not a child impersonating an actor.

The earliest scene of a comic actor in a performance context is on a chous of about 420 BC (FIGURE 1.10).[83] Perhaps the most interesting – certainly the most unusual – of all Attic representations of drama, it is also one of the most damaged.

It is here presented in a reconstructed drawing.[84] This is the only Attic vase to show a stage or an audience and the first to focus upon a performing actor (the diminutive figure behind the altar on the Basel krater, FIGURE 1.2, probably an actor, is marginal to the choral scene). Worried by its unique subject matter, its poor condition, and its inaccessibility, scholarship has attempted to ignore or downplay its importance to theater iconography, either by assigning the performance to a non-theatrical genre (mime, pantomime, farce or freak-show) or by denying that it is a theatrical performance altogether (private performance, rehearsal, murder trial).[85] Albeit unique, the main features of the vasepainting are not unparalleled (something that definitely cannot be said for the fanciful scenarios scholars have dreamt up in an attempt to defuse the vase's importance to theater history).

On the left, two figures seated in wooden chairs (*klismoi*) watch a stage performance. The front row seating of the later, stone "Lycurgan" theater in Athens imitates the form of these wooden chairs, probably in allusion to the earlier practice of placing such chairs at the edge of the *orchestra* for celebrity seating (*prohedria*). The first of the spectators is bearded, muffled in a cloak, and wears a garland, apparently of laurel. The other is beardless and his (?) hair is banded by a ribbon; he turns to face the bearded man. The bearded figure is paralleled in Attic pottery from 450 to 420 BC by several seated and garlanded men who often (but not invariably) carry the long staff of judges and umpires and watch musicians perform on a low platform (*bema*).[86] The transference of this schema from a musical to a stage performance is a natural if creative step. Perhaps a specific identity was intended for these two figures (judges? choregos and poet? Dionysus and Ariadne?), but they function, in any case, as a synecdoche for the audience.

On the right side of the vase a ladder with three rungs leads up from the level of the *orchestra* to a low stage. If unique in Attic art, both ladder and stage are amply paralleled in West Greek comic vasepainting beginning as little as two decades after the production of this vase.[87] On top of the stage we see a performer who carries the sickle and magic bag that are the standard attributes of the mythical hero Perseus. A line on the performer's raised right wrist (and probably at the right ankle) gives a clear indication that he wears the body tights that are standard and invariable costume for theater performers and which represent "stage-nakedness."[88] In addition his stance emphasizes his "looped" phallus, a familiar manner of arranging this feature of comic costume.[89] There can be no doubt that a comic actor is intended (the chorus only performs in the *orchestra*: in this image both chorus and *orchestra* are elided in order to focus on the interplay between actor and audience).

Despite all these details, scholars have remained skeptical about the Perseus actor. They declare themselves unsatisfied with the dimension of his phallus (it seems too small for comedy) and his stomach seems to offer no trace of the padding that normally indicates the comic *somation*. His head seems large enough with respect to his body that many are content to suppose him a dwarf, but for others it is too small to indicate a mask. And though his mouth is open, it is not as wide open as many seem to expect for a representation of a comic mask. But perhaps this is because Attic vasepainters have not yet developed a standard idiom for representing masks, oversized comic phalloi, and padding.[90] I suspect rather, though it may come down to the same thing, that this Attic vasepainter is still to some extent depicting the story behind the performance. Along with the comic actor we see the mythical hero Perseus that he represents. And although his head is larger than those of his audience, and the unusual strand by strand representation of his hair draws attention to its artificiality, as well as its mussiness, Perseus is represented by no mask, but by a heroically handsome face, with features untouched by the distortions we would expect to find on a comic mask.

The situation is just the opposite on an Attic chous of *c.*410 BC that depicts a comic Heracles and a snub-nosed Victory together in a chariot pulled by four centaurs.[91] In front of the centaurs is a man (Iolaus?) who dances in front of the centaurs as if to suggest that he is leading the team. This figure is "stage-naked" because he clearly wears comic tights (there are lines at the wrists and ankles and an abundance of wrinkles on his legs). He also has a phallus that would satisfy the most theater-skeptical viewer (though his belly is not more pronounced than was Perseus'). But, apart from these costume details, there is nothing to signify a comic production. On the contrary, the centaurs, although caricatured, are presented as real centaurs, not pantomime horse-men as we might have expected to see in a comedy. Just possibly the vase gives us a somewhat mythicized scene from a comic production featuring Heracles and a chorus of centaurs.

More probably, the subject of Heracles in a victory chariot gives us a parody of epinician painting. The vase draws directly upon the imagery of the Ascension of Heracles and indirectly upon the homecoming rituals of athletic victors.[92] I argued above that the "introduction" imagery was directly borrowed from Heracles iconography in the Pan Painter's vase celebrating a choral victory in tragedy (FIGURE 1.8). Several passages in Archaic Greek literature make it clear that the chariot imagery was directly applied to victors in musical contests. Simonides dedicated a painting or relief upon which an epigram boasted that upon winning a life total of fifty-six victories in the circular chorus he "stepped onto the brilliant chariot of Victory."[93] Pindar makes reference to himself or other poets mounting the chariot of the Muses.[94] A (probably early fifth-century) choregic epigram, describes the choregos for a circular chorus being "borne about in the chariot of the Graces."[95] It is possible, therefore, that the image of the comic Heracles in the chariot of Victory plays with generic imagery from choregic victory monuments: the rare depiction of a choregic painting mounted in Dionysus' sanctuary in FIGURE 5.5, below (just behind Dionysus), consists of nothing more than a winged Victory driving a chariot. In the case of the comic chous, it could be argued that no specific comic production lies behind the image, but that it is a vasepainter's fantasy of a mythical scene in comic dress (though possibly a mythical scene selected for its association with victory and specifically a comic victory). Nonetheless, the painting does render realistic production details in its depiction of comic costume, most particularly in the comically distorted faces and the indication of comic tights and a phallus on the centaur who leads the chariot. Moreover Heracles' face is indistinguishable from the type of the comic Heracles we find in vasepainting and terracotta figurines (some only a decade later than this vase). However, even if much in the painting is due to painterly elaboration, one cannot discount the possibility that it alludes to a specific comedy in which Heracles tamed a chorus of centaurs. Nichochares produced a comedy called *Heracles Choregos* at about this date.

The very best connection with a known comedy comes from a crudely painted winejug (*oinochoe*) fragments of about 410 BC, with two labeled figures in comic costume (FIGURE 1.11).[96] Preserved is "..onysos" which can certainly be restored as "Dionysos," left, and "Phor" which can with high probability be restored as "Phormio," right. The oinochoe almost certainly shows a scene from *Taxiarchoi*, a comedy by Eupolis, first produced in Athens probably around 415 BC, in which we are told that Dionysus "learns from Phormio the ways of generals and wars."[97] Much of the play's humor derives from the contrast between Dionysus, who in comedy is usually portrayed as soft, lazy, and effeminate, and Phormio, an Athenian general with a reputation for being an old-fashioned disciplinarian (in the play he proclaims that his nickname is "Ares"). The fragments preserve, among other things, lessons that Dionysus receives in holding a shield, making camp, living in squalor, dining on olives and raw onions, and rowing. Phormio's posture on the oinochoe suggests a lesson in oarsmanship. We have a fragment from the play with the complaint "hey you at the bow, will you stop splashing us?" and, if the speaker is Dionysus, it might be delivered at a moment very close to that here represented.[98] On the oinochoe, enough of "Dionysus" survives to suggest the standard comic body suit with breast, belly and buttock padding, and the large head and gaping mouth hint at a mask, but generally speaking, as the original publication notes, "an accurate portrayal of a comic actor does not seem to have been intended."[99] Indeed, the painting is fast and crude and nothing very accurate was intended. But the contours suffice to show that a comic figure is meant.

Within the last decade of the fifth century Athens begins to produce the first terracotta figurines of comic actors. These were probably intended primarily for sale to foreign tourists attending the Athenian Dionysia and are found widely

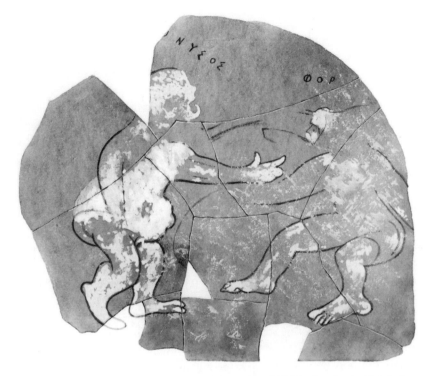

Figure 1.11   Attic polychrome oinochoe, *c*.400 BC, Agora P23985. Drawing by Piet de Jong. Courtesy, Agora Excavations, The American School of Classical Studies.

dispersed throughout the Greek world.[100] The few (only four) that can be assigned a fifth-century date, however, were all found in Athens.[101] The production of figurines increases significantly at a time when Attic vasepainting is in decline and the export of Attic vases comes to an end. From the first quarter of the fourth century there survive at least twenty-six different bronze and terracotta figurine types of comic actors, which survive in hundreds of copies, and reproduce the masks, costumes and gestures of comic actors with uncompromised realism – and all apparently are the work of a single Athenian coroplast.[102] Statuettes of satyrs and silens with indications of costume also begin to be produced at the same time, but apart from these the terracotta production is entirely concerned with actors, not choreuts.[103] No tragic figurine is datable before the Hellenistic period and when tragic figurines do appear they are also exclusively actors. Early fourth-century BC Athens also saw the manufacture of representations of comic masks.[104] Except in the case of stone sculpture, which either comes from a choregic dedication or imitates the choral subjects of choregic dedications, all representations of comic masks are actors' masks.[105]

Conclusion

Attic art has some subjects that can be treated with uncompromised realism. Among them theater scenes have an important, indeed privileged, place. They begin with choral scenes, a reflection of the fact that for these subjects vasepainters took their inspiration from the art of choregic monuments, which are above all designed to commemorate the victory of a chorus. Commemorative dedications of this sort are a very likely source for the development of realistic images of theatrical performance. The function of a dedication is to commemorate a specific victory by specific people in the contemporary world. It may play with the dramatic illusion or may emphasize the performers' service to the god Dionysus through pictorial analogies between the chorus and Dionysus' mythical thiasos, but it is nonetheless the performers, not the drama's heroes, that are the chief object of interest.

Himmelmann signaled the importance of votive art in the development of Greek pictorial realism.[106] I hope to have indicated that choregic art was one of the most productive of all votive forms in this process. Choregic art took a greater interest in depicting a chorus as real citizens (sometimes, as in the case of the Pronomos vase inscribing real names beside them) than as the anonymous mythical or fictional group of people or creatures evoked by a dramatic narrative. But the choregos commissioned the monument not just to commemorate the contribution of individual choreuts. He commemorated his own contribution. For this reason choregic art had a special interest in not just the performers but the performance. It certainly suited the choregos to display his contribution in realistic detail: the costumes he commissioned, the dancers he paid to train, the dances for which he paid, the trainers he paid, the pipers he paid, and all the other personnel directly involved with the chorus, even (it would appear from the evidence of FIGURE 1.3) the piper's assistant.[107] All of these might appear in choregic art and all were susceptible to treatment in a realistic style that might at times approach the quality of a visual inventory of choregic outlay. Actors on the other hand had little or no direct share either in the chorus' victory or the choregos' largesse and are present, if at all, only indirectly, and with nothing approaching the realism with which Attic art treats the chorus and its attributes.

Attic vasepainting has no interest in actors before about 430 BC, at a time when theatrical realism in the depiction of choral scenes is in its fullest maturity. Representations of actors are admittedly rare (considerably rarer even than the surviving representations of choral subjects) but they do exist. Though scenes with actors are produced in the same realistic (or in some cases quasi-realistic) idiom as choral scenes, this fact should not blind us to their very different background and significance. Choral scenes appear primarily in marble reliefs or the free-standing paintings of choregic dedications, and then only secondarily on vases, but for the most part large vases created for the symposium. Actors, by contrast, appear only on small vessels, particularly choes and the rather roughly produced polychrome oinochoe of FIGURE 1.11, or in terracotta figurines, which were also very inexpensive. On the one hand, we have expensive upmarket products that have imagery that is choral, elaborate, and shows a very clear preference for the higher status genres of tragedy and satyrplay. On the other hand, we have distinctly downmarket vessels which show actors and are exclusively comic. While the choes do occasionally also draw upon choregic subjects and motifs, the larger vessels never display actors except, if at all, as mere adjuncts to the representation of a choral performance.

The reason for the subject preference of the larger sympotic vessels is not difficult to guess. Choral imagery's association with choregic art gave it the proper sociological status for vases intended for use at drinking parties whose secondary purpose was to display the wealth of the house. Choral motifs had snobappeal because they alluded to the activities and lifestyle of the choregic classes, a lifestyle that had no less appeal because few if any of the consumers of ceramic sympotic vessels could actually afford it. Choes by contrast are not designed for showing off. They are inexpensive and designed for private use (people who attended the drinking parties at the Anthesteria were required to bring their own choes and, unlike ordinary symposia, wine was not shared). Theirs is a much more demotic art, designed for use at popular festivals (just as figurines probably served as souvenirs of the Dionysia). We do have several choes that draw upon choregic art: the painters of choes showed no reluctance to draw upon high-status Dionysian imagery.[108] But – and this is the significant thing – the imagery was not in any way limited to high-status subjects. Comedy evidently suited the hilarity appropriate to day two of the Anthesteria. However, the choice of actors, as opposed to choral subjects, and realistic depictions of actors, as opposed to the narrative or mythical characters they represent, shows a popular interest, for the first time, in the men behind the masks, and an awareness of their skills. The emphasis is not upon the artistic illusion, but upon the art that produces the illusion, and not for any commemorative purpose, but from delight in the actor's art.

Notes

1   Small 2003.52, cf. Small 2005.
2   Gombrich 1960, ch. 4.
3   Ferrari 2003; cf. Ferrari 2002, though with a heavy dose of (post)structuralism's real-world phobia (on which see Eagleton 1996; Csapo 2005.276–90).

4   For a deeper understanding of the artistic and literary style implied by "realism," I have found the writings of Raymond Williams most useful, esp. Williams 1977, Williams 1976.216–20. The term is, of course, at home in Western cultural production of the eighteenth and nineteenth century and applied only by a partial and imprecise, but nonetheless helpful, analogy to ancient art and drama (see further Chapter 4, where some of the limitations are explored). Both the style and many of the social, economic and ideological conditions that gave rise to modern realism are anticipated in antiquity, but this is not the place to pursue this question. Himmelmann 1994 sees a general dropping off in artistic realism from the mid fifth century until the Early Hellenistic period, but notes that the tradition persists in some quarters, and particularly in comedy-related artifacts (1994.19). The observation is in part determined by Himmelmann's focus on low life, vulgarity and ugliness as the most conspicuous manifestations of realism. The fact that deformity and ugliness no longer function as a marker of low sociological status in serious art is surely due to the more democratic ideology of the late fifth to late fourth centuries, when even handworkers could portray themselves as gentlemen (Himmelmann 1994.29). It is paralleled in dramatic writing and acting styles and is not inconsistent with the growth of other aspects of realism (see Chapter 4).

5   Steinhart 2004.

6   *P&P* 7.

7   Wilson 1996.

8   See esp. Green 1991; Taplin 1997; Förtsch 1997.

9   *P&P* 15.

10 Attic red-figured calyx krater, *c*.400–375 BC, Berlin Antikensammlung 3974, *P&P* 206 no. 75.

11 See Chapter 2, pp. 55, 65.

12 For discussion of the tragedy's climactic scene, see Preiser 2000.89–92, 99–109. For the two pre-Euripidean depictions, see Csapo 1990. For depictions of different episode of the Telephus myth, not related to Euripides' play, see Preiser 2000.98, 109–15; *P&P* 210–11.

13 See in particular Hedreen 2007.

14 Attic red-figured hydria, Leningrad Painter, 475–450 BC, Boston MFA 03.788, *MTS* AV 14.

15 Munich 1871 inv. 6025, a black-figured lekythos, is sometimes included in this group, but has not even a piper: it shows young men kneeling in a line with uniform gestures of lamentation in front of an unusual pillar with a human head, perhaps an icon.

16 Attic red-figured pelike, *c*.460 BC; Berlin 3223 (*MTS* AV 15).

17 Attic red-figured hydria fragments by Leningrad Painter, *c*.460 BC, Corinth T620 + T1144, *MTS* AV 13. Most recently discussed by Miller 2004.

18 Attic RF column krater in the Mannerist Style, *c*.500–490 BC, Basel BS 415.

19 On this question, see Csapo 2008.280–4.

20 Taplin 1977.447–8.

21 I thank Margaret Miller for this observation. Compare the Anavyssos chous with the Perseus dancer (FIGURE 1.10), where, as here, special attention is given to the hair as part of a deliberate attempt to make the heads look artificial (i.e. masklike).

22 Froning 2002.72, fig. 88; *P&P* 30, fig. 9.

23 Froning 2002.72; Revermann 2006a.87–8, n. 64.

24 The first, an Attic red-figured calyx krater, once Malibu 82.AE.83, has now been returned to Italy by the Getty Museum. It was first published by Green 1985 and has been much discussed since then (see following notes). The second, an Attic red-figured pelike, Atlanta 2008.4.1, was first mentioned in print in *Burlington Magazine* Jan. 2008.

25 There are good reasons why cocks in Greek art are sometimes ithyphallic and they have nothing to do with satyromorphism: see Csapo 1993b.

26 See Krumeich 1999.54 n. 56.

27 The theory has been spun out of a suggestion in Taplin 1993.104 that Taplin himself characterised as "very far-fetched." It is pursued by Revermann 2006a.218–19; Rothwell 2007.57–8; Bakola forthcoming.

28 Comedies with satyr choruses: Storey 2005.

29 Studied by Green 1985a.

30 Green 1985a, Förtsch 1997, and others refer to them as "comic," "precomic" or "protocomic." For their connection with the *komos,* see Csapo 2003.86–90; Rusten 2006; Csapo and Miller 2007b.22–4; Hedreen 2007.161–3, 185–7; Seaford 2007.380; Csapo 2006/7. Rothwell 2006 rightly stresses the importance of the komos but is wrong to associate the komos exclusively with the aristocratic symposium.

31 Boston MFA 20.18; see Csapo 2008.

32 See esp. Steinhart 2004.22; Rothwell 2007.52–8.

33 Cf. Berlin 3223 and discussion in Rusten forthcoming.

34 Green 1985a dated the vase to *c.*415 BC (Aristophanes' *Birds* was first produced 414 BC). Most experts I have consulted would date the vase at least a decade earlier, and German scholars would update it by two decades or more (cf. Himmelmann 1994.124 "deutlich früher;" Krumeich 1999.42, n. 8 "um 450/440 v. Chr.;" Steinhart 2004.22 "um 440/30 v. Chr.").

35 See Taplin 1993.102.

36 As suggested by Taplin 1987 and Csapo 1993.

37 Marble reliefs: Athens, Agora Museum S1025 + S1586 + S2586 (*SEG* 28.213, *MMC³* 118–19 AS 3); Agora S2098 (*MMC³* AS 4).

38 For details, see Csapo forthcoming A.

39 Attic red-figured chous fragments, Benaki 30895: Pingliatoglou 1992; Fotopoulos and Delivorrias 1997, figs. 208–9; Froning 2002.89, fig. 123.

40 See Csapo forthcoming A, for a more detailed typology of choregic reliefs.

41 Athens NM 1500, *MTS* AS 1. The problems posed by the relief are discussed in detail by Csapo forthcoming A.

42 Micheli 1998.3 has detected traces of a mask on the leftmost choreut's head.

43 St. Petersburg B 201 (St. 1538); Schmidt 1967; Green 1995a.

44 Green 1995a.77.

45   *IG* I³ 840; *IG* II² 3023; *IG* II² 3089; *IG* II² 4572.

46   As earlier suggested by Schmidt 1967. Voting tablets are clearly attested for Athens by Lysias 4.3, for Sicily in the fifth century by Epicharmus (*PCG* 1 F 237), and for Euboea in the fourth century by *IG* XII 9, 207 etc. (Le Guen 2001a, vol. 1, no. 1, l. 34). Epicharmus' expression "the decision rests on the knees of five judges" implies the use of tablets: it is difficult to see why the judges' knees should be evoked unless the voting tablets normally rested upon them (see Chapter 3, p. 97). Cf. Aelian *VH* 2.13. It is probably voting tablets rather than crowns (or money bags) that appear on the table of the judges representing the Rural Dionysia on the image for Poseideon on the Calendar Frieze of the Little Metropolitan in Athens (Simon 1983.101, pl. 3.3). An Etruscan relief from Chiusi appears to show a scribe with a writing tablet (*grammateion*) standing beside the judges' tribune: Thuillier 1985. 139–40, fig. 52; Colonna 1976.187–8 (I thank J.-P. Thuillier for this reference).

47   Csapo forthcoming A.

48   Burkert 1966.93–102.

49   Plato in the *Symposium* is careful to distinguish the victory celebration for personal friends at Agathon's house from the *epinikia* which took place the night before in which Agathon and his choreuts gave sacrifice (173a6, 174a7). For the epinician feast in general, see Wilson 2000.102–3.

50   There appears to be no specific literary reference to the *epinikia* taking place in the Temple of Dionysus, but this almost certainly follows from the normal practice of athletic victors offering sacrifice at the site of victory, even if banquets are later offered in their own homes: Buhmann 1975.55–6; Wilson 2000.348 n. 250. Aristodemos' description of the *epinikia* in Plato's *Symposium* (see previous note) shows that it took place in a large, public space in which other dramatic victors, their friends and well-wishers were present (note that at the end of Aristophanes' *Assemblywomen*, lines 1141–2, Praxagora's maid invites the spectators and the judges to join the feast). Aristodemos complains that he was frightened by the size of the crowd (*ochlos*) at the *epinikia* (174a 7), and Agathon complains that he looked for him in vain in order to to invite him to a private (and less boisterous) victory party at this own home on the following day (174e).

51   Ar. *Ach.* 1087, with Olson 2002.335, and *Frogs* 297, with Dover 1968.230; Biles 2007.32–5. For the general metatheatrical play between Aristophanic comedy and the *epinikia*: see Revermann 2006a.113–18; Biles 2007; Wilson 2007a.

52   See Golden 1998.141–75; Csapo 2005.304–9.

53   For the *eiselasis*, see Buhmann 1975; Slater 1984; Kurke 1993. Eiselastic imagery seems to have appeared on dedications for musical victories as well, see below, pp. 27–8.

54   Boardman 1990.

55   Attic black-figured cup, by the Phrynos Painter, *c.*560, London B 424, *ABV* 168.

56   Scholl 2000 discussing Ny Carlsberg Glyptotek 3306. His suggestion that it is a dedication by an actor or a poet is highly unlikely: see Green 2008.181. Cf. Sande 1992 on the "Motya youth."

57   Cf. also the Attic relief, Louvre Ma 756 which is thought by some to represent dithyrambic choreuts, but is just as likely to be a dramatic monument (closely related in style to the probably dramatic relief from Sphettos, Athens NM 2400, with which it is probably contemporary): see the discussion in Csapo forthcoming A.

58   **Tragedy.**
1.   Attic red-figured *oinochoe* fragments, Near Hermonax, *c.*470 BC, Agora P 11810, *MTS* AV 9, Moore 1997.232, no. 623; Froning 2002.72, fig. 89.
2.   Attic red-figured bell krater, 460–450 BC, Ferrara T 173C, *MTS* AV 9 and pl. 1a, Pickard-Cambridge 1968, fig. 33.
3.   Attic red-figured pelike, Phiale Painter, *c.*450 BC, Boston MFA 98.883–11, *MTS* AV 20, Pickard-Cambridge 1968, fig. 34.
4.   Attic red-figured volute krater fr., *c.*400 BC, Swiss Private Collection, Froning 2002.84, fig. 112.
5.   Attic red-figured bell krater fr., 375–350 BC, Agora P 24828, *MTS* AV 38 and pl. 1b, Pickard-Cambridge 1968, fig. 52.
6.   Attic volute krater fr., Near Pronomos Painter, *c.*400 BC, Würzburg H 4781, Froning 2002.73, figs. 90–1.
7.   Attic red-figured pelike, Circle of the Pronomos Painter, *c.*400 BC, Barcelona 33, *MTS* AV 36, Csapo forthcoming A.
Satyrplay.
8.   Attic red-figured oinochoe or chous fr., *c.*430 BC, Agora P 32970, Camp 1999.257, fig. 2.
9.   Attic volute krater, Pronomos Painter, *c.*400 BC, Naples NM 81673, *MTS* AV 25.
10.   Attic cup fr., Dresden Albertinum AB 473, 390–380 BC, Froning 2002.83, fig. 110.
Comedy.
11.   Attic red-figured bell krater, Heidelberg B 134, 390–370 BC, Pickard-Cambridge 1968, fig. 85.

59   No. 9 in the list in the previous note. Taplin and Wyles forthcoming is devoted to this vase.
60   Attic relief, Cagliari MN 10918, fourth century BC. See Csapo forthcoming A.
61   Excellent discussion of iconographic contrasts between ritual and mythical choruses by Hedreen 2007.
62   Fragmentary Attic red-figured volute krater, *c.*400 BC, Near the Pronomos Painter, Samothrace 65.104E +, Dinsmoor 1992; fragmentary Attic red-figured pelike, *c.*400 BC, Circle of the Pronomos Painter, Barcelona 33, *MTS* AV 36; Attic bell krater, *c.*400 BC, Ferrara T161C. All three vases are illustrated and discussed in Csapo forthcoming A.
63   See above, note 58.
64   Peiraeus Museum, later fifth century BC, from Salamis. Clairmont 1993.1.233–4 no. 1.075; Scholl 1995, fig. 14; Steinhauer 2001.301 fig. 447. Base for a funerary lekythos, from Vari, Athens, NM 4498, 380–370 BC; Vierneisel and Scholl 2002, fig. 15. Fragmentary marble grave relief, Copenhagen, Ny Carlsberg Glyptotek 1939, 330–320 BC; *MTS*² AS 4.
65   Revermann 2006b.

66   Explored in Csapo 2008 and Csapo forthcoming A.

67   The reliefs are studied by Micheli 1998, though she does not distinguish between actors and choreuts.

68   Rather surprisingly, the poet's beard was trimmed in the late fourth century BC; see Scholl 1995.

69   *MMC* regards the masks as different (AS 1).

70   Rumpf 1961.

71   See Csapo forthcoming A.

72   [Plut.] *X orat.* 841, which seems to draw upon Philochorus *Atthis,* written about 261 BC (cf. schol. Ar. *Ran.* 218). The Lycurgan revival is only otherwise mentioned by Diog. Laert. 3.56; Philostr. *VA* 4.21. The evidence for a spectacle at the Chytroi is collected by Hamilton 1992.38–42.

73   Callim. *Hekale* fr. 85 Hollis; cf. Parker 2005.297.

74   Parker 2005.297–301.

75   Agora P 15116c, Moore 1997.238, no. 675, pl. 72.

76   On a bell krater by the Kleophon Painter (Copenhagen 13817) and in a processional scene with children on a chous in New York (MMA 24.97.34). I doubt that it is intended to be a kottabos stand, as argued by Reilly 1994, or an agricultural implement as argued, among others, by Vatin 2004.40.

77   Athens NM 17752. *MMC* AV 9 recognizes the mask as a standard Old Man mask (E).

78   Attic red-figured chous, *c.*420–410 BC, Louvre CA 2938, *MMC* AV 5.

79   Attic red-figured miniature chous, Class of Athens 1227, *c.*400 BC, Hermitage Фα 1869.47, *MMC* AV 8; Rusten forthcoming.

80   Compare the dress of the choregos (?) who stands beside his tripod on the Attic rf chous, Class of Athens 1268, *c.*415–400 BC, Louvre N2703 ED 73, van Hoorn 1951 nr. 836 fig. 142.

81   As shown by Rusten forthcoming.

82   Fragment of an Attic rf cup, possibly Painter of London E 777, *c.*430 BC, Agora P 10798a, *MMC* AV 3, Moore 1997.326 no. 1449.

83   Attic chous, Painter of the Perseus Dance (name vase), *c.*420 BC, Athens BΣ 518, *MMC* AV 4.

84   Malyon's reconstruction (FIGURE 1.10) is based on photographs and the drawing by Gilléron *fils,* whose accuracy of detail has been vindicated in a recent study of the chous by Hughes 2006.

85   Literature reviewed in Hughes 2006.

86   Hughes 2006.427–8; relevant illustrations collected and discussed by Shapiro 1992.

87   Hughes 2006. 421–3. See Chapter 2 below.

88   The details are confirmed by Hughes 2006.425.

89   Hughes 2006.425.

90   Padding seems slight on the cup fragment, Agora P 10798a, discussed above; cf. Green 1991.31.

91   Attic red-figured chous, Louvre N3408, *MMC* AV 6.

92   See above, p. 17.
93   Simonides 27 P = 145 Bergk, *AnthPal* 6.213.
94   P. *P.* 10.65; *I.* 2.2, cf. *I.* 8.62.
95   *Palatine Anthology* 13.28. See Wilson 2000.120–3.
96   Attic polychrome oinochoe, Athens, *c.*410 BC, Agora P 23985, *MMC* AV 14.
97   ΣArist. *Peace* 348. See Storey 2003.246–60 for discussion of the date and contents of the play.
98   *PCG* F 268.50–1.
99   Crosby 1955.8.
100   Wilson 2008.117–18, who compares souvenirs sold at the Great Panathenaea, especially the "pseudo-Panathenaic" amphorae which appear at precisely this period: see Shear 2001.432–51.
101   *MMC* AT 1–4: Agora T 1468 and 1575; Agora T 3507, same type as Louve CA 376; Agora T 3070. Nicholls 1995.470 dates the earliest to 405 BC.
102   Green 1991.32; Himmelmann 1994.125–35.
103   *MTS* AT 1–3.
104   *MMC* AT4, 31–4. Attic tragic masks are much later, although earlier fourth-century examples are produced outside of Athens: *MMC* AB 1, AT 6–8; Bernabò Brea 1995; Todisco 2002.102–3.
105   Marble reliefs with masks: Athens, NM 1750, MTS² 34, AS 5 (375–350 BC); Athens, NM 4531, SEG 32 [1982] 248 (350–308 BC); Athens NM 382, *MTS* AS 27 (Imperial imitation). See further, Csapo forthcoming A.
106   Himmelmann 1994.9, 23–7.
107   The expense of the piper seems to have been assumed at least initially by the choregos (see Wilson 2000.69), though this may have changed sometime before 348 BC (as suggested by the allotment of pipers by the archon attested by Dem. 21.13–14).
108   See above, notes 39, 71, 83 and 91.

2

A Portrait of the Artist II
Theater-Realistic Art in the Greek West, 400–300 BC

Greece was invented in the Classical period. The Archaic period, it is true, began the work: Archaic epic and lyric laid the foundation of a common ancestry, history, religion, and rituals. But the work of cementing a common bond through language and culture was greatly accelerated in the century and a half following the Persian wars. It happened so quickly that it sometimes takes us by surprise.

Drama became the primary vehicle of cultural Hellenization. West Greek pottery shows that by the last quarter of the fifth century the Greek colonists of Southern Italy had a close familiarity with Attic tragedy. By 400 BC West Greek pottery delivers an even more startling revelation (so startling that scholarship has been very slow to accept it). It preserves images that show scenes, figures or masks of Attic comedy, even Attic Old Comedy, and not just Attic Old Comedy, but Attic Old Comedy in what had seemed its most insular and parochially Athenian form, the political comedy of Aristophanes and Eupolis. Scholarship was so unready for this discovery that in the two decades since proof emerged, it has expended far more energy trying to contain and limit the impact of the evidence upon its conceptual habits than to rethink the prejudices that made the irrefutable facts once seem impossible.

We have been taught to worry about being too Athenocentric in our assessments of Greek culture and to worry about the domination of our evidence from the Classical period by Athenian sources. The modern postcolonial era's antihegemonic sensibility prompted many to take a far greater interest than ever before in the material remains of other Greek states. Paradoxically, however, the largest extant corpus of non-Athenian cultural production from the Classical period, the 20,000 or so extant pieces of painted West Greek pottery, now tell us that in many ways we have not been Athenocentric enough.

Hindsight shows that we might have expected this. The common culture that emerges in the Hellenistic period as the *koine* is in fact mainly Athenian. It is this fact, after all, that resulted in the near exclusive selection, canonization and preservation of Athenian texts (and primarily dramatic texts) from the Classical period. Indeed the Hellenistic cultural *koine* was not only Athenian (in much the same way that our present-day "global" culture is American) but also "classicizing" in the strict sense of the word (fifth and fourth century authors and artists formed the canon in almost every sphere of Hellenistic literature and art). But the art shows us, astonishingly, that the tragic canon existed in the Greek West even before the fifth century ended. Aeschylean, Sophoclean, and Euripidean plays account for close to 75 percent of all tragedy-related vasepaintings.[1] And it is a notable fact that the only identifiable scenes on West Greek comic vases from the first half of the fourth century BC relate to plays by Aristophanes and Eupolis (who later became, along with Cratinus, the canonical triad of Old Comic authors). Who would have thought that the translation of Athenian drama into Greek classics could begin so early? And who would have thought that the evidence for it would come not from Athens or Athens' colonies, empire, or neighbors, but from the distant and (in the late fifth century) mainly hostile states of the Dorian West? Scholars continue to worry that our Athenocentricity is causing us to ignore evidence of differences – differences fostered by the survival and continuance of the native dramatic culture we know to have existed (and persisted) in Sicily. But the problem may rather be our persistence in categorizing fourth-century drama in regional terms. Why does a distinctly Sicilian comedy after its early fifth-century efflorescence with Epicharmus and Phormis appear to vanish without a trace? Why are other regional forms ("Doric" and "Megarian farce") so elusive in the historical period? Why does the Greek West appear to be so interested in "Athenian" drama? The answer may be that the questions are wrong. To anticipate an argument we will take up in Chapter 3, it may be that there was no "Athenian" or "Sicilian" drama by 400 BC, only "Greek" drama? The question then is rather why the earlier fifth-century dramas that seem so Athenian and Athenocentric were reperformed as "classics" in the Greek West. But then did the Western Greeks necessarily think that even early fifth-century dramatic classics were something foreign, quaint, or alien to their culture?

What seems undoubtedly Athenian drama to us may not have seemed so very foreign to a late-fifth or fourth-century Sicilian. Aeschylus, our sources tell us, frequented Sicily and chose to spend the last years of his life there. He wrote at least one play, *Aetnian Women,* specifically for a Sicilian audience, and performed the *Persians,* a drama, if any, with Panhellenic aspirations.[2] Epicharmus's *Persians* is probably a parody of Aeschylus' play.[3] Ancient scholars found Aeschylus' work to be full of Sicilianisms.[4] Partly because of the dense concentration of doricisms, Radt thinks Aeschylus' satyrplay *Diktyoulkoi* was an imitation or parody of Epicharmus' *Diktyes.*[5] Epicharmus' fragments contain at least one Aeschyleanism.[6] One ancient commentator found Aeschylus "in a way, a native" of Sicily; another "definitely a Sicilian."[7] How foreign did fifth-century

Sicilians think Aeschylus or tragedy? Aeschylus – possibly even his tragic rival Phrynichus – died in Sicily.[8] His body, buried in Gela, was a Sicilian treasure: they built a shrine for him, and mounted an annual theater festival in his honor. If the many sources that report Aeschylus' sojourns and emigration to Sicily were fabrications (and there is no good reason to believe that they are), they are evidently fabrications with which Sicily was complicit, and the existence of the story, to say nothing of the shrine, is enough to show that Sicily laid some claim to fostering early tragedy. The theatrical family of Carcinus, the tragedian, who won first prize at the Athenian Dionysia of 446 BC, appears to have had close connections with Sicily; in any case his grandson, also a tragedian was born in Acragas in the last decades of the fifth century and is known to have spent much time in Syracuse.[9] Aristotle tells us of another native Acragantine tragedian, Empedokles, grandson of the mystic philosopher, who wrote twenty-four "political tragedies," possibly in the Aeschylean and Phrynichean tradition sometime in the late fifth century and probably in Sicily.[10]

Sicily also rivaled Athens' claims to being the birthplace of comedy. Aristotle had few doubts about the high sophistication of the Sicilian comedy at a time when Athenian comedy was little more than lampoon; indeed he attributes the maturation of Attic comedy in the mid fifth century BC to the influence of Sicilian Epicharmus.[11] Histories of drama generated in the Greek West had by the fourth century established and in fact overdetermined the Sicilian paternity of both tragedy and comedy.[12] If comedy is to our eyes very Attic it did not look that way to the Western Greeks. We perhaps underestimate late fifth- and fourth-century Greek interest and knowledge of Athenian politics and culture, and the degree to which they viewed Attic culture as a common Greek property. It was, after all, about this time that a non-Athenian, Timotheus of Miletos, dubbed Athens "the Greece of Greece," an expression which doubtless pleased because it encapsulated the paradox that if Athenian cultural hegemony had made the rest of Greece more Athenian, it had also made Athens considerably less so.[13]

Tradition and Innovation: the Case of the Tarporley Painter

In general West Greek vasepainting shows the influence of drama far more commonly than Athenian vasepainting. There are limits to this statement, and we will want to qualify it later, but, viewed globally, West Greek vasepainting shows a greater awareness of drama than Attic. Recent estimates number about 400 tragedy-related and over 250 comedy-related vasepaintings.[14] On these estimates 3.5 percent of all surviving West Greek pottery (estimated at about 20,000 pieces) is decorated with theatrical subjects. This is quantitatively and of course proportionally far greater than Attic vasepainting.

Some controversy attaches to the degree to which West Greek theater-related pottery develops the Attic tradition. The issue of West Greek pottery's dependence has, rightly or wrongly, been entangled with another controversy: what is the ultimate source of the images? Oliver Taplin, who most cogently urged the case for taking the pottery as evidence of dramatic production in the Greek West, has been accused of downplaying West Greek vasepainting's continuity with the Attic tradition.[15] Jeff Rusten's recent hypothesis is that some of the most theater-realistic comic pottery in West Greek vasepainting is inspired by or copies Attic vasepainting and does not furnish evidence of comic performances in the Greek West.[16] The Attic tradition of theater-realistic art is, as we have seen, not negligible. There is need therefore for a reassessment of the relationship of West Greek and Attic theater-related art keeping in mind the impact this relationship may have on the question of contemporary dramatic performance in the Greek West.

No one denies the *general* influence of Attic upon West Greek pottery and iconography. Even before they began to produce their own red-figured pottery Italy and Sicily were an important market for Athenian vases. Among fifth-century imports were dramatic vases of nearly every variety (tragedy-related mythological vases, tragic and comic choruses in performance, and many genre scenes – the one exception, probably fortuitous, is vasepaintings of comic actors). Of tragic subjects alone Catucci lists 89 Attic red figure vases found in South Italian or Sicilian contexts.[17] Athenian potters apparently emigrated to pursue the economic opportunities offered by the Italian markets (their emigration to Dorian cities like Metapontum and Tarentum is not easily explained by the normal patterns of Athenian colonization).[18] When Metapontum and Tarentum began to produce their own red-figured pottery about 440 BC, it was contiguous with Attic production in every way. As Luca Giuliani puts it:

> the technique is Attic, Attic is the shape of the vases, Attic their iconography; the first potters and painters must have been of Attic origin, having had their training in the Athenian Kerameikos. For about one generation the connection between Apulian and Attic vase-production remains rather close: but around 400 BC the immigration of Attic vase painters as well as the import of Attic vases comes to a sudden end: from this time at the latest vase-production in Apulia develops to become a phenomenon of its own.[19]

Given the continuity with Attic pottery, and given the evident marketability of vases with theatrical subjects in the Greek West, it is a bit surprising to find that it is precisely around 400 BC that vases with dramatic subjects begin to appear. Of the more loosely theater-related vases that are based on versions of myths originating in tragedy we have only a dozen before about 400 BC.[20] What is true of Apulia is also true of other West Greek fabrics. It was around 400 BC that the red-figured technique spread from the Italian instep to Greek cities in Sicily, and around 360 BC that it spread from there to the mixed Greek and Lucanian city of Posidonia (Paestum) and the mixed Greek and Oscan cities of Campania. On the face of it, then, chronology as well as the quantity of West Greek theater iconography tells against the view that West Greek artists simply copied Attic theater subjects. A close look at some of the earliest theater-related vases, however, tells still more convincingly against those who deny any continuity between West Greek and Attic theater-related vases.

The career of the Tarporley Painter is particularly instructive in weighing the debt West Greek vasepainting owes to the Attic tradition. He is the successor of the Sisyphus Painter who, under the direct influence of Attic artists, specialized in scenes of everyday life as well as Dionysian subjects. The Tarporley Painter's theater-related vases, which belong to his early work, creatively combine both the subject-fields pursued by his predecessor. There are only six theater-related vases (out of over seventy known vases painted by his hand), but most of them are strikingly original. Though he was hugely influential, setting the standard for one of the three main schools of Apulian vasepainting, and though, in Trendall's opinion, "he set the fashion at Taranto for decorating vases with scenes connected with the theatre,"[21] some of his experiments in theatrical art were never copied by West Greek vasepainters. Of those experiments that never caught on in Western Greece, most – and this is the most significant point for our purposes – follow the Attic tradition closely, if also creatively.

The Tarporley Painter's most famous piece, a bell krater in Sydney, shows three satyr choreuts, two of whom hold their masks in hand, and one wears his mask and adopts the stance of a dancing satyr.[22] This is a doubly unique piece among West Greek vasepaintings. It is the only (likely) scene showing dramatic choreuts in West Greek art. It is also the only realistic depiction of satyr-performers. And one might add that it is one of relatively few genre-scenes showing actors and masks. Yet all of these subjects are prominent in the Attic tradition. Indeed, the schema of the Sydney bell krater adopts the most typical format of all Attic choral genre scenes: the realistic treatment of the two unmasked choreuts contrasts with the illusionistic rendering of the masked choreut in the Sydney krater (typical examples were discussed in the last chapter in relation to the Piraeus relief, FIGURE 1.7, and the Pronomos vase, FIGURE 1.9).[23]

One of the earliest works by the Tarporley Painter (possibly as early as the last decade of the fifth century BC) is a bell krater with Dionysus holding a tragic mask and facing a satyr who dips an oinochoe into a wine krater decorated with dancers.[24] This is the first vasepainting depicting Dionysus holding a theatrical mask, a subject, with variations, that becomes very popular in later Apulian and Paestan art.[25] But despite its uniqueness it too follows a well established schema in contemporary Attic art. "Monoposiast" scenes with Dionysus seated or reclining appear first on Attic reliefs, among them four choregic monuments.[26] Typically the god has a young servant serving wine, and is often accompanied by a female companion who sometimes holds a theatrical mask. On two of the choregic reliefs he is approached by representatives of the chorus holding masks (FIGURE 1.7). At the time the Tarporley Painter produced this painting, Attic vasepainters, most prominently the Pronomos Painter and artists associated with him, were also developing the monoposiast schema and creatively combining it with the scheme of the theatrical genre scene and other Dionysian and theatrical motifs (FIGURE 1.9).[27] It is likely that the Tarporley Painter was responsible for transferring both the monoposiast and choral genre scenes to West Greece where artists freely developed it for the Dionysian and epinician connotations of symbols derived from choregic monuments.

Another bell krater by the Tarporley Painter, "clearly a companion piece" to the one just discussed, shows a Victory crowning a naked youth who holds a tragic female mask.[28] Behind the Victory a pan holding a bird looks on. This also is a first in West Greek art, though it was often imitated in later Apulian art.[29] Once again, however, the subject owes much to Attic genre scenes and in particular to the creative experimentation with the epinician imagery of choregic monuments that we find in the art of the Pronomos Painter and his associates (much of which was found in Italy). Ribbon- or garland-bearing Victories are particularly common in the imagery of dithyrambic monuments and related vasepainting.[30] Ribbon-bearing Victories also appear on the richly developed genre scenes of a pelike of the Circle of the Pronomos Painter in Barcelona and of a bell krater in Ferrara: though in these cases it is Dionysus, not an actor, who is garlanded.[31] As Erotes very frequently substitute for Victories on choregic monuments, it is no surprise to find one flying with a victory garland on the Pronomos vase (FIGURE 1.9). In the Attic art, however, the focus of such imagery is on the chorus and choreuts. The generic quality of the Tarporley Painter's victory imagery does not encourage us to decide whether a choreut or an actor is intended. This is often the case with the West Greek genre scenes. The later examples show that many of the vasepainters interpreted these figures as actors rather than choreuts, a shift that was probably much easier outside Attica where the traditions of choregic art made the imagery more fixedly choral. It is in any case sometimes clear in West Greek vases that actors, not choreuts, are intended: the figures are sometimes accompanied by more than one mask; or as on the famous Würzburg fragment, which is a more distantly related example of the genre scene, the performer is shown as aged or clothed in a costume appropriate only to actors.[32] Indeed, West Greek genre scenes after the Tarporley Painter seem to encourage one to see actors (or poets) in that they normally show a single performer. Closely related, however, are the Apulian and Paestan banquet scenes that show several performers celebrating (a victory) with their masks hanging above them. Erotes with victory garlands further develop the victory symbolism. But here too, we are evidently meant to think of actors, not choreuts: each celebrant is associated with a different mask type.[33]

Even if the figure on the Tarporley Painter's krater is intended to be a choreut, he nonetheless represents a uniquely creative application of the Attic formula. The Tarporley Painter is to our knowledge the first painter to have extended to human actors the constellation of motifs associated with Dionysus. In Attic art, Victories (or Erotes) carry ribbons to choregic monuments or wreaths to Dionysus.[34] The reason for this is doubtless because the images are derived from monuments celebrating group victories (and in drama, choral victories) and individuals could not be singled out this way without arousing indignation. We come very close on the Pronomos vase (FIGURE 1.9), where a winged Eros (who often substitutes for Victory) carries a wreath in the general direction of an actor, but the actor is seated on Dionysus' couch and the Eros seems not in fact to be moving to the actor.

The Tarporley Painter's image may therefore depict an actor. The fact that in West Greek art human figures holding mask are normally depicted as youths does suggest a certain indifference on the painter's part to any precise distinction between actor and choreut, or indeed between actors and other members of the Dionysian entourage. Indeed, the figure of the "actor" and of Dionysus are easily interchangeable in the scenic configurations of later West Greek art: one can find reclining human "actors" in the monoposiast pose served by satyrs,[35] or youthful actors in such scenes substituting for satyrs who bring the wine to Dionysus.[36] The mask itself sometimes seems incidental and sufficiently interchangeable with other Dionysian symbols that one might wisely shy away from any overdirect and literal explanations of this particular group of images and in particular from the common assumption that pots with human figures holding masks were designed to mark the burials of actual dramatic poets and actors.[37] (This is an especially unlikely conclusion given the findspot of many of these vases in the tombs of the warrior classes of native Peucetians and Messapians on the periphery of Tarentum and Metapontum). In the last chapter we saw that by the late fifth century the choreut holding (or juxtaposed to) a mask became a motif on grave stelae symbolizing the dead man's service and devotion to Dionysus, who was also the god of the underworld and afterlife. Athenian vasepainting associated with the Pronomos Painter begins to play with such symbolism at about 400 BC and these are very likely the symbolic resonances of theater art that were exploited by the Tarporley Painter and perceived by the purchasers of his vases.

The Tarporley Painter included in his repertoire two vasepaintings with mythological scenes, both ultimately inspired by the story of Orestes' refuge at

Delphi. This was, so far as we know, a detail in the story of Orestes that was entirely invented by Aeschylus.[38] A bell krater in Oxford shows Orestes being pursued by a Fury.[39] The scene is well established in Attic iconography and one of red figure's more popular mythical subjects.[40] The Tarporley Painter's Fury is even winged like most Attic Furies, and quite unlike later Apulian Furies (and also quite unlike the actual Furies that appeared in Aeschylus' *Eumenides*).[41] In contrast to this uncreatively Atticizing piece, another of the Tarporley Painter's earliest works presents a detail of Aeschylus' tale of Orestes at Delphi that is without iconographic precedent. A bell krater in Melbourne shows Orestes taking refuge on the altar, now clearly located in Delphi by the presence of the omphalos, while Apollo cleanses him with the blood of a piglet.[42] The cleansing of Orestes of blood-pollution by Apollo is referred to, though not enacted, in Aeschylus' *Eumenides*. The text gives explicit reference to purification through flowing water and the blood of suckling animals (280–5, 445–52). The scene is imitated five times in later Apulian and Paestan art, first by the Eumenides Painter, a close follower of the Tarporley Painter.[43] From the hand of the Eumenides Painter we have one vasepainting with Apollo sprinkling water on Orestes, and two vasepaintings with Apollo dripping the blood of a suckling piglet over Orestes' head. The suckling piglet versions add several other details that indicate their close adherence to the narrative of Aeschylus' play: the sleeping (this time wingless) Furies, for example, and the ghost of Clytemnestra.[44] It is likely that the Tarporley Painter provided the model for the Eumenides Painter and the other painters who imitated this scene.[45]

In comparing the mythological scenes in Attic and Apulian vasepainting Giuliani uses the iconography of Orestes at Delphi to exemplify general characteristics of the two fabrics. Attic scenes, he says, attempt to render the story as a whole. Apulian scenes "follow the drama closely, offering a literal reflex of one particular scene;" Attic scenes provide a "simple summary" of a whole story and are consequently "easy to decipher," but Apulian vases "rely closely on a particular text" and as a consequence are far more difficult to understand unless we know the text.[46] The Melbourne krater indicates knowledge of the wording of Aeschylus' text, whether known through reading or performance. Giuliani argues that, because the purification scene was not shown on stage, the Tarporley Painter's source must have been a written text. Taplin argues that the visually richer expansion of the scene by later Apulian followers of the Tarporley Painter are more likely to depend on a performance. This is a controversy we will address later. What is important for our purposes is the vase's relatively clear indication that the Tarporley Painter is adapting a traditional schema of Attic mythological vasepainting and bringing it into closer conformity with narrative details known from a particular drama.

The most stunningly original of the Tarporley Painter's works is also one of his earliest (*c*.400 BC), a calyx krater, now in New York, containing one of the

Figure 2.1   Apulian red-figured calyx krater, Tarporley Painter, *c.*400 BC, The Metropolitan Museum of Art, Fletcher Fund, 1924 (24.97.104). Image © The Metropolitan Museum of Art.

most extraordinary scenes in West Greek art (FIGURE 2.1).[47] The subject is a comic performance. It shows three actors performing: an old woman on a stage to the right, and in the *orchestra* an old man with his hands raised in the air, approached by a thuggish young man with a stick. As in a modern cartoon, the words of each character emanate from their mouths. The old woman says "I hand him over to you," a legalistic formula of the sort one uses when offering a slave up for torture by a civic authority (the only condition under which evidence from slaves was admissible under Athenian law). Something like this actually happens here, I suspect. The man in the center of the *orchestra* on tiptoes with his hands raised says "he has tied up my hands." It was normal to suspend a slave before giving him lashes. The fellow behind him holding a switch is presumably going to do the work. He is clean shaven to show that he is young. He says "Noraretteblo" which means as much in Greek as it does in English. In Athens, Scythians were used as police, and his barbarism might indicate that he is supposed to be a Scythian.

This is the first of well over a hundred scenes of comic performance in West Greek art. Yet there are several unique features in this painting which are never matched by the Tarporley Painter's followers. The painting tries in various ways to capture the specificity of theatrical performance. It is the only vasepainting to transcribe dramatic dialogue. It is the only vasepainting to capture an interaction between actors on stage and actors in the *orchestra*. Indeed it is the only attempt to render the full topography of the theater, including the skene doors, the stage, the *orchestra* and possibly the theatron. The figure of the naked youth watching on the left seems to float as if rising in the theatron. He bears the puzzling label *tragoidos,* that in a theatrical context is more likely to refer to a tragic choreut or actor than a poet. Neither meaning, however, suffices to make him part of the play. Whoever he is he is also clearly a spectator, not a performer.

Most remarkable of all, however, is the stark theatrical realism of the vase. Costumes and masks are rendered without any compromise. The detail of the buckle that joins the buttocks to the belly of the old man's body suit is never reproduced in ancient theater art. We noted above that the Tarporley Painter was interested in the contrast between theatrical (and artistic) illusion and reality. Here he has chosen a subject that vividly presents the performance reality behind the dramatic illusion. Most strikingly, at the very center of the scene, the old man in the *orchestra* tells us that he has been strung up for a beating, but there is no sign of ropes nor of anything to tie him to. Here both the humor and the art of the actor's performance depend precisely upon the viewers' (and audience's) awareness that the actor is posturing and dancing about like a man suspended without actually being so.[48]

The originality of this scene is breathtaking. There is, however, Attic precedent, especially in the Perseus Dance vase (FIGURE 1.10) for the majority of its most striking features: the detailing of mask and costume, the representation of the stage, the attempt to capture the full sweep of the theater from the stage to the theatron. The main difference is that the Tarporley Painter does it much better, much more consistently and with a level of specificity and detail that is unprecedented. The Tarporley Painter captures on the surface of a pot the very fullness of the theatrical experience. We are left with the impression of seeing not just a scene but as it were a film clip of an ancient comedy: the characters speak, interact and even move (Marshall observes how the script emerging from the old man's mouth rises up as if leaving a trail as he is hoisted in the air) – even the floating mask may point to another character who appears earlier or later in the narrative.[49]

There are, however, no iconographic precedents for the specific details of this scene. The unusually detailed presentation of the scene urges us to suppose that the Tarporley Painter takes his inspiration from a specific drama. It has what Taplin calls a "scene specificity" about it that goes far beyond anything we find in the comic art of Athens. Later West Greek pottery offers examples of generic scenes from comedy, designed evidently to give an impression of the type of thing one would see at a comic festival, with typical comic figures and situations, for the most part easily recognizable and unlikely to provoke much curiosity about their narrative context: a running slave, two actors engaged in conversation on stage, a cook carrying a small table with a cake on it, Heracles stealing a cake – generic images that are increasingly common after about 370 BC. The Tarporley Painter's scene has the opposite effect. It advertises itself as a specific moment in a comedy with a rather complex and elaborate plot and it engages the viewer to supply the broader narrative context. Taplin has argued that scene-specific dramatic vasepainting presupposes purchasers who will be attracted to the image because they recognize the visual details of the performance of the comedy from which the scene is taken. Conversely, one could suppose that potential purchasers will be confused and disinterested if they do not understand what it is they are looking at. Since the Tarporley Painter's experiment in comic vasepainting was extremely influential – many other West Greek vases approach the same degree of specificity – scene-specificity in effect becomes a proof that the West Greek purchasers of the vasepaintings were well acquainted with the performance of the comedies illustrated. The main problem with this argument is that, while West Greek pottery was not widely exported, much, especially Apulian (and presumably including comic vases), *was exported* to non-Greek communities in the broader hinterland. The presumption of consumer recognition would then have to be applied to the non-Greek purchasers. For this reason Taplin's perfectly reasonable argument has encountered considerable skepticism. Edward Robinson has, however, recently marshaled evidence that suggests that native Italians in the hinterland of the main production centers were indeed familiar with comic performance.[50] This may be just another area in which we have underestimated the rate of cultural Hellenization.

It is possible, however, that scene-specificity does not necessarily imply local production. The appeal of vasepaintings such as FIGURE 2.1 might conceivably be their puzzling strangeness, rather than the spark of recognition that they generate.[51] The Tarporley Painter might then have copied an image from an Attic source, with little concern that it would be unfamiliar to his viewers, or he might, as the more extreme iconocentrists would like, have spun the whole image from his painter's imagination stimulated either by the reading of a comic text or indeed have created it entirely unaided, but for the most superficial knowledge of comic performance, filling it with a misleading particularity of the detail that merely creates "an effect of the real." There are few firm footholds to guide us through this controversy. And yet there are a few.

At first sight, the preservation of lines from a comedy might seem to confirm the view that the Tarporley Painter copied a text illustrated by Attic artists, in line with a hypothesis developed by Mingazzini and Bertino, or that the Tarporley Painter created an image based on the reading of a text, in line with Giuliani's theory.[52] Indeed, if Beazley's editing and re-arranging of the lines is accepted, they formed one and a half iambic trimeters, seemingly direct from the text of a play.[53] But Beazley's editing forces the text into a metrical straight-jacket that it does not easily fit. To produce a continuous line and a half of comic iambics (which is not as hard as it may seem – comic iambics have a very loose structure!) Beazley takes the words of the old man first, those of the thug second, and those of the old woman third: but this defies the normal reading convention of left to right and top to bottom or any systematic directionality that can be gotten from the position of the texts. Secondly, Beazley arbitrarily lengthens two syllables in the speech of the thug by turning omicrons into omegas (one at least must change if the utterance is to fit into iambic verse). It is true that in labeling the Tragoidos our painter has written an omicron rather than an omega, but the error is particularly unlikely in the transcription of metrical verse in which syllable lengths are fixed for the ear as well as the eye, and especially unlikely in a transcription of verse in which three omegas otherwise correctly appear.

Indeed, the details of the inscriptions on FIGURE 2.1 give every indication that they were not copied. Quite the opposite. The fact that, at least as they stand, they are not in verse, shows that the words are not the exact words of the play, but words written to fit the moments in the drama that the artist is specifically remembering (or more likely words calculated to explain the scene rather than give a precise record of the dialogue). This would not have happened if the artist were working from a text (whether illustrated or not). Another feature of the inscription helps corroborate the view that this is memory work. The dialect is Attic, because this is evidently the language of the comedy, but the alphabet is the local alphabet of Tarentum where the pot was produced: the form of the heta in the old woman's lines is peculiar to the Tarentine alphabet (it also appears in the name-labels on another Apulian comic vase and three Apulian tragedy-related vases).[54] In other words, it appears that the Tarporley Painter is not copying a text but sounding out the Attic dialect words in his head and writing them down in the way that comes naturally to him.[55]

A remarkable confirmation that we are dealing with a performance tradition, not a text, comes from an Apulian bell krater painted by a different artist, the McDaniel Painter, as much as thirty years after the Tarporley Painter's krater, though he is probably an apprentice of the Tarporley Painter (FIGURE 2.2).[56] The McDaniel Painter's bell krater shows two male characters with very nearly the exact same costume and masks as the Tarporley Painter's calyx krater. The thuggish young man still carries his stick. The feisty old man oils himself because he is about to wrestle him. The reappearance of the same masks does not, of course, suffice to show that we are dealing with a different scene from the same play as the Tarporley Painter's calyx krater. It is rather the baskets at the lower right of each vase that establish this beyond reasonable doubt. Each vase shows two goats in baskets and on each a goose stands or lies beside them. (On the Tarporley

Figure 2.2   Apulian red-figured bell krater, McDaniel Painter, *c.*370 BC, MFA Boston, Otis Norcross Fund 69.951. Photograph © 2009 Museum of Fine Arts, Boston.

Painter's vase [FIGURE 2.1], there is damage to the face of the rightmost goat, but its ears, and the back of its head are clearly visible.)[57] Moreover, the baskets appear both to be yoked double-baskets: though the Tarporley Painter's baskets are seen in profile, he is careful to outline the edge of the second basket. Since this is anything but a standard prop in Greek comedy, it can leave no serious doubt that we are dealing with a different scene from the same comedy.[58] If we can judge by the life-cycle of the goose, the Tarporley Painter's scene is the earlier one since in his painting the goose is still alive.

   If these two extraordinary scenes cohere so closely in detail it is surely not because the McDaniel Painter simply imagined an earlier scene to a scene of a comedy imagined by the Tarporley Painter. In all likelihood the McDaniel Painter had never seen the Tarporley Painter's vase: its condition suggests that it had been sold and sealed in a tomb soon after its production. The retention of the precise details of the appearance of costumes and props over thirty years (if Trendall's dating is correct) surely tells against Giuliani's theory that our painters are working from texts: the texts of plays rarely provide descriptions of what is visually obvious in a production, and could not provide it with the precision that is manifest in these vasepaintings. Does FIGURE 2.2 then offer proof of a hardcopy transmission, either from Attic vasepainting or from illustrated texts? There is no evidence that illustrated books of any sort were circulating in this period, which represents the extreme infancy of the book industry. Even for the Hellenistic period there is no evidence for elaborately illustrated dramatic texts. On the contrary, we find only crude sketches, when we do find illustrations: elaborate illustration is scarcely suited to the impermanence of papyrus and rarely found before the use of parchment.[59] Nor are there very promising parallels in extant Attic pottery to suggest that imported vases served as a model. The few Attic vasepaintings that focus on actors appear on very small vessels that could scarcely have contained the detailed images, let alone the texts, that we find on FIGURES 2.1 and 2.2. Moreover, if the vasepaintings do copy Attic paintings, we might expect to have duplicates of the more popular scenes, but this we never have.[60] Each comic vase has an entirely unique scene. The easiest conclusion is that artists and consumers knew their comedies from local performance.

If, as some think, the Tarporley and McDaniel Painters were each inventing their images on the basis of a text of a play, it could not conceivably have resulted in the close correspondence of masks, props and details of costume that we find in FIGURES 2.1 and 2.2. But the very minor differences between the costumes and the props are no less revealing. If it were a case of copying two closely related images, as, for example, from a single illustrated manuscript, one might have expected absolute consistency. But here the baskets, though close, are not identical in their shape or weave; the thug has the same mask but different hair length and a ribbon on the McDaniel Painter's vase; the old man's hair has changed color; and the stage's are very different. The images sooner testify to the continuance and conservatism of a local performance tradition.

The Tarporley Painter's generation, if not the Tarporley Painter himself, established the popularity of theater-related subjects. In doing so, he was well aware of and much influenced by Attic theater-related art. The Sydney krater with the satyr choreuts and the Oxford krater with Orestes pursued by a Fury are both squarely within the Attic tradition. But there can be no question that he is merely a copyist. Unless the extant material is entirely deceptive in this regard, the Tarporley Painter goes well beyond his Attic models in the production of his other four theatrical paintings. The Dionysus holding a mask, and its companion, the actor or choreut holding a mask and crowned by a Nike draw upon the victory-imagery of Attic choregic monuments, but they also go well beyond anything we find in Attic vasepainting in developing the Dionysian and eschatological symbolism of the mask and the theatrical performer. We do find considerable play in this direction by contemporary Attic vasepainters, especially the Pronomos Painter and his associates, but the Tarporley Painter's composition is entirely different from their products in most other respects, and later West Greek vasepaintings of Dionysus or actors with masks owe far more to his simple and direct style than the busy and complex compositions near the Pronomos Painter. It is above all, however, in the Melbourne krater showing a detail of the story of Orestes, known only from Aeschylus, and in the rendition of the comic scene in New York that we find clear evidence of the new departures in theatrical vasepainting that are the distinctive contribution of West Greek production. The Melbourne krater, as Giuliani puts it, does not attempt, like Attic mythological narratives to somehow summarize an entire story in a single visual plain. Rather, it captures a moment known only from tragedy and requires the viewer to fill out the narrative from his own knowledge and memory of the play. The comic calyx krater (FIGURE 2.1) does much more than this. It is an attempt to capture the experience of theater in its fullness, showing the interaction of stage, *orchestra*, and audience, and rendering costume, action, movement, and even dialogue with a fullness of detail that is never fully matched by any later painter. Scarcely a single detail is lost to the narrative illusion (the floating mask and the floating "tragoidos" expand the viewer's awareness of the play and the theater, not of a story). One only misses a reference to music and the chorus. Some may, with Giuliani, continue to contend that antiquity's most successful attempt to render an experience of comic theater was produced by a painter who had never seen drama and for a public that knew theater only from books, but the balance of probabilities (and the balance of the evidence) is against them.

The Lessons of West Greek Comic Vasepainting

For well over a century West Greek comic vases were referred to as "phlyax" vases, or in the plural, "phlyakes." Heydemann, the author of the first study of the pottery in 1886, identified them with a preliterary form of comedy said by an ancient scholar to be native to Southern Italy.[61] This view still lives on. Such recent works as the third edition of the *Oxford Classical Dictionary* (1996), Inge Nielsen's *Cultic Theatres and Ritual Drama* (2002) or *The Oxford Encyclopedia of Theatre and Performance* (2003) seem unaware of any other possibility.[62] But comic vases of the sort created by the Tarporley and McDaniel painter have grown in numbers and with new examples, quite a different picture has emerged. The standard catalogue of *Phlyax Vases* by Dale Trendall dates back to 1967 and numbers 185 items, but J. R. Green's catalogue now has 592 comic vases from the Greek West. Of these 342 show mere masks (or masks in non-dramatic scenes) and 118 show single actors in costume alone or in a Dionysian setting. But as many as 132 show complete scenes of comic performance. The corpus is still growing.

The first serious challenge to the *phlyax*-theory, however, came as early as 1948. T. B. L. Webster pointed out: that the costumes worn by the West Greek comic performers were identical to those of contemporary Attic terracotta figurines of comic actors; that the paintings suggest plots not very different from those found in contemporary Attic comedy; and that Attic tragedy, at least, was well known in Southern Italy.[63] All of these reasons led Webster to believe that the comedy depicted on West Greek vases were not *phlyakes* or any other form of "preliterary Doric farce" but contemporary Attic Middle Comedy. In addition to these general considerations, Webster made a most compelling observation. Many pots are accompanied by inscriptions. These inscriptions are usually character labels – only in the case of the Tarporley Painter's calyx krater do we have lines of dialogue (FIGURE 2.1). Though the centers of production for these vases were all cities that spoke the Doric dialect, the form of the names and words in the inscriptions are almost always in Athenian dialect. Webster argued, quite reasonably, that this was because the comedy was Athenian.

For some forty years Webster's observation was politely acknowledged but generally rejected. Too much had already been invested in the "indigenous Italian" roots of *phlyax* performance. Histories of the theater regarded it as the missing link between Attic comedy (which they believed to be too insular for export) and the Roman comedy of Plautus and Terence that provides the earliest substantial remains of Latin literature. Part of the reason for keeping Athenian comedy at bay was Italian nationalism and part, perhaps the larger part, was secured by trends in the study of Latin literature, which, especially since the middle of the twentieth century, was in serious reaction against a tradition of "explaining" Latin literature (and especially Latin comedy) by listing its Greek models. The scholarly agenda turned toward exploration of Latin literature's uniquely Italian roots. Beyond this, postcolonial and postmodern hostility to cultural-derivation models probably played a part. The most important work on West Greek vases was being carried on in the ambivalently British antipodes. But Australian and New Zealand universities had also been colonized by Webster's students, whose interests, like their mentor's, were not favoured by the Classical establishment in Britain at the time.[64] Professional and global politics here interacted in interesting ways.

The problem of just what comedy appears on West Greek vasepainting took a significant turn after the University Museum of Würzburg acquired an Apulian bell krater in 1978, by the Schiller Painter (a painter strongly influenced by the Tarporley Painter, FIGURE 2.3).[65] This tiny bell krater shows two comic actors atop a raised groundline. The actor on the right, whose body-tights are clearly visible, kneels astride an altar. His right hand holds a sword, his left a wineskin.

Figure 2.3   Apulian red-figured bell krater, Schiller Painter, *c.*370 BC, Würzburg H5697.
Courtesy, Martin von Wagner Museum der Universität Würzburg (Photo: K. Öhrlein).

The wineskin is fitted with baby-booties. From the left an actor in female costume rushes in carrying an oversized skyphos. Above and between them hangs a mirror in profile. The mirror's reflective surface faces the figure on the altar.

It is not entirely clear whether the actor on the altar is playing a male or female role. On other vases and on figurines of this date the standard comic costume for mature male characters includes a beard and a very short tunic (though they can also wear a *himation* over the tunic). The standard comic male tunic is designed not to cover but to reveal the phallus. The character atop the altar has no beard and a knee-length tunic. He is in fact sexually indeterminate, and, on the evidence, deliberately so: though beardless, there are a dozen clearly marked splotches about his mouth rendering what appears to be razor stubble; and while his garment is too long to be male it is definitely too short to be female, but it is nevertheless girded above the waist like female dress. Other feminine features of the costume are the headband and the rather fluffy hairdo, both of which are paralleled by female characters on other Apulian vases.[66]

The actor's stance on the altar is well known to iconographers as the *position agenouillée*.[67] It characterizes mythological scenes showing heroic suppliants fleeing to take sanctuary at altars, and often, as in the case of Telephus (or Orestes at Delphi), with swords drawn (see FIGURE 1.1). The stance probably originates with, and is in any case most closely associated with Telephus taking the baby Orestes as hostage. As we know this incident was invented by Euripides, we can guess that the performance of *Telephus* ultimately inspired the painters' kneeling position.[68]

The Würzburg krater has numerous correspondences with Aristophanes' parody of the climax of the Telephus in *Thesmophoriazusae*. In Aristophanes' play Euripides' "in-law" is shaved, and then disguised with an effeminate headband, fancy shoes, and a dress in order to infiltrate the Thesmophoria (an exclusively women's festival characterized by fasting and abstinence) where the women of Athens plan revenge against Euripides for his misogyny. News comes that a man has infiltrated the rites and suspicion falls upon the in-law who is discovered to be male when they lift his tunic. The in-law then grabs what appears to be the baby of one of the women and jumps upon an altar threatening it with a sword. As several women run in search of kindling to burn the in-law off the altar and away from his sanctuary, the following dialogue takes place (lines 730–55):

IN-LAW: *(to the women)* Go ahead, kindle! Burn! *(to the baby)* But you, off with this wrap right now! For your death, child, you have only your mother to blame. Hey, what's this? The girl has turned into a skin full of wine and wearing booties at that! O most flagrant women! O most bibulous of creatures, stopping at nothing to contrive an opportunity for a drink! Great boon for the bar-tender; great bane for mankind! Bane too for dishes and the loom!

MIKA: *(to her servant)* Mania, throw lots of brushwood beside the altar!

IN-LAW: Go ahead throw it down alongside. But you! Answer me this question! Do you claim to be the mother?

MIKA: To be sure I bore her for ten months!

IN-LAW: YOU bore her?

MIKA: Yes, by Artemis!

IN-LAW: At three pints an obol, or what?

MIKA: What have you done? You've stripped my child naked, tiny as she is, you pervert!

IN-LAW: Tiny! I'll say she's tiny!! How old is she? Three or four Wine Pitchers? [The reference is to the annual drinking contests on the second day of the Anthesteria.]

MIKA: About that, plus however many months to the Dionysia. But give her back!

IN-LAW: No, by this Apollo here!

MIKA: We'll set you on fire, then!

IN-LAW: Go ahead! Burn! But this baby's going to get her throat cut, this instant!

MIKA: No! I beg you! Do whatever you like to me, but spare her!

IN-LAW: I see you have a very maternal nature. But her throat will be cut nonetheless!

MIKA: Oh my child! *(to her servant)* Mania, give me the sacrificial basin so that
I can at least save the blood of my baby.

The details on the vase correspond accurately to the implied action: the *Telephus* parody on the altar, the wineskin with booties, the woman rushing toward the threatened wineskin with a vessel to catch the "blood," the headband of the figure on the altar, the longish tunic which hides the actor's phallus, the beardless face and razor splotches. Even the mirror has a place in the shaving scene just before this episode. It is clear that we have something very close to what we might legitimately call a representation of the climactic moment in the performance of Aristophanes' *Thesmophoriazusae*.[69]

There are, however, also discrepancies. Austin and Olson list several details that show that the artist is not giving us a perfectly accurate representation of every detail that from the text we know a stage-production must have included.[70] Our scene, for example, does not show the brushwood that the text suggests was already by this point in the dialogue piled around the altar. An omission of this sort does not cast doubt upon the connection between this painting and a scene from Aristophanes' play. It does, however, demonstrate that vasepainters are generally less interested in accurately documenting every detail of a performance than in producing an attractive, clear and recognizable image. One must first take into account the fact that artists and actors have different resources at their disposal. On stage there could be no doubt that the in-law is on an altar: the audience sees him take refuge on the altar and then the brushwood is piled up around it. The viewer of the vasepainting, however, does not share the knowledge that an audience would gain from the sequence of action seen in a performance. The painter needs to show that the in-law is on an altar and it would be counterproductive to obscure or hide the altar by surrounding it with brushwood. Indeed, as Austin and Olson remark, the recognition of this scene as the climax of *Thesmophoriazusae* depends on the iconic clarity with which the configuration of the altar and suppliant conform to the visual patterning of Euripides' play. This would only be frustrated by the addition of such incidental performance details we can infer from the text, such as the presence of brushwood, a servant, a statue of Apollo and the very un-beggar-like (and hence un-Telephean) effeminate shoes we know were worn by the in-law. In other words, many (on the whole minor) discrepancies between the painter's image and the actors' performance may arise, paradoxically, out of the painter's very desire to provoke recognition of the specific performance from whose details he deviates.

The details that are in the text, but not in the painting, are much less revealing than the details that are in the painting, but not in the text. On this vase, there are two types of added detail that I find interesting. The first is detail that recalls or foreshadows moments elsewhere in the narrative. Though it is true that West Greek vases in general aim to capture a single important moment within a narrative, deviations from the temporal unity of the image may actually aid in the recognition of the scene. There is, for example, no reference to a mirror at this point in the play. The mirror does, however, appear in an earlier scene in which the in-law is shaved and dressed in female disguise. In the painting the mirror appears to allude to the dressing scene for the sake of imparting essential background to the visual narrative, because it is important that we recognize that the person of ambiguous gender is only "dressed up" as a woman. The mirror, in other words, is added as a clue to the interpretation of a scene to which it does not strictly belong. (There is no need to suppose that the mirror was left hanging on the stage at the end of the dressing scene and continued to be visible in this one.). The razor splotches on the in-law's face are also there by the painter's art and not by the mask-maker's: a mask in production might well have had such splotches, but they would not be easily visible to even the closest members of the audience. These too, by alluding to the shaving scene, appear to serve as clues to facilitate recognition.

But there are also some details that are not in the text at all, not even hinted at, though they make perfect sense once we see them. The bibulous woman in the *Thesmophoriazusae* asks for a *sphageion* which is a large basin employed in sacrificial ritual to catch the blood of a sacrificial victim. Instead, we see the old woman rushing forward with a giant drinking cup or *skyphos*.[71] The substitution is perfectly consistent with a text that systematically confuses the language of sacrifice and the language of wine-tippling, but nothing in the text would have justified our extension of this pattern of incongruity to the shape of the vessel used to collect the "blood" of the wineskin. The detail surely reproduces the stage-action of the play in production – it is unlikely that a vasepainter invented the detail in the expectation that his customers would remember that the text called for a *sphageion*.

Another detail that enriches our knowledge of the stage action beyond anything we might have guessed from the text is the fact, evident from the mask, that Miko is an old woman well past the age of childbirth. In light of this detail the in-law's incredulous "YOU bore her?" has an extra dimension of comic meaning. It is also noteworthy that it is particularly old women who are caricatured as winos in Greek comedy.

Both the absence of details in the text and the presence of details not in the text indicate that the artist is not in fact illustrating a text. Details imported from earlier moments of the play show that he is concerned to enhance the recognizability of an action that would simply be "given" in the case of a book illustration. Other details, however, that cannot be inferred from the text cannot plausibly derive from any source other than a stage production.

Here is a very clear example of an image that makes direct reference to a known comedy. Yet in the years since Oliver Taplin and I independently recognized that the vase gave decisive confirmation to Webster's theory, scholars have made every effort to limit and control the damage this evidence presents to the traditional view that Attic comedy was insular, unexportable and of little interest to anyone outside Attica.[72] Giuliani in an unargued footnote blandly declares the failure of "Taplin's attempts to connect some comic Apulian vases with particular scenes from comedies by Aristophanes" and asserts that "no comic scene in Apulian iconography shows a demonstrable relation to any given Attic comedy."[73] Virtually everyone else finds it more difficult to deny the correspondences between the vasepainting and some sort of production connected to *Thesmophoriazusae*. But even that allows plenty of wiggle room for scholars who find the adjustment to old habits of thought too difficult. Some maintain that this is a Telephus parody like *Thesmophoriazusae*, but not exactly *Thesmophoriazusae*, or that it is a Telephus parody with borrowings from Aristophanes but otherwise inserted in an unAttic drama, or even simply staged by itself, as if this would have made it easier for Tarentines to understand.[74] To these suggestions we must reply that the vase shows not just a moment in a play, but a moment in the sequence of a tightly-woven and complex plot that necessarily implies (and carries the visual allusions to) shaving, cross-dressing, infiltration into a space accessible only to women, discovery, hostage-taking, "murder" of the false hostage – in short a plot that cannot be either distinguished from the plot of the *Thesmophoriazusae* or meaningfully extricated from it. Others suggest that the Würzburg krater is just an oddball or an exception that proves the rule.[75]

But there are other West Greek comic vases that depict known comedies. In *Comic Angels*, Oliver Taplin defended two such connections that seem to me highly probable, though there are problems. One of the connections was made as early as 1849 between an Apulian bell krater of 375–350 BC that "disappeared" from the Berlin museum during the war and Aristophanes' *Frogs* (FIGURE 2.4).[76] Only one photograph and one drawing of the vase are known. The drawing is from the original publication by Panofka in 1849 and is inaccurate in several details. The photograph shows the vase had suffered much surface damage. It may also be misleading in places, since the vase has very probably been "touched up" either before or since its acquisition. From left to right one sees a Doric pilaster or column representing a building, apparently a porch since the figure

Figure 2.4   Apulian red-figured bell krater, 375–350 BC, formerly Berlin F3046, Kriegsverlust (lost during WW II). Courtesy, Staatliche Museen zu Berlin.

immediately to the right rises up to enter (despite the high variability of the ground-line in this painting). The figure appears stage-naked (with body-tights and *somation*). There are apparently remnants of an original phallus, but the rest of the phallus was either eradicated or not restored: it appears that the two lines marking its projection over the body-tights were assimilated to wrinkles, but the phallus in the line-drawing, which was not meant to be seen by the general public, is more explicit, if impossibly small. The figure has a thick beard and bushy hair and a face close enough to what *MMC* identifies as Mask J, the Heracles mask. J. R. Green draws my attention to the white aura around "Heracles"' head, which may be the remnant of the head of the lion skin. He holds a club in his right hand, evidently to beat the door. His left hand holds an animal skin by one leg. On the line drawing this is interpreted as a bow, but that is doubtful, given the appearance of the skin's other legs. Under the animal skin that falls awkwardly from the actor's back is an altar. J. R. Green points out to me that the white circles strung across the top of the scene do sometimes appear in Apulian sanctuary scenes. Behind the altar is a donkey ridden by another actor. On the photograph one can just make out a line running up the inside of the donkey's raised foreleg. It may suggest a seam and be a reminiscence of a panto-mime ass. The unnatural spots on the legs may also suggest artifice. The lines of the actor's tights at the wrist and ankle are distinct. Over his shoulder is an exaggeratedly large bundle. It could only be attached to a stick though the lines of the stick are barely visible behind the figure's chin.

At the beginning of Aristophanes' *Frogs*, Dionysus, disguised as Heracles with a lion skin and club, makes his way to Heracles' home to ask directions to the Underworld. There is nothing in the text of the play to suggest that Heracles lives in a shrine, but the idea that a god lives in his temple is natural enough. Dionysus' slave sits on a donkey, but absurdly also carries a large pack suspended on a pole which presses against his shoulder. Dionysus then proceeds to bang violently on Heracles door with his club. Despite the condition of the vase when photographed, the details that correspond to this scenario are clear enough: a comic actor dressed as Heracles in a lion skin bangs at a door with a club, while a slave carrying a heavy pack sits on a donkey behind him. The general configuration of the scene conforms in every detail. Doubt attaches only to the details of the costume worn by the figure who bangs at the door with his club. His costume appears to be that of Heracles rather than that of Dionysus disguised as Heracles: the text of *Frogs* makes it certain that Dionysus is supposed to be wearing boots and a diaphanous gown beneath his lion skin. Indeed, the figure's face appears to be that of Heracles rather than Dionysus.

The problem appears insuperable if one expects perfect conformity between an image of a theater scene and the production details indicated by a text.[77] It is considerably less severe, if we accept, as we had to with the Schiller Painter's image, that West Greek painters might omit and even alter details to enhance the beauty, clarity, or recognizability of their paintings. The painter of this scene may well have balked at the confusion likely to result from an attempt to render an actor disguised as Dionysus disguised as Heracles and for the sake of clarity have chosen only to render the beginning and end-points of this chain of impersonation.[78] It is, after all, difficult iconographically to signal a "Heracles" if you add boots, an effeminate gown and someone else's face.

How much weight can we give to the minor costume details when we throw them in the balance beside the general outline of the scene? Hoffmann suggests that this precise scenario might have appeared in any number of ancient comedies.[79] Even supposing that scenes juxtaposing a Heracles-like figure clubbing a door and a slave carrying a large pack on his shoulders while seated on a donkey were all the rage in Classical Greece, there are good reasons why *Frogs* might particularly be represented by this scene. Not only is it the opening scene of the play, but the dialogue draws particular attention to the details. The violence of Dionysus' knocking generates one of the most brilliant "gatekeeper" scenes in Greek comedy; Dionysus' Heracles-costume is the object of a good deal of ridicule by Heracles himself; and finally the detail of the slave carrying a pack while sitting on a donkey is important because the slave complains about the pole pressing into his shoulder, which elicits an elaborate joke as Dionysus tries to prove that it is the donkey and not the slave who is doing the work. The details we see in this image generate the humor of the opening fifty lines of *Frogs*. But are we seriously to entertain Hoffmann's hypothesis that there were many lost Heracles-banging-at-the-door-with-his-club-accompanied-by-the-pack-bearing-donkey-riding-slave comedies? The jokes do not really bear repeating and certainly not to this length. It is hard to imagine Aristophanes winning first prize with such an opener if the joke was as stale as the hyperskeptics suggest.

I should perhaps for methodological reasons avoid pointing out that our painter is not a consummate artist, but was, to his credit, at least aware of his limitations and wisely did not attempt to render the triple disguise required by the performance. The manner in which the lion skin floats behind the Heracles figure with no connection to his body and the manner in which the pack carried by the slave floats above the slave in relative independence of his stick or his back all inspire little faith in the artist's skill. But though a poor picture may obscure the importance of his image, it cannot compromise it. One should, however, acknowledge the possibility that such desired minor costume details as a diaphanous gown on a figure that is otherwise obviously Heracles were mis-recognized and omitted when the vase was restored in the nineteenth century. We will never know really know unless the missing vase resurfaces.

A third reasonably secure connection with Attic comedy is provided by a Paestan bell-krater (FIGURE 2.5).[80] The vasepainting shows two figures in masks and comic costume. On the left is a younger man with a laurel crown. He holds a concert kithara in his left hand and a plectrum in his right. The kithara is hung with ribbons indicating a victory in a musical contest. He resists being dragged off by an old man with the mask and costume, albeit comic, of a respectable citizen (his phallus is covered and he carries a walking stick). Both characters are labeled. The musician is the famous singer and composer "Phrynis." This Phrynis can be not other than the dithyrambic poet and kitha-rode from Mytilene, active throughout Greece in the second half of the fifth century BC.[81] His appearance on a Paestan vasepainting by Asteas more than half a century after his death is no surprise: he was canonized as one of the founders of the controversial "New Music." Phrynis' musical innovations are the object of jokes in several Old Comedies: a personified "Music" names him in a list of composer/poets who have violated her in Pherecrates' *Cheiron*; his innovations are ridiculed in Aristophanes' *Clouds*; and the Suda says he was "often" named by the comic poets.[82] An afterlife on the comic stage as well as notoriety in West Greece is indicated by a recently published Apulian bell krater, probably a little later than this one, that shows a comic mask of a man with the laurel crown of a victor juxtaposed to a kithara and inscribed "Phrynis."[83] The sash in the upper right of the picture may suggest a sanctuary

Figure 2.5 Paestan red-figured bell krater, Asteas, Salerno, *c.*350 BC, Museo Provinciale Pc 1812. Courtesy, Direzione, Musei e biblioteche, Provincia di Salerno, and Jeffery Rusten.

setting. This, together with the ribbons on the kithara, may indicate that Phrynis has just been performing at a festival.

The elderly gentleman appears to be dragging the resisting Phrynis away.[84] He is named "Pyronides." Few now believe that the name is a comic distortion pointing to the Athenian general "Myronides."[85] The connection with an Old Comedy depends mainly upon this label. "Pyronides" is the name of the main character of Eupolis' *Demes*, a partially extant comedy produced sometime between 417 and 410 BC.[86] *Demes* is largely concerned with restoring the virtues of the simple and virtuous old order to a troubled and degenerate Athens. The hero brings up from the underworld the great statesmen of the past and together they rid Athens of various personifications of its ills: at least we still have the text of a scene in which a sycophant is arrested and further fragments to suggest that other undesirables suffered a similar fate.[87] Pyronides possibly drags Phrynis away for punishment for offences against traditional music.[88] Green argues that the Maltese dog at Phrynis' feet is normally associated with musicians, women and children and may indicate effeminacy.[89] Contemporary music critics were very generous in accusing the New Music and its practitioners with this vice.

Alexa Piqueux has recently expressed the view that "onomastics do not allow one to connect this image with a known play."[90] I think they do and it is worth setting out the evidence in some detail. "Pyronides" is an extremely rare name. As a fictional name it is attested three times: on Asteas' vase, in Eupolis' *Demes,* and in Lucian's totally fictitious *True Histories.*[91] As a historical anthroponym it appears only once in all the historical and epigraphic texts of antiquity: in Athens and in the late fifth century, at the time of the production of Eupolis' play.[92] There is no need to suppose that Eupolis means to spoof this Pyronides, though it is not impossible: this Pyronides was a wealthy and well-connected citizen and possibly well enough known to serve Eupolis as a model for his comic hero. The name is not only extremely rare but somewhat improbable.

Eupolis and Lucian exploit "Pyronides" as a speaking name, as if it came from the root *pyr,* meaning "fire" and suggesting ardor in the case of Eupolis' hero, and, in Lucian, suggesting a more literally combustible gentleman (Lucian's Pyronides appears in a list of humorous speaking-names given to leaders of the people of the Sun and Moon where Pyronides is, of course, one of the Sunnies). As a real anthroponym it derives not directly from *pyr* but from *pyrrh* a root meaning ruddy or red-headed, from which several other names are derived, most notably "Pyrrhos."[93] We do, in fact, have one and only one (not very securely attested) Pyrrh[on]ides from early fifth century Athens and one and only one (possibly fictional) Doric variation, Pyrrhonidas, dubiously reported to be the father of the lyric poet Pratinas.[94] Pyrrh- names do sometimes appear as Pyr-names, but as Chantraine notes the phenomenon is "tardif." For example, the five volumes of Fraser and Matthews *Greek Personal Names* attest 196 different people named "Pyrrhos" from Greek antiquity, but only 14 named "Pyros." Moreover at least 5 of these 14 are treated by the experts as simple spelling mistakes (they appear in semi-literate graffiti) and the remaining 9 all date to the first three centuries AD, with a single possible exception from third-century BC Crete.

It is worth laying out all this information because several scholars suggest that the "Pyronides" on the Asteas krater could be any old Pyronides (just as FIGURE 2.4 could be any old comedy with a Heracles figure banging at the door in the company of a slave carrying a pack and riding a donkey).[95] But it is very surprising to find any historical Pyronides at all, especially in the Classical period. The Athenian Pyronides attested by the Vienna papyrus had a name that was not only extremely rare, but spelled in a form that was, so far as we know, unique but for its comic exploitation. Pyronides is no John Smith. The odds are overwhelming that an ancient purchaser, even in Paestum, recognized that a kitharode named Phrynis must be the famous kitharode Phrynis and that a citizen named Pyronides must be the famous Pyronides, even if the first was

Figure 2.6   Apulian relief guttus, *c.*330 BC, Naples MN Santangelo 368. Courtesy, Soprintendenza Archeologica Napoli e Pompei.

ultimately historical and the second ultimately a comic fiction, just as surely as we in purchasing a cup with the image of a wizard named "Dumbledore" could not fail to realize that the image referred to the famous master of Hogwarts and not some Dumbledore we managed to dig out of the Edinburgh telephone directory. Gould and Lewis were correct therefore it to take the presence of the name as an almost certain link with Eupolis' play, and all studies of the *Demoi* written since the Würzburg *Thesmophoriazusae* krater came to light are right to regard Asteas' dependence upon the play as a virtual certainty.[96] In this case, onomastics do help.

Astonishingly little notice has been taken of the most certain example, after the Würzburg krater, of a West Greek imagery connected to a known comedy. This is partly because the image is not on a painted pot, but on a series of Apulian mould-made oil cans (*gutti*) of the late fourth century BC. Taplin confined his investigation in *Comic Angels* to vasepainting.[97] It is, moreover, small and ugly. But truth is not always found with beauty. FIGURE 2.6 is one of three ceramics known from the same mould.[98] On them we see a single comic actor (the stomach padding and the phallus are immediately visible and one can make out the wrinkling of the actor's tights). The actor is not in any generic pose: the action is "scene specific." He kneels upon an altar in a position that is easily recognizable as a parody of Euripides' *Telephus* (cf. FIGURES 1.1 and 2.3). He holds a sword in his right hand and in the other he holds a bucket. One can also barely distinguish the outline of a *pilos* or felt cap upon his head. Hats of this sort are conventionally associated with travelers, poor men or beggars, and all associations are appropriate to the hero of Euripides' tragedy who disguises himself as a beggar when he comes to Agamemnon's palace. Literary testimonia associate the *pilos* with the hero in the performance tradition of the play.[99] FIGURE 2.6 is in fact a representation of *the* other extant parody of Euripides' *Telephus*, namely the scene from Aristophanes' *Acharnians* where the hero, Dikaiopolis takes hostage and threatens to kill a charcoal-bucket (a *larkos*) which is notionally a friend and neighbour of the chorusmen from Acharnae (to get the joke you have to know that charcoal burning was a major industry in Acharnae). Some scholars have said that the oval object he holds in his left hand is a shield, not a bucket, evidently without the benefit of a careful inspection of the object which is clearly concave (with the concavity here facing outwards), far too small for a shield, and not held like any shield known to military science – the actor's fingers are wrapped around the rim.[100] An Attic vasepainting shows a man pouring charcoal onto a fire from a vessel of just this size and shape.[101] Sparkes tentatively identifies the vessel as a *larkos*.[102] The Apulian guttus confirms the identification.

West Greek pottery thus yields images relating to four known comedies. All of them are what we traditionally recognize as Attic and all seem to vindicate Webster's claim that the comedy we find on West Greek pottery is not of a different species from the comedies whose texts survive on manuscripts and papyri from antiquity. The most surprising thing, however, is that the comedies are all Old Comedies, and some had their debut as much as a quarter century before the creation of the first comic vase in West Greece. It is, of course, only because they are scenes from Old Comedy that we can recognize them at all. Our meager fragments of so-called Middle Comedy would be unlikely to conjure up production scenarios that we could recognize in a vasepainting. West Greek vases may show contemporary fourth-century comedies, but this may never be demonstrable.[103]

Close examination of a few comic scenes has yielded some clues about the how and why of West Greek comic scenes. The artists are, as Giuliani argued, mainly focused upon a single moment in a play. But quite unlike what Giuliani found in the case of vasepaintings influenced by tragedies, they are not in any sense illustrating the story narrated by the comedy. The comic scenes are primarily illustrations of theatrical productions. The comic stories are important too, but secondary. We can see this from the very beginning in the Tarporley Painter's evident concern in FIGURE 2.1 to create the feel of theater, its vast extent of space, its acting surfaces, its ways of creating illusion through costume (down to the last detail of how the comic *somation* is buckled between the belly and buttocks) and the physical dexterity of the players (dancing on tiptoes like a man suspended from ropes), and capturing its unique blend of voice and action, even something of the quick pace of its action, and all this without ever succumbing to the narrative illusion and compromising its performance realism. This is not the approach one would expect from a book illustrator, and surely not an approach available to one who has only a remote idea of what theater is like. Add to this the presence of details, like the giant skyphos held by the old woman in FIGURE 2.3, that could only be known from an actual production. The artists are drawing upon the memory of a specific production, not from a text (as we can see, for example, in the oddities of the Tarporley Painter's inscription in FIGURE 2.1), just as their Attic colleagues did before them.

For all that, there are obvious differences between what one sees on a West Greek comic pot and what one would see in a comic production. But these differences in no way compromise the specificity of the images. Details may be added (such as in the splotches on the in–law's beard or the floating mirror) or omitted (such as the *Thesmophoriazusae's* brushwood, or a layer of costuming in the *Frogs)* to enhance the recognizability of certain scenes. The artists main concern was evidently not just to provide a convincing image of a scene of comedy, but an image that his customer's could immediately recognize as belonging to a specific comedy that they knew. Indeed, two of our known scenes are Telephus parodies, not just because they were memorable climactic scenes in their comedies, but because iconography (and doubtless also the theater) had given the suppliant scene an iconic form that was immediately recognizable and could be used to make the *Telephus* parodies in *Thesmophoriazusae* and in *Acharnians* also immediately recognizable. In the case of scene-specific comic images the artist has made every effort to make his painting recognizable to his consumers as *this* specific scene from *this* specific comedy. Evidently, the specific pleasure of these vases for the consumer was the pleasure of recognition and a recognition that was triggered primarily through imagery evoking the visual impact of a theatrical production (not the imagery that we would readily ascribe to a reader's imagination): name labels for characters do sometimes appear and we even have a snatch of dialogue, but in all the theater-related artifacts from West Greece or, for that matter, Attica, no label ever names the play from which the scene appears. The vasepaintings, in sum, give every indication of belonging to a culture which knew theater intimately and knew it from sight.

Historians of the theater are adjusting their impression of how fast and how wide it spread, but not, as we saw, without growing pains. The majority, however, still balk at the notion that Aristophanes and Old Comedy were performed in the Greek West. And yet, we only have evidence for the production of fifth-century drama in the Greek West in the fourth century. This has a lot to do with the fact that our texts are mainly fifth-century texts and so the odds are very much against recognizing a scene from later drama. But that is not a complete explanation. In the case of our most explicitly tragedy-related vasepaintings we noticed that 75 percent were from plays by Aeschylus, Sophocles and Euripides. West Greek vasepainting gives us clear evidence of the early onset of the same process of canonization that ensured that of many centuries of tragic and comic production most of our textual remains are of four fifth-century authors. I do not, however, believe that these statistics reflect a disproportionate focus in West Greece in the fourth century upon fifth-century classics. Without doubt, they were performed often, but probably not with the degree of exclusivity that a numerical count of vasepaintings suggests. My guess is, rather, that these classics made good subjects for vasepainting precisely because the on-going process of canonization brought Aeschylus, Sophocles, Euripides, and, yes, even Aristophanes into the mainstream of popular culture and the popular imagination, with the result that painters of theatrical vases preferred them as more likely to trigger easy recognition from their customers, and therefore as more marketable.

Theater-Realistic Scenes of Tragedy

The Tarporley Painter, despite being the very earliest of West Greek painters to paint theatrical subjects in a realistic style, also represents the apogee of West Greek theater-realism. It is a curious fact, and one that needs explanation, that the vasepainting of tragic subjects only begins to approach this kind of realism at the very end of the production of theater-related vasepainting in the Greek West, only so far as we know in the 330s BC, and only in Sicily.

The most remarkable of these is a calyx krater excavated in Syracuse in 1969 and attributed to the Capodarso Painter or a close associate (FIGURE 2.7).[104] Architectural details in Greek vasepainting signify that the scene takes place in an unusual location whose identity is important for an understanding of the visual narrative. Here the columns are emphasized by added white. They are all somewhat different from one another, possibly drawing attention to the artificiality of the environment. That on the left descends to the very edge of a platform, even overhangs it somewhat, and thereby emphasizes the confined and narrow nature of the platform. The three-dimensionality of the ground is marked by lines showing the depth of the floor boards, and, lest anyone fail to get the point, the front edge of the floor joists are clearly outlined underneath.

Figure 2.7   Sicilian red-figured calyx krater, Gibil Gabib Group, probably Capodarso Painter, *c.*340–330 BC, Syracuse, Museo Archeologico Regionale "Paolo Orsi" 66557. Courtesy, Assessorato Beni Culturali e Ambientali e P. I. della Regione Siciliana.

The treatment is very similar to the calyx krater of the Adrastos Group, except only the abruptness with which the platform ends at the back and sides.[105] The details signify that the action takes place on a wooden stage in front of columns that represent the palace. This fragment is one of two West Greek vases that show the performance of a tragedy on stage. Both are Sicilian. Both produced around 330. Both are probably by the Capodarso Painter. Clearly depicted stages otherwise appear only on vasepaintings related to comedy.

Atop the stage stand six figures: from left to right an old man, a young girl, a younger man, a girl, a woman, and on the far right, not visible in the reproduction a second woman who runs away from the scene. Details of stage-costume are clearest in the character of the old man. His arms clearly show the actor's tights, outlined in black, emerging from underneath his cloak (compare also the younger man's right arm). A mask is suggested by the vacant look in his face, emphasized by the rare frontal view, though this may also serve to signal his extreme old age as do the pupils of his eyes that are rendered with vertical strokes. He wears the cloak and boots characteristic of the "*paidagogos*" figure that Green and Taplin regard as an iconographic index in West Greek vasepaint-ing of tragic action.[106] The *paidagogos* or old nurse frequently serves as a mes-senger in tragedy and New Comedy. A mask is also suggested by the stiffness, angularity and the larger-than-life size of the younger man's head.

Most of all, however, it is the configuration of the scene that suggests a stage action. The old man to the left stares straight out toward the viewer, but makes a conventional "speaking-gesture" toward the younger man and woman at center stage. In non-dramatic scenes people look as well as gesture toward those to whom they speak. But this odd bi-directionality is a common feature of the comic messenger known from the highly-realistic theater art of the Hellenistic period.[107] The New Comic messenger delivers his narrative "up-front," looking toward the audience, but gestures with his left hand toward the characters he notionally addresses. The younger man, at center stage, strokes his beard in thoughtful puzzlement at the old man's words; the woman to the right holds her left hand to the side of her cheek in an expression of shock (their stance and gestures are also paralleled by Hellenistic representations of dramatic messen-ger scenes).[108]

The Capodarso Painter very probably intends to show a performance of the climactic messenger scene of Sophocles' *Oedipus the King,* where an old shep-herd from Corinth brings news of the death of Oedipus' presumed parents. Upon questioning he reveals that they were not Oedipus' natural parents: the infant Oedipus was given to the old man by a slave of Laius and taken to the childless Corinthian couple. Jocasta's gesture captures the moment of her recog-nition soon after the old man releases the vital information at line 1042.

Even in this most realistic of all tragic scenes, however, there are illusionistic details. Tragic vases never achieve the degree of realism that comic vases show from the start. The mouths of the actors are not quite as open as we expect from a tragic mask. Moreover, the stage-realism is compromised, paradoxically, by some of the standard forms of theatrical "rhetoric" one finds on the mythologi-cal vases. Oedipus' daughters Antigone and Ismene are added for pathos, even though they are not part of this scene in Sophocles' play (though they do appear later). The anonymous woman just behind Jocasta turns away with a gesture of alarm, like many other female onlookers who typically register emotional reac-tions on the margins of South Italian mythological scenes. Yet in this scene it is only Jocasta and the audience who have the requisite knowledge to feel alarm. The anonymous running woman simply serves as the concrete and conven-tional symbol of tragic horror. The artist's desire to show the production is compromised by a desire to tell the story. He possibly felt the daughters neces-sary to show that this recognition scene was that of Oedipus (in Sophocles' play Oedipus' children/siblings do not appear until much later but they are symbolically important to the present moment that marks the first recognition of the confusion of the natural order of generations that Oedipus' crime represents).

The other vase adopts a much simpler method of signifying a stage. This second calyx krater by the Capodarso Painter shows a platform raised on two posts (we are left to imagine two more behind them) and supported in the center by a column.[109] On top of the platform are four figures, one of whom is a messenger figure with a distorted mask-like face and wearing sleeves and high boots like the old man in FIGURE 2.7. Three women react to his news, one kneeling with a very loud gesture of despair, and one turning away. At least two of the women also have sleeves or lines at the wrist indicating actors' tights. Their faces, however, have no mask-like qualities and even the old man's mouth is closed. Moreover, the woman at the left edge of the stage, who turns away, probably to be read as another one of the "running women" favored by West Greek vasepainters to register an emotional reaction and indicate that the news is bad.

These two Sicilian kraters are as close as West Greek vasepainting gets to representations of tragedy in performance, yet all of them succumb to illusionistic mythical representation, especially in the rendering of faces, or in their narrative enrichments.[110] None attests the flawless performance realism attained by Attic vasepainting (esp. FIGURE 1.3).

Conclusion: a Synkrisis of Attic and West Greek Theater-Related Art

The appearance in the last few decades of a great many West Greek vasepaintings, some with surprisingly strong and unexpected connections with known drama, has contributed to a sense of paradox. The more we became aware of the degree to which theater was celebrated in West Greek pottery, the more keenly we felt its absence in Attic. Theater, after all, was an Attic invention. Or so, at least, it appears to our eyes. Oliver Taplin spoke of Attic vasepainting's reticence or avoidance of dramatic subjects.[111] Förtsch speaks of Attic's "non-representation" of drama.[112] Maffre goes so far as to characterize the disparity as a "total divorce" between comedy and Attic vase-painting.[113] Taplin suggests that this reticence has something to do with the general avoidance of subjects dealing with the public and political life of Athens, such as depictions of the Assembly, Council, or lawcourts. It may be true that political subjects are avoided, but it is surely arbitrary to include drama within the category of "political life" as opposed to, say, Dionysian scenes, or religious life, not to mention musical or choral subjects, of which we have many representations on Attic vases. There is indeed both a quantitative and a qualitative difference in Attic vasepainting's receptivity to theater, but it is less stark and more subtle than the language of "avoidance" or "divorce" allows.

In general, Classical art depicting theatrical performance and theatrical performers comes in disparate clumps, so much so that the very unevenness of the material seems to require explanation. In concluding this chapter, I will outline two ways in which scholars have attempted to impose a pattern of order and sense upon the material and then offer one of my own. The latter is not meant to replace, but to supplement the former. There is merit, I think, in all three ways of dividing the pie.

Attic vs West Greek

Oliver Taplin's work on the theatrical art (restricted to vasepainting) has always stressed the qualitative differences between Attic and West Greek products. In his three principal surveys of the subject he has treated Attic only as a background to West Greek.[114] Some, most recently Jeffrey Rusten, feel that he downplays the quantity and quality of the Attic material. In *Comic Angels,* for example, he allowed "only one Attic vase-painting which is clearly signaled as showing tragedy in performance."[115] Of Attic comic precedents fourteen were named but all problematized. Taplin's main point, however, is unaffected by specific exclusions. There is unquestionably a difference in the way these two regions responded to drama. The sense of a quantitative difference depends mainly in how one organizes and reads the statistics.

Taplin estimates some four hundred West Greek tragedy-related vasepaintings. The relationship to tragedy is indirect, but follows explicit criteria: a combination of subject matter, explicit visual signals, and possibly inscriptions. Most important is to know that certain story details were invented by specific tragedians (as in FIGURE 1.1). Secondly, visual details contribute to an impression of "staginess," such as dress reminiscent of tragic costume, background details reminiscent of the architecture of the stage building, or the presence of distinctly tragic characters like *paedagogoi.* Lastly, many vasepaintings contain name labels in Attic dialect. These are all, in my view, valid criteria, even if they are "subjective" (i.e. require judicious rather than mechanical application). But he makes no estimate about how many Attic mythological vasepaintings could also satisfy these criteria, or other equally valid criteria that might be more specific to Attic. Todisco *et al.* (2003) using criteria not very different from Taplin, produced a list of one hundred and forty Attic tragedy-related vases. My guess is that West Greek tragedy-related vasepainting, though generally more exuberant in its use of tragic signals, is more copious, but not vastly more copious than Attic.

If, however, one is as restrictive in the admission of West Greek tragic vasepaintings as Taplin was with Attic, namely allowing only those that are "clearly
signaled as showing tragedy in performance," which I take to be the strict criterion of theater-realism that I have adopted in Chapter 1, then we find no more
than two West Greek vasepaintings that take tragic production as their subject
(and do so in a not entirely satisfactory manner) as opposed to four Attic vases
(one with impeccable realism) that show tragedy in performance.[116] If the category is expanded to genre scenes showing tragic actors, then the Attic count is
still higher (fourteen as opposed to a possible five) and still more so if we permit
reliefs (giving Attic art nineteen).[117]

If we were to include satyrplay (despite the difficulty of establishing connec-
tions between satyrs and drama) Attic vasepainting's interest in depicting theatrical subjects would appear vastly greater. Carpenter's recent study of West
Greek satyrplay-related vases found only four serious candidates, while over
three hundred Attic satyrplay-related vasepaintings are listed by Brommer.[118]
Attic prevails even on the strictest criteria for theater-realism. There is only one
West Greek vase that unquestionably depicts satyr-performers, the Tarporley
Painter's genre scene with satyr choreuts, as opposed to three Attic genre scenes
with satyr-choreuts.[119] It is only in the production of comic scenes and scenes of
comic actors that West Greek vasepainting with 250 examples makes Attic comic
art with its 11 vasepaintings seem small.[120] But again, if we were to shift our gaze
from vasepainting to theater art generally, we could add two Attic reliefs and
hundreds of figurines from the fourth century, enough to nullify any general
claims that West Greece invented realistic representations of comedy.

Indeed, attention to theater art in general suggests quite a different picture
from that offered by vasepainting alone. The real divide seems not so much
determined by the different mentality of Athenians and West Greeks as determined by the different mentality of Greeks in the fifth century and Greeks in the
fourth century BC. The interest in theatrical subjects seems to grow rapidly from
the 420s to blossom after about 400 BC. At this time however Attic vase production was dwindling and, except in the case of a few small groups like the
Pronomos Painter and his associates, Attic vasepainting was growing moribund
and repetitive. West Greek vasepainting was at this date expanding both its production and its iconographic repertoire. It is only because of the conspicuous
artistry of West Greek comic vasepainting, as opposed to Attic coroplastic art
(that was also expanding), or the longevity of pottery as opposed to free painting or glyptic, that Attic theater art seems slim in comparison with the Greek
West. The contrast between Attic and West Greek art cannot easily be reduced
to a plus/minus index of theater receptivity

But even if we confine our discussion to the corpus of twenty-six Attic vases
(all but one red-figured) showing performers or scenes of tragedy or comedy,

and even if we admit that these vasepaintings represent a miniscule percentage of the estimated corpus (0.00026 percent of extant Attic red-figured vases), it is large enough to obviate the claim that theater art is virtually a West Greek invention, especially given the observable debt West Greek vasepainters, like the Tarporley Painter, owed to Attic models. If there is avoidance of certain theatrical subjects we could sooner find it in West Greek art. Only one West Greek artifact, for example, certainly relates to the production of satyrplay. Only one relates to a dramatic choral performance (the same one). Indeed the same vase, by the Tarporley Painter, is one of only two relatively clear genre scenes within West Greek art where theatrical performers hold masks. Finally, it must be noted that West Greek tragic art, at its best, never achieves the stark realism offered by the Attic fragment in Kiev (FIGURE 1.3). If the Attic repertoire is less numerous in terms of theater-realistic artifacts it is at least more inclusive. There are, on the one hand, Attic parallels for everything we find in West Greek vasepainting, with the notable exception of a scene with tragic actors (as opposed to choreuts) in performance. On the other hand, the most common types of theatrical scenes in Attic are unparalleled or rare in West Greek production (tragic choruses, comic choruses, genre scenes with choreuts of any variety). There is unevenness in the clumping of the evidence, but I do not think that speculation upon differences in the collective responses of Athenians and West Greeks to the political contents of drama will explain it. The most overtly political drama reflected in our artifacts is surely the scene from Eupolis *Taxiarchoi*, and that is Attic, though admittedly it is not red-figure (FIGURE 1.11).

Tragedy vs Comedy

Green slices the pie differently. In Green's view the difference is not so much in how different Greeks reacted to drama as in how Greeks reacted to different dramatic genres.[121] The artist's most basic instinct is to mythicize his material. Tragedy was a dramatic representation of myth (satyrplay much more so) and the genre was therefore perceived as the mythical story created by the dramatic illusion. Comedy, by contrast, had reference only to the contemporary and real world, and therefore lent itself, as a genre, to realistic representation. Moreover, as Green points out, Attic Old Comedy freely breaks the dramatic illusion and so is less illusionistic by virtue of its form as well as its content. The validity of Green's simple observation can be perceived in the explanation of the differential treatment we find in such paintings as the Choregos vase, where the mythical hero Aegisthus is rendered much more illusionistically than the comic characters who share his stage, or in the Perseus Dancer vase (FIGURE 1.10) where the comic hero, as he happens also to be a mythical hero, is less realistically rendered than other contemporary comic actors.[122] It might also explain why the earliest realistic depictions of theater performers are the choruses, the ordinary men and women of tragedy, and not the mythical heroes, or why choreuts holding their masks are more realistically rendered than choreuts wearing them. Best of all, of course, is the power of Green's observation to explain comedy's overall domination of the corpus of theater-realistic artifacts.

The problem is that the genre distinction too often works the other way. Our earliest theater-realistic artifacts are tragic.[123] Tragedy dominates the corpus of realistic representations for over half a century. Indeed our most theater-realistic artifacts are tragic (I refer to the Kiev fragment, FIGURE 1.3, again), setting a standard of realism by 430 BC that comic artifacts do not again approach for almost thirty years. Moreover, tragic subjects by far dominate our Attic representations in all media but the terracotta figurines. At the other end of the timescale we find tragic vasepaintings around 330 BC rendered in a far more realistic idiom than any comic vases of this date (West Greek comic realism seems to decline sharply from about 350 BC).

Chorus vs Actors

Most of the Attic theatrical artifacts are choral. Only six or seven of the Attic vasepaintings depict actors (not including the possibly incidental actor on FIGURE 1.2) and in two of these (Pronomos vase [= FIGURE 1.9] and Heracles and the centaurs) the actors are incidental to choreuts; all the others depict choruses. The Attic reliefs are also choral: one shows a poet; probably none show actors. By contrast all of the terracotta figurines are actors and the West Greek artifacts show, with very rare exceptions, only actors.

The unevenness of this pattern of distribution may not, however, reflect the subject preference of different artistic media, so much as chronology. This is quite clear in Attic vasepainting which gives us the fullest chronological spread. Choreuts are of interest to Attic vasepainting from the very beginning of the organized tragic contests at the Dionysia, about 500 BC (FIGURES 1.2, 1.8). If we discount the figures incidental to choral scenes, we do not have any representations of actors, certainly none that focus upon the actor, until 430 to 420 BC (when we have two, including FIGURE 1.10). Another six representations of tragic and comic actors date from 410 to 400 BC. The actor does not become an object of interest until fairly late in the production of Attic red-figured pottery, and the very end of its creative phase. It is precisely from this period (410 to 400 BC) that we can trace the earliest production of theater-realistic terracotta figurines in Athens and the production of theater-realistic vasepainting in the Greek West: and these are exclusively focused upon actors.

Artistic medium is an important factor in this development. In Attic art the preference for chorus or actor depends very much on the prestige and expense of the medium and – one might infer – sociological differences in the target market for the different products upon which theater-realistic art appears. The eight theatrical Attic reliefs appear to show only choreuts (along with gods, choregoi, pipers and minor adjutants), with the exception only of the Lyme Park relief, which probably shows a poet.[124] Of the twenty-seven Attic vasepaintings we have discussed, choral subjects are only found on large sympotic vessels (mainly kraters), the one major exception being the latest of all our vasepaintings, the chous of about 350 BC that showed a comic chorus.[125] By contrast, of the seven Attic scenes that focus upon actors, all appear on minor vessels, the largest a cup, and the others choes or (in one case an oinochoe). In many cases too, actor vases are of a strikingly inferior quality (esp. FIGURE 1.11). The terracotta figurines, all actors, are also classifiable as downmarket merchandise.

This division is not likely to be a function of the greater compositional challenge of rendering a chorus. Some actor's scenes are quite elaborate, and our latest choral vase is a chous. Clearly, the subjects themselves had different sociological appeal. As noted earlier, many of the choral reliefs are from monuments commemorating a choral victory in drama. Choral imagery was endemic to choregic art and its place in choregic art lent considerable glamour to the imagery when it migrated to other media. Choral imagery evidently appealed to those who could afford to buy kraters and who aspired to the lifestyle of genteel entertainment that a krater (a symposium vessel) implied. Choral imagery carried with it associations of the lifestyle of the super-rich (Athenians in the top 1 percent income bracket who were eligible to take on the responsibility of funding a chorus). In short, pictures of choruses had a snob-appeal that pictures of actors lacked. The status-consciousness of large symposium vessels is also expressed in the preference of tragic and satyric over comic choruses, a factor of seventeen to three. The cost of a tragic/satyric chorus was nearly twice that of a comic chorus, and the prestige of victory proportionately greater.

The starkest contrast between Attic and West Greek theatrical vasepainting is the dominance of choral subjects in Attic and their virtual absence in West Greek.[126] West Greek pottery offers only one choral vasepainting (the Tarporley Painter's genre scene with satyr-choreuts). The absence of choral subjects is all the more striking because West Greek scenes showing actors appear mostly on large, sympotic vessels of the sort Attic potters reserved for choral subjects

It would be dangerous to conclude from the absence of choral subjects from West Greek vasepaintings that drama in Italy and Sicily was performed without a chorus. The popularity of Aeschylus and Old Comedy tells against this, as do the titles of plays that were written for performance in Sicily, such as Aeschylus' *Aetnian Women*, or indeed. Epicharmus' *Choreuts*.[127] Recent epigraphic evidence makes certain the existence of some kind of choregic system in Sicily.[128] Moreover, the tragedy-related vasepaintings do sometimes suggest choruses, through the appearance of identical incidental figures, sometimes inscribed with plural names, and more abstractly through the marginal presence of running women, registering an emotional reaction to the central tragic action.[129] The production of comedies like Aristophanes' *Acharnians* or *Thesmophoriazusae* is unthinkable without a chorus – the chorus is a main character in both plays and indispensable to the action. It would appear, rather, that the symbolism of choral imagery was less valued in Italy and Sicily: possibly because choregic memorialization took on a different form in the Greek West (there are no traces of choregic monuments in this part of the world); or, conversely, the actor and his domain, the stage, had a much higher symbolic prestige in the Greek West than at Athens. But the general impression left by theater-related art in Athens and West Greece is that from about 420 BC actors began to catch the popular imagination in a way they had never done before. In the next two chapters we will explore other evidence that confirms this view.

Notes

1 Todisco 2003 is a mine of statistics for tragedy-related vasepaintings. Todisco 2006.246–50 gives more readable tables for breakdown by author and region.
2 For Aeschylus in Sicily, see Herington 1967; Bremer 1991.39–41; Taplin 2006; Wilson 2007c; Kowalzig 2008; Duncan forthcoming. For the context and content of *Aetnian Women,* see Poli-Palladini 2001.
3 Kerkhof 2001.136.
4 Athen. 402b; Stanford 1937–8; Herington 1967.78; Griffith 1978.
5 Radt *ad* A. *TrGF* 3 pp. 161–2.
6 Schol. A. *Eum.* 626 (= Epicharmus *PCG* 1 F 221). For parody of the *Prometheus Bound* in Epicharmus, see Kerkhof 2001.136–40 with further literature.
7 Schol. Venet. Ar. *Peace* 73; Macrob. *Sat.*5.19.17; Herington 1967.
8 **Aeschylus:** *Life of Aeschylus* 10–11; *Marm.Par.* esp. 59. **Phrynichus:** Anon. *de com.* pp. 8, 36 Kaib., *TrGF* T 6.
9 Suda s.v. *Karkinos.*
10 Suda ε 1001; Diog. L. 8.57.1.
11 Arist. *Poet.* 1449b 5–9.
12 Arist. *Poet.* 1448a 29–b 3; schol. Theocritus, pp. 2.21 ff. Wendel.
13 *Vita Euripidis* p. 3 Schwartz.
14 Todisco 2003; *P&P* 15.
15 Csapo 1994.56–7; Rusten forthcoming. See Chapter 1, p. 1.
16 I am grateful to Jeff Rusten for forwarding to me the outline of an as yet unpublished lecture delivered in Göttingen. The claim is specifically limited to reperformances of Old Comedy (which we will examine in the following section).

17   Catucci 2003.

18   See Robinson 2004 [2006].196.

19   Giuliani 2001.17 = Giuliani 2003.231–2.

20   Only two of the vases in *P&P* (nos. 24, 56) significantly predate 400 BC; however, in a contribution to a conference in Michigan in 2008 Taplin discussed fifth-century West Greek vessels with tragic subjects beginning as early as the 420s BC (to appear in Bosher forthcoming).

21   Trendall 1988.138.

22   Apulian red-figured bell krater, Tarporley Painter, *c*.400 BC, Sydney, Nicholson 47.05, *MTS* TV 18, *RFVAp* no. 15.

23   Interest in the tension between reality and representation is characteristic of the Tarporley Painter's work: Lissarague 2008.440–1.

24   Apulian red-figured bell krater, Tarporley Painter, *c*.400 BC, New York MMA 63.21.5, *ARVAp* no. 2, *P&P* fig. 1.

25   In Apulian: Trendall 1988, nos. I 3, I 5, I 7–18, I 15–20, I 23–5, I 30–3, I 36, II 2–3, 7, III 2. In Paestan: calyx krater by Asteas, Paestum MN 21306, *PP* 104.137, pl. 59a–b; calyx krater in Lipari 9604, *PP* 44.91, pl. 11a–b; oinochoe, Workshop of Asteas, Paestum MN 104378 (from tomb 197 di Gaudo 1990); bell krater, Naples private collection, *PP* 64.9, pl. 173e–f; see Pontrandolfo 2000, figs. 22, 23, 29. Several new Paestan examples appear in Schauenburg 2003.37–9, figs. 91a, 94a, 95, 96 and Schauenburg 2005.52–6, 66, figs. 134a, 135a, 137a, XLIX–L, LI–LII.

26   Athens NM 1500, *MTS* 33, AS 1 (our Figure 1.7); Cagliari, Museo Nazionale 10918, *MTS* 34, AS 6; Athens NM 1513; Eleusis no. 30, *MTS* 113, AS 29. These reliefs are all discussed and illustrated in Csapo forthcoming A.

27   The female companion of Dionysus holds a mask on three vasepaintings of *c*.400 BC, the Pronomos vase (FIGURE 1.9); a fragmentary volute krater, Near the Pronomos Painter, Samothrace 65.104 E+; bell krater, Ferrara T141C. The later relief from Cagliari (see previous note) has the same female figure with the mask. See Chapter 1, pp. 14, 19.

28   Apulian bell krater, Tarporley Painter, 400–390 BC, London BM F 163; *MTS* TV 29. The quoted words are from Trendall 1988.140.

29   Trendall 1988 lists (in addition to the Tarporley Painter) four Apulian examples of solitary human figures with tragic masks (nos. I 26–8 and postscript p. 154) and two Apulian examples with comic masks (nos. I 35, II 4). In a class by itself is Apulian gnathia krater fragment, Konnakis Ptr., *c*.340 BC, Wurzburg H 4600.

30   Csapo forthcoming A.

31   Fragmentary Attic red-figured pelike, Circle of the Pronomos Painter, *c*.400 BC, Barcelona 33; Attic red-figured bell krater, *c*.400 BC, Ferrara T161C. Both vases are illustrated and discussed in Csapo forthcoming A.

32   Multiplicity of masks: Apulian red-figured bell krater, *c*.370 BC, Brindisi, Faldetta coll., *P&P* fig. 2. Age or costume: Apulian Gnathia bell krater fragment, *c*.340 BC, Würzburg L832.

33   Trendall 1988, nos. II 9–11. Paestan red-figured calyx krater, signed by Asteas, *c*.350, in the Fujita collection, first published by Simon 2002, Simon 2004, fig. 9.7–8;

Schauenburg 2003, Abb. 115a–b, XVIII. The general schema reworked by Python in a red-figured bell-krater, Vatican 17270, discussed by Green 1995b.111–12; Simon 2004.120–1; and the very similar Paestan bell-krater recovered from the wreck of the HMS Colossus, Smallwood and Woodford 2003, pl. 72, 99. Simon 2002.120–1 takes the vasepaintings to show a staged mime, but there is no indication of a stage, albeit the frame around the image is suggestive, nor any parallel for vasepainting depicting mime.

34   The Attic krater by Nikias ($ARV^2$1133, no.1) seems not to be a significant exception. There the Victory carries a ribbon to a sacrifice celebrating a victory in the Panathenaic torch race: see P. Wilson 2000.254–5, fig 26; Bentz 2002.242 fig. 2.

35   Trendall 1988, nos. I 27–8.

36   Trendall 1988, nos. I 29, II 1. Cf. the Comic actors who serve as cupbearers to Dionysus on Paestan craters in Tampa (Zewadski collection, PP 74.63, pl. 31a–b) and Paestum (MN 32113, PP 64.10, pl. 18a); Pontrandolfo 2000.127.

37   See Trendall, PhV, p. 75; Dearden 1988.38; Taplin 1993.92; Schauenburg 2000.44; and the doubts of Lohmann 1979.55 and Hoffmann 2002.1131.

38   Sommerstein 1989.1–6; P&P 58.

39   Bell krater, Oxford 1917.65, RFVAp no. 4.

40   LIMC Orestes 7–10, 22; P&P 59 with further bibliography.

41   Giuliani 2001.28–33; Giuliani 2003.249–52.

42   Apulian bell krater, Tarporley Painter, c.400 BC, Melbourne, Geddes Collection A 4:8; Trendall 1990, fig. 36.

43   Apulian bell krater, Eumenides Painter, 390–380 BC, London BM F 166, RVAp I 97, no. 232; Apulian bell krater, Eumenides Painter, 390–380 BC, once Milan market, Finarte Cat. 5 (1963) pls. 42–3, RVAp I 97, no. 4/230; Apulian bell krater, Eumenides Painter, 390–380 BC, Louvre ED 710, RVAp I 97, no. 4/229; Apulian bell krater, Painter of the Long Overfalls, 370–360 BC, Leningrad inv. 298 (St. 1734), RVAp I 83, no. 127; Paestan squat lekythos, Asteas, 350–340 BC, Paestum 4794, RVP 109, no. 142, pl. 62a.

44   See the discussion in Giuliani 2001.32–8; P&P 62–4.

45   Trendall 1990.214.

46   Giuliani 2001.28–35; Giuliani 2003.243–61.

47   Apulian calyx krater, Tarporley Painter, c.400 BC, New York, MMA 24.97.104, RVAp 3/7, P&P 13, fig. 5.

48   I agree with Marshall 2001.59 that the "magical" interpretation of the scene, suggested by Beazley 1952 and followed by Taplin 1993 and Schmidt 1998, cannot stand. Beazley was reacting to Trendall's concern about the apparent contradiction between the central character's complaint that he was tied up and the absence of visible ropes in the painting. Though the Greek verb katadein can mean "to cast a spell," its normal meaning is simply "tie." The adverb ano is a problem for Beazley's interpretation: "tie up" is far more likely than "hex up." For an excellent account of the implications of the gestures and lines of dialogue, see Marshall 2001.60–2.

49   Marshall 2001.

50   Robinson 2004. Cf. Carpenter 2003, Carpenter 2009.

51 Giuliani 1995.152–8.
52 Mingazzini 1965/6.69–71; Bertino 1975.17–28; Giuliani 2001, Giuliani 2003. 243–61.
53 Beazley 1952.
54 Jeffery 1990.29; *PhV* 81, *P&P* nos. 68, 81 and 96 (I thank Oliver Taplin for bringing these other hetas to my attention).
55 In addition, the fact that the retrograde script contains many letters with an orthograde stance shows a certain casualness that one would not expect to find in any book illustration.
56 Apulian bell krater, McDaniel Painter, *c*.370 BC, Boston MFA 69.951, *RVAp* 4/251.
57 The Tarporley Painter's second goat is regularly overlooked in the literature: Taplin 1993.30; Schmidt 1998.24.
58 The only known comedy that comes close is Cratinus' *Dionysalexandros,* and only on Körte's supplement to the papyrus hypothesis, according to which Dionysus turned Helen into a goose and himself into a ram (not a kid!) and hid in a basket. Nothing else in the play is easily reconcilable with the details of the scenes.
59 Green 1994.112.
60 The tradition behind images of Hellenistic comedy offers a significant contrast: see, below, Chapter 5. The moulded relief gutti, discussed below, are also, by the nature of the product, a special case.
61 "Phlyax" drama, performed by "phlyakes," is a form of Doric comedy, attested for Greek Italy by the historian Sosibius (*c*.250 BC, *ap.* Athen. 621f). Literary versions of this comedy were produced by Rhinthon, according to *AP* 7.414, St. Byz. 603 and Suda s.v. "Rhinthon." On Rhinthon, see Taplin 1993.48–52,
62 *OCD* p. 1172 (W. G. Arnott); Nielsen 2002.156–7.
63 Webster 1948.
64 Taplin 1993.52–4 makes most of these points with different emphases. See also Robinson 2004.207.
65 Apulian red-figured bell krater, Schiller Painter, *c*.370 BC, Würzburg H5697, *P&P* fig. 6.
66 See esp. the woman on the Apulian bell krater, *c*.400–380 BC, Milan AO.9.284.
67 Moret 1975.101.
68 On Euripides' play, see Chapter 1, pp. 3–4.
69 Detailed argument in Csapo 1986 and Taplin 1987.
70 Austin and Olson 2004.lxxvi–lxxvii list five departures of which one must be rejected. They suppose that because the in-law has by this point been exposed as male, his phallus should be visible. But this is without warrant because the inlaw, as they admit (2004.233), continues to wear the same garment he did earlier.
71 For oversized props in Attic comedy: Revermann 2006a.244–6.
72 Csapo 1986; Taplin 1987.
73 Giuliani 2001.37, n. 39.
74 Kossatz-Deismann 1980; Dearden 1999.242.
75 Keuls 1997.324; Hoffmann 2002.170–5; Small 2003.
76 Once Berlin St. Mus. 43046. The history is given by Taplin 1993.45–7.

77   See Taplin 1993.45 n. 37 and more recently Hoffmann 2002.175.

78   Cf. Handley 2000.158: "If the choice is to simplify Dionysus-Herakles to Herakles at a moment when Dionysus is at his most Herakles-like, the vase will have to have sold on its recall of that key moment, and with neglect of the double identity of its principal which has so great an impact in the theatre. Unfortunately, perhaps, the interests of theatrical historians and those of vasepainters and their clients do not always coincide in matters of documentary realism."

79   Hoffmann 2002.175.

80   Paestan red-figured bell krater, Asteas, c.350 BC, Salerno, Museo Provinciale Pc 1812, *PhV*² 58.

81   For the sources and chronology for Phrynis, see Telò 2007.28–33.

82   Pherecrates *PCG* F 155; Ar. *Clouds* 966–72; Suda s.v. Phrynis. A comedy might also lie behind Istros' claim that Phrynis' father was a cook for the tyrant Hieron.

83   Apulia bell krater attributed to the Winterthur Painter, c.340 BC, Budapest 97; Vandlik 2002.

84   The suggestion by Goulaki-Voutira 1999 that the old man is a tutor is answered by Piqueux 2006, who still nonetheless allows the tutorial hypothesis some validity. Goulaki-Voutira's parallels are very weak.

85   Plepelits 1970.116–32; Heath 1990.154–5; Storey 2003.117–19.

86   For Pyronides as a character, see Storey 2003.116–17. For the date of Eupolis *Demoi*: Telò and Porciani 2002; Storey 2003.112–14.

87   See Storey 2003.165–74.

88   Storey 2003.170 thinks of an intruder scene after the model of Cinesias in Aristophanes' *Birds*. Telò thinks that Phrynis must be among the dead brought back to Athens from the Underworld in the play. I am, however, disinclined to his conclusion that the vase shows a forcible abduction to the upper world. A literal *apagoge* for punishment before a magistrate for musical offences by (the perhaps, on acquaintance, disillusioned) Pyronides better suits the disciplinarian fantasies of anti-New Musical discourse: see Csapo 2004a.244; Piqueux 2006.

89   Green forthcoming.

90   Piqueux 2006.3.

91   Luc. *VH* 1.20.13.

92   Lysias frr. 26, 29 Carey. The reading depends on *PGraecVindob* 29816 fr. 2, col. ii, lines 5–6 which preserves "Pyron..o." and fr. 3, col. ii 3–4 which preserves "..ronidou." The initial pi is unmistakable: see Carey 2004.126.

93   Chantraine 1974.959.

94   Pyrrh[oni]des is a suggested reading for *Agora* XXI D 37 (the broken ostrakon has "Pyrrh" on one side and "des" on the other and one has to assume that they form different parts of the same name). Pyrrhonidas is said by the Suda to be an alternative name, along with Enkomios, for the father of the dramatic poet Pratinas: but Enkomios is clearly fictional and Pyrrhonidas may be as well.

95   Many who make the claim unwittingly refer to a false reading from an inscription in South Italy. The supposed Pyronides from Licata (Dearden 1988.36; cf. Hoffmann 2002.175; Piqueux 2006.3) is a free invention by Kaibel in *IG* XIV 256, 45 based

on Dorville's reading of PYRRONM, which Feyel (1935.384), the next person to study the actual stone, corrected to PYRROMM, cf. Dubois 1989.185; Manganaro 1990.405–7.

96   Gould and Lewis in Pickard-Cambridge 1968.219; Storey 2003.169–70; Revermann 2006.318; Telò 2007.28–36.

97   The importance of the gutti was urged by Csapo 1994 and Pöhlmann 1998 in their reviews of Taplin's Comic Angels and pressed by Green 1994, and more forcefully by Csapo 2001, Preisser 2000.100, and Revermann 2006.

98   Apulian relief guttus, c.330 BC, Naples MN Santangelo 368. The two other examples are: Tampa Museum, Zewadski collection; Private Collection, Westfalia, Germany. See Csapo 1994.

99   Ar. Ach. 439 with scholia. See further Csapo 1986.382 n. 6.

100   Small (2003.67, following LIMC Telephus 83) identifies the object as a wineskin, a claim that no professional iconographer could endorse, and elsewhere pretends to know that though "the object held by the figure kneeling on the altar is difficult to make out, it is definitely not a 'charcoal-basket'" (2003.195).

101   Attic black-figure stand, Acheloos Ptr., Toledo 1958.69; Para 169, Add 101.

102   Sparkes 1975.134, fig. 17d.

103   The best candidate is perhaps that discussed by Green 2003. But nothing prevents the sigma, theta, epison from being an abbreviation not for "Sthenelos" but something like "Syrakosion therapon."

104   Sicilian calyx krater, c.330, attributed to the Gibil Gabib Group, probably the Capodarso Painter, Syracuse 66557; LCS Suppl. 3.275/46f; RVSIS fig. 428, pl. 236; P&P 90–2, no. 22.

105   Sicilian calyx krater, Adrastos Group, c.340 BC, Lipari 10647; P&P 257–8, no. 103. This vasepainting should perhaps be regarded as a third tragic vase with a realistic stage.

106   Green 1999 and Taplin 2007.40–1.

107   Csapo 1993a.

108   Csapo 1993a.

109   Sicilian calyx krater, Capodarso Painter, c.300 BC, Caltanisetta 1301bis, MTS SV2, P&P 261–2, no. 105.

110   The fragment of a fourth candidate listed in P&P (no. 106, a fragment of a Sicilian red-figured krater, Lentini-Manfria Group, 330 BC, Contessa Entellina Excavations E856) is shown by Green 2007 to belong to a comedy. Taplin tells me he is now certain that his interpretation of it as a tragic scene is an error.

111   Taplin 1997.88–90.

112   Förtsch 1997.

113   Maffre 2000.286.

114   Taplin 1993, 1997, P&P.

115   Taplin 1993.7, raised to two "showing beyond any reasonable doubt, a scene of tragedy in performance," after the publication of the publication of the Kiev fragment (P&P 29) but oddly changing from the hydria found in Corinth (T 1144) to the Basel krater (BS 415) mentioned above, pages 6 and 6–8.

116   See above, pp. 6–9 and 67–70.

117   Attic discussed above, pp. 12–23; West Greek discussed above, pp. 42–4.

118   Carpenter 2005; Brommer 1959; Brommer 1978–9; Brommer 1983.

119   Apulian red-figured bell krater, Tarporley Painter, *c*.400 BC, Sydney, Nicholson 47.05, *MTS* TV 18.

120   Above, pp. 23–31, 45–66, esp. 52–3.

121   Principal discussion in Green 1991.

122   Choregos vase: Apulian bell krater, 400–380 BC, Choregos Ptr., once Getty 96.AE.29: Taplin 1993.55–63, fig. 9.1; Taplin 2007.28, fig. 7; Csapo 2001.33–5, fig. 18.

123   Green, however, would disagree, see on the komos vases above, Chapter 1, n. 30.

124   A relief from Nemea, Athens, NM 1492, recently revived by Vierneisel and Scholl 2002, fig. 22, and said to be of Pentelic marble, of the fourth century BC and related to comedy, would be unique as a sculpture apparently focussed on actors. If it is comic at all, however, it must be related to Hellenistic New Comedy.

125   Benaki 30895. Another probable exception is the very late Attic bell krater, Ferrara T1612, a type of genre-scene fantasy related to those of the Pronomos Painter and his close associates, but where a figure more like an actor than a choreut keeps company with Dionysus.

126   Taplin 1993 urges a choral interpretation for the "Choregos vase" and the "Bari Pipers." On the first of these the case rests purely on the strength of the inscription "Choregos" over the heads of two men, differently costumed, and not dancing, so the case is not strong. The case for the Bari Pipers is stronger, but the similarity of costume and the music are more easily explained as a form of *agon* (choreuts sing, they do not play instruments). The objection that the action is on stage seems an insurmountable obstacle to both choral interpretations (choruses are confined to the *orchestra*). Taplin 1993.75–8 names a further four possibilities, but himself voices the weaknesses of each case.

127   See Kerkhof 2001.151–5.

128   For this and other evidence: Jordan 2007; Wilson 2007c.

129   *P&P* 39, 64, 67. 82, 85, 103, 126, 131, 148, 152, 158, 178, 192, 242, 245; Taplin 2007.

3

The Spread of Theater
and the Rise of the Actor

We do not often think of ancient theater as a business, let alone consider the many unique features it had as a business in its day.[1] From the time, at least, of the democratic reorganization, *c.*508 BC, the Athenian Dionysia differed from other musical festivals in frequency, in scale, and in the variety of economic interests directly involved in its operations.[2] We know of no other annual musical festival before the Dionysia. Its venue, the Theater of Dionysus, was also larger than any other, holding in the fifth century even on more restrictive current estimates, probably close to 7,000 spectators in the seating area (*theatron*) and possibly many more on the hillside above it.[3] Financing the festival combined money from the state, from donors, from private investors, and, for the very first time in the history of Greek religious festivals, there were admission charges.[4] By the late fifth century BC, the Athenian Dionysia caused some thirty talants to change hands, most of it during the five days of the festival itself.[5] This goes well beyond the means of the traditional aristocratic or sanctuary patronage that sponsored earlier athletic and musical festivals. It amounts to more money than five times the annual income of Hipponikos, the richest man in fifth-century Greece.[6] As Bremer noted, the complexity of this kind of funding made drama less "sponsor-directed" and more "audience-oriented" than the cultural products patronized by aristocrats and tyrants.[7] At the same time, the complexity and scale of the investment introduced monetary interests with a direct financial stake in maximizing public participation in the festival. This was, most conspicuously, the chief interest of the *theatronai* or *theatropolai,* entrepreneurs who paid the city for a franchise to build and manage the theater and to profit from the collection of admission fees.[8] Maximizing attendance was thus also in the interest of the city that sold the franchise (for as much as an estimated two talants). From the beginning theater had at least an impulse to expand into the mass-entertainment industry we know it to have been by the end of the Classical period. But just how early did that expansion begin?

Oddly, the expansion and diffusion of the theater has only recently become an object of serious interest. Most scholars take it as axiomatic that fifth-century drama was produced only once, at Athens, for a single audience. Webster gave this view its most authoritative expression. He even inferred from the extreme brevity of ancient drama's performance-life that playwrights really wrote with a reading public in mind: "The Greek dramatist could only be certain of a single presentation of his tragedy on the stage."[9] The single-performance theory has become a bland dogma and if the claim ever receives qualification by scholars troubled by ample evidence to the contrary, it is normally in the form of exceptions that prove the rule: Pickard-Cambridge notably excepts reperformances of "unsuccessful plays in revised form," while Starr would except only "more successful works."[10] By the late 1980s scholarship had built, on the foundation of this putative fact, a vision of drama (now no longer "Greek" but "Athenian") as a form of internal propaganda created uniquely by Athenians uniquely for Athenians (most monumentally in Winkler and Zeitlin's *Nothing to Do with Dionysos?* where we are urged to "remind ourselves that fifth-century plays were written for single performances").[11] Even Calder, when arguing against Webster's essentially "literary" conception of drama, felt obliged to concede that "the single performance was a necessity forced upon the ancient dramatist by the social and economic conditions of his time."[12]

What Calder, nonetheless, calls the "single-performance fallacy" is of a piece with a systematic effort to deny or downplay the economic dimension of theater. The academic élite of the great age that saw the initial collection of data about material aspects of the theater was often profoundly out of tune with the growing "economization" of their contemporary cultural life. Mark Golden has produced an illuminating study to show how the crucial late nineteenth- and early-twentieth century collections of the realia of ancient athletics were marked by a profound disdain for the growing professionalization of sports in their own era and that this disdain led them to insist, nostalgically and quite incorrectly, that athletes at the ancient games struggled only for glory and a crown of leaves.[13] Doubtless for similar reasons, the gentleman-scholar Pickard-Cambridge was reluctant to pursue evidence of the availability of more substantial material rewards in the theater. In this case a desire to keep this utopic image of ancient Greece alive and untainted from any implicit comparison with the big-money economy that was taking over theater and cinema in his own day probably accounts for Pickard-Cambridge's reluctance to commit himself to the notion that ancient poets earned money (a fact which he further misrepresented with the term "honorarium"), and yet the pay received by poets at the Athenian Dionysia was substantial, calculated at at least a talant by Bremer and at a little under a talant by Wilson.[14] Multiple productions too go very much against the grain of the romantic notion, still dear to classical scholarship, that all the expense and labor that went into the production of an ancient drama was sacrifice designed for a single immolation – a potlatch for the god Dionysus and the glory of Athens.

In the past fifteen years, however, there have been many effective challenges to the Athenocentric view of Classical drama. This came partly as a reaction against the vision generally promoted by the volume *Nothing to Do with Dionysos?*, published in 1989 (at the end of the Cold War), in which some of the essays seemed to urge a Nürnberg-Rally-like image of Classical drama by reducing its social function to official state propaganda geared to the creation of good Athenian soldiers and citizens. Much scholarship since then has been dedicated to correcting this view and pointing out that not all the passages in tragedy seem designed to promote xenophobic nationalism and that much in fact seems to presuppose an audience not only sympathetic to more panhellenic ideals but familiar with other states – indeed some passages in drama, even some whole dramas, seem designed with a non-Athenian audience in mind.[15] Others have salvaged some of the biographical and anecdotal information about poets and actors traveling passed on by ancient sources from the deep skepticism left in the wake of Mary Lefkowitz's *Lives of the Greek Poets*.[16] Still others have vindicated the relevance of undoubtedly historical testimony to Sicilian and Megarian comedy, which past generations have tended to disparage as belonging to a "primitive type of buffoonery" with no influence on true drama.[17] But the main impetus for re-examining the question of the Athenian monopoly on drama comes from the material record. The number of early theaters being found outside of Athens has steadily increased over the years. So have the number of artifacts depicting the performance of Aeschylean and Euripidean drama in the Greek West. Oddly, however, it was the Würzburg Telephus (FIGURE 2.3) and the reassessment of the "phlyax" genre that it entailed (see Chapter 2) that proved the catalyst for the first studies of the spread of Greek theater. The studies by Green, Taplin, Dearden, Allan, and Scodel, all appeared in the years immediately spanning the advent of the new millennium.[18] None of these scholars is very precise about the timing of the spread; they are especially non-committal about when it begins. Taplin, Dearden, and Allan do not see much expansion of theater outside Athens before the end of the fifth century and Scodel extends this to "the last decades."[19] This chapter aims at a clearer map of the process of the spread of drama from Athens and at an appraisal of the implications of this spread for the reperformance of drama and the rise of the acting profession.

Theater and Actors from about 370–300 BC

Let us begin with an overview of a period where the fact of the expansion of theater is not controversial.[20] From about 370 BC we have plentiful evidence for the internationalization of drama. The names of many non-Athenians appear in the records of performance at Athens. Among poets, Antiphanes, probably the most prolific comic poet of all time, is said to have been of foreign origin (Kios, Rhodes, Smyrna, or Larissa). He performed his first play about 385 BC, won eight victories at the Athenian Lenaea and a further five at the Dionysia.[21] Theodectas (better known by his atticized name, Theodectes) was a prolific tragedian who came from of Phaselis (in Lycia) and won seven times at the Athenian Dionysia, the first time soon after 372 BC, but he is also known to have put on tragedies in Caria in 353 BC.[22] Dionysius, tyrant of Syracuse, reportedly after many attempts at Athenian festivals, won with his last tragedy at the Lenaea in 367 BC.[23] Alexis of Thurii won his first Athenian victory at the Lenaea some time in the 350s and at the Dionysia in 347 BC.[24] Amphis the comic poet may be the subject of an honorary decree of 332/1 BC; if so it shows him to have been of non-Athenian origin (from Andros).[25] Philemon of Syracuse (or Soli in Cilicia) won the competition at the Athenian Dionysia in 327 BC and Apollodorus of Gela wrote comedies in the late fourth century.[26] Many of the most celebrated actors of the fourth century are also originally non-Athenians. The comic actor Satyros, a native of Olynthus, won at the Lenaea about 375 BC and was well known by 348 BC when he is mentioned as a participant in Philip's games celebrating the capture of Olynthus.[27] Judging from their placement on the Lenaean Victors' List, the tragic actors Aristodemos of Metapontum and Neoptolemos of Skyros were victorious in Athens about 370 BC and 350 BC respectively.[28] The comic actor Lykon, who came from Scarphe in Locris, won twice at the Athenian Lenaea, c.350.[29] The tragic actors Archias of Thurii and Polos of Aegina performed in Athens and elsewhere in the last quarter of the fourth century BC.[30] Many fourth-century theatrical performers who are assumed to be Athenian probably are not, and many who are reported to be Athenian will have been awarded citizenship late in life as it was a conscious policy, at least from the time of Lycurgus, to award citizenship to talented theatricians in an effort to promote the Athenian industry.[31]

Athens needed to actively promote its theater by the second half of the fourth century because of competition from Greek cities that were acquiring theaters at an ever accelerated rate. We have architectural, epigraphic, or literary evidence of over ninety-five permanent theaters built by the end of the fourth century.[32] Moreover, permanent theaters or regular festivals were not the only venues for dramatic performance. Philip, Alexander, and the wife of Mausolus especially made good use of occasional festivals and sometimes temporary theaters to celebrate royal weddings, military victories, or funerals.[33] As a result, the demand for good actors grew with such rapidity that it clearly outstripped the supply. Even the Athenian Dionysia found it necessary to secure actors by paying appearance fees, tendering large advances and imposing fines for non-appearance. We have no actual sums, but Plutarch's sources found them impressive enough to think it worth recording that Alexander paid off a fine for Athenodorus when he failed to honor an engagement at the Athenian Dionysia but showed up at one of Alexander's impulse-festivals instead – the anecdote is told in order to illustrate Alexander's liberality to actors and is juxtaposed to another anecdote about a spontaneous gift of ten talants to the comic actor Lykon.[34] On another occasion, when Athens wished to make Aristodemos part of an embassy to Philip, Demosthenes proposed "that ambassadors be chosen to send to the cities in which Aristodemos was to compete in order to request that he be exempted from his fines."[35] One would like to know how many made up the plural "cities," but even if it was only two, it is a fitting testimony to how busy a star actor might be in 346 BC, since the embassy probably only lasted at most three weeks between late February and mid March.[36] The Scholiast to Aeschines tells us that the fine imposed on Aristodemos was twice the advance he had received for his appearance: in Hellenistic times the fines for breaking a theatrical engagement ranged from 200 to 1,000 drachmas.[37]

By the end of the fourth century we see the impact this expansion of the theater industry had upon actors' incomes. An anecdote, traceable to Critolaus in the early second century BC, tells us that Polos (or Aristodemos) could gain a talant "for two days' competition."[38] This is a very large sum. Supposing that at this period 2 drachmas is an average daily wage, a talant (= 6,000 drachmas) is ten years' wages. It is therefore generally and reasonably assumed that the anecdotes exaggerate. However, a much more secure index of the actor's bargaining power comes from a Samian inscription of 306 BC in which Samos heaps fulsome honors upon Polos for agreeing to take lower than usual fees and defer payment in exchange for all of the box-office proceeds.[39] But Polos was a superstar and one wonders how less illustrious actors fared. Some idea comes from the Euboean decree of about 290 BC. Here prospective actors are awarded 1,600 drachmas for a five-day appearance, not including expenses and prize-money. Each takes over 100 drachmas per performance.[40]

Clearly the fourth century provided the necessary conditions for the development of a star-system of Hollywood proportions. But just when acting became so lucrative is a much more difficult question. We have only indirect anecdotal evidence for the personal wealth of star actors in the earlier fourth century. Already in 352 BC Theodoros was able to make a contribution to the rebuilding of the Temple of Apollo at Delphi almost five times larger than that of any other private individual and larger than that of many states.[41] Neoptolemos could afford repeated gifts of money for public works to the city of Athens, beginning some time before 348 BC.[42] These are the earliest indications of the wealth that might be acquired by actors. To trace the economic factor most responsible for this wealth, namely, the expansion of the theater industry, we need to go a good deal farther back in time.

The Earliest Actors in the Fifth Century BC (down to about 430 BC)

The Great Dionysia alone, and even together with the Lenaea (after *c*.440 BC), could presumably not by itself sustain a class of specialized laborers, namely actors, who (unlike, for example, pipers) could not market their skills in any other forum. Acting seems, in fact, originally to have been an activity dominated by Athenians of independent or semi-independent means. Sutton shows that early actors and poets came from the same family groups, indeed the early theater was dominated by theatrical clans who were in many cases demonstrably families of wealth and position.[43] But though known Athenian actors, poets and also chorus trainers (*chorodidaskaloi*) generally came from a restricted number of family groups, these groups were strictly divided on generic lines. Family groups can be shown to include poets, actors and chorus trainers of tragedy or comedy, but not practitioners of both genres. Sutton thinks this is the result of home schooling, and this is surely right, but not, I think, the whole explanation. Ancient sources tell us that the principal actors were initially the poets themselves. They presumably directly engaged their second and third actors. Later, we are told, poets stopped acting but were responsible for hiring the actors. The sources (which are mostly late) look as if they are forcing a variable practice into evolutionary stages in order to conform with the dictates of Aristotelian evolutionary cultural history. The evidence for actual practice in the early fifth century suggests that the poets were responsible for hiring the actors, sometimes choosing to take on roles themselves (note that the word *tragoidos* is the standard Greek word for "tragic poet," "tragic actor," or "tragic choreut," and *komoidos* is the standard word for "comic poet," "comic actor," and "comic choreut" – in origin, perhaps, the difference was neither important nor always obvious).[44] In normal practice, this frequently meant hiring one's own sons and nephews, or the sons and nephews of other poets. Our evidence shows theatrical families strictly divided between tragedy and comedy, because poets were strictly divided between tragedy and comedy and the generations were linked by the kind of family collaboration and networking with colleagues that one might expect to find in all skilled occupations at this date. For example, no less than eleven known tragic poets and tragic actors are direct offspring of Aeschylus' father, Euphorion; no less than four tragic poets and actors are known offspring of Sophocles' father, Sophilos; no less than nine tragic poets and actors are known offspring of Carcinus' father, Xenotimos; Euripides had at least one son who was a tragic actor; Aristophanes probably had six offspring who were comic poets or actors.[45] All these poets belonged to well-to-do families and it follows, therefore, that this was the norm for early actors as well.[46]

The archon at some point took over the responsibility for selecting and paying the actors. This, at least is implied by the practice of assigning actors to poets by lottery (i.e. they chose lots for first choice from the archon's list). The state of Athens is unlikely to have intervened in this way if it was not also bearing the financial responsibility. We have no proof that this change is in place, however, until 341 BC.[47] The same state intervention appears in the distribution of pipers by 350 BC, at latest.[48] In the case of both actors and pipers, it seems likely that the state intervened in order to ensure that the best performers competed at the Dionysia. This assumes competition for performers at other venues and it is my contention here that such conditions certainly existed in the fifth century BC.[49] Indeed, employment opportunities in a number sufficient to allow an actor the power of refusal seem to me to be the necessary condition for the development of an actor's profession in our modern sense of the term, by which I mean an employment from which a person can receive a livelihood without any other means of support. Plenty of employment opportunities are, of course, required before the next stage of professional development is possible, namely the development of a star system which might give some actors status and salaries far above the norm.

The Expansion of Theater in Attica

The earliest evidence for the spread of Athenian drama comes from the immediate periphery of Athens: we find it in inscriptions, theater architecture, and snippets of information culled from Greek prose authors. The earliest evidence is theater architecture. The remains of the theaters at Ikarion and Thoricus may be as early as the late sixth or early fifth century and as old as the Theater of Dionysus in Athens.[50] From the late fifth century there is evidence for a theater at Peiraeus (literary sources show it existed by 411 BC), a theater at Trachones (Euonymon), and probably from the late fifth or early fourth are a rectilinear theatron at Oropus.[51] Possibly early are remnants of the theater at Acharnae.[52]

Theater buildings by themselves, unfortunately, do not prove the existence of theater in the abstract sense. The desire to produce drama is a strong motive for building a theater, but theaters were employed for many other purposes in antiquity. Many served as venues for meetings of the local legislative assemblies. They also served as viewing areas for non-dramatic musical performances. Herodotus, for example, attests the existence of a theater in Sparta as early as 491–480 BC, but he names it as the venue for the choral dances of the *gymnopaidia,* and the little we know of Spartan culture in this period would not encourage us to think that anything like Athenian drama was produced there until very much later.[53] Even in Attica it is conceivable, especially at this early date, that the principal motive for building a theater was to put on "men's choruses" and "boys' choruses" (the official name for what we call dithyramb), or even more purely ritualistic performances: phallic processions, or competitions in drunken processions (*komoi*) such as those attested for the demes Acharnae and Xypete as late as 330/29 BC.[54] For certain or probable evidence of the performance of drama in rural Attica we require epigraphic or literary testimony.

Three of the most important inscriptions to our question are generally ignored, or avoided, because they fly in the face of a long-standing prejudice about the city's virtual monopoly on high-quality dramatic performance.[55] All three of these inscriptions were found in the Attic countryside and all three appear on marble bases or columns that supported statues. Both of these details would normally be taken as evidence that the inscriptions refer to the Rural Dionysia. Marble statues were the most common form of choregic dedication commemorating dramatic victories at the Rural Dionysia. For victories at the City festivals, by contrast, dramatic choregoi normally dedicated reliefs or paintings in or near the sanctuary of Dionysus in Athens.[56] We in fact know quite a lot about dramatic performances in the demes, precisely because of the more elaborate stone monuments: they lasted longer than paintings and, because they were further from the center of population, they were less likely to be destroyed in later years. From the city we have the remains of only one statue base (in this case holding herms) commemorating a victory in drama; however, this is no choregic monument at all, but a dedication by the Archon Basileus who presided over the Lenaean contests.[57] Nonetheless, these three choregic statue bases have generally been referred to the City festivals. The main reason for this is the fact that they list famous poets as the directors (*didaskaloi*, more literally "chorus trainers"). It is almost universally assumed that if drama was produced in the demes, it was by second-rate performers. This assumption is both groundless and disprovable.

Of the three inscriptions mentioned above as subject to prejudicial miscategorization, *IG* I[3] 970 is a choregic dedication by two *synchoregoi* (= "joint-choregoi"), found in Eleusis, and dated by Lewis between 425 and 406 BC (evidently dated to the careers of Aristophanes and Sophocles), fifty years before any other evidence for drama at Eleusis.[58] Aristophanes was director of the victorious comedy and Sophocles directed the victorious tragedy:

> [G]nathis, son of Timok[ed]o[s A]naxandrides, son of Tima[g]oros
> while serving as choregoi won in the comedy competition
> Aristophanes was d[i]rector.
> Another victory in the tragic competition
> Sophocles was director.

The verb used here for "was director," ἐδίδασκεν, in inscriptions specifically refers to the "director of the chorus," and never simply means "was poet." The stone therefore indicates the physical participation of Aristophanes and Sophocles in the production here commemorated.

Assuming that the Dionysia of Eleusis was an unworthy venue for such luminaries, scholarly opinion until 1943 inclined toward supposing that the inscription commemorated a victory at the City Dionysia on a monument set up in the local deme theater of Eleusis. The critical evidence against this view came in the publication of a fragment of the *Fasti* which enabled Capps to show that the entire inscription allowed only room enough to report a single *synchoregia* at the City Dionysia.[59] That *synchoregia* was in 405 BC on the testimony of Aristotle.[60] We cannot, however, ascribe both victories on this stone to the Dionysia of 405 BC: Sophocles the Elder died sometime after midsummer 406 BC; his grandson Sophocles the Younger is certainly also to be excluded – he is not known to have been active until 401 BC, when he produced his grandfather's *Oedipus at Colonus*, and otherwise not until 396 BC when we are told "he began to produce tragedies."[61] The Lenaea should also be excluded. We know of no *synchoregia* there and the scholiast's evidence shows that he also knew of none. But *synchoregoi* are as common as single choregoi at the Rural Dionysia. A majority of experts now concedes that *IG* I³ 970 probably refers to the Dionysia at Eleusis.[62] On the available evidence, this is the only reasonable conclusion.

IG I³ 969, an inscription dated by Lewis to c.440–431 BC, was found at Anagyrous, antedating by a century other evidence for drama in this deme:[63]

Sokrates made the dedication.	
Euripides was director.	
Tragedians	Amphidemos
Python	Euthydikos
Echekles	Lysias
Menalkes	Son
Philokrates	Kritodemos
Echyllos	Charias
Meletos	Phaidon
Emporion	*vacat*

We find the names of the choregos, the director Euripides, and a list of fourteen *tragoidoi*. The latter term can only be read here as "tragic chorusmen."[64] Since all the chorusmembers are named without patronymic and demotic, we must assume that they are all demesmen of Anagyrous.[65] In fact we know of a Sokrates of Anagyrous from this period, and evidently of choregic class, since he served as a general in the Samian War, and later as a candidate for ostracism.[66] The inference that the choreuts also all come from Anagyrous is partly confirmed by a fourth-century inscription in which a Son is identified as a member of that deme (the name "Son" is extremely rare).[67] I find it very unlikely that all the choreuts for tragedy at the City Dionysia would be selected from Anagyrous, but this, of course, was mandatory for the deme's Rural Dionysia.

An inscription (*IG* II² 3091), found near Halai Aixonides, lists four dramatic victories:[68]

> E[.... serving as choregos won in co]medy
> Ecphantides was director of *The Attempts.*
> Thrasyboulos serving as choregos won in comedy
> Cratinus was the director of *The Cowherds.*
> Thrasyboulos serving as choregos won in tragedy.
> Timotheus was director of *Alcmeon, (A)lphesibo[ia.]*
> Epichares serving as choregos won with traged[y]
> Sophocles was director of *The Telepheia.*

These victories must begin about the middle of the fifth century, though they may run as late as its final decade, judging from the appearance and close juxta-position of Ecphantides, Cratinus, Timotheus, and Sophocles. The presence of famous poets is the main argument for referring these victories to a festival in the city.[69] Wilson suggests that even the Timotheus named here as director may be the famous Timotheus, namely the lyric poet.[70] Luppe notes that the trage-dian Achaeus is known to have written an *Alcmeon* and an *Alphesiboia.*[71] This makes it still more likely that the Timotheos in question is a professional direc-tor and not the poet who also acts in the capacity of director (as in the case of the other three directors mentioned in this inscription). We have no evidence of the number of tragedies normally produced by each group of contestants at the Rural Dionysia, so it is a matter of indifference that this inscription names two and possibly three tragedies per set (*Telepheia* should refer to a group of plays about the mythic hero Telephus).[72] The two tragedies directed by Timotheus, however, do definitely exclude the City Dionysia where a set of four plays (four tragedies or three tragedies and a satyrplay) was an invariable norm until prob-ably sometime around the middle of the fourth century BC. The evident fifth-century date of the victories is also no obstacle,[73] since we have other evidence of very active festivals in Ikarion and Thoricus, quite apart from the Eleusinian and Anagyrasian inscriptions discussed above.[74]

All the internal and contextual evidence indicates that these stones refer to the Rural Dionysia. Taking them to refer to the City Dionysia or the Lenaea involves some insuperable problems. As the monuments make no explicit refer-ence to either of these city festivals, we would have to suppose that any demes-man reading the stone would immediately conclude, like modern scholars, from the presence of "big-name" directors that the victory was in the city and not in the township. But what right have we to suppose that élite theatricians would not perform at the Rural Dionysia? Ghiron-Bistagne, who concedes that the Eleusinian inscription, *IG* I³ 970, must refer to the Rural Dionysia, nonetheless argues that Sophocles and Aristophanes are named as *didaskaloi* on this inscription only in their capacity as poets and not as the actual directors of the deme performance. Why? She can only state *a priori* that "if we consider the organization of the Rural Dionysia, it would seem completely outlandish to suppose that the poet was the real director."[75] It is true that the only non-epigraphic evidence for top poets directing at the Rural Dionysia is Aelian's anecdote about Euripides directing at Peiraeus (the historicity of which we may well doubt).[76] But the Nikostratos listed as *didaskalos* on an inscription (*IG* II² 3094) relating to the Rural Dionysia at Ikarion from the beginning of the fourth century is probably the one whose plays survive in some forty fragments from twenty-one plays and who is said to be a son of Aristophanes.[77] Of particular interest in this regard is a choregic inscription for the Dionysia at Acharnae from the same period or a little later:[78]

Mnesistratos, son of Misgon,	Mnesimachos, son of Mnesistratos,
Diopeithes, son of Diodoros, were choregoi.	Theotimos, son of Diotimos, were choregoi.
[Di]caeogenes was director.	Ariphron was director.
	Polychares, son of Komo[n], was [di]rector.

On the right hand side of the monument.

> Theoti[mos, son of Diotimos]
> Mnesi[machos, son of Mnesistratos, were choregoi.]
> Thersa[ndros was director].

The inscription names Dicaeogenes, a writer of both tragedies and dithyrambs, whom Aristotle praises for his recognitions and whom the same Aristotle or one of Aristotle's students praised for writing songs second to none.[79] (This inscription may be for dithyramb: only dithyramb and comedy are independently attested at Acharnae's Dionysia.)[80] Moreover, Ariphron is also known for lyric composition, a particularly famous paean to Health.[81]

Poets often enlisted the help of other professionals to undertake the directing. This is well known from the scholarly production notes (*hypotheses*) that have come down with the plays of Aristophanes: these all refer to the City Dionysia or the Lenaea, but we can see that other theater people frequently step into the role of chorus trainer even at the Rural Dionysia, as in the case of Timotheus directing plays of Achaeus at Halia Aixonides (mentioned above).

Thersandros on the Acharnian inscription may be the man identified by Polyaenus and Xenophon as an aulete.[82] Sannion, who specialized as a chorus-trainer, is said by Demosthenes to have been so sought after (sometime around the 370s BC) that ambitious tragic choregoi in the city hired him to train their choruses, even at the risk of violating the law against employing disenfranchised citizens; and yet we know that Sannion directed tragic choruses at the Rural Dionysia in Kollytos.[83] Even pipers might assume the task. The famous piper Telephanes directed Demosthenes' dithyrambic chorus in 348 BC, but we find the same Telephanes named as the piper for boys' dithyramb on a choregic dedication in Salamis at the beginning of the fourth century (the Dionysia of Salamis, though Salamis is not technically a deme, is placed on much the same footing as the Rural Dionysia).[84] The fact that Telephanes is the very first piper ever to be named on a choregic inscription is a secure index of his fame, which is otherwise well attested: one ancient author compares Telephanes' virtuosity to that of Orpheus, Nestor, and Homer in their respective specializations.[85]

Famous actors are also known to have performed at the Rural Dionysia. A mid-fourth century choregic dedication from Thoricus, the only choregic monument to list actors, names "[..]odoros" as the actor for tragedy.[86] This is almost certainly the great Theodoros, most famous tragedian of the fourth century.[87] From literary sources we can add Parmenon, one of the most celebrated comic actors of the fourth century, whom Aeschines names as a performer at the Rural Dionysia of Kollytos.[88] Because of a lot of bad press from Demosthenes, Aeschines is generally supposed to have been one of the third-rate actors who typically performed the rural circuit, and Demosthenes leaves us with some memorable sketches of bad acting in rural contexts. But even this most unobjective of witnesses Demosthenes lets slip that Aeschines was good enough to perform with the greatest talents of his day, Theodoros (whom we already suspected, above, to have performed in Thoricus) and Aristodemos.[89]

Although most of this evidence belongs to the fourth century, this is precisely the time when we might have expected the theater industry to be large enough to support the kind of inferior artist we are supposed to imagine haunted the deme theaters. The fact that so many familiar and famous names appear on deme inscriptions, or are connected to the Rural Dionysia by the orators, should show, rather, that the same performers who worked the city festivals also worked the deme festivals. *IG* I³ 970, *IG* I³ 969, and *IG* II² 3091 show that they did so from as early as the mid fifth century.

These inscriptions attest the performance of drama at the demesites of Halai Aixonides from about 450 BC, at Anagyrous from about 440–431 BC, and at Eleusis by 425–406 BC. Other inscriptions fill out this picture of a fairly rapid spread of drama from about 440 BC throughout Attica. The earliest inscription attesting drama at Ikarion is dated 440–415 BC.[90] At Thoricus, despite the early date of its theater, the first evidence of choregic activity is a monument, dated to 435–410 BC.[91] This could refer to dithyramb rather than drama, but fourth-century inscriptions (from as early as 375 BC) attest tragic and comic, but not dithyrambic performances, and to that extent drama is most likely.[92] Inscriptions show the full program of Dionysian performances at the deme theater of Acharnae from about 400 BC.[93] Literary sources add drama at Peiraeus in the late fifth century and at Kollytos by *c.*370 B.C.[94]

A relief from Brauron gives strong iconographic evidence for comedy at its rural festival around the mid-fourth century BC (it shows the precinct of Dionysus and Artemis hung with choregic dedications of comic masks).[95] We cannot be sure of drama at Paiania and Rhamnous until *c.*350 BC.[96] Choregiai of unspecified genre (hence conceivably dithyramb rather than drama) are attested at Aigilia and Myrrhinous sometime before the middle of the fourth century BC and at Halai Araphenides just a little after.[97] Inscriptions attesting comedy at Aixone may belong to the Dionysia of 340 BC.[98] A choregic relief from Sphettos celebrating a victory in tragedy has been dated to the late fourth century, but we do have a mid-century decree awarding front-row seats (*prohedria*) in the theater, thus making it probable that Sphettos also had drama by about 350–330 BC.[99] Unfortunately the evidence from Athmonon is only vaguely dated to the fourth century BC, and the inscription names only a piper and director.[100]

While evaluating this evidence we should keep in mind the fact that few deme sites have been properly excavated and that most theater inscriptions are chance finds: we would know nothing of drama at Thoricus, for example, if it were not for the Belgian and Greek excavations. How many more of Attica's 139 deme sites had regular dramatic competitions is anyone's guess. The fact that Plato can speak, in what is obviously meant to be hyperbole, of theater lovers "running around to all of the Dionysia and omitting none, whether in the cities or in the villages" shows that by *c.*370 BC, the likely date of Plato's dialogue, there were many Dionysia that offered drama.[101] The passage also suggests that the festivals were co-ordinated to allow the same audiences, and doubtless the same performers, to appear.

The Expansion of Theater Beyond Attica

Unfortunately in the Classical period few cities shared Athens' "epigraphic habit." Inscriptions are little help in tracing the early expansion of drama outside Attica. Here we rely almost exclusively on the architectural remains of theaters, theatrical artifacts, and literary attestations. All of these sources are far more problematic than the inscriptions that offered us a relatively solid foundation for mapping drama's spread through Attica. The presence of a theater building is no proof of drama, for reasons explained above: theaters have many uses. But it must be said that the absence of a theater at any given date is also proof of nothing, since most early theaters were of wood and vanished without a trace, especially those that were later dug out to be rebuilt in stone. Theatrical artifacts need to be examined for their specific contexts and contents. Drama-related vases, as we have seen, can be appreciated for their mythical content, and are highly variable in the degree of theatrical acculturation they presuppose. Yet, as we saw in Chapter 2, the requisite theatrical acculturation even for the appreciation of tragedy-related vases can be very high, but it is consistently so for comedy-related vases, and seems indispensable for theatrical genre scenes. In the same way the potential utility of literary attestations of drama are highly variable. Reasonable caution requires one to be suspicious of anecdotes by late authors even when the theatrical information content seems credible enough. Such for example is the story in the *Life of Sophocles,* based on the testimony of the third-century BC biographers Istros and Neanthes, that Sophocles died choking on a grape-pip when the actor Kallippides, returning from an engagement in Opous, brought him a gift of fresh grapes.[102] Final acts and words are too important to be trusted: and one must be especially cautious about the symbolic significance of an anecdote that insists that Kallippides killed Sophocles.[103] Biographical information, even by late sources, can, however, be both plausible and consistent with other information. Fourteen different sources tell us of Aeschylus' relocation to Sicily. Though these texts are often mixed with silly anecdotes (e.g. voluntary exile because his Furies in *Eumenides* were so frightening that they caused women to abort, or because the seats collapsed, or because he was jealous of Sophocles or Simonides), his move to Sicily is a given in every case and the silliness extends only to the explanation for his relocation. They include some of our most trusted authorities: men like Eratosthenes and Plutarch. To reject such information offhand because of methodical or generic doubt is unreasonable.

Each of the three sources of evidence attests an early expansion of theater into Sicily and South Italy. Most unhelpful are the archaeological remains of theaters. Most stone theaters in Sicily, outside Syracuse, were not built until after the middle of the fourth century, so that early wooden theaters are impossible to trace through the archaeological record.[104] The dates of the earliest architectural remains are hotly disputed. Dates assigned to the theater at Syracuse range from the early fifth century to the mid third BC.[105] Some also ascribe traces of a fifth-century-BC theater to Catana (the location of Hieron's Aetna and a likely location for the performance of Aeschylus' *Aetnean Women*, performed, the *Life of Aeschylus* informs us, to celebrate the city's inauguration).[106] The theaters at Morgantina and Iaitas are more securely dated to the mid to late fourth century; the theaters of Herakleia Minoa, Heloros, Lato, Solous, Tyndaris, and, according to recent reports, Hippana are possibly fourth century, but, if so, probably later than the period of greatest interest to this investigation; the theater at Iaitas can be dated stratigraphically to the end of the fourth century.[107] Plutarch sets a speech by Dion in the theater of Leontini in 355 BC; Diodorus' attestation that in 339/8 BC Timoleon made the theater at Agryrion "the most beautiful in Sicily after Syracuse" is more reliably set in the context of a massive urban renewal program (though the language does not exclude the rebuilding of an earlier construction).[108]

The earliest specific historical reference to the theater at Syracuse is not till 406 BC, when Diodorus informs us that the Syracusans were gathered in the theater to watch a "spectacle."[109] There can, however, be no doubt that drama was performed in Sicily from the earliest fifth century. We have many fragments of Sicilian comic poetry, some of it certainly of the early fifth century, handed down under the name of Epicharmus; we also know of two other comic playwrights, Phormis and Deinolochus. From a fragment of Epicharmus ("the decision rests on the knees of five judges") we know that drama was performed in regular festival competitions from the beginning and used, it seems, a similar system of reaching a decision to that practiced at Athenian festivals: as Hesychius says "Five judges: this many judged the comic choruses not only in Athens, but in Sicily."[110] An early fifth-century curse tablet from Gela confirms the existence of competitive choral performances in that city and also suggests close analogies to the Athenian system of finance and regulation.[111] We also have reliable evidence for early performances by Athenian playwrights in Sicily. Aeschylus, and possibly Phrynichus were not the only Athenian dramatists to spend time in Sicily.[112] The anonymous *Life of Aeschylus* tells us that Aeschylus' grave was turned into a hero shrine and "all those who gained their livelihood from tragedy used to visit the monument, both to make offerings to his spirit and to perform his dramas." Unfortunately there is no indication of how early this kind of pilgrimage took place. The survival of so many of Aeschylus' plays and fragments must be due to a strong reperformance tradition: we have no other significant remnants of drama from the first half of the fifth century. But we know that a reperformance tradition for Aeschylus' plays existed at Athens, and even at the City Dionysia apparently by a special concession.[113] A strong performance tradition at Gela would explain the huge popularity in Sicily of vasepaintings showing myths invented and/or popularized by Aeschylus' plays. Todisco, for example, enumerates 401 vases of West Greek manufacture that show subjects related to tragedy: of these 96 or 24 percent are of Aeschylean plays.[114]

The popularity of Aeschylus in the Greek West is surpassed only by the popularity of Euripides who accounts for 34 percent of tragedy-related vasepainting in the region, on Todisco's reckoning. This fits in well with the anecdotal evidence for Euripides' popularity in Sicily in the last two decades of the fifth century.[115]

Some confirmation of Euripides' popularity at this time comes from the fact (attested by the excellent authority of Aristotle) that Euripides was sent as an ambassador to Syracuse to beg their friendship, an early use of the common practice of using celebrities particularly in sensitive diplomatic missions.[116] Euripides' popularity, attested by all these sources, is certain evidence for the continued contact with "Athenian" tragedy throughout the fifth century BC.

The vasepainting evidence is much stronger and earlier for Tarentum and Metapontum (of Todisco's list of tragedy-related vases, only 20 are Sicilian, but 243 are "Apulian," probably all produced in Tarentum, and 56 "Lucanian," meaning probably Metapontum and Thurii) and begins as early as the 420s BC.[117] As we saw in Chapter 2, the Apulian and Lucanian vasepainters are, from c.400 BC at latest, thoroughly conversant with the details of mask, costume and stage, and are not likely to have come by this knowledge through any means other than frequent contact with living theater (though theater scenes also die out very early here as well). Underneath the late fourth century BC theater at Metapontum are the remains of a building with the unusual shape of two concentric theatra meeting a square orchestra between them.[118] It is usually referred to as an *ekklesiasterion* (legislative assembly building), but it is clear that it could function as a theater. It dates back to about 550 BC. Euripides' *Captive Melanippe* deals with a South Italian version of the myth and ends with a prognostication of the founding of Herakleia (Policoro) in the Italian instep by Metapontum: it is a reasonable speculation that the play was written with production in Herakleia or Metapontum in mind.[119] The play *Thurio-Persians* by the comic poet Metagenes (active in the last decade of the fifth century BC) apparently had a chorus of Persified citizens of Thurii and contained lavish praise of Thurii as a land of abundance: a strong case has been made for its production in Thurii.[120] Other theater remains in Apulia and Lucania are disappointing: there are no remains of a theater dating any earlier than the mid or late fourth century BC (Locri, Rhegion, Castiglione di Paludi).[121] The possible exception is Elea where, beneath the Hellenistic theater, traces of an earlier theater dating to the first half of the fourth century have been found.[122] Iamblichus' attestation of a fifth-century theater in Croton is not reliable.[123] The literary testimony is helpful only to the extent that it makes it clear that Tarentum had a theater by about 320 BC.[124] It should be noted that theater culture was sufficiently entrenched that Lucania was able to produce some of the most famous poets and actors of the fourth-century theater, including the tragic actor Aristodemos of Metapontum, who won at the Athenian Lenaea about 370 BC, the comic poet Alexis, who won the Lenaea by the 350s, and the tragic actor Archias of Thurii, whose Lenaean victory was about 330 BC. This at least reinforces the very strong iconographic evidence showing that theater was widespread in the region by c.400 at the latest.[125] Plato, who knew Sicily and South Italy well, having spent much time in Syracuse

and Tarentum between 380 and 360 BC, was able to speak of "the modern custom in Sicily and Italy that permits the majority in the theater audience to des-
ignate the winner by a show of hands."[126] The general extension of the practice
to the entire region is not likely to have been due to careless expression.[127]

Both mainland Megara and its Sicilian colony of the same name laid claim, in
antiquity, to the invention of comedy.[128] The early history of Megarian comedy
is much distorted by the schematizations and free inventions of later literary
history. It is clear, however, that the Megarian comic tradition in mainland
Megara was probably well established by the middle of the fifth century when it
is mentioned by the Attic Old Comic poet Ecphantides, and certainly by the last
quarter of the fifth century when it is ridiculed for its lack of sophistication by
Aristophanes and Eupolis.[129] On the strength of this testimony, Megarian comedy is frequently dismissed as "primitive" comedy or "farce" and therefore left
off the literary (and dramatic) map. Anyone who trusts the characterizations of
Megara's rival comedians must contend with the evidence that not only are
many of the jokes in Old Comedy of Megarian origin but so are two of the
masks known from New Comedy.[130] Aristotle's evidence suggests the existence
of a choregic system in Megara, and certainly indicates the use of a chorus and
some similarity in structure to Attic comedy; indeed, his testimony suggests that
Megarian comedy's most serious deficiency was underfunding.[131] Discounting
the bias of our sources, it is likely that Megarian, like Sicilian and indeed Attic
drama, whatever its original epichoric flavor, was at least by the end of the fifth
century less easily distinguishable from the mainstream than the Attic carica-
tures encourage us to believe.

In mainland Greece we have the archaeological remains of theaters at Argos,
dating to the mid-fifth century BC, at Dion, dating to the late fifth, and possibly
also of fifth-century date at Charoneia.[132] Macedonian interest in drama is confirmed by the remains of theaters at Aegae (Vergina) which Drougou has dated
to the early years of the fourth century BC and Philippi as early as the mid fourth
century BC.[133] Arrian places Archelaus' theatrical festival dedicated to Zeus and
the Muses in the theater of Aegae, although Bosworth takes this to be an error
for "Dion."[134] Both are certainly possible, but Aegae is the most probable location of the first production of Euripides' *Archelaos* as the play contains an aetiol-
ogy for the foundation of that city.

Despite the methodical skepticism some scholars reserve for all ancient biographical information about poets, the sojourn of Euripides and Agathon at the
court of Archelaus is based on testimony as reliable as any we have from antiquity.[135] Euripides' presence at Archelaus' court is attested, among many other
sources, by Aristotle, who was at the Macedonian court as a boy (where his
father was a physician to King Amyntas) and who was hardly likely to have
depended on lurid tales invented by armchair scholars for his knowledge.[136]

Plato in the prologue to the *Symposium* writes "Don't you know that Agathon hasn't lived in Athens for several years now?" and in the *Republic* denounces Euripides and other tragic poets for being in the pay of tyrants: both comments are scarcely intelligible unless Euripides and Agathon spent time in Macedon (these dialogues are set in the last decade of the fifth century).[137]

In the Peloponnese, the remains of the theater at Isthmia can be dated *c.*400 BC.[138] Many would date the theater at Corinth also to the fifth century, but in any case the testimony of Xenophon ensures its existence before 392 BC.[139] The theaters of Megalopolis, Mantinea, Tegea, Epidauros, Aipion, Elis, Arcadian Orchomenos, Leontion, Phleious, and Sicyon are probably fourth- or early third-century constructions, but none of them datable to any earlier than about 330 BC.[140] Literary testimony adds a theater and a Dionysia in Phigalea (Arcadia) in 375/4 BC.[141]

Thebes had an independent tradition of what might be best called ritual comedy performed at the Cabeirion. The existence of a form of "ritual drama" is amply attested by Boeotian black-figured pottery from about 425 BC, though there are no traces of a theatral area that can be dated even tentatively before the fourth century. A theater is attested before 362 BC, but we have no evidence of mainstream drama being produced in Thebes (despite the fact that a disproportionate number of theatrical pipers for drama and dithyramb were native to the city).[142] The theater at Cheironeia has been dated as early as the fifth century BC.[143] A coin deposit appears now to permit a mid-fourth-century date for the theater of Thebae in Phthiotis.[144] Pausanias reports a theater at Skotoussa (Thessaly) by 369–358 BC, though in his report it functioned as an Assembly.[145] Not datable until the last quarter of fourth (at the earliest) are Orchomenos, Ambracia, Delphi, Kassope, Makyneia, Stratos, and Neandria.[146] Byzantium certainly had tragedy by 306 BC.[147]

When Athens planted colonies and clerouchies it normally also transplanted its religion and festivals.[148] We would therefore expect Athenian colonies to be among the earliest to build theaters and hold dramatic performances. This is certainly true at Thurii and Salamis, mentioned earlier. Though most clerouchies probably had a Dionysia with some form of drama by the end of the fifth century, proof of dramatic performance is only found in the fourth century BC or in some cases the third. Samos first received Athenian cleruchs in 440 BC, but neither the Dionysia nor tragedy are epigraphically attested until about 350 BC.[149] Similarly, in the case of Lemnos, home to an Athenian clerouchy from at least the 450s BC, we cannot be sure of a Dionysia with a tragic competition until 348 BC.[150] Andros had an Athenian clerouchy from 450 BC, but offers no sure evidence of tragic competitions until well into the third century BC.[151] Eretria received Athenian cleruchs in 446 BC but the remains of its theater date no earlier than 330 BC and the epigraphic attestation of choral performances for Dionysus, among them boys' dithyramb, comes still later in the fourth century.[152]

It is not, however, until about 290 BC that we have firm evidence for tragedy and comedy at Eretria, Chalkis and two other locations on the island of Euboea – and yet Euboea was the home of some of the earliest non-Athenian dramatists, the actor Mynniskos of Chalkis, and the poet Achaeus of Eretria, the former active from the time of Aeschylus and the latter from about 445 BC.[153] A choregic system is in place in Mytilene even before the Athenian clerouchy was established in 427 BC, and we have information of a Dionysia in the fifth or fourth century at Antissa, also on Lesbos, but as yet no firm evidence for drama.[154] No date has been established for the inscriptions attesting a theater and a Dionysia at Naxos, which had a clerouchy from about 450 BC.[155]

Evidence for theater in the Classical period on the other islands and in Asia Minor comes from a variety of sources.[156] The first book of the Hippocratic *Epidemics*, of fifth-century composition, mentions a theater in Thasos, although no firm epigraphic and architectural evidence exists before c.300 BC.[157] We have epigraphic evidence for a tragic competition in Rhodes between the tragic actors Kleandros and Aristomedes that cannot be any later than the first quarter of the fourth century BC.[158] A theater appears to be attested for Cos by Eudoxus of Cnidus who died c.340 BC.[159] Keos' theater is not very reliably attested for the early fifth century, but one of its cities, Karthaia, had a choregic system (for dithyramb) possibly as early as the fourth.[160] Otherwise, there are several fourth-century theaters that can only be securely dated to the last decades of the century (if not later): Priene, Tenos, Delos, Erythrai, Ephesus, Ialysos, Kastabos, and Paphos.

Theater was to some extent known even in the farthest corners of the Greek world in this period. Stucchi thinks the foundations of a wooden *skene* building in Cyrene go back to the late sixth century and Chamoux finds archaeological evidence of dramatic performance there by the late fifth century in the form of a funerary sculpture inspired, he thinks, by Euripides' *Alcestis*: secure evidence of performances of tragedy does not come until about 335 BC where it is mentioned in official accounts inscribed on stone.[161] A theater at Herakleia on the Black Sea is unfortunately attested for the fourth century only by an absurd anecdote preserved by Diogenes Laertius that we should probably disregard, but the Black Sea area is surprisingly well represented, statistically, as a findspot for artifacts relating to tragedy and comedy from the fifth century and the first quarter of the fourth BC.[162]

The importation of vases painted with scenes related to tragedy or comedy is not perhaps the strongest index of interest in or knowledge of drama, since the vessels have a use-value and an aesthetic appeal that goes well beyond the dramatic decoration, but the importation of comic figurines could have little point except as a symbol of comedy. Comic figurines were exported throughout the Greek Mediterranean in the first half of the fourth century BC. The twenty-six

Table 3.1   Attested Venues for Drama from *c*.440 to *c*.340 BC (excluding performance venues at one-off festivals)[163]

By	Certain	+Probable	+Very Possible
c.440	Syracuse	Gela	Thoricus
	Athenian Dionysia	Megara (Sicilian)	Catana
	Athenian Lenaea		Metapontum
	Halai Aixonides		Anagyrous
	Megara (Mainland)		Ikarion
			Sparta
			Argos
c.420	Anagyrous	Ikarion	Eleusis
		Thoricus	Thebes
c.400	Ikarion	Peiraeus	Elea
	Thoricus	Thurii	Euonymon
	Acharnae	Tarentum	Oropus
	Eleusis	Metapontum	Cheironeia
	Dion (or Aegae)		Isthmia
			Thasos
			Cyrene
c.370	Euonymon	Rhodes	Corinth
	Kollytos		Phigalia
			Salamis
			Aegae
c.340	Peiraeus	Cyrene	Locri
	Brauron		Aixone
	Paiania		Sphettos
	Rhamnous		Morgantina
	Aigilia		Iaitas
	Myrrhinous		Leontini
	Halai Araphenides		Thebae Phthiotides
	Lemnos		Philippi
	Rhodes		Cos
	Samos		

different figurine types known from the first quarter of the fourth century are all originally Athenian, most apparently produced by a single Athenian coroplast. They were not only imported but came to be imitated by local manufacturers in such diverse locations as Corinth, Olynthus, Akanthos, Thasos, Asia Minor, Cyprus, Cyrene, Egypt, Naples, Paestum, Lokroi, Tarentum, Herakleia (Policoro), Lipari, Sicily (especially Syracuse), and even Emporion (Ampurias) in Spain by the middle of the fourth century BC.[164]

Putting all this evidence together, we have by *c*.440 BC certain evidence for five regular festivals where dramatic performances took place, and certain to possible evidence for fourteen. By 400 BC we have eleven festivals certainly offering theater, seventeen certain to probable, and twenty-eight that are either certain or, on the evidence, likely to have included drama. By 370 BC there are thirteen festivals certainly offering drama and thirty-five for which there is certain to plausible evidence. By 340 BC our meager remains guarantee twenty-three festivals offering dramatic performances in the Greek world and as many as fifty-five for which the evidence survives to show a strong likelihood of drama. The volume of evidence does not, of course, suffice to generate reliable statistics, but on present evidence we can say that the number of employment opportunities available to actors of the third generation (assuming a beginning of "tragedy as we know it" sometime around 500 BC in Athens and "comedy as we know it" about the same time in Syracuse) doubled during their lifetime and then doubled again in the fifth and sixth generation of actors. Although this expansion was small compared to that which appeared immediately in the wake of Alexander's conquest, it is enough to give a fairly convincing context for the rapid growth of the acting profession from about 430 BC. There is every reason to believe that these numbers represent only the view of the "tip of the iceberg" permitted by the random and fortuitous survival of the evidence.

Some More Direct Evidence for the Emergence of an Actors' Profession

I have tried to show that there were enough opportunities to act that one could make a living as a professional actor in the later fifth century and perhaps even make a living without wandering very far. Nonetheless, a willingness to travel, and even to cross the Adriatic, certainly helped. It is about this time that we begin to have reliable evidence of actors (as opposed to poets) traveling. In Demosthenes' speech *Against Euboulides*, delivered around 345 BC, a speaker, Euxitheos, whose Athenian citizenship was impugned because his father had foreign mannerisms, reports that "They have denounced my father as displaying foreign ways, but they omitted to say that he had been caught by the enemy during the Decelean War (413 BC) and sold off to be a slave in Leucas, where, after many a year, he chanced to meet the actor Kleandros and was brought home safe to his relatives."[165] Euxitheos may, of course, be lying about his father. If he is not lying, the encounter with Kleandros is most likely to have happened in the late fifth or very early fourth century BC. But if Euxitheos and his witnesses *are* lying, then it is noteworthy that the scripted rescue of Euxitheos' father is given added plausibility by casting a traveling actor as the Athenian who discovered him (the island of Leucas is a natural stop for an actor traveling from the mainland to South Italy). This is almost certainly the same Kleandros whom we find competing in Rhodes in the same period or perhaps a little later and who won the Athenian Dionysia in 387 BC.[166] Aelian, much less reliably, also reports actors traveling across the Peloponnese to Cythera in 407 BC, probably en route overseas.[167] We also have stories of the tragic actor Kallippides performing in various locations, from Sparta in the time of Agesilaus, to Opous (in Locris) in 405 BC, to Aeolis in Asia Minor in 399 BC.[168] The sudden efflorescence of foreign-born actors and poets from the 370s BC indicates that festivals outside Athens even in the late fifth century probably ran at least partly on local talent.[169]

Ironically, the surest evidence for the professionalization of actors is probably the record of scorn that Athenian (and Greek) élites began to direct toward them from the 420s onwards. Elites resented the new professional classes who had risen from humble origins and began to acquire wealth and glory in a realm that had once been dominated by respectable (i.e. élite) Athenian families.[170] The situation precisely parallels the élite resentment of the "New Music," an invasion of a once élite cultural preserve, by professionalized theater musicians that began only one or two decades earlier.[171] By the 420s we get our first anecdotes about actors. For earlier tragic actors we have little more than names and occasionally dates. But for the great tragic actors of 425–390 BC, Kallippides and Nikostratos, we have as much information as for any of the great stars of the fourth century.[172]

For Kallippides, at least, these anecdotes are mostly hostile. They make no attempt to deny his celebrity. The point is rather to show just how little actors merited the success that the gullible theater audiences lavished upon them. The sources for Kallippides speak of his "name and fame" (ὄνομα καὶ δόξα) even if the scene is set in Sparta:

> Kallippides the tragic actor, whose name and fame was known among all Greeks and who was the object of universal enthusiasm, at first encountered and greeted Agesilaus. Then, pompously thrusting himself forward among Agesilaus' entourage, he began to show off, thinking this would elicit some sign of courteous recognition. Finally, he said: "Your majesty, don't you know who I am?" Agesilaus, glancing up at him said "aren't you Kallippides the buffoon?" This is what Spartans call imitators.[173]

The anecdote, certainly too good to be true, features the blunt and deeply conservative Spartan king Agesilaus, a man famously out of touch with the popular enthusiasms of his day, from a city famously indifferent to the winds of cultural change, taking the stuffing out of the acting profession's first superstar and knocking him down to size.[174] Other anecdotes emphasize Kallippides' pomposity, his incompetence, and his vulgarity.[175] Though many of the stories are only preserved by later antiquity, the trend for mocking Kallippides as a gross and pompous upstart is certainly contemporary with the actor: his vulgarity is ridiculed already by Aristophanes; Strattis devoted an entire comedy to him; and Xenophon makes his boasting the subject of a joke.[176] This wealth of anecdotes confirms what we learned from studying Athenian iconography in Chapter 1, namely, that from the 420s onwards actors had suddenly, and for the first time ever, captured the popular imagination. The nature of the anecdotes, however, also shows that the brilliance of their success had also upset the theatrical establishment. Actors soon acquired a stigma as wage-earners (by contrast with the citizen choregoi, choreuts and poets, who came to be represented as volunteers and amateurs competing for honour, not material rewards, though they did get these in abundance).[177]

It is difficult to determine when actors acquired the poor reputation that stuck to them for the rest of antiquity. The problem is that the official language and records of drama always appear to have ignored the actor. In official terminology, the chorus generally stood for the entire performance. Tragedy, comedy and satyrplay are simply the *tragoidoi*, *komoidoi*, and *satyroi*, meaning, as the last instance shows, "the choruses of the tragedians/comedians/satyrs." Even the poet is known only in his relation to the chorus as its "teacher" and he is said to "apply for a chorus." The archon is said to "grant a chorus." At the beginning of the performances the herald invited the poet to "bring on the chorus." At the end the festival judges "judged the choruses" (their oath apparently enjoined them to give the prize "to the one who sang well"). By contrast, the actor is merely the one who "responds," *hypokrinetai*, presumably to the chorus.

It was the chorusmen, along with the choregoi, who represented the Athenian people in the theater. By law chorusmen were citizens, at least for the Dionysia, or citizens and metics for the Lenaea (and perhaps Rural Dionysia). The nationality of actors, by contrast, was a matter of indifference.

Official records were also slow to notice the actors. Victorious poets, choregoi and choruses were recorded for fifty years before anyone thought, it seems, to record the name of an actor. It is true that the institution of the actors' contests, about 449 and 432 BC at the Dionysia and Lenaea, gives actors official recognition, but it it did so in such a way as to give an official stamp to the great divide that isolated the actor from the chorus, poet and choregos, for the actors' contest is entirely separate from the contest for the productions.

Private monuments dismiss actors altogether.[178] Choregic inscriptions regularly credit poets and identify choruses by tribe, if not the choreuts by name. They even, by the fourth century, list pipers. But among the many score of Athenian choregic dedications that survive, only one ever names an actor

(Theodoros at Thoricus).[179] Artifacts are no less dismissive. As we saw in Chapter 1, Athenian painted pottery and reliefs with theatrical subjects, when they show performance, almost always depict the chorus, and when they show performers before or after a performance, also almost always depict the chorus. One of the few exceptions, the Pronomos vase (FIGURE 1.9), most eloquently proves the rule. It presents the cast of Demetrios' satyrplay. The choreuts are shown, mostly with their masks off to reveal their real faces and names, the choregos is shown with his real face and name, even the chorodidaskalos, even the piper is shown with his real face and name, but not the actors. Beside the image of the actors is listed nothing more than the name of the characters they play, and not only that, but their faces are those of the masks that they carry in their hands. The image of one actor who played a female role is not even graced with his own gender.[180]

One gets the strong impression that actors were barely noticed until long after the dramatic festivals' official language and customs of recognition had been set. When actors do get noticed by the late fifth and in the fourth centuries BC, it is too often for the wrong reasons. If our fifth-century writers are largely indifferent to actors, our fourth-century writers are for the most part openly hostile and the most conspicuous focal point of their hostility is the issue of money. This was the most popular subject of anecdotes about fourth-century actors, as we saw above. Actors, like musicians, came to symbolize the invasion of cultural pursuits, the traditional preserve of the leisure classes, by money.

It is against this background that one must weight the significance of an event recorded by the Athenian inscription known as the *Fasti*. By the early fourth century actors had sufficient consciousness of their common identity and their power that they were able to organize and co-operate in pursuit of common interests. In 386 BC tragedians were well enough organized as a profession to produce and donate an "old tragedy" to the festival program (to be produced preliminary to the festival competition):

ἐπὶ Θεοδότου
παλαιὸν δρᾶμα πρῶτο[ν]
παραδίδαξαν οἱ τραγ[ῳδοί]

"In the archonship of Theodotus the tragedians [as a group] first produced alongside the competition an old play."[181]

This event marks a watershed in the relations between actors and other actors, between actors and poets, and between actors and their public. It is the first time we see actors assuming a corporate identity, acting in concert (so to speak) and organizing the entirety of a production, thus asserting their independence of sponsors, poets and state bureaucracy. But most important of all, it is the first time that actors collectively rise above the conditions of their money economy to participate in the élite gift economy that official representations relating to the theater had reserved for the "voluntary" contributions of citizen choregoi, choreuts, and poets. With this "gift" to the Athenian people, actors collectively made a gesture of largesse that inaugurated a habit of euergetism, for which we have many examples from the days of the Hellenistic actors' unions.[182] It is a powerfully assertive public relations exercise on the part of a group whose status official and élite Athens had come to regard with a certain ambivalence.[183]

Notes

1   This chapter expands upon sections of Csapo 2004b. I revisit the material with the kind permission of the editors, C. Hugoniot, F. Hurlet, and S. Milanezi, and of the Presses Universitaires François-Rabelais of the University of Tours. Le Guen, forthcoming, is the first volume entirely dedicated to matters of finance for theater and games in antiquity.

2   The clearest impression of the Dionysia's scale and complexity is offered by Wilson 2008.

3   For the rationale behind the estimate see Csapo 2007, esp. 97. For the hillside: Roselli 2007.113–16 and Roselli forthcoming.

4   Wilson 2008.92.

5   Wilson 2008.

6   Davies 1971.260.

7   Bremer 1991.59.

8   Csapo 2007; Wilson 2008.91–6.

9   Webster 1956.xi–xii.

10 Pickard-Cambridge 1968.99; Starr 1991.320. Cf. e.g. N. W. Slater 2002.54, Garland 2004.3.

11 Winkler and Zeitlin 1989.394 (N. W. Slater).

12 Calder 2006.3.

13 Golden 2009.105–39; cf. Golden 1998.141–75. For the monetary value of prizes for athletes at the Panathenaea, see Shear 2001.388–98, Shear 2003b, Wilson 2008, n. 95.

14 Pickard-Cambridge 1968.90; Bremer 1991.56; Wilson 2008.105.

15 Esp. Hall 1989; Easterling 1994; Taplin 1999; Allan 2001; Scodel 2001; Zacharia 2003; Taplin 2006; Hall 2007.

16 N. G. Wilson 1999; Revermann 1999–2000; Wilson 2007c; Kowalzig 2008; Duncan forthcoming.

17 Pickard-Cambridge 1927.273 (quotation). The study by Kerkhof 2001 is somewhat more positive; Bosher 2006.67–80 argues that the conditions of production in Syracuse were not only similar to Athens but in many cases developed earlier.

18 Green 1994.49–88, Taplin 1999, Dearden 1999, Allan 2001, Scodel 2001.

19 Taplin 1999.37 seems to put the spread to the rural Dionysia much earlier, but is firm only on "the time of Herodotus;" Scodel 2001.218.
20 Taplin 1999 is the fullest general treatment to date.
21 Anon. *de com.* 45 p. 10 Koster; Suda s.v. *Antiphanes; IG* II² 2325, l. 146.
22 1 *TrGF* 72 T1–10.
23 Diod. 16.73.5; Ephippus *PCG* F 16; Tzet. *Chil.* 5.178, etc.
24 Arnott 1996.3–18.
25 *IG* II2 347; Lambert 2008, no. 2.
26 Suda s.v. *Philemon;* Strabo 14.671; Marm. Par. *FGrH* 239 B 7; on Apollodorus, see Capps 1900.45–50.
27 *IG* II² 2325, l. 190; Pickard-Cambridge 1968.114; Stephanis 1988.392–3 no. 2235.
28 *IG* II² 2325, ll. 259, 266; Stephanis 1988.76–7 no. 332, 321–2 no. 1797.
29 *IG* II² 2325, l. 195; Stephanis 1988.286–7 no.1567.
30 Stephanis 1988.95–6 no. 439, 382–4 no. 2187.
31 This was probably the case with the poets Antiphanes, Amphis, Philemon, Apollodoros of Carystos, and the actors Neoptolemos and Aristodemos. See Wilson and Csapo 2009.64–5.
32 See Frederiksen 2002 to which further additions can be made.
33 See Chapter 6, n. 29.
34 Plut. *Alex.* 29.
35 Aesch. 2.19.
36 See Rhodes 2006.310.
37 Schol. Aesch. 2.19; *IG* IX 9, 207 (= Le Guen 2001a, 1, TE1) ll. 42–3; *IG* IX 1, 694, l. 113; *IG* IV 1, 99–100; *IK* 28.1, 152 (= Le Guen 2001a, 1, TE 53); Le Guen 2001a, 1, 54; Lightfoot 2002, 14–5. Cf. Pollux 4.88.
38 [Plut.] *Ten Orators* 848b; Gellius 11.9, cf. 11.10.6. Cf. Dion Chys. *Or.* 66.11, which inflates the cost of an appearance of "a Polos" to five talants.
39 *SEG* 1.362.
40 *IG* XII 9, 207 (= Le Guen 2001a, 1, TE 1) l. 22, with Le Guen 2001a.2.71–4.
41 *FD* III 5.3.67, *SIG* 239 B.
42 Demosthenes 18.114, cf. 5.8, with Wilson and Csapo 2009.64–5. Neoptolemos later dedicated gold-plated cups worth the notice of Polemon's guidebook to the Athenian Acropolis (Athen. 472c).
43 Sutton 1987.9–26.
44 For poet-actors after the 440s BC, see Wilson 2008.106, n. 98.
45 Sutton 1987.12–19.
46 Aeschylus: *Vita Aesch.* 1; *IG* II² 3029 (the Pythodoros son of Melanthius, choregos for dithyramb at the City Dionysia in the early fourth century is very probably the grandnephew of Aeschylus); for the élite context of the *kalos*-inscriptions naming Euaion, son of Aeschylus, see Shapiro 1987. Sophocles: *Vita Soph.* 1–11. Carcinus: Davies 1971.283–5, no. 8254; Olson 2000.66–7. Euripides: Roselli 2005.8–9; Aristophanes' social status is more elusive: see Welsh 1983; Lind 1985; Olson 1998.xxi.
47 *IG* II² 2320. Cf. Hesych., Suda and Photius, *Lex.* s.v. *nemesis hypokriton.*

48 [Plut.] *De Mus.* 1141d; Ath. 617b–c; Wilson 2000.69, 336–7 nn. 85–6; Wilson 2008.108.

49 Cf. Wilson 2008.106. Despite frequent claims to the contrary, the existence of an actor's prize, first attested for the Dionysia about 449 BC, may have contributed to, but does not in itself imply, the economic independence of the actor, nor the independence of his art, nor the high social staus that could be achieved by a professional man.

50 Ikarion: Goette 1995a.10; Moretti 2000.278–9. Thoricus: Hackens 1967.75–96, esp. 95; Goette 1995a.12–13.

51 Peiraeus: Goette 1995a.18; Travlos 1988.342; Thuc. 8.93.1; Lys. 13.32; Xen. *Hist.* 2.4.32. Trachones: Pöhlmann 1995b.139; Lohmann 1998.196; Tzachou-Alexandri 1999.421. Oropus: Goette 1995b; Tzachou-Alexandri 1999.421.

52 Acharnae excavations are reported in *AR* 53 (2007) 8 on the basis of newspaper reports from February and March of 2007: "Finds (sherds) and architecture indicate a date of construction certainly by the mid fourth century BC, and possibly as early as 450 BC." But no basis for dating was known to the excavator when I spoke to her in May of 2007. The remains from Rhamnous date to the third or second century BC, though inscriptions show it is older (Moretti 1991.16). The remains of a possibly early theater were also found at Halimous in Attica. Associated pottery suggest that the theater served the Thesmophorion as a venue for cultic performances from the seventh century BC before it began to serve as a regular theater by some as yet indeterminable time in the fourth (there are fragments of what appears to be the base of a choregic monument): see Kaza-Papageorgiou 1993.70.

53 Hdt. 6.67.3.

54 Semos *FGrH* 396 F 24; *IG* II² 3103, 3104.

55 The authority of Pickard-Cambridge (1968.47–50, 54–6, 87, 361) and Ghiron-Bistagne (1976.92–3, 119–21) looms large in general discussions of the diffusion of drama. Following this tradition, Dearden (1999.223) and Scodel (2001.222) only mention Eleusis (the first of the three we will examine); Taplin (1999.37) briefly draws upon all three of these inscriptions in his discussion, but draws no inferences about the identity and the quality of performers outside of Athens.

56 See Wilson 2000.30–1, 236–62; Csapo forthcoming A; Goette 2007.

57 *SEG* 32.239; Wilson 2000.30–1, fig. 1. Another possible candidate is also very exceptional in that the possible reference to a victory at the Dionysia appears on a monument built to commemorate a victory in *pyrrhikhe* at the Panathenaea: Athens, NM 3854 (*SEG* 23.103); Wilson 1997; Wilson 2000.236–7; Kaltsas 2002.127, no. 242; Shear 2003a.174.

58 *IG* II² 1186 (mid fourth century BC, attesting dithyramb and tragedy); *IG* II² 3100 (mid fourth century BC, attesting comedy); *IG* II² 3107 (fourth century BC, unspecified choregia). Cf. *IG* II² 1194 + 1274. Note also the fourth-century relief of a choregic type: Eleusis no. 30; Dentzer 1982, R 236 fig. 489; *MTS*² 113, AS 29; Csapo forthcoming A.

59 Capps 1943.5–8.

60   Schol. Arist. *Frogs* (= Aristotle fr. 630 Rose): "he appears to imply that the poets were already being poorly served by the choregoi. In the archonship of Callias, at any rate, Aristotle says that it was decreed that the office of the choregia for the tragedy and comedy of the Dionysia would be assigned to pairs of choregoi, so that there was perhaps some retrenchment too in the case of the Lenaean contest." Quite apart from the epigraphic evidence, it is easy to infer from the scholiast's words that the Dionysia never saw more than one year of *synchoregiai*. Apart from the "fact" he has gleaned from Aristotle, he makes no attempt to disguise his statements as anything but pure speculation. He was indeed looking for evidence for *synchoregiai*, but could find no firm evidence of it outside of the archonship of Callias. His words "poets were already being poorly served by the choregoi" show that he is working within the confines of the standard Hellenistic theory that the abolition of the choregia brough on "Middle Comedy" (cf. Csapo 2000). Afterward he goes on to claim that Cinesias abolished the choregia once and for all and his "proof" is the fact that Strattis called Cinesias a "chorus-killer." The point of the epithet is, however, purely musical. The interpretation is a fine example of the manner in which ancient scholarship arbitrarily manufactured the grand scheme of literary and dramatic history (normally employing the organic model of the birth, maturation, decline and death of genres) and then set about finding the evidence to prove it. In Hellenistic times the *Frogs* was the last "Old Comedy" regularly read in schools, and so a likely place to look for evidence of the genre's impending doom.

61   *Marm. Par. FGrH* 239.64; 1 *TrGF* p. 51, DID D2. Pickard-Cambridge (1968.48) says that, if the inscription from Eleusis refers to an Athenian festival, the plays would almost certainly have been *Frogs* and *Oedipus at Colonus*. But there is no reason to doubt the didascalic notice that *Frogs* was produced in 405 at the Lenaea by Philonides. It would be better, if one is determined to fit it into a City festival, to suppose that the stone refers to the reperformance of *Frogs*, probably in 404 (see Dover 1993.74–5). The problem with Sophocles remains, however.

62   Pickard-Cambridge 1968.47–8; Ghiron-Bistagne 1976.92–3; Whitehead 1986.217; Makres 1994.350–1; Wilson 2000.375, n. 164.

63   *IG* II² 1210, *IG* II² 3101.

64   I do not believe, with Gould and Lewis in their addendum to Pickard-Cambridge 1968.261, that fourteen choreuts might suggest rural economy vis-à-vis the usual number, fifteen, for the City festivals. I think the correct interpretation is given by Wilson 2000.353 n. 90: "In a number of sources, the number of tragic *khoreutai* is actually given as *fourteen*: the *koryphaios* is almost certainly excluded: Souda s.v. 'Sophokles;' Pollux, IV.109; Scholia to Ar. *Knights* 589." In the present case, Wilson thinks it most likely that fourteen are listed because the choregos, Sokrates, served as the chorus-leader (*koryphaios*, 2000.133). I would urge Wilson's other hypothesis (2000.133), that the *koryphaios* was frequently, perhaps regularly, a paid operative (sometimes functioning also as chorus trainer, *chorodidaskalos)*, not a volunteer, and so not always conceptually part of the chorus, and in any case not among those whose services need to be thanked by public recognition (as opposed to cash). Some evidence in favor of the view that the leader of the chorus might be paid

labor is provided by the case of Sannion mentioned by Demosthenes (*Meid.* 58–61). Sannion functioned as a chorus trainer, but is also clearly envisioned as performing in the theater with the chorus (despite being disenfranchised); cf. Csapo and Slater 1995.352–3. Demochares, *FGrH* 74 F 6a also suggests that Sannion was performing in the orchestra, since he was in a position to help Aeschines to his feet when the latter slipped during a performance.

65 Makres 1994.355–7. Cf. Wilson 2000.132–3, although Wilson thinks it refers to the City Dionysia despite the probability that all choreuts come from the same deme as the choregos.

66 Thompson 1950.337; Androtion *FGrH* 324 F 38. If the late-fifth-century date assigned by Mitsos (1965.164) and Matthaiou (1990–91.181 n. 3) is retained, then the Sokrates is likely to be another Sokrates of Anagyrous, the presumed grandson of the general, who was a councilor in the first half of the fourth century (see *IG* II² 1697, l. 16).

67 See Matthaiou 1990–91.181.

68 Earlier literature assigns it to the deme Aixone. See the discussions of Wilson 2000.248; Makres 1994.359–61; Luppe 1969. Eliot 1962.35–46 identified the deme as Halai Aixonides. The only other possible evidence for drama (or dithyramb) at Halai Aixonides is the undated fragment *SEG* 38.263 (cf. Wilson 2000.367 n.14).

69 Wilson 2000.248: "although the force of this argument has rightly come to be seen as overrated."

70 Wilson 2000.375 n. 164 (cf. Pickard-Cambridge 1968.55). This is an attractive suggestion, though Timotheos is a fairly common name in Attica (J. Traill kindly informs me of some two dozen from this period).

71 Luppe 1969.141.

72 *Pace* Makres 1994.361: "Whereas one would think that, at the rural contests, tragic poets would more likely have presented single plays." Wilson 2000.248 rightly notes that "there is no good reason to deny [multiple dramas presented by the tragedians] to the Rural Dionysia."

73 Wilson 2000.248.

74 On Icaria and Thoricus, see further below. Perhaps the strongest argument for these victories referring to the city are those by Luppe 1968.148 (cf. Luppe 1973) who urges that the selection of these particular victories makes little sense in a commemoration of deme victories in the deme where there were any number of victories to choose from, and more sense if these four represented the sum total of city victories by choregoi from Halai Aixonides. It is true that we do not know what motivated this unusual monument, but Luppe's explanation seems to me to explain *obscurum per obscurius*. We cannot, to take an obvious counter-scenario, exclude the possibility that the two or three choregoi here listed all belong to the same family. Most editors and commentators print the conjecture "Epichares" in the first line (as in line 7) leaving only two choregoi, or alternating generations of a family.

75 Ghiron-Bistagne 1976.133.

76 Aelian *VH* 2.13.41–5.

77 Nicostratus *PCG* 7 T-13, F 1–40.
78 *IG* II² 3092 + *SEG* 45.250. See Makres 1994.371–3; Wilson 2000.306–7.
79 Dicaeogenes 1 *TrGF* 52 T 1–3.
80 *IG* II² 3106; Summa 2004.
81 Ariphron 1 *TrGF* 53; *PMG* 813.
82 Polyaen. 6.10; Xen. *H.* 4.8.18–19; Stephanis 1988.217–18, no. 1193.
83 Demosth. *Meid.* 58–61. Compare Demochares ap. *Life of Aeschines* 7 (*FGrH* 75 F 6a) and Demosth. *Cor.* 180, 242.
84 Demosth. *Meid.* 17; *IG* II² 3093; Arist. *AthPol* 54.8.
85 Nicarchus, *AP* 7.159. For Telephanes, see Stephanis 1988.424–5, no. 2408.
86 *SEG* 34.174.
87 Stephanis 1988.210–12, no. 1157. It appears that the stele found in the theater of Thoricus, *SEG* 40.167, and thought to be a list of winners of the acting competition is most probably a list of choregoi, so that the Pindaros named there is not likely to be the tragic actor known from Aristotle *Poet.* 1461b 35: see: Summa 2006; Makres 1994.348.
88 Aesch. *Tim.* 157; Stephanis 1988.355–6 no. 2012.
89 Demosth. *False Embassy* 246–7.
90 *IG* I³ 254.
91 *IG* I³ 1027bis. *SEG* 34.107 a Thorician decree on the auctioning of the choregia is not later than about 400 BC: see Wilson 2007d.
92 *SEG* 34.174; *IG* I³ 258bis; cf. *SEG* 40.167.
93 *IG* II² 3092 (ca. 400, tragedy); *IG* II² 3106 (fourth century BC, dithyramb and comedy); Summa 2004 (second half of fourth centruy BC, comedy). Cf. *SEG* 63.26.
94 Aelian *VH* 11.13; Demosth. *Cor.*180, 262. Aelian is not a trustworthy source; the earliest reasonably secure attestation of drama at Peiraeus is the Law of Euegoros, which, if genuine (as it appears to be), predates Demosthenes' speech of 346 BC and certainly the event of 348 BC which gave rise to the trial.
95 Vierneisel and Scholl 2002 date it *c.*360 BC, but J. R. Green (*per litteras*) would put it as much as thirty years later.
96 *IG* II² 3097; *SEG* 48.129 (tragic contest at Rhamnous ca. 350 BC; *IG* II² 3108 is evidence of comedy at Rhamnous, but only dated vaguely to the fourth century BC).
97 *IG* II² 3096; *IG* II² 1182; *SEG* 53.1, 227; *SEG* 46.153.
98 *IG* II² 1202; *SEG* 36.186.
99 van Straten 1995.87 and fig. 92 (cf. Csapo forthcoming A); *SEG* 36 (1986) 187.
100 *SEG* 51.193.
101 Pl. *Rep.* 475d.
102 *Vita Soph.* 55–8 (= Istros *FGrH* 334 F 37; Neanthes *FGrH* 84 F18). Cf. also Polyaen. *Strat.* 6.10 where an ad hoc festival is called in order to trap the population of Aeolis in 399 BC. This seems too early for an ad hoc festival of this sort: see Chapter 6, p. 173.
103 See Chapter 4.

104 Mitens 1993.93; Marconi in Bosher forthcoming.
105 Polacco and Anti 1981 date an early phase of the large theater at Syracuse to the early fifth century, but Bernabo Brea 1967, Mertens 2004.32, argue that it was constructed after the middle of the fourth century BC. Gentili 1962 and Ginouvès 1972 identify a theater with rectilinear theatron as the fifth-century theater. Moretti 1993.83–6 dates the theater to the mid third century BC.
106 Fifth century date for theater: Mitens 1988.100–3, Courtois 1989, ad loc., Ciancio Rossetto and Pisani Sartorio 1994.2.428–30, Dearden 1999.245; Todisco 2002.170–1.
107 See in general Mitens 1988; Moretti 1993; Ciancio Rossetto and Pisani Sartorio 1994; Todisco 2002.167–92. For Solous, see also Wiegand 1997. For Hippana, articles by Vassallo and Marconi in Bosher forthcoming.
108 Plut. *Dion* 43.1.1; Diod. 16.83.3.
109 Diod. 13.94.1.
110 Epicharmus *PCG* 1 F 237; Hesych. s.v. *pente kritai*. Cf. Schol Ar. Birds 445; *POxy* 1611.30–7; Wilson 2007c.355; and for procedure in Athens generally, see Marshall and van Willigenburg 2004.
111 Jordan 2007; Wilson 2007c.
112 See Chapter 2, pp. 39–40.
113 Ar. *Ach.* 9–12 (with scholion), *Frogs* 868 (with scholion); Quint. *Inst.* 10.1.66; Philostr. *Apoll.* 6.11; *Life of Aeschylus* 12. Biles, forthcoming, is skeptical.
114 Todisco 2006.246–50. The statistics are based on the lists compiled by Catucci, Gadeleta and Roscino in Todisco 2003.769–800. Cf. also Kossatz-Deissmann 1978; *P&P* 48–87. For reperformance in Gela, see, further, Wilson 2007c.356–8.
115 Satyrus, *Life of Euripides* (*POxy* 1176, fr. 39, col. 19); Plut. *Nicias* 29. Cf. *Life of Euripides* 5 (= Hermippus, *FHG* 3.52, fr. 73b).
116 Arist. *Rhet.* 1384b15 (with scholion).
117 Todisco 2006.246–50.
118 Ciancio Rossetto and Pisani Sartorio 1994.2.500–3; Todisco 2002.149–56.
119 Collard, Cropp and Lee 1995.245. Cf. Taplin 1993.16–17; Allan 2001.85–6, n. 75.
120 Revermann 2006a.71–2.
121 Ciancio Rossetto and Pisani Sartorio 1994.2.427, 490–1, 578; Todisco 2002. 139–66.
122 Krinzinger and Gassner 1997; Todisco 2002.141–4.
123 Iambl. *VP* 126.9.
124 Aristox. fr. 28 da Rios (with Robinson 2004.209). Late testimonia: Polyb. 8.30; Livy 25.10.4; Dio 9.39 fr. 52; D.H. 19.5.3; Val. Max. 2.2.5; Florus *Epit.* 1.13.3; Orosius *Contra Pag.* 4.1; Zonaras 8, ch.2. p. 370; Hesych. s.v *dromos*.
125 Alexis: Arnott 1996.3–17; Archias: *IG* II² 2325, col. 3; Stephanis 1988.95–6, no. 439. For Aristodemos, see above, notes 28, 35–6, and 89.
126 Pl. *Laws* 659a–c.
127 Though vase-painting is the main witness to theater in the Greek West, there is dispute about the degree to which the Paestan manufacture (about 30 "theatrical vases") shows close familiarity with performance or simply copies motifs from the

Sicilian tradition (from which the Paestan school evidently derives): Hughes 2003; Green 2008.214–15. There is much more doubt about Campanian wares: *P&P* 20. The degree to which non-Greeks in South Italy were familiar with theater is only beginning to receive serious consideration: see Carpenter 2003; Robinson 2004 [2006]; Carpenter 2009.

128 On Megarian comedy generally, see Kerkhof 2001.13–50 with earlier literature.

129 Ecphantides *PCG* F 3; Ar. *Wasps* 54–66; Eupolis *PCG* F 261; Kerkhof 2001.17–24.

130 Kerkhof 2001.17–24, 30–38.

131 Arist. *NE* 1122b 23.

132 Argos: Ginouvès 1972. Dion: Polacco 1986; Pandermalis has apparently found proof of a fifth-century date (not yet published); Chaeroneia: Anti and Polacco 1969.19–44; Ciancio Rossetto and Pisani Sartorio 1994.2.146.

133 Aegae: Drougou 1997. Philippi: Samiou and Athanasiades 1987; Moretti 1991. 28–9; Ciancio Rossetto and Pisani Sartorio 1994.2.243–4.

134 Arrian 1.11.1; Bosworth 1980 ad loc.

135 Scullion 2003 is the most recent to cast a skeptical eye in this direction, though it is not always clear whether he means to cast doubt on Euripides' presence in Macedon or his "exile" and "death" in Macedon. He is right to reject as myth the characterization of Euripides' soujourn in Macedon as an "exile." But his primary evidence, jokes *not* made by Aristophanes, seems a poor basis for rejecting the possibility of Euripides presence or death in Macedon: it should be noted that Aristophanes does not joke about Aeschylus' presence or death in Sicily, events that are apparently accepted as fact by Scullion, since he treats them as a model for the supposed Euripidean fiction. See the more balanced discussion by Hanink 2008.

136 Arist. *Pol.* 1311b30–40. Scullion 2003.396 suggests that "Aristotle is doubtless drawing on such collections of anecdotes."

137 Pl. *Symp.* 172c, *Rep.* 568a–b, n.b.: "I think [the tragic poets] will go around to the other cities, gathering crowds, hiring those who have good, loud, and persuasive voices, and dragging states into tyranny and democracy." "Very likely." "In addition, then, they will be paid and honored by them, especially, in all likelihood, by the tyrants, but secondly by the democracies…" For Archelaus' patronage, see Chapter 6, p. 172.

138 Gebhard 1973; 1974.438; Moretti 1992.84–7. Plut. *Mor.* 79e places it in the fifth century BC, but the anecdote about Aeschylus is not credible.

139 Ciancio Rossetto and Pisani Sartorio 1994.2.152–5; Xen. *Hell.* 4.4.3.

140 Of these Megalopolis has been most controversial. Some (e.g. Goette 1995a.34–5 and Wiles 1997.36–8) date it to between 368 and 362 BC, but see now Lauter and Lauter-Bufe 2004, who would date in the late years of the fourth century.

141 Diod. Sic. 15.40.2.

142 Plut. *Mor.* 799e–f. For Boeotia and pipers: Wilson forthcoming.

143 Anti and Polacco 1969.19–44; Ciancio Rossetto and Pisani Sartorio 1994.2.146.

144 See works cited by Green 2008.55, 64.

145 Paus. 6.5.2–3.

146   I leave aside mention of the theater of Abydos assumed by a breezy anecdote in Arist. *Mir.* 832b 18: the work is not by Aristotle and not likely, in any case, to date to the fourth century.
147   *IG* II² 555.
148   Parker 1994.
149   *IG* XII 6.253, l. 11.
150   *IG* XII 8.4; Parker 1994.343 n. 18; Wilson 2000.388, n. 104; Cropp 2003.138.
151   *IG* XII 5.714; Reger 1994.
152   Isler 2007; Wilson 2000.283–4, 387.
153   Le Guen 2001a.1, no. 1.
154   Ant. 5.74; [Arist]. *Oec.* 2.26; Wilson 2000.284, 387 n. 97.
155   *IG* XII 5.35 and 46.
156   The spread of theater on the Aegean islands, mainly after the time of Alexander, is well documented by Le Guen 2001b.
157   Hippoc. *Epid.* 1.2.9.55 Littré. Proskenion inscription: *IG* XII Suppl. 399; *I.Lampsakos* 1.21. See Grandjean and Salviat 2000.105–6.
158   *IGUR* I 223, 229. Stephanis 1988.82 no. 363, 258 no. 1413. See also Alkimachos (= Stefanis 1988.41, no. 139 with *IG* XII 1.125).
159   Unfortunately the point of Antig. Car. *Mir.* 161 is unclear: he appears to complain that in speaking of the stones used to build the theater at Cos Eudoxus did not mention the stream that was the main source of their production (= fr. 363 Lasserre).
160   Athen. 456f; *IG* XII 5.5344, 1075; Wilson 2000.285–6.
161   Stucchi 1975.34–6, 69–70; Chamoux 1998.134–5; Ceccarelli and Milanezi 2007. Cyrene also imported the comic vase discussed in Chapter 1, pp. 27–8.
162   D.L. 5.91; Green 1994.68. Cf. the Attic choral fragment from Olbia, Chapter 1, pp. 8–9.
163   The discussion above and the chart exclude occasional dramatic festivals put on by Philip and Alexander to celebrate weddings, funerals, and military victories. These are discussed in Chapter 6, pp. 173–4.
164   Green 1995c.152–3; Green 2008.20, 215. See *MMC* pp. 39–66.
165   Dem. 57.18.
166   See above n. 158, and *IG* II² 2318, l. 200.
167   Ael. *HA* 11.19 with (N. G.) Wilson 1999.
168   Plut. *Ages.* 21.4, *Apophth. Lacon.* 212f; *Vita Soph.* 14; Polyaen. *Strateg.* 6.10.
169   See above, pp. 85–6.
170   See above, p. 88.
171   See Csapo 2004a.
172   Stephanis 1988.245–7 no. 1348, 331–2 no. 1861. On Kallippides, see Braund 2000, and Chapter 4.
173   Plut. *Ages.*21.4.
174   Plut. *Ages.* 21.3.
175   Arist. *Poet.* 1461b 34, 1462a 9 (discussed in detail in Chapter 4); Plut. *Alcib.* 32; Athen. 535d; *Epist. Socr.* 14.3 (p. 620 Hercher);

176   Ar. *PCG* F 490; Strattis *PCG* T1, F 11–13; Xen. *Symp.* 3.11.
177   On which, see Wilson 2000, *passim* and Wilson 2008.
178   With the exception of a third century monument from the Kerameikos: see Hallof and Stroszeck 2002.
179   See n. 86.
180   See Chapter 1, pp. 20–1.
181   *IG* II² 2318, lines 201–3.
182   See Le Guen 2001a, TE 5 (with vol. 2, p. 90), TE 10, TE 13, TE 53, and the inscriptions mentioned in vol. 2, p. 91 n. 443.
183   There is insufficient evidence to show if this donation of a tragic performance continued regularly after 386 BC (it was annual by 341, cf. *IG* II² 2320). Similarly the first comedy to be donated by "the comedians" was in 339 BC (*IG* II² 2318), but we cannot tell if it was annual before 311 BC (*IG* II² 2323a).

Kallippides on the Floor Sweepings
The Limits of Realism in Classical Acting

Our sources offer little direct comment on acting and production in the Classical Greek theater.[1] If we omit the schematic and dubious claims, mainly in the scholia and poets' biographies, which are derived from Hellenistic and later authors, and confine ourselves to Classical authors, we are left with a few comments by Aristotle, many anecdotes, and some extended but distorted descriptions in comedy. Among these, three independent *testimonia* give evidence for broad developments in acting and production and all three indicate that in the late fifth century BC there occurred a significant movement toward something we may provisionally call "realism."

Mynniskos vs. Kallippides

Mynniskos called his fellow actor, Kallippides, an "ape."[2] Mynniskos was the senior colleague. He had begun his career in the time of Aeschylus – is even said to have been "Aeschylus' actor."[3] Kallippides was the *enfant terrible* of the new generation. Mynniskos probably delivered his insult, if at all, in the 420s BC. The anecdote gives direct testimony to controversy already within the third generation of tragic actors.

The value of the anecdote does not depend on its historicity. Whether Mynniskos really called Kallippides an ape is beyond proof. Though anecdotes (and comedy) are not reliable as concerns specific truths, they usually owe their survival to success in expressing general perceptions. The anecdote neatly captured a perceived shift in aesthetic sensibilities between generations. This is why Aristotle tells the tale – it illustrates "how the older actors perceived the younger generation of actors." Even if the anecdote is not much older than Aristotle, we will see that it perpetuates a debate that goes back to the late fifth century BC.

The meaning of Mynniskos' insult is frequently misunderstood. In Aristotle's words Mynniskos called Kallippides an ape "because he went too far" (ὡς λίαν ὑπερβάλλοντα). The Greek expression can mean either overdoing something or transgressing some boundary. Translators almost invariably take Aristotle's words here to indicate overacting, i.e. the use of grotesquely loud gestures. But the broader context of the passage in Aristotle's *Poetics* shows that he understood the slur to refer not to excessive or exaggerated gestures, bur rather to an *excess of gesture,* i.e. excessive *mimesis*; not overacting, but imitating actions that are best not imitated at all:[4]

> One may well be at a loss to decide whether epic imitation is better than tragic. For if the less vulgar is the better – the less vulgar being always that which is directed to the better part of the audience – it is only too clear that the vulgar art is that which *imitates everything*. Supposing that their audience will understand nothing unless they *incorporate it in their representation,* some artists *will produce any gesture* … Now tragedy is just this sort of art. So too the older actors perceived the younger generation of actors: Mynniskos used to call Kallippides an ape because he went too far; the same opinion might be held of Pindaros. The relation of these actors to their older contemporaries is arguably the same as tragedy generally to epic. Epic, so the argument goes, is directed to the superior audience that has *no need for such gestures and postures,* but tragedy is directed toward an inferior. If then tragedy is vulgar, clearly it would be worse. We may answer, first of all, that this charge has nothing to do with poetry but with acting, since one can be intrusive with one's use of gestures even in an epic recitation … Secondly, *not all movement is objectionable – one would not condemn dance, for example – but only that which is in imitation of inferior people: Kallippides was censured, as are others today, for representing lower-class women.* Tragedy does its work even without movement, just like epic: by reading it you can tell what kind of tragedy it is. If then tragedy is superior in other respects, it is not necessarily subject to this fault.

Kallippides is not an ape because he immoderately reproduced gestures which might have been acceptable in moderation, but because, like an ape that "imitates everything" and "will produce any gesture," Kallippides produced gestures that non-vulgar sensibilities would rather not see in tragedy, specifically the gestures of the non-élite.[5]

Taken in context, it is clear that the complaint about Kallippides has less to do with some transhistorical criterion of good taste (who would argue for excessive gesture?), than with the specific disgust of an upper-class Greek at seeing heroes behave with the mannerisms of social inferiors. Even for Aristotle *mimesis* has its limits, in this case ideological ones, which are difficult to reconcile with the strict logic of his theory of art, and especially tragic art, as a form of *mimesis*.[6] In the past, scholars and translators have attempted to reconcile Aristotle's words with their own middle-class ethical standard by interpreting the words I translate as "lower-class women" as referring to sluts or harlots (who never actually appear in tragedy).[7] But the expression "οὐκ ἐλευθέρας γυναῖκας" refers, in

Aristotle's sociolect to all women below leisure class, and hence lower than the élite status appropriate to tragic heroines and Aristotle's readers.[8] What Aristotle complains about is not what we would term the unseemly or pornographic, but imitation of the simple gestures of ordinary women.

It is worth insisting upon a contextual reading of this anecdote because the usual reading in terms of "excessive gestures" is often inserted into a traditional picture of tragedy's decline in the fourth century when Aristotle claimed "the actors are more important now than the poets," and when Plato deplored the rise of the vulgar masses, who "once silent, became vocal, pretending to know what is good art and what not, and instead of aristocracy in the arts a degenerate theatrocracy came into being."[9] According to this theory, an increasingly self-assertive mass audience came to exercise a form of democratic control over music and drama (which meant that the mob dragged it down to the level of their vulgar tastes). The theory is of little value for cultural history beyond attesting the cultural alienation of the élite in the fourth-century Athenian democracy and is based on the problematic assumption that actors (who by this time were definitely non-élites) were more inclined to cater to the masses than poets (who still were).[10] For the modern reader (for whom realism is perhaps still a default style), it is not easy to sympathize with the notion that the first step to tragedy's moral and aesthetic decline was due to "excessive *mimesis*." In effect this must mean "too much realism," if not simply "too much acting." Modern proponents of the theatrocracy theory must contend with the fact that Kallippides and his generation did what they did to drama at the time of the first production of the majority of Euripides', if not Sophocles', extant plays, and that these poets are not usually encompassed by the theory of decline.

Possibly Mynniskos' slur on Kallippides was meant to signify something other than the meaning Aristotle sets upon it. If so, that is beyond our control. Certainly nothing encourages us to doubt that Mynniskos intended what Aristotle implies. Indeed, a comic fragment of the fifth (or very early fourth) century, and so contemporary with Kallippides, makes a similar complaint about the actor's style. The fragment is cited from Aristophanes' *Skenas Katalambanousai* ("Women who take Control of the Stage-Building" [or possibly "of the Tents"]): "Like Kallippides I sit upon the ground on the floor-sweepings."[11] Kassel and Austin point out that the language is similar to the description in the *Odyssey* of Odysseus as a helpless suppliant to the Phaeacian court, "sitting on the ground at the hearth in the dust," and Kock was doubtless right to suggest that Aristophanes alludes to Kallippides' role in a tragedy, Euripides' *Telephus*, for example, in which Kallippides portrayed the hero as a suppliant or a beggar.[12] If this is right, Aristophanes ridicules Kallippides for realistically portraying the degradation of a mythological hero which an older actor like Mynniskos would have shown, if at all, with genteel restraint. This willingness to "imitate anything" doubtless also contributed to the proverbial tale of Kallippides' dismissal as a "buffoon" (*deikeliktas*) by the Spartan (hence very conservative) king Agesilaus.[13]

Aeschylus vs. Euripides

The contest of Aristophanes' *Frogs* sets Euripides against Aeschylus for the "chair" of tragedy in the underworld. It is our first extended extant piece of ancient dramatic criticism. What most strikes the modern reader is that the criticism is entirely axiological (i.e. who is the better poet?) and that the criteria for deciding the question of poetic superiority are predominantly moral and political, not aesthetic. It has sometimes been asked why Aristophanes did not make Sophocles part of this debate. Some even infer that *Frogs* was substantially written before Sophocles' death and that Aristophanes' lines (786–94) excusing Sophocles' non-participation in the contest were last-minute additions. But the assumption that Aristophanes would have pitted Euripides against Sophocles, if only death had made him available in time, fails to see that the power and resonance of this debate, at least for the Athenian audience, went far beyond merely dramatic values. Aeschylus and Euripides represent positions, not poets, and these positions have all the social and ideological depth we find in other Aristophanic debates, that of *Clouds*, for example, where classes, generations, moral codes and conceptual universes clash head on.[14] The choice of Aeschylus and Euripides to represent the poles of the debate in *Frogs* had a sociological and political logic that overshadows the poetic. Aeschylus is already here a classic. He represented tradition and the values of a heroic past, especially because of his connections with the Persian Wars (through his *Persians* and the fact that he himself fought at Marathon). Euripides represented modernity and the values of a "radically" democratic present.

A very prominent feature of this structured opposition is the contrast between Aeschylus' silent restraint and Euripides' unbridled speech. The first dramatic criticism, by Euripides of Aeschylus, is that he introduced (911–15) "some Achilles or Niobe, never showing their face, and sat them down alone, a mere pretense of tragedy, not uttering a syllable… Then the chorus would ram the audience with a chain of four successive odes sung without interruption. But the actors remained mute." At this point Dionysus interrupts with "I used to like the mute actors: they pleased me no less than do the chatterboxes nowadays" (196–7). Euripides, by contrast, proudly claims that "he left no one idle, but the wife spoke and the slave no less, and the master, the maiden and the old crone" (949–50). The comic poet even represents Euripides as the author of the loquacity of modern audiences: Euripides boasts that "I taught these people [the audience] to chatter" (954). The claim is later taken up by Aeschylus who charges Euripides with having "taught the audience to chatter and drivel" (1069).[15] Earlier in the *Frogs* loquacity is treated as a characteristic of *all the modern poets:* Why go to Hades to fetch Euripides? Heracles asks Dionysus, when "there are here more than ten thousand young tragedians, bigger chatterboxes by a mile than Euripides" (89–91). Dover warns that the translation of "chatter" and "chatter-boxes" for the Greek words λαλία, λαλεῖν, λάλοι "is sometimes too strong" and that the words "are more like what we mean by pronouncing the word 'talk' in a contemptuous or impatient way: talking out of turn when prompt and silent compliance is needed."[16] Dover points to parallels in the *agon* of *Clouds* where the Greater Argument accuses the Lesser of teaching the young to prac-tice "mere chatter" rather than undergoing the physical training required of citizen soldiers.[17] For Aristophanes "chattiness" was the distinguishing charac-teristic of Euripidean tragedies – elsewhere he calls them "chat-about tragedies" (τραγῳδίαι περιλαλοῦσαι), whereas Aeschylus' mouth in *Frogs* is described as "incapable of chatter" (ἀπερίλάλητον).[18] Just as Kallippides was condemned as vulgar by Mynniskos for acting without restraint, so "Euripides" is con-demned as vulgar by "Aeschylus" for writing without restraint.

In the world of comedy, poets are cut from the same cloth as their drama. In *Frogs* it is therefore not surprising to find a strict homology embracing the char-acteristics of everyone involved in the performance of Euripidean drama – the whole communication chain – the poets, their characters, their audiences, and their actors, all chatterboxes. Aeschylus, like his characters, is the opposite. He is portrayed as glowering in silent indignation, so much so that Dionysus repeat-edly has to command him to speak (832, 866, 1020, 1125, 1151, 1170). When he does speak he bursts forth in a frenzy of rage (838, 855, 859) and then Dionysus has to command him to shut up (843, 851, 926, 1132 f., cf. 922, 927). This is another side of Aeschylus that makes for a nice contrast with the always glib and ready Euripides. Aeschylus is brought to speak primarily when overcome by powerful emotions, when provoked by a sudden access of madness (816), rage (856, 994, 998, 1006) or spleen. These angry impulses constitute a primitive sort of inspiration welling up (cf. 1005) from the "guts" as befits the pupil of a bel-licose muse (844, 1006). Later critics liked to think of Aeschylus as an "inspired" rather than a technically accomplished poet: Sophocles was said to have described Aeschylus as writing poetry without really knowing what he was doing (οὐκ εἰδώς), and the late fourth century critic Chamaeleon claimed that Aeschylus wrote his dramas while drunk.[19]

Euripides, by contrast, is the epitome of magisterial polish and control. He has no need for external sources of inspiration. No traditional Muse gives breath to his verse, but the instrumentalities of his own speech: in place of the goddess he invokes "intellect, pivot of tongue, and nostrils" (892–3, cf. 819, 826–7). His poetry is all art and artifice. His versification is characterized in terms that liken him to a lowly craftsman. His words are described as if they were the products – or rather the useless by-products, "chips and shavings," of a carpenter (819, 881, 901). Aeschylus' words are wrapped in military metaphors which liken them to armor, fortifications and especially weapons of assault, verbal projectiles (818, 821, 824, 854–5, 902, 924–5, 928–9, 1004, 1018). Aeschylus does not unsheathe his tongue except to draw blood. His speech is the speech of action – archetypal, heroic action, as if it were powerful and efficacious speech as opposed to "mere chatter."

But the opposition of chatter to silence, or the opposition of sophistic virtuosity to bardic inspiration, merely lie at the surface of a much deeper and more serious opposition, the opposition of the moral and political character of old and new tragedy. Aristophanes' Aeschylus is the stereotype of a staunch, militaristic, elitist conservative; Euripides is the versatile, clever, and modern democrat. Euripides' audiences chatter because he has taught them to question authority. Aristophanes has him sum up his contribution thus: "I introduced thinking to the audience and put ratiocination (λογισμός) into the art [of dramatic poetry] and critical doubt" (971–4). Authority resides in the individual: it has become a matter of personal knowledge and discernment. Aristophanes' Aeschylus, on the other hand, would put it back in the social hierarchy. Euripides' audiences have learned to question and quibble where Aeschylus' audiences were trained to silent obedience.

In this ostensibly poetic discourse Aristophanes is really opposing, albeit fleshed out in the form of their respective culture heroes, the ideologies of the political camps that, at the time of the production of *Frogs* (405 BC), had placed Athens on the verge of civil war: new radical democrats and old oligarchs. Euripides is low class (947), self-professedly democratic (951), and supported by the demos of the underworld (779). He is likened to a sophist, giving exhibitions of his skill to the bedazzlement of the degenerate "mob" in the underworld (771–6). Aeschylus by contrast is presented as a friend of the élite of the underworld (783), hostile to the leaders of the democracy, whom he refers to as "demo-chimps" (1085), and no friend of the Athenian majority (807–8). His advice for saving Athens is to turf out the current democratic leaders and bring back the exiled aristocrats and oligarchs (1446–8) – and as this is essentially the same advice as Aristophanes puts into the mouths of the chorus in the parabasis, we may suppose that this is where Aristophanes' own sympathies lie.[20] The political color of Aeschylus' portrait is best marked in his complaint that Euripides taught the sailors of the ship *Paralos* to talk back to their superiors (1071–2). *Paralos* is a revealing example. At the time of the oligarchic coup at Athens in 411, the ship played a leading role in the democratic mutiny of the Athenian fleet at Samos, and this mutiny eventually led to the restoration of democracy at Athens. The sailors of the *Paralos* were "all of them free men and Athenians," says Thucydides, "and all eternally opposed to oligarchy even when it did not exist."[21] We may guess that the real Aeschylus would not have been particularly happy with this characterization – nor Euripides for that matter, but both were safely dead. Aristophanes reduces them to fit the guiding stereotypes of current Athenian social discourse. They are simply the poles of a structured opposition between tradition and modernity, self-restraint and self-indulgence, unquestioning obedience and individual responsibility, and government by one's social betters and democracy, all trained upon an organizing opposition between old tragedy and new.

As such, the *Frogs* is an invaluable witness to the social and ideological resonances perceived by Athenian audiences in 405 BC to different production styles in tragedy. *Frogs* gives the (entirely misleading) impression that Aeschylus wrote only on military themes in an imposing style, with verbal and visual magnificence designed to stun the audience (833–4, 862, 911–20). Its Aeschylus maintains that heroes should wear uncommonly elegant costumes (1061) and use "bigger words" than ordinary mortals (1060). Euripides and Dionysus find his language pompous, grandiose, and unintelligible (923–6, 929–31, 940, 1056–7), while at the same time primitive and inarticulate (836–9).

Euripides, by contrast, boasts that he introduced to the stage the things of everyday life, which the audience knew and could judge for themselves, from their own experience, to be true to life or not (959–61). Aeschylus claims that, unlike Euripides, he never introduced anything as unseemly as women in love (1043–4). Here the poet of Ares is opposed to the poet of Aphrodite (1021, 1045). Euripides defends himself by insisting that Phaedra's love for Hippolytus was a "true story;" Aeschylus replies "yes, true, by Zeus, but a poet must hide what is unseemly and not bring it on stage nor produce it" (1053–4). One must at least hide the real if one cannot improve upon it. This criticism also applies to the realistic portrayal of lame heroes and the "rags" with which Euripides costumed his down-and-out (or disguised) heroes (842, 846): Aeschylus charges that Euripides "first dressed kings in rags, so that they would seem more piteous" (1064). Showing their halting gait is characterized as an act of "impudence" (*thraseia*), and a transgression of proper restraint.

Not only does Aristophanes' Euripides pride himself upon presenting actions beneath the threshold of moral dignity, and upon presenting clothing and movements beneath the threshold of social respectability, he also prides himself on having lowered the threshold of representable speech. Euripides boasts that he "reduced the tumescence" of tragic grandiloquence to make his heroes speak "like ordinary human beings."[22] He is charged with having modeled his verse on language of different registers: literary genres (943), speech genres (841, cf. *Ach.* 398), and musical genres, especially those that are low and common (843, 1297).

Euripides claims that his use of language was "democratic" (952) insofar as he gave equal voice to women, slaves, young and old (949–50). For this audacity, says Aeschylus, he should have been killed (951).

Sophocles vs. Euripides

We might compare a third document. Chapter twenty-five of Aristotle's *Poetics* is devoted to celebrated problems in ancient literary criticism and chiefly the defense of poetic authorities against the charge of representing immoral, improbable, or impossible objects. Such charges, says Aristotle, can often be dismissed by recognizing that an artist may imitate three different categories of objects: "either the way things were or are, or the way things are said or seem to be, or the way things ought to be" (1460b 10–11). To illustrate the point Aristotle reports that "Sophocles said he portrayed men as they should be, but Euripides portrayed them as they are" (Σοφοκλῆς ἔφη αὐτὸς μὲν οἵους δεῖ ποιεῖν, Εὐριπίδην δὲ οἷοι εἰσίν, 1460b 34). The meaning of the passage is much disputed. Suffice it here to say that more controversy attaches to the first term of the opposition than to the second: Euripides portrayed people "realistically," but what is the sense of "should" in Sophocles' alleged portrayal of people as they "should be?" The statement is often over-interpreted as an unqualified opposition between "idealism" and "realism."[23]

Aristotle introduces the statement as a possible defense against the charge of "false reproduction" and an appeal to idealism is no defense in Aristotle's books against amimetic practice.[24] Verisimilitude (τὸ πιθανόν) is a central concern of Aristotle's theory of art, and verisimilitude is produced by what is possible, and, since we do not consider things possible that have never happened, real models are indispensable if art is to have its proper effect.[25]

Nevertheless, Aristotle surely understood some aspect of what we mean by "idealization" to lie behind the statement ascribed to Sophocles. This is probably the same kind of cosmetic surgery upon the real that Aristotle himself recommends to the tragedian. Tragic heroes, he says, should be both like ordinary men and better than ordinary men.[26] In creating them, the poet should act as do good portrait painters, who "while making men similar, paint them more beautiful." "In the same way," continues Aristotle, "a poet imitating men who are irascible or too easy-going or of some other such quality, makes them good, while yet such as they are."[27] Tragic heroes must be believable, but also better, in order to arouse pity and fear. There is also some concern for what Aristotle imagines to be the cognitive function of tragedy. The cognitive function of poetry in general requires the excision of unnecessary details of material reality (particularly trivial or unattractive ones such as Alcibiades' lisp): where history is concerned to represent particular truths, poetry is more serious and philo-sophical insofar as the poet attempts, by stripping his models of all that is con-tingent and idiosyncratic, to represent a universal truth.[28] Thus, some have interpreted Sophocles' self-assessment to mean that he portrayed characters "as they should be [portrayed]." In this case "should be" has less to do with an ideal world, than with a different criterion for accessing the real.

If Sophocles ever made such a statement he is likely to have meant consider-ably less by it than did Aristotle. Since Aristotle gives no context for Sophocles' putative statement, we may guess that Sophocles intended his opposition to be taken morally. This is suggested by the context supplied by the *Gnomologium Vaticanum* where the *bon mot* is Sophocles' response to the question: "Why, Sophocles, do you make human characters good, while Euripides makes them worthless?"[29] A moralizing context is also implied by a version in which Philoxenus responds to the question why his women are worthless, while Sophocles' are good.[30]

However Sophocles may have conceived his own practice, the anecdote once more associates Euripides with a style of production which was perceived by contemporaries or near-contemporaries as "realistic" and placed in opposition to a more restrained style of production that only admitted what was consistent with good taste or moral decency.

The anecdotes and the comic contest in *Frogs* attest to a perceived opposition in dramatic values, diachronically between generations, and synchronically between individual actors and poets. They indicate, further, that the period of greatest polarization was approximately 425 to 405 bc, and that the second term of this opposition can be characterized as the rise of "realism" in the use of lan-guage, costume, gesture, and characterization on the tragic stage.

In contrasting Euripides to the other tragedians, comedy to tragedy, or New Comedy to Old, classical scholars have never hesitated to use the term "realism," or the often synonymous "naturalism" (beyond occasionally placing the terms in "scarequotes" as I have done), particularly in discussions of characterization, stagecraft, and the dramatic use of time and space.[31] The terms are indeed help-ful for understanding the development of Classical drama, notwithstanding the occasional error (necessary to realists, but fatal to their critics) of confusing the art-historical term with its ontological cognate. One must keep in mind, however, that the term is a metaphor comparing developments in ancient drama to a dominant style that emerged in Western art and literature in the eighteenth and nineteenth centuries. Like all metaphors, it has its utility – in this case I think enormous – but also its limitations. Like its more modern counterpart, ancient drama developed a rich typology of human character, and a variegated means of portraying its diversity. Unlike its modern counterpart, ancient drama was far more selective in the types of social diversity it described.

This selectivity is all the more striking because, as we will see, some of the criteria of selection and avoidance change *toto caelo* from the late fifth to the late fourth century BC.

Performing Language

Some recent scholarship denies that ancient acting included verbal mimicry. It argues that, because the protagonist (leader of a troupe of actors) competed for a prize, his chief interest lay in remaining conspicuous behind the roles he played.[32] Given the convention of masked acting, actors were most readily identified by their voices. It would seem to follow therefore that the actor's interest in winning the competition prevented him from altering his natural speaking voice to suit any particular role – his professional success as an actor, in effect, depended upon his avoidance of acting.

This argument wildly exaggerates the difficulty experienced by ancient audiences in following the main actor's part in a drama where a total of only two or three actors played a very limited number of speaking characters. Indeed, most fifth-century drama tends to focus the action upon a single dominant character, who in practice was generally played by the protagonist.[33] But quite apart from this, the premise is wrong. Not the protagonist, but the acting troupe competed for the prize. True, only the name of the protagonist was officially recognized, but he won the prize not for his individual performance in competition with his subordinates, but for the performance of his troupe in competition with other troupes. It was therefore never imperative that the identity of any individual actor be transparent behind his mask.[34] Yet even supposing that these scholars are correct in their claims relating to the practice of the tragic protagonists, there is still nothing to justify their generalized claim that ancient actors never altered the character of their voice. Moreover, their argument permits no conclusions about the practices of subordinate actors, who generally played far more roles than the protagonists, and no conclusions about the practices of comic actors. The actor's competition is indeed irrelevant for many comedies: the comic actor's prize was not introduced to the Dionysia until after 329 BC.[35]

Comedy provides ample evidence for vocal mimicry. Here characters frequently impersonate others. At times instruction in the art of mimicry even forms part of the comic action. At *Thesmophoriazusae* 267–8 the In-Law (the protagonist) is instructed to "feminize the tone of his voice" (ὅπως τῷ φθέγματι γυναικιεῖς εὖ καὶ πιθανῶς), and then immediately enters the Thesmophorion chattering like a housewife to an imaginary maid;[36] in *Ecclesiazusae* the disguised women, exhorted to speak "like men" (149), march out singing an "old man's song, imitating the manner of countrymen" (277–9). In some cases the alternation of the actor's voice is necessary to avoid confusion. The sharing of a single role between two actors, though generally avoided in tragedy, is frequently necessary in comedy (which functions with a larger character set) and especially in the New Comedy of Menander.[37] The audience would presumably have difficulty recognizing the identity of the character unless both actors sharing the role acted with one voice. At *Lysistrata* 879 the actor playing Kinesias must supply the voice of the baby he holds by "ventriloquism" – unlikely to succeed, one would think, if the actor refuses to change the quality of his voice.[38] In Menander's monologues, characters frequently quote one or more other characters in direct speech, sometimes with no introductory words such as "he said," an act impossible to follow unless all the voices employed by the actor were audibly different.[39] Quintilian indeed complains of precisely this excess of mimicry in Menander's speeches: "even if [comic actors] play the part of a youth they nonetheless speak with a quavering or effeminate voice when reporting in a narration the speech of an old man, as for example in the prologue of *Hydria*, or a woman, as in *Georgos*."[40] Quintilian's direct testimony for voice modulation by actors belongs to a much later epoch, but Menander is unlikely to have written this way unless mimicry were already an established part of the actor's art. Similar juxtaposition of different voices appears in Agathon's song in *Thesmophoriazusae* (101–29), where only the modulation of the voice could show that Agathon is singing both parts of an exchange between a priestess and a female chorus (and both voices are described as effeminate at lines 131 and 192). The texts of Old Comedy also represent dialect and non-standard speech in direct quotation by Athenian characters of non-Athenians or the speech patterns of known individuals.[41] Are we to imagine that comic poets freely indulged an appetite for linguistic realism shunned by their actors? In antiquity dramatic poets wrote for dramatic performers, and it is an old, bad habit of traditional philology to suppose otherwise. We should rather infer that the poets' motive for introducing into their dramas such a medley of often clearly differentiated speech patterns was precisely to allow actors to display virtuosity in parading a patter of distinct voices. Clearly vocal mimicry was an important part of the comic actor's art by the late fifth century BC.

Slight and unevenly scattered as it is, the evidence shows an overall growth of interest in vocal mimicry among comic actors from the later fifth to the fourth and third centuries BC. This emerges not only from the evidence for the form of delivery (as above), but from changes in the form and structure of the comic narrative. Increasingly common from 411 BC are comedies involving themes of disguise and (especially cross-gender) role-playing, which make large demands upon the actor's mimic talents. There is also a striking change in the pattern of role distribution in our extant Aristophanic comedies. Earlier comic protagonists were content with a single dominant role, but after 405 BC Aristophanic comedy assigns the protagonist a much greater diversity of roles. Vetta explains the change as a response to the chief actor's desire to display his powers of mimicry.[42] In the fourth century BC, skill at vocal mimicry might be the basis of an actor's claim to fame, as in the case of the comic actor Parmenon (said to have been "emulated by many"), whose imitation of a squealing pig became proverbial. By this time, even tragic actors cultivated such skills: Theodoros, the most famous tragic actor of the century, was particularly remembered for his success in imitating the sound of a windlass.[43] Plato cites these actors in a complaint about the tendency of narrative in direct speech, of which drama was the most extreme form, to involve "imitation of voice and gesture" requiring "every kind of pitch and rhythm if it is to be delivered properly, since it involves all manner of shifts."[44] Such effects were evidently popular among contemporary theater audiences – like Aristotle, Plato associated this mimetic excess with the tastes of men of low birth and breeding.

The refinement of the actor's powers of vocal mimicry was only part of a series of developments in the language of dramatic performance. The texts of the plays show a marked turn toward realism in vocabulary and speech rhythm, especially from the last quarter of the fifth century onward. Aristophanes' Euripides justly boasted that he tamed the high-flown language of tragedy and brought it closer to ordinary speech. Aristotle recommends natural speech to orators as most convincing and least likely to arouse suspicion – the illusion of natural speech "succeeds when one composes from a vocabulary chosen from normal conversation" – and he adds that "Euripides was the first to do this and showed the way."[45] As Aristotle implies, later dramatists followed Euripides' lead: Menander's vocabulary is far closer to ordinary speech than that of either Aristophanes or Euripides.[46] Euripides also led the way in modifying the iambic trimeters (and trochaic tetrameters) of tragedy to sound less stiff, deliberate and artificial.[47] This loosening of metrical forms increases radically and consistently from the 420s until the time of Euripides' death. Speech rhythms are also measurably freer in the late plays of Sophocles. The concern to bring dramatic verse closer to natural language finds its proper culmination in Early Hellenistic comedy, which avoids meters other than iambic trimeter and trochiac tetrameter, and nearly dispenses with song altogether.

The dramatic texts also show an increasing interest in language as a vehicle for characterization, especially from the 420s onward. Scholarship tends to treat this phenomenon in isolation as a more or less fortuitous poetic or literary achievement. Historical explanation is only really possible if we view the "literary" evidence in the larger context of the trend toward realism in dramatic *performance*. In large part, the growing realism of the language of our texts presupposes the developing skill of contemporary actors in capturing different personalities through voice and gesture. The actor's interest in developing the precision and diversity of his mimetic talents is in turn largely driven by the large economic incentives of the developing star system. The initial most powerful stimulus was the spread of theater from Attica to the rest of Greece, which can be dated to the final decades of the fifth century BC.[48] For this reason, the characters of Euripides and New Comedy are generally better individualized by their vocabulary, style, register, dialect, mode of delivery, meter, and syntax than the characters of Aeschylus and Sophocles, tragedy and Old Comedy, respectively. By the time of Menander the mimicry of individual speech patterns is systematic and extensive.[49]

Despite this, ancient "realism" falls short of its modern counterpart in the extent of its development. This is partly because it also differs in kind. Modern realism strives to reveal character inwardly as a private and unique essence. But, as Bakhtin acutely observed, the ancients generally constructed character outwardly as a public person defined by a broad typology oriented less to psychological than to the sociological distinctions that define one's *état civil*.[50] In the fifth century BC the differentiation of language is generally limited to broad categories of sex, age, ethnicity, and social class. Even in New Comedy, the most realistic of the traditional dramatic genres, linguistic portraiture seems only to have diversified within this received typological framework, and especially in the category of social class, where it added more precise markings to distinguish the citizen from the slave, and the leisure-class gentleman from various representatives of the working class (the latter is curiously divided into a limited set of "professions"). Yet by contrast with the universal and more steadily incremental development toward familiar vocabulary or freer verse, the development of realism in the linguistic representation of character shows interesting anomalies over the course of the fifth and fourth centuries BC.

The Limits of Ancient Realism

Interest in representing women's speech seems to have grown steadily in the fifth and fourth centuries BC: several recent studies demonstrate that women's speech is more distinctive in Euripides than in Sophocles or Aeschylus, more distinctive in Aristophanes than in Euripides, and most distinctive in Menander.[51] Linguistic realism was nonetheless subject to social and ideological pressures that made its development both uneven and incomplete. The greatest unevenness appears in linguistic differentiation by ethnicity or class.

The direct representation of foreign speech is not attested in any genre of Greek literature before tragedy.[52] Paradoxically, it is our earliest tragedian, Aeschylus, who offers the most extensive representations of the tone, syntax, and vocabulary of barbarian speech. *Persians* attempts to imitate the Greek spoken by Persians through formalities, frequent Ionicism, and the use of Persian words, names, and exclamations.[53] In the highly emotional choral song preceding and accompanying the attack made by the Egyptians on the Danaides in *Suppliants* (776–871), we find Egyptian and North African Greek (Cyrenean) words, as well as a number of "unusual, archaic, and cacophonous" words, all peppered with a great density of "cries, repetition, and alliteration to substantiate his Egyptians' claim to be heterophone."[54] Such characterization is uncommon in the later tragedians. "Only one reference to the fact that a character speaks a foreign language exists in the extant plays of Sophocles (*Ajax* 1263) ... Tecmessa's foreignness might ... have been developed by drawing attention to her speech, but Sophocles does not raise the point."[55] Three fragmentary plays of Sophocles, not certainly tragedies, included items of foreign vocabulary.[56] Euripides revives some of the Aeschylean effects in his late monodies and choral odes, especially those influenced by the New Music (which had an Eastern flavor), but not in dialogue.[57] Realism in the characterization of foreign speech in tragedy can therefore be said to decline in tragedy over the course of the fifth century. Moreover, despite incipient realism in the characterization of foreign non-Greek speech, foreign Greek dialect is never used to characterize non-Athenians in tragedy. Even after he announces in the *Libation-Bearers* that he will "imitate the Phocian dialect," Orestes speaks a perfectly normal poetic Attic.[58] Late fifth-century comedy is, by contrast, very free in it representation of both non-Greek and non-Attic speech: Colvin finds "no example in extant Old Comedy of a non-Athenian Greek or barbarian whose speech is not marked as foreign in some way" (and he argues that dialect imitation, at least, has more to do with the genre's realism than with humor).[59]

The representation of sociolect presents a still more anomalous picture. Stevens found that Aeschylus was most concerned to differentiate the speech of lower-caste characters, which he did "partly by colloquial expressions, partly by touches of naïveté, garrulity or sententiousness."[60] The same is true of Sophocles, where "colloquialisms are sometimes admitted, particularly in the speech of servants or messengers" as in Aeschylus, but more rarely.[61] Low-caste characters account for 60 percent of Aeschylus' colloquialisms but only 24 percent of Sophocles'.[62] Yet even when Sophocles gives colloquialism to upper-caste heroes, it is frequently for the purpose of revealing them to be vulgar and undignified, like Menelaus in *Ajax,* or to be losing their composure through such emotions as anger or excitement.[63] Colloquialism thus remains associated with plebeian qualities more often than the bare statistics suggest. Satyr drama may also use colloquialism to distinguish the bestial (satyrs, Silenus, ogres) from heroic characters who speak a more uniformly tragic language.[64] By contrast, Euripides and Aristophanes are very free with colloquialism and apply it indiscriminately to both high- and low-caste characters, contributing "to a general scaling down of heroic splendour to something nearer to the ordinary life of men."[65]

Here is a paradox for any who might have expected to see a steady progression in the realism of linguistic portraiture. Euripides may be said to champion the trend insofar as it involves a general devolution of style to the level of common speech. Yet in the use of language to differentiate social status the opposite is true. As Stevens says, "there is a much greater degree of realism [in Aeschylus and Sophocles] than in much of the work of Euripides, whose tendency is to reduce the legendary heroes and heroines to a more everyday level both in thought and in speech, so that there is less room for distinction between them and the characters of humbler status."[66] Similarly, students of Old Comedy have not failed to contrast the exuberant characterization of non-Greeks and speakers of other Greek dialects with the surprising fact "that comedy did not exploit the humorous potentialities of solecism and malapropism in the language of slaves or illiterate citizens ... even the Sausage-seller of *Knights,* whose hold on reading and writing is shaky (188–9), speaks as well as anyone else."[67] That Old Comedy was capable of such realism is shown by its use of non-standard Attic to characterize prominent real-life Athenian politicians like Cleophon and Hyperbolus when the comic poets wished to intimate their foreign birth or poor education. Non-standard Attic was also used to mock the high social pretensions of real-life celebrities like Alcibiades. The odd thing is that sociolect, which was freely used to (mis)represent specific (élite) individuals, was avoided in the linguistic representation of social groups within the polis.[68]

New Comedy, by contrast, offers the fullest and freest dramatic representation of sociolect in the traditional dramatic genres. Plutarch, indeed, found Aristophanes' use of language completely inept in contrast with Menander's genius for discriminating the language appropriate to each age, gender, class, and profession.[69] Unlike Aristophanes, Menander was careful to mark the language of slaves and working-class characters with obscenity, frequent oaths, vivid, colorful, colloquial, or technical language, and, especially in the case of poor rustics, laconic, syntactically disjointed, or rhetorically inept speech.[70] Conversely, however – and, once again, in total contrast with Old Comedy – New Comedy shows little interest in portraying foreign speech, even despite the fact that many plays are set outside Athens or revolve around non-Athenian characters. The one notable exception seems to prove the rule: in Menander's *Aspis* a character puts on a Doric accent, but only because he is pretending to be a doctor: the dialect sooner characterizes the working-class professional than the foreigner.[71]

The history of dramatic costume and gesture shows a similar pattern of developing realism combined with a highly selective and shifting focus. The best evidence is provided by comic costume. Barring props and clothing, Old Comic costume allowed no closer social distinctions than male and female, old and young, citizen and foreigner (though specific individuals received portrait masks). The comic *somation* created a uniform body for all Old Comic characters, male or female.[72] The comic *somation*, with its enlarged breast and buttocks that suggest a female body, and its pot-belly and phallus that signal a male body, was of cultic origin, but had the very practical consequence of allowing the actor to change gender simply by changing mask and clothing (see, for example, FIGURE 2.1).[73] The main determinant of gender was whether or not the *chiton* revealed the phallus (though more respectable male characters might also cover up with a cloak (*himation*)).[74] The iconographic evidence shows that a more naturalistic costume developed over the course of the fourth century BC, but, significantly, at different rates and to different degrees, depending on the sociological status of the character involved. The phallus, padding, and the more grotesque facial features of the traditional comic masks become markers of social inferiority. They disappear first (ca. 350 BC) in the costume of the young man of good family who becomes the focal point of audience sympathy. Some time later, old men (of the sort who in New Comedy are normally of the leisure class or wealthy merchants) acquire decent shin-length tunics, shed all their body padding, beyond a residue around the belly, and lose the more grotesque of their facial features. At the other end of the social hierarchy, slaves always retained pot-bellies, though, by the late fourth century BC, there was a general reduction in the volume of body padding and especially the (for males) improbably prominent breasts and buttocks. Similarly, though the slave's tunic grew just long enough that the phallus was not normally visible, it was still short enough to expose the (now smaller) genitals when the slave adopted a seated position, and short enough that the phallus could easily be withdrawn for the purpose of an occasional joke.[75]

The physiognomy of the free working-class males in New Comedy was carefully positioned somewhere between the poles of upper-class decency and servile deformity. Parasites (a "profession" in later comedy) often, soldiers and pimps sometimes, and cooks generally retained bellies. The tunic of parasites, cooks, farmers, and soldiers is shorter than that of élite characters. Moreover, the distorted features of fifth-century comic masks, which differed only in terms of sex, age, or ethnicity, became highly differentiated in the later fourth century in conformity with currently fashionable physiognomic ideas. For example, the toadies and parasites (i.e. free unemployed dependants of the élite families) have a hook nose that is said to denote shamelessness, a short neck that indicates treachery, raised eyebrows to show malevolence, and to these the actor added hunched shoulders to indicate an "unfree" disposition.[76] His semi-servile status is further emphasized by his broken ears (frequently boxed by his patron) and the strigil and oil bottle that serve as his regular attributes (he uses them to rub down his patron). In this world, an undistorted body was the privilege of the free, and freedom meant the economic independence of the leisure class.

Though New Comedy also admits foreign physiognomies, they are only visible in the masks of slaves and working-class characters. Of the latter category, the best attested is the foreign cook called the "Cicada" (*Tettix*), who has an African physiognomy. He appears in the Mytilene mosaic of *Samia*, FIGURE 5.1 (the description of the mask by Pollux is a precise fit for the image), but there is nothing in his language in the text of that play that would allow us to guess that he is not Greek. Even so, "the monuments make it clear that the foreign cook [i.e. the Cicada] was a far less common – or conceivably less interesting – character in the plays than his native fellow tradesman."[77] Similarly, the other foreign characters, the "Sicilian" parasite and the foreign "Portrait-Like" masks, both attested by Pollux, are still more rare, if they appear at all, in the monuments.[78] New Comic costume, like New Comic language, showed little interest in ethnicity for its own sake, and used foreign physiognomy primarily as a marker of social status.

The history of tragic costume, though much more elusive, seems consistent with this pattern. For fifth-century tragic costume and gesture we must rely on Aristophanes and Aristotle to capture some the sense of scandal that accompanied the leveling of the tragic hero's dignity when Euripides dressed him in rags and Kallippides portrayed him with the gestures of commoners. By the mid-fourth century, however, the iconographic evidence shows that the costumes of the non-heroic caste, of tragic messengers, for example, are clearly differentiated from the growing magnificence of the masks and costumes of heroes. From about this time there is also a concern to use gesture to mark "respectability" and to distinguish the restrained, graceful and inexpressive gestures of heroes from the loud and busy movements of social inferiors.[79]

Conclusion

In seeking an explanation for the anomalous development of ancient realism we should recall the self-consciously political and ideological terms with which ancient contemporaries expressed their attitudes toward the growth in acting realism (as discussed in the first section of this chapter). When Kallippides mimicked the language and behavior of lower-class women, or imitated the manners of real beggars in performing the part of a king reduced to mendicancy, he did much more than offend against good taste. He uncovered deep divisions in the Athenian body politic about both the constitution of reality and the etiquette of its representation. We find evidence of the same divisions not only in conservative hostility to performance realism, but in the partiality and gaps in "realist" representations. Aeschylus experimented with the means of distinguishing characters both by class and by ethnicity. For Sophocles, the most important distinction was the horizontal division between the heroes and the lower classes, and relatively little attention was paid to the vertical divisions between different ethnicities and linguistic groups. Euripides and Aristophanes, by contrast, are much more interested in representing the vertical divisions between Athenians and non-Athenians and even go so far as to erase the horizontal divisions between strata within Athenian society.

Within the context of the political and ideological polarization of Athens during the time of the "radical democracy" in Athens, the debate surrounding Kallippides can now be seen to have less to do with an opposition between "realist" and "idealist" aesthetics, than with two opposed concepts of the real, one belonging to a conservative, residually aristocratic-hierarchic mentality, the other to an emergent democratic-egalitarian mentality. The anecdotes with which we began this investigation criticize Euripides and the younger generation of actors for erasing the horizontal division separating tragic heroes from characters of low social status. The language of Euripidean and Aristophanic performance in the last decades of the fifth century tended toward social realism in the representation of common speech, but this produced no "slice of life," since the diversity of language within the polis was misrepresented as a homogeneous common speech without social distinctions. The emergent aesthetic was a realism limited by the perspective of the democratic citizen whose "other" was an outsider, a foreigner, or possibly a woman. But he shunned the linguistic representation of social difference within the citizen body, and even within the resident population. This was a distinction that appealed, rather, to anti-democratic or conservative élites who readily equated the cultural difference between élite and mass with that between citizen and slave.[80] The erasure of social difference stands in stark contrast to the growing realism in the linguistic portraiture of women and foreigners (abetted doubtless by the sexist and xenophobic tendencies of Athenian democratic ideology).

Both trends left their mark on later dramatic performance. Though Kallippides' techniques were imitated by later actors, his contribution seems generally to have been contained within the framework of the more conservative aesthetic. Our evidence suggests that Kallippides' later imitators tended to raise rather than lower the profile of the heroic caste by using his gestural realism to mark the mannerisms of low characters within the world of tragedy.

The élite aesthetic came to dominate comedy as the status of the comic genre began to rise within the dramatic hierarchy. The homogenizing tendencies of Old Comic linguistic portraiture of the citizen classes was reversed by Menander's style of New Comedy, which paid much closer attention to sociolect and idiolect, particularly in the characterization of slaves and working-class professions.

This change is often ascribed to widespread changes in political structure, theatrical organization, and spectatorship at the time of Demetrius of Phaleron (317–307 BC). The renewed focus upon the realistic depiction of difference within the social composition of the polis certainly brought dramatic representation in closer harmony with the viewpoint of a new governing élite, defined by wealth and breeding (though it appropriated many of the values and attitudes of the early fifth-century aristocracy). The artifacts, however, suggest that the representation of social difference in costume began two or three decades earlier than Demetrius and indicate a more complex causal relationship between the ideological and political changes that occurred in Athens in the later fourth century BC.

Notes

1 This chapter draws upon material from my "Kallippides on the Floor-Sweepings: the Limits of Realism in Classical Acting and Performance Styles," pp. 127–147 in Pat Easterling and Edith Hall, eds. *Greek and Roman Actors: Aspects of an Ancient Profession* (2002) © Cambridge University Press 2002, reproduced with permission.

2 Arist. *Po.* 1461b 34–5.

3 *Vita Aesch.* 15.

4 Arist. *Po.* 1461b 26–62a 14. I italicize important phrases. "Excess of gesture" is the rendering of Pickard-Cambridge 1968.174.

5 "Ape" in the late fifth century BC was a colloquial synonym for *panourgos*, namely someone who knows no limits to his behavior: see Taillardat 1962.19, 227–8; Eire 1997.202.

6 Cf. the puzzlement of Lucas 1968.251 on the expression in the *Poetics* translated above as "imitates everything:" "ἡ ἅπαντα μιμουμένη: a strange phrase, since it is the business of a mimetic art to imitate. Possibly *mimesis* here is impersonation … In the light of what follows the meaning seems restricted to over-playing of parts by actors."

7 E.g. Dacier 1692.505: *les gestes des femmes deshonêtes et corrumpues*; Butcher 1929.109: "representing degraded women;" Potts 1962.60: "imitate women who are not respectable;" Hutton 1982.78: "their women were anything but ladies." This interpretation of Aristotle is doubtless influenced by Aristophanes' portrayal of Euripidean heroines as "whores" (*Frogs* 1043), to say nothing of his Muse (*Frogs* 1305–63), and of Euripides himself as an aged procuress (*Thesm.* 1172–1231), a comic distortion of characters like Phaedra's nurse in *Hippolytus*.

8 Cf. in particular Aristotle's use of ἀνελεύθερος. For *eleutheros* meaning "leisure-class," as more frequently *eleutherios*, see the comments by Wood 1996.129–31; Csapo 2005.302–4. This usage is most common in discussions of aesthetics, where it is less likely than in political or ethical discussions to generate confusion with the technical sociological sense of "free," antonym to "slave" (see Arist. *Rhet.* 1367a 30,

Pol. 1341b 13, 1342a 19, *Prob.* 918b 21). If Aristotle simply meant "slave women," he would have written *doulas*.

9   Arist. *Rhet.* 1403b 31. Pl. *Laws* 700e 6–701a 3. Modern scholars who insert the anecdote in this devolutionary framework include Haigh 1907.277 and Lesky 1983.401–2. Vetta 1995.66–7 alone correctly reads the anecdote as evidence of the development of gestural realism.

10   Cf. Chapter 3, pp. 104–7. The view that drama declined in the fourth century BC because of greedy actors and "*theatrokratia*, that tyranny of the spectators" is repeated most notably by Ghiron-Bistagne 1974.1335. Wallace 1997 has a partly (and in my view excessively) sympathetic discussion of the *theatrokratia* theory and its reception in modern scholarship (on his own evidence, the audience of the fifth century BC differed little from that of the fourth). The theater did not, in fact, degenerate in the fourth century BC (cf. Easterling 1993).

11   There are difficulties with the text. Kassel and Austin (*PCG* F 490) print the reading of the manuscripts of Pollux ὥσπερ ἐν Καλλιπίδῃ ἐπὶ τοῦ κορήματος καθέζομαι χαμαί, which must mean "I sit on the ground upon the floor-sweepings as in *Kallippides*," a reference to the play *Kallippides* by Aristophanes' contemporary Strattis. I prefer Brunck's emendation which is printed by Kock (fr. 474): ... ὥσπερει Καλλιπίδης etc. "like [the actor] Kallippides ..." For the metatheatrical (and paratragic) reference to tragic actors, cf. Eubulus *PCG* F 134 "I will do everything in the style of Nikostratos," presumably said by a comic messenger in reference to the tragic actor Nikostratos' famed skill in delivering messenger speeches. Either text supports the present argument. With Kassel and Austin's text we would have to imagine a character in Aristophanes' play (which, judging by the title, may have been about the theater) who also appeared in an undignified posture in Strattis' play, and this character would surely be none other than the comic butt of the play, Kallippides himself.

12   Hom. *Od.* 7.160. For the *Telephus*, see Chapter 1, pp. 3–4.

13   See Chapter 3, p. 104.

14   Cf. Dover 1993.32: "Comparison with *Clouds* indicates that Aristophanes had assimilated the contrast between Aeschylus and Euripides to the generalized contrast between old and new ..."

15   Pl. *Gorg.* 515e says that it was the demagogue Pericles who taught the Athenians to chatter.

16   Dover 1993.22. Cf. Ar. *Frogs* 1492 with Dover 1993 *ad loc.*; Arist. *Or.* 46.133.

17   Ar. *Clouds* 931, 1002, 1053.

18   Ar. *PCG* F 392, *Frogs* 839.

19   Athen. 428f; Chamaeleon F 40a Wehrli.

20   *Frogs* 718–37. See Dover 1993.75 who notes that the advice is set in cautiously ambivalent terms.

21   Thuc. 8.73.

22   Ar. *Frogs* 939–43, 1058 (Dover's translation of ἀνθρωπείως, 1993.325).

23   See the discussion by Halliwell 1986.135–6, n. 39.

24   Though it might have satisfied Plato: cf. *Rep.* 472d.

25 Arist. *Po.* 1451b 16–19.
26 Arist. *Po.* ch. 15.
27 Arist. *Po.* 1454b 10–13.
28 Arist. *Po.* ch. 9.
29 Soph. *TrGF* T 53b.
30 Soph. *TrGF* T 172.
31 See, for example, the excellent discussion of tragic time and space by Fantuzzi 1990.
32 Pavlovskis 1977; Jouan 1983; Damen 1989. Ringer 1998 speaks confidently of "non-naturalistic delivery" in the ancient theater. Their views are criticized by Vetta 1995.68–78 and Sifakis 1995.
33 Pickard-Cambridge 1968.135–53.
34 Sifakis 1995.
35 This is not to diminish the importance of the Lenaea, where a comic actor's prize was awarded from about 432 BC.
36 Handley 1985.393–6.
37 Pickard-Cambridge 1968.154; Gomme and Sandbach 1973.18; Revermann 2006a.129–32, 141–2.
38 Marshall 1997.
39 E.g. Men. *Sam.* 256–7, *Sik.* 257–8, 264–6, *Mis.* 698–700, 799 (Arnott). The sparse use of "quotatives" in direct speech is a distinctive feature of Menander's drama (Bers 1997.117–18). Cf. Handley 2002; Nünlist 2002 (with emphasis on precedents in fifth- and fourth-century comedy).
40 Quint. *Inst.* 11.3.91. Cf. Plut. *Mor.* 711c, Luc. *Nigr.*11.
41 Colvin 1999.265–95.
42 Vetta 1995.77.
43 Plut. *Mor.* 18b–c; cf. Pl. *Rep.* 397a–b, *Laws* 669c–d.
44 Pl. *Rep.* 397a–c. Further evidence for tragedy is hard to find, but it is perhaps noteworthy that Dickin 1999 finds that tragic messengers usually use direct quotation for characters played by the same actor (presumably to get the voice just right?). The scholiast to *Orestes* 176 (a play whose musical notation may have survived till the Roman period) informs us that Electra's monody is "sung on the top and very high." Cf. Hall 2002.10. I have not seen Dickin 2009.
45 Arist. *Rhet.* 1404b 24–5.
46 Arist. *Rhet.* 1404a 20–5; Del Corno 1979.280–1.
47 Devine and Stephens 1981, 1983; Cropp and Fick 1985.
48 See Chapter 3.
49 For Menander's individualization of speech: Sandbach 1970, Del Corno 1975, Arnott 1995.
50 Bakhtin 1981.130–46. Cf. Duncan 2006.
51 Bain 1984 (Menander); McClure 1995 (Euripides); Sommerstein 1995 (drama in general); McClure 1999 (drama in general); Willi 2003.157–97 (Aristophanes).
52 The fragments of Hipponax contain Lydian and Phrygian words. Since he is an Ephesian, this could equally be characterized as colloquialism. See Colvin 1999. 39–54, esp. 50–2.

53 Hall 1989.76–84; Hall 1996.22–3; cf. Colvin 1999.77. The high incidence of words with long alphas may also represent an Aeschylean attempt to imitate the aural impact of Iranian: see Morenilla-Talens 1989.

54 Hall 1989.120, 118; cf. Colvin 1999.78.

55 Bacon 1961.64.

56 Phrygian and Persian words appear in *Shepherds* (*TrGF* F 515, 519, 520), *Wedding of Helen* (F 183), both of which may be satyrplays – see Heynen and Krumeich 1993.391–3 – and *Troilus* (F 631, 634), which is more probably but not certainly a tragedy. Eastern coloring is also attested in *Prisoners of War* and *Triptolemos*, where the word "Ionian" was used for "Greek" after the Persian manner (F 56, 617). See Colvin 1999.81–3.

57 Hall 1989.119–21, 126–7.

58 A. *Cho.* 563–4. See Dover 1987.240 *contra* Stevens 1945.96. It would be a disturbing anomaly if Orestes' lines were delivered in Phocian dialect despite our text: see Colvin 1999.75–6; Revermann 2006a.54–5.

59 Colvin 1999.295, 302–6. Cf. Willi 2003.198–225; Hall 2006.225–54.

60 Stevens 1945.95; cf. Arnott 1995.160–1. According to West 1990.5, the use of colloquialism as a means of characterization appears to be a diachronic development even within Aeschylus' oeuvre, and does not appear in any significant form before the *Oresteia*: "minor characters in the earlier plays do not seem to be treated to these touches of the demotic," but "on the contrary … seem to speak with a rather stiff formality." For colloquialism in Aeschylus, see also Zangrando 1997.200.

61 Stevens 1937.183; cf. Zangrando 1997.200–1; Petrovic 2003.

62 Stevens 1945.95.

63 Fraenkel 1977.34–7, 44–5, 49, 52, 61, 64–5, 69–72; Rossi 1989. Resolution is sometimes also used by Sophocles to mark vulgar and undignified characters: see, for example, Webster 1970.161; Fraenkel 1977.75–6. Disjointed syntax usually shows flustered or exasperated speech (e.g. *OT* 350–3, 603–4), but occasionally seems to be employed as a caste marker to show simplicity or naivety (e.g. *OT* 1135–7).

64 Seaford 1984.47–8; Seidensticker 1999.15–16.

65 Stevens 1945.97. Cf. Stevens 1937.182–3. The incidence of colloquialism does vary between plays, being proportionately much higher in *Orestes* than elsewhere: Stevens 1976.64–5. Stevens' collection of Euripidean colloquialism is now supplemented by Collard 2005. For Aristophanes, see the following notes.

66 Stevens 1945.95.

67 Dover 1987.19, cf. 241–4. See also Halliwell 1990; Del Corno 1997; Colvin 1999.295; Willi 2002a.

68 Colvin 1999.281–94. One exception may be the precious speech of the upper-class youth, Pheidippides (Ar. *Clouds* 872–3), but the passage is not easy to interpret. A passage of the comic poet Plato's *Metics* may be another, but there is no reason to suppose that the chorus was composed of metics, rather than, say, citizen *komodoumenoi* abused as "metics," nor any reason to suppose that the solecism of *PCG* Plato F 83 was spoken by one of them.

69 Plut. *Comparison of Aristophanes and Menander*, *Mor.* 853d–e.

70 See esp. Arnott 1995, though his catalogue is by individual rather than type.
71 Men. *Asp*. 430–64. The chief medical schools were in Doric Sicily and Cos. It is not known whether Plautus or Alexis is responsible for the pseudo-Punic in *Poenulus* 930–49, though Plautus is the more likely candidate.
72 Green 1994.37.
73 For the cultic and Dionysian origins of this bisexual body-costume, see Csapo and Miller 2007b.13–21, and for Dionysian sexual ambivalence, Csapo 1997a.
74 See the discussion on FIGURES 2.3 and 2.5 in Chapter 2, pp. 54, 61–2.
75 E.g. *MNC* 1AT 3. For possible remnants of New Comic phallus humor in Roman comedy, see Marshall 2006.62–5. It is not clear that the phallus ever disappeared entirely from comic costume. For the general development, see Green 2006.
76 For the description of the mask and attributes, see Pollux 4.148, 120, with *MNC* vol. 1, pp. 22–3. The physiognomic "readings" appear in [Arist.] *Physiognomonica* 811a 4 (hunched shoulders), 17 (short neck), 34–5 (hooknose).
77 *MNC* vol. 1, p. 32.
78 *MNC* vol. 1, p. 25.
79 Green 2002.105–11.
80 See esp. Raaflaub 1983 and Raaflaub 1984.305–13.

5

Cooking with Menander
Slices from the Ancient Home Entertainment Industry?

A superficial survey of the modern archaeological literature might give you the impression that Menander, rather than being an early Hellenistic comic poet, was one of the beautiful people of the Middle to Late Empire, a kind of ancient Aristotle Onassis or Dodi al Fayed, with houses in all the best places: there are so-called Houses of Menander in Pompeii, in Antioch, and on the island of Lesbos, at Mytilene.[1]

The most important for students of ancient drama, for any number of reasons, is the House of Menander at Mytilene, although here the allusion to Dodi al Fayed is misleading. The house is that of a provincial bourgeois, not one of the jet-setting élite. In the dining room or triclinium, there is a mosaic floor with ten panels, seven of which illustrate scenes from comedies of Menander (FIGURE 5.1).[2] All face the *lectus medius,* or central couch. The *lectus medius* was normally occupied by the owner of the house and his most distinguished guest. This is the privileged position from which to view the floor. The floor as a whole was never photographed – the excavators were anxious to get it safely under lock and key and so uncovered, photographed, and removed into storage each panel one by one – so my crude montage is the first attempt to understand the overall pattern.[3] From left to right, top to bottom, all neatly labeled, there are: a portrait bust of Menander, followed by Act 2 from Menander's *Plokion,* then a scene from Plato's *Phaedo,* then a bust, with comic mask, of the comic Muse, Thalia, then Act 3 of Menander's *Samia,* then the opening scene of Menander's *Synaristosai,* then Act 2 of Menander's *Epitrepontes,* then Act 2 of Menander's *Theophoroumene,* then Act 4 of Menander's *Encheiridion,* then Act 5 of Menander's *Messenia.* In the adjoining portico, that can be reached by a small door in the east corner is another mosaic floor with five panels (FIGURE 5.2).[4] These are to be viewed from the open courtyard to the south: from left to right we have a comic mask, Act 3 of Menander's *Kybernetai,* an unidentified act from Menander's *Leukadia,* Act 5 from Menander's Misoumenos, and Act 2 from Menander's *Phasma.* Later clearing of the west side of the portico revealed that the comic mask began

Figure 5.1   Reconstruction of the mosaic floor of the triclinium of the House of Menander in Mytilene. Photos courtesy of the editors of *Antike Kunst.*

a series of three mosaic masks, all oriented in the same way, followed by a maritime scene.[5]

All of these panels are of some interest to theater historians, even, as we will see, the panel from Plato's *Phaedo,* which appears to keep such odd company, for, to our eyes at least, there is a world of difference between this very sober philosophical dialogue and comedy. It did not take long for scholars to propose explanations for the novelty of this floor pattern. The explanations characteristically involve inferences about the recreational and intellectual habits of the homeowner. He had, they guessed, a great passion for the theater.[6] Mytilene's theater, they observed, was only an (unremarkable) half kilometer's distance. Or the owner was bookish: the *Phaedo* panel was an obscure allusion to some unknown event he had read about in the life of the comic poet, possibly an illustration from the very book, or maybe it was allusion to the philosophical character of Menander's art.[7] Or maybe the owner had a grand passion for theater and a 91 percent less grand passion for philosophy.[8] Perhaps the man was a reactionary pagan

Figure 5.2 Reconstruction of the mosaic floor of the portico of the House of Menander in Mytilene. Photos courtesy of the editors of *Antike Kunst*.

making, as Berczelly suggested, "a declaration of affection for and allegiance to the philosophical and literary traditions of the past, in the face of victorious Christianity."[9] Whatever the case for the homeowner's strange choice, commentators were and are still generally agreed that these mosaics reproduce in some way the homeowner's enthusiasm for performances of comedy, and since such enthusiasms must imply actual experience of the object of enthusiasm, these mosaics therefore give good evidence for the life of the theater at Mytilene during the Late Roman Empire.[10] Indeed these panels have been treated as virtual windows onto performances seen by the mosaicist and admired by the master of the house.

It is after all not so odd to find evidence of Menandromania even in a small provincial town in the late Roman Empire. Soon after Menander's death, if not during his lifetime, his comedies became literary classics. Statistics from papyrus-finds make Menander the third most purchased or copied poet after Homer and Euripides. He would probably be second, if the ascription of anonymous fragments of New Comedy were a little easier. Bits of Menander's plays survive in over a hundred papyri dating from the third century BC to the seventh century AD. But his popularity was highest in the first three centuries AD, whence come over 60 percent of them. Menander's plays were school classics. More often than Euripides, Menander was copied in writing exercises in elementary schools, quoted in writing exercises of the grammar schools, and performed and imitated in the rhetorical schools. More critics of the first to third centuries paired Homer with Menander than with Euripides. We know of eight ancient commentaries on Menander's plays. The evidence of ancient art gives an even more favorable assessment of the poet: no other dramatist – indeed, no other author – was so often portrayed (about 80 portraits, many more than Sophocles and roughly twice as many as Homer and Euripides).[11] No other dramatist's plays were so often illustrated. But the statistical curve for representations of plays by Menander otherwise resembles the papyrus statistics for his popularity among readers. Of about 180 illustrations or extracts from illustrations of Menander's plays listed by Green and Seeberg, some 75 percent come from the first three centuries AD.[12]

The House of Menander at Mytilene is probably a full century later. Although the excavators proposed a date around 270 AD, stylistic analysis of the mosaics sooner suggests a date in the later fourth century AD.[13] If the date offers no obstacle to our portrait of the homeowner as an aficionado of Menander, it might raise some doubts about taking his floor decoration as evidence for the continued performance of tragedy or comedy. Despite all the proofs of Menander's popularity, we have no secure evidence of a performance of Menander in any theater after the early second century AD.[14] Public performances of any comedy or tragedy are attested by inscriptions and literary sources only as late as the early third century AD and by papyrus to the end of the third century AD.[15] You will look in vain in Stephanis' list of ancient stage artists for anyone who calls himself a *komoidos* or *tragoidos* after that date.[16] So it does make a difference for the history of the reception of ancient drama whether or not we believe artifacts showing scenes of comedy or tragedy are in fact evidence for contemporary performances of tragedy or comedy. It is a still more important question, if we allow the evidence of extracts from such scenes. For though the Mytilene mosaics are among the latest illustrations of scenes of comedy in performance, we will see that there are extracts from such comic scenes that appear in art as late as the sixth century AD. Could the evidence of art permit us to extend the life of the reperformance of classical drama in antiquity by another three centuries? Let's approach this question by first considering whether the performances here illustrated really do refer to the theater, and if so in what way.

That these scenes are "theatrical," there can be little doubt. They definitely show actors acting in masks and full costume, with props, and sometimes we even get a glimpse of stagey backdrops (better represented on, for example, FIGURE 5.8 (below) than in Mytilene). Yet almost all of our dramatic scenes (as well as our portraits of Menander) come from the walls and floors of private houses, not from the decoration of public buildings and not from theaters.[17] Most of the houses are considerably more sumptuous than the House of Menander at Mytilene. Typical of the kind is one of the other houses "of Menander" from Daphne in Antioch. Daphne is described as "gracious and shaded with trees," a suburb "where élite citizens made their homes." And this particular house is described as one of the most luxurious in all Antioch.[18] Among its many dining spaces there is a smallish room with an unusual portrait of Menander dated to between 250 and 275 AD (FIGURE 5.3).[19] This is not exactly a scene of drama in performance, but it is clearly related to our theme, and provides a helpful vantagepoint from which to examine our problem.

For reasons already mentioned, it is not surprising that a wealthy and well-educated élite of third-century Antioch might want to portray Menander in his dining room. But the way he does it is more unusual and interesting. Menander is not portrayed, as elsewhere, on a relief in the Vatican for example, in the act of creating his dramas (FIGURE 5.4). There are no masks or scrolls in hand. Instead, we find him on a dining couch. For all we know – the central patch of the mosaic is modern reconstruction – he may have had a cup of wine in his hand. And there are other indications to show that Menander is not exactly at the office – unlike the Vatican relief which Bieber entitles "Menander in His Studio."[20] On the Daphne mosaic Menander has his mistress, the prostitute Glykera, on the couch beside him. That a man of wealth and education should put a picture of Menander on his

Figure 5.3 Mosaic emblema from House of Menander, Daphne, 250–275 AD, Princeton y1940–435. Courtesy, Princeton University Art Museum. Gift of the Committee for the Excavation of Antioch to Princeton University. Photo: Bruce M. White.

Figure 5.4 Marble relief, first century AD copy of a Hellenistic original, Vatican 9985 (ex Lateran). Photo: akg-images/Werner Forman.

floor is readily intelligible, but it is not so readily intelligible why his passion for theater should be expressed iconographically by the representation of Menander as a guest at a cocktail party.

As with the Mytilene mosaics, early scholarship instinctively grasped at biographical explanations. Studniczka, at least, had explained the Vatican relief on the left through researching the pseudo-biographical letters of Menander, written by Alciphron, to discover a passage in which Menander's mistress Glykera claimed to prepare his masks and costumes for him. The lady to the right in the relief is therefore, in his view, Glykera fetching masks.[21] But despite an extensive search, Friend despaired of finding a similar factoid of Menandrian biography to explain the Daphne mosaic.[22] With dismay, he simply noted that it was a variation of a scheme normally depicting Dionysus.

Let us have a closer look at the Daphne mosaic. Menander may not be in his studio, but he is not entirely given to the sensual pleasures of the banquet either. The table in front of him, which is partly reconstructed, probably held not food, but another mask. The woman at the end of his couch is not a second trollop, but the personification of Comedy. And she bears not evening dress, but the costume and – in her hand – the mask of a comic old man. In front of Comedy is another mask on top of a box containing papyrus rolls. Also unusual is the location of this mosaic – not in the library or study, but on the floor of a room which "appears to have been dedicated to dining and entertainment."[23] The costume, three masks, one for each person, and the box of papyri, suggest that they are about to entertain us with a performance of a scene from one of Menander's plays.

Rather than digging for obscure and unknowable biographical data about the artist, patron, or subject of the mosaic representation, we should look to a social practice that has, until fairly recently, been ignored by art and theater historians. I refer to the practice of mounting dramatic performances for the entertainment of one's guests at a formal dinner or symposium. Though rooted in the culture of the royal court of Macedon, this practice first became relatively widespread in the Late Hellenistic and Late Republican period.[24] By widespread, however, I do not mean popular: the custom of private performances of comedy and tragedy appears to have been limited to the political and cultural élite of Rome and the Empire. In the most conspicuous form of this custom, very wealthy owners of palaces and villas would mount performances of tragedy, comedy, pantomime, or mime on their own private stage, often for the entertainment of hundreds of guests at a time, and normally with trained professional, often even star actors. Less ambitious private performances were also, of course, possible. At the time of Trajan, Pliny speaks of being entertained by comedians when dining alone with his wife or with a few friends, but throughout its long history, we have little evidence for private drama below what we might call the imperial governing class.

There are good reasons for connecting our frescoes, mosaics, and sculptures showing scenes of dramatic performance, not with the theater, but with private drama. *First of all*, we should note that there is a rough but reassuring contemporaneity between the spread of private drama and the appearance in domestic art of scenes of drama. Theatrical motifs generally, though they may appear in room decoration earlier, only really become popular in the Late Republic and under the Empire. *Secondly*, theatrical motifs and especially mosaics, paintings, and reliefs of tragic or comic performances are normally found, as stated, in domestic art, and by preference in the decoration of the public rooms of the house and especially the dining rooms and colonnades around the interior courtyards where private theater entertainments normally took place. *Thirdly*, we are assured by Plutarch that Menander was a clear favorite for symposium and dinner entertainment, at least at the beginning of the second century AD. *Fourthly*, Pliny, Plutarch and, a century later, Athenaeus attest a fashion for performances of Platonic dialogues at private dinner parties.[25] This highbrow entertainment probably had its roots in the philosophical mime, a form of drama known even in the Republican theater: Cicero mentions a play based on an imaginary and highly anachronistic dinner conversation between Menander, Euripides, Socrates, and Epicurus.[26] Surely it is this vogue which accounts for the presence of a scene from *Phaedo*, among the scenes of Menander in Mytilene.

There is something then to recommend the hypothesis that domestic theatrical decorations allude in some way to private theater. The hypothesis is not an old one: I have been able to trace the first suggestion of such a link to T. P. Wiseman in the 1980s.[27] David Parrish and I independently argued the case more fully in the 1990s.[28] More recently Kondoleon and Huskinson have argued that the Daphne mosaic relates directly to plays of Menander performed or recited in the dining room.[29] George Harrison has even suggested that the triclinium in the house of Menander in Mytilene served as a kind of menu from which honored guests would choose their evening entertainment.[30] That there is some relationship between domestic theater art and the practice of domestic theater is an attractive hypothesis and in general a far better explanation for the presence of such comic scenes in dining rooms than speculation about the personal psychology and life history of people known to us only by the floors and foundations of their houses. But even with this solution, the old problem remains. The artifacts may have some general connection with the practice of private performances but are they specific evidence for performances in the spaces decorated with the paintings and mosaics? Do the Mytilene mosaics provide evidence for private performances of Menander in the late fourth century AD? Or are they evidence of any contemporary performance? Almost all those who study this material assume an answer in the affirmative, but the assumption is more problematic than they are generally able to recognize or willing to admit.

Though scenes of dramatic performance first appear on house walls in the Late Hellenistic and Late Republican period, the connection between the imagery of drama and symposia is much older. And in its earlier form, the connection between drama and symposium is imaginary and symbolic and has little to do with social practice. The particular scheme we find in the Antioch mosaic could be said to go back to Attic and West Greek art of the late fifth and fourth centuries BC. Usually, it is Dionysus who sits on the dining couch and is surrounded by dramatic performers. The iconographic type begins with choregic reliefs that show Dionysus on a couch, often with a woman at his feet holding a mask, or with masks on the wall or held by figures near the couch.[31] Most often, Dionysus is being approached by worshippers who are clearly marked as chorusmen by their costume or marked as the choregos or a representative of the chorus either by inscription or by the carrying of a mask (FIGURE 1.7). The Pronomos Vase notoriously adapts this dedicatory imagery (FIGURE 1.9). Here Dionysus, still on a couch which he shares with two women, one at his feet carrying a mask, presides over the victory festivities of a group of performers in his sanctuary. J. R. Green has shown how South Italian pottery picked up on this imagery to combine masks, actors, dining couches, and symposium entertainments, in a powerful evocation of the two realms of Dionysus, theater and symposium, in images of the actors' victory parties.[32] From here it was a fairly small step to reverse the original imagery: in the more anthropocentric Hellenistic world, instead of the choregos leading his chorus to pay tribute to Dionysus, it is the victorious poet or performer who reclines on a kline with a girl at his feet (and masks under the couch) while Dionysus approaches leading his chorus of satyrs to bind the poet's head with a victory ribbon (FIGURE 5.5).[33] From here it is an even smaller step to reach our point of departure: the image of the poet reclining with women and masks (FIGURE 5.3).

The image of the actor reclining to drink in the flush of victory becomes an archetype of celebration, joyful unwinding after enormous exertion. Even a third realm of Dionysus was added to the mix, the realm of death and the afterlife. Vasepaintings of choreuts and actors celebrating a dramatic victory served as grave goods since Dionysus, as god of the mysteries, as well as of wine and theater, linked life's brief moments of triumph and repose with the more lasting triumph and repose of death. By the second century BC theater motifs came to be used in the decoration of tombs as well as the dining rooms of private houses.

The evidence for continuity should not, however, blind us to the quantitative and qualitative changes in the art. From Late Hellenistic times, the villas of wealthy Greeks and Romans display imagery that more specifically evokes not sanctuary and celebration but theater: statues and portraits of poets and actors, frescoes of stage scenes, and especially the paintings, mosaics, and

Figure 5.5   Marble relief, Roman copy of Hellenistic original, Paris, Louvre 1606. © 2006 Musée du Louvre/D. Lebée et C. Déambrosis.

reliefs of scenes of drama in performance. The scenes of drama in performance are the most distinctly new item in the repertoire. We find them first in the main reception room of the House of the Comedians at Delos in the late second century BC.[34] Contemporary with these are the famous Dioskourides mosaics of Menander's *Synaristosai* and *Theophoroumene* which were later lifted from a floor in Samos and transported to Pompeii (FIGURES 5.6 and 5.7).[35] And it is from Late Republican and Early Imperial Pompeii and Herculaneum that we get the best impression of the popularity of scenes of drama in performance. The excavation of the cities buried by Vesuvius yielded more than thirty-five painted or mosaic scenes of drama in performance, to say nothing of the abundant masks, stage scenes, and portraits of actors and poets. This theater imagery functions very differently from the celebratory symbolism we found in earlier art. It evokes not the actors' victory celebration in the sanctuary, but the performance of plays. To this extent nothing hinders drawing a direct connection between the art and the practice of private drama. But there is another new aspect to this art, which we might describe by the term "classicism."

The dramatic imagery from Late Republican and Imperial houses follows strict rules of selection. Domestic art limits its theatrical imagery to the Classical genres of tragedy, comedy, and satyrplay. Yet this is at a time when the literary record makes it clear that mime and pantomime dominated the public stage – from these contemporary genres imagery is exceedingly rare or absent altogether.

Figure 5.6   Mosaic scene from Menander's *Synaristosai*, Dioskourides, 125–100 BC, Naples, Museo Nazionale 9987. Alinari Archives, Florence.

Indeed, this conservatism is particularly marked in the Greek East, where domestic art not only excludes pantomime and mime but eschews even such contemporary and popular entertainments as horse-racing, gladiators, and wild beast shows.[36] It appears, moreover, that the restriction is not only to the genres of tragedy and comedy, but to a very restricted canon of Classical authors. Contemporary authors are excluded altogether. Of some two hundred scenes of drama in performance in wall-painting, mosaics and reliefs, perhaps a third are identified by inscription or otherwise identifiable with confidence, and they are all plays of Euripides or Menander. There is every reason to think that all the as-yet-unidentified scenes also belong to plays by one of these authors.[37]

The spirit of classicism determines not just the subject matter of theatrical imagery, it determines the image itself. The scenes of dramatic classics which decorate domestic spaces are also artistic classics. Most if not all of the performance imagery goes back to famous paintings of the Early Hellenistic period. In a recent article, Axel Seeberg lays it down as a rule of thumb that: "the existence of two copies indicates an 'old master,' an original a good deal older than the copies."[38] In the case of comic scenes, we can often do better than just two copies.

Figure 5.7   Mosaic scene from Menander's *Theophoroumene*, Dioskourides, 125–100 BC, Naples, Museo Nazionale 9985. Alinari Archives, Florence.

The third edition of *Monuments Illustrating New Comedy (MNC)* estimates that a limited set of fifty-two comic scenes is copied and adapted by over one hundred and eighty artifacts. For example Menander's *Theophoroumene* is one of our most frequently illustrated plays. We find illustrations of it in fourth-century AD Mytilene (FIGURE 5.1), in second- or third-century AD Crete, in first-century AD Stabiae, and (two or three times) in first-century BC to first-century AD Pompeii.[39] But one of the Pompeian artifacts (FIGURE 5.7) was itself taken, probably robbed as plunder, from Greece, where it was created in the late second century BC. This is not the original either, as is shown by five terracotta copies of the two young men, some of which are likely to be earlier than the mosaic. On the basis of the copies, Rumpf dated the original to the early third century BC.[40] Indeed, Green has presented strong arguments for believing that the originals of most, if not all, of the other Menandrian scenes were a coherent series of large-scale Early-Hellenistic paintings or reliefs.[41]

In one case we have tangible proof of an early Hellenistic origin. A comic relief in Naples (FIGURE 5.8), perhaps of Imperial date, copies an original that served as a model for a cameo of about 100 BC (FIGURE 5.9), but the pair on the

Figure 5.8 Marble relief, first century AD copy of Early Hellenistic original, Naples, Museo Nazionale 6687. Courtesy, Soprintendenza Archeologica Napoli e Pompei.

Figure 5.9 Cameo, *c.*100 BC, Geneva 21133, © Musée d'art et d'histoire, Ville de Genève. Photo: Jean-Marc Yersin.

right of each scene, a drunken young man supported by his slave, was also copied by no less than seven terracotta figurines.[42] The earliest of these is certainly datable to before 280 BC, and J. R. Green would put it before 300 BC, which is well within Menander's own lifetime.[43] Indeed, a number of features in the style and selection of these scenes suggest that, behind most, if not all the scenes of comic and tragic performance in late Hellenistic and Imperial art there lies a single set of paintings depicting tragic and comic classics, Euripides (possibly Sophocles) and Menander, and that this set was produced about 280 BC, very soon after Menander's death if not before.

Other scenes from the House of Menander in Mytilene have copies: the *Synaristosai*, for example, the centerpiece of the triclinium mosaic (FIGURE 5.1), was a favorite, perhaps because it is a dramatic dining scene and so admirably suited as a decoration for dining rooms. The Mytilene version presents in inverse order the same characters that we find in the mosaic from Pompeii (FIGURE 5.6). The recent emergency excavations at Zeugma uncovered another copy, probably from the early decades of the third century AD. This copy, like that in Mytilene, formed the centerpiece of the dining room of a large provincial house.[44] Rumor has it that yet another copy has been found at Daphne.

The representations of scenes from tragedy and comedy thus display a subtle but general shift in purpose. The tragic, comic, and satyric imagery that adorned the sympotic vessels of Classical or earlier Hellenistic reception rooms functioned to create a Dionysiac ambiance, with a particular stress on the values of celebration and repose, such as we found on the vessels showing actors or chorusmen celebrating in the temple of Dionysus.[45] In the domestic art of the late Hellenistic to Roman period, theatrical motifs are less concerned to model the dining room after the temple of Dionysus than to signify the homeowner's adherence to classicism and the élite culture classicism implies.

The shift in emphasis from the Dionysiac to classicism in the first centuries BC and AD is nicely expressed by Roger Ling in a study of the art from the dining rooms of the houses of Pompeii.[46] Contrary to the pattern established in earlier Greek art, Ling determined that only a minority (though a sizeable minority) of Pompeian triclinia were decorated with Dionysiac themes. What does determine the choice of subjects for painting and mosaics is according to Ling a simple "appeal to the literary taste of educated diners."[47] Under the Roman Empire, domestic art showing scenes from Homer, Euripides, or Menander advertised standards of taste and a cultural attainment high above the common level. Scenes from tragedy or comedy thus have a double snob-appeal: they advertise the classicizing tastes of a cultural élite, whether in classics of drama or art; but they also allude to an activity, private drama, which was a plaything of the super-rich. In light of the copy tradition behind these dramatic scenes, I am inclined to doubt, however, that our wealthy bourgeois from Mytilene, or even his wealthier and less provincial counterpart in Antioch, actually had the kind of performance in their dining rooms that the paintings suggest.

Those who maintain that these illustrations give evidence of contemporary performance can point to literary and textual evidence for performances of mime or pantomime which continue on both the public and private stage until at least the sixth century AD.[48] Yet the evidence for even private performances of tragedy and comedy take us no later than the evidence for public theater. Literary and epigraphic sources only attest to *tragoedi* and *comoedi* at private functions up to the time of Hadrian, the first half of the second century AD.[49] We could push this date much later, to the end of the third century AD, if we understood better the function of various tragic and comic papyrus texts that have been called actors' texts or performance texts. Six of these have speaker assignments not to characters, such as "Moschion," "Laches," and "Daos," but to "First," "Second," and "Third," meaning the actors. It is often supposed that these were for actors performing on the public stage, but one of the latest, a second-century AD papyrus of New Comedy, includes notation for a fourth actor, which was never allowed in the Greek theater as we know it.[50] They are thus possible evidence for domestic performances, though performance in the schoolroom seems at least as likely: a letter of Libanius makes it clear that students of the *rhetor*, even in the fourth century, regularly gave dramatic readings of plays in the classroom; in fact he is elsewhere explicit that tragedy survived only in the classroom.[51]

Another worry I have about drawing too close a correspondence between art and social practice in the present case is the troubling fact that most of the rooms in which these artworks are found are simply too small to accommodate the kind of performance to which the artworks allude. Katharine Dunbabin points out that "the standard dining-room [of the Late Republic and Early Empire] is still designed for a *triclinium* of the traditional size, and allows only limited space for entertainers: a little music, recitation, a couple of dancers, but nothing really fancy."[52] And although larger and better appointed dining arrangements appeared in the later Empire, few of the decorated dining rooms sporting dramatic scenes are of the necessary scale and type. At Mytilene, for example, barely two meters separate the couches from the wall. Wealthy homeowners who did not have large dining rooms often provided meals and entertainments in the courtyard or in the garden.[53] For example, at least two houses in Pompeii seem to have stages opening onto their peristyle gardens.[54] The peristyle garden of the House of the Golden Cupids (VI.xvi.7), where "sculptured decorations with theatrical motifs abound," including comic and tragic masks and a portrait head of Menander, has on its west side an elevation with its central space framed by Corinthian pilasters and a pediment, which, according to Jashemski, "definitely suggests a stage."[55] The House of the Faun (VI.xii.2–5), an unusually luxurious house, also has a raised area in the portico of the peristyle north of the garden.[56]

The extension of the mosaics of the House of Menander at Mytilene into and around the peristyle probably alludes to the same usage. In some later Roman villas, dining spaces even opened out onto the courtyards, offering an unobstructed view for diners within of the entertainments that might be provided there.[57] But this is clearly not the case at Mytilene, where the narrow doorway from triclinium to courtyard looks onto a wall. Though we cannot say that the House of Menander never offered dramatic entertainments to its guests, it is extremely unlikely that these took place in the triclinium, and so the dramatic imagery in the triclinium is to that extent void of any reference to actual activities practiced in that space. And so too are most of the triclinia yielding dramatic scenes.

Another probable limitation to the use of the theater scenes as direct evidence for practice is financial. Almost all the evidence for private drama points to the upper crust of the upper crust, and not so much the economic as the political élite of the Empire (although economics certainly have a great deal to do with it).[58] Now this may be due to the fact that our literary sources are mainly interested in political élites. Though well below the standards of a Harris poll, papyri give us the closest thing we have to a random demographic survey in antiquity. We have a reasonable sampling of papyri relating to private and public performers: contracts, letters and accounts. One document from the second century AD, apparently receipts for a single public festival, lists the wage of a mime and a Homeric mime at 496 and 448 drachmas, while a dancer gets only 100 and some drachmas.[59] The latter is comparable to the cost of castanet dancers or pipe girls in Egypt some twenty and fifty years later, the former of whom performed in a private house, and the other for the festivities of a private club.[60] The important thing to note is that despite a couple dozen papyri relating to hirings by private individuals and private clubs, with very few exceptions, the hiring of tragedians, comedians, mimes, and pantomimes is limited to city officials contracting for the public theater. Hirings by private individuals and by clubs relate to musicians and dancers, including *kinaidoi*, comic and obscene dancers, who are sometimes classified as mimes, but are not drama.[61] The four exceptions are all from the accounts of large estates. We can identify the owners of three of these.[62] The Zeno papyri of the mid-third century BC include disbursements to a comic actor, a *kinaidos*, a piper, poets, and even a lecturer on Homer.[63] These accounts are from the estate of a minister of King Ptolemy II, one Apollonius, "the man in charge of the economy for Ptolemy II Philadelphus," and one of the richest and politically most powerful men in Egypt, even if there is some disagreement about his precise rank: "the first person in the State after the king," "the manager in the name of the king of the economic life of Egypt," or no better than sixth at court, and perhaps as low as tenth.[64] From the early fourth century AD, we have an inventory of wine consumed during a private reception. In addition to the guests wine was given to cooks, sausage makers, a baker, pastry chefs, charioteers, acrobats, and mimes. The estate belonged to Theophanes, a native of Hermopolis, who was a high official, probably on the staff of the prefect of Egypt, and the guests were the provincial governor and his retinue.[65] A third papyrus, of c.566 AD, incidentally the latest documentary source for mime, is an account recording disbursements of wine to servants and tradesmen as New Year's presents: the recipients include mercenaries, guards, Goths, cooks, pandoura players, cooks, waiters, trapeze artists, and "the mimes of the two companies."[66] The accounts are from the estate of the Apion family one of the most illustrious and politically powerful patrician families of the Eastern Empire.[67]

I doubt that even our Menandromaniac in Antioch belongs to this class, but I am pretty sure that his counterpart in Mytilene is not, and neither are any of the other medium-sized house owners of later antiquity, who boasted scenes from Menander on their mosaic floors, in Chania, Zeugma, or Ulpia Oescus.[68] It is, of course, possible that our man in Mytilene did not put on full-scale dramatic performances, but only had readings and recitations, such as those provided to Pliny by his slave Zosimos (who was, however, a trained actor).[69] Maybe he and his friends read and discussed drama together, like Aulus Gellius and his literary coterie.[70] But recitations are a far cry from what are depicted on the mosaics.[71] It is just as likely that our man from Mytilene, despite the pavement semiotics, was happiest with a piper and a dancing girl. His mosaics probably refer to a cultural and economic ideal which he could neither afford nor inwardly digest.

There is just about every reason to doubt that the floor mosaics showing scenes of drama in performance are contemporary reflections of real practices in the spaces where they appear. Before I conclude, however, there is an argument, used by those who urge the contrary, that I need to address here, however briefly. It is often claimed that, although the archetypes of these scenes may originate in the Early Hellenistic period, the scenes nevertheless show changes, and these changes must reflect later performances of the drama. There are two varieties of this argument: one relates generally to changes in the configuration of a scene, and another relates specifically to changes in costume.

Let me deal first with the claim that reconfigured scenes reflect different performances of a play. The argument gains some plausibility from the fact that theater scenes are exceptionally conservative. More than any other type of scene, they follow a close copy tradition that presupposes fairly precise and immediate models in the form of copybooks.[72] But even despite the use of direct visual models the copies reveal much of the fluidity one associates with reproductions based merely on memorized formulae. I can do no better than to quote a few highly-relevant phrases of Roger Ling, discussing Roman art generally:[73]

Underlying most of the pictures were certain established iconographic formulae which were reinterpreted according to ... the requirements of the context ... Scenes are reproduced in mirror-image, figures are omitted or deliberately altered ... the places of figures within a composition are switched round. Sometimes figure-types are transferred to different actors ... The chief fact which seems to have dictated the choice of pictures in a given room was the possibility of achieving a formal balance ... [The patron] was primarily concerned that [panel pictures] could be made to look right together, even if this meant allowing or encouraging the painter to alter the number and arrangement of the figures, adjust the colours and change the settings.

There can be no doubt that the mosaicist at Mytilene treated his originals with all the freedom Ling describes. One has only to look at the general floor design. With the exception of the balanced portraits of Menander and Thalia, all of the panels in the triclinium (FIGURE 5.1), including the *Phaedo* picture, show the interactions of three main figures (others are greatly reduced in size, and have generally been thought to be children, though we may note that one apparent little girl, in the *Epitrepontes* scene, is the wife of one of the main characters). Note also that in all these scenes the composition is arranged in such a way as to guide the eye from left to right. In every case there are two characters on the left who look right, overbalancing the character on the right who looks left. This happens in all the panels except the last which reverses this stance as if inviting the viewer's eye to go back to the top and read the panels over again. Moreover there are pairs which provide a kind of rigid formal balance. The configuration of the *Plokion* mosaic reproduces with only slight variation the *Samia* mosaic, the next Menander scene in sequence. Similarly the *Theophoroumene* scene which follows the *Epitrepontes* reproduces its configuration almost exactly. The last pair also share a psi-like configuration despite the reversal of the gaze. You need only look at the portico mosaics (FIGURE 5.2) to see that this is no accident. This time all the panels have two figures on the right who look left and one figure on the left who looks right. They direct the viewer away from the east perimeter wall counterclockwise around the portico. Even the mask in the corner helps the viewer turn as he follows its gaze. Such considerations as these explain the difference, for example, in the direction of the arm gesture and stance of the old man at center in the *Samia* mosaic here and in the other copy from Pompeii;[74] or the reversal of the *Synaristosai* scene, where the archetype, with the small slave looking left and the more-or-less frontal gaze of the two central characters (as seen in FIGURE 5.6) might have spoiled the rightward thrust of the series; the Mytilene mosaicist has tucked the small slave behind the old woman's chair (his head sticks out awkwardly above her right shoulder) and turned the gaze of the two women on the left to the right.[75] The same reason, with some evident further corruption of the image, lies behind the reversal of the *Theophoroumene* mosaics (compare FIGURES 5.1 and 5.7).[76] This has nothing to do with incorporating the details of a putative reperformance and everything to do with a copyist's sense of interior design.

I need now to address the argument that changes in the costume reflect contemporary performance standards and that therefore most of the dramatic scenes, however late, give evidence of contemporary performance. A clear statement of this argument appears in a very recent book by Blake Leyerle. He states that "new evidence in the form of mosaics, like those from Daphne, suggest that [classical drama] was indeed still performed [in late fourth century theaters] since only ongoing performance would explain why the style of costumes and masks was carefully updated."[77] The most authoritative statement of the argument that up-dated costume is a sign of a healthy performance tradition can be found in the writings of J. R. Green and Axel Seeberg.[78]

But we have no evidence for the appearance of dramatic costume in this period except from the artifacts, and so no means of knowing whether changes in the dress of actors are indeed related to the evolution of the costume used in stage performances. There are other and better reasons why a copyist might change the style of the costume he finds in his model, far short of inspiration by contemporary performance. He might simply translate his visual archetype to suit contemporary fashion outside the theater, deliberately for aesthetic reasons, or simply because his eye interprets or misinterprets his model in accordance with familiar standards. Even if the copyist changes one distinctive form of theatrical costume into another distinctive form of theatrical costume, it may have nothing to do with a contemporary performance tradition. I will give some specific examples.

From 384 AD the consuls in Rome and Constantinople were accorded the exclusive privilege of celebrating their year in office by the production of diptychs, a custom which survived in Constantinople until 541 AD. As the consuls' duty was to organize public spectacles and entertainments, these diptychs typically depicted either the consul himself or his games or both and are, therefore, a rich source of imagery for circus entertainments, wild beast hunts, mimes, and musicians.[79] They are not, however, likely to be representations of the games actually organized by the respective consuls. As Walter Puchner puts it, "it is unlikely that the reliefs reproduce the actual celebrations which were held in honor of the new consul, given that diptychs of different date are identical in parts."[80] Klaus Neiiendam is more direct: "the carvings on the Byzantine diptychs are so stylised that exactly the same scenes could be used again by later consuls."[81] Three of these diptychs show what appear to be actors (probably all comic). One is an actor who holds his mask.[82] The other two offer the two latest dramatic scenes from antiquity. It is probably no coincidence that both are on diptychs created for the same consul, and both appear to reproduce two of the most copied scenes of Menander in antiquity.

Figure 5.10   Detail of an ivory consular diptych of Flavius Anastasius Probus, 517 AD, St. Petersburg ω 263 (Byz 925/16). Courtesy, The State Hermitage Museum, St. Petersburg. Photograph © The State Hermitage Museum.

The drunken figures found in the relief in Naples (FIGURE 5.8), and known from eight copies in antiquity, reappear, as Green has shown, on an ivory diptych made for the consul Anastasius dated to 517 AD (FIGURE 5.10).[83] They are the two characters to the lower right. Their costume shows they are actors. But note also the strange hat on the main figure. It is an iconographic confusion for the tragic *onkos*, the elevator hair-dos one finds on tragic masks from the Hellenistic period onward (the elevator boots worn by tragic actors from the Hellenistic period onward are, however, missing).[84] The *onkos* was never used for comedy, but here it is employed by the artist to signify that the actor belongs to one of the classical genres. Green takes this as evidence that contemporary comedians were now wearing costumes that imitated the tragic style. But in this case, because of the very late date, he rightly hesitates to take it as evidence for a "full-length" performance, suggesting either "that the group stands for recital of extracts from classical theater, or even that it simply

Figure 5.11   Detail of left leaf of an ivory consular diptych of Flavius Anastasius Probus, 517 AD, Cabinet des Medailles 55–296bis. Courtesy, Bibliothèque nationale de France.

stands as a symbol for theater and festivity."[85] I would definitely opt for the second possibility. Sooner than showing contemporary comic costume, the diptych seems to me to provide evidence that the artist in 517 AD knew little of tragic costume, and much less about comedy, but copied or produced an image in which his main concern was to distinguish the performers as actors from the acrobats to the left of them. He did this by giving them the hairdo that he knew, from his acquaintance with the iconographic tradition, signified classical drama.

More recently Axel Seeberg argued that the *Synaristosai* scene, known from three or four copies in antiquity (e.g. FIGURE 5.6), is reproduced on another ivory diptych made for Anastasius in 517 AD (FIGURE 5.11).[86] I find this suggestion irresistible. We see, once again, in the lower right hand corner, three seated women. The table is gone, but they are still positioned as if around it. Once again, they are wearing hats that are misreadings for tragic *onkoi*, and this time they are also wearing the elevator boots of tragedy. Once again, the actors are marked off from the mimes performing to the lower left as performers of a classical genre, albeit with tragic not comic attributes. Seeberg takes these strange hats as evidence for a change in comic costume and as an index of the survival of performances of Menander's comedy into the sixth century.[87] But surely this tells us nothing about comic costume. It is a clumsy confusion of genres, and it shows that the artist had no real understanding of the image before him, quite likely because he had never had the opportunity to see either a tragedy or a comedy in performance.

We have to look to the medieval traditions of manuscript illustration to find anything comparable to the copybook tradition that lies behind our scenes from Menander. Kurt Weitzmann studied the manuscript illustrations long ago.[88] He found that no matter how much the copyist tried to imitate his model, it was changed by the process of copying to reflect the stylistic tendencies and fashions of the day. The relatively stable elements in the process are the gestures, spatial relationships between figures, and the stance of the human body.[89] The most changeable element is costume.[90] Costume is invariably reinterpreted in light of contemporary fashion. Sometimes it may be for ethical reasons, to cover up nudity, since most copyists were bashful monks. Notice the "decentification" of the figures of Cassiopeia and Aquarius on the left columns of Weitzmann's Plate 44 (FIGURE 5.12). But most often, costume change occurs because current fashion governs the copyist's eye as he interprets the scene before him, or because he thinks it makes his image more attractive, or because obsolete fashions are likely to be misinterpreted, either by the copyist or his patrons. This is clearly the case with the illustrated Terence manuscripts on the right column of Weitzmann's plate. These manuscripts go back to an archetype of c.400 AD and survive in thirteen copies ranging from the ninth to the twelfth century. They show radical changes of costume, yet no one would argue that these changes are inspired by contemporary stage productions. In this particular case we may note misunderstandings like the pillbox military hat ("Pannonian beret") on the boasting soldier who is the leftmost figure. This is properly reproduced from the archetype by the Carolingian copy, but turned into a royal crown in a twelfth century copy in the Bodleian.

In the mid-seventies I had a job framing paintings in Greenwich Village in Manhattan for an artist who made good money from the sale of "derby paintings" to decorate the offices of lawyers and dentists. Derby paintings are pictures of horse-races and jockeys, and elegant nineteenth-century gentleman wearing tophats in stands. The type alludes to an art made popular in the time of Degas. But the lawyers and dentists who bought these copies, however well paid, did not breed or race horses, and most of them, I suspect, had never been on a horse, let alone to a derby. Theses images expressed the kind of lifestyle and activity about which bored dentists might well dream while drilling teeth but would never either have the money or the leisure ever to pursue. The images were not arbitrary. British aristocrats and American plutocrats kept horses, like

148. LEYDEN, UNIV. LIB. COD. VOSS. lat. quart. 79. Fol. 28ᵛ: Cassiopeia

149. VATICAN. Cod. gr. 1291. Fol. 22ᵛ: Aquarius

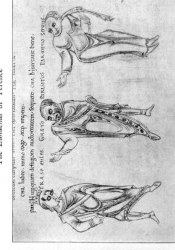

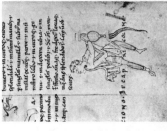

150. PARIS, BIBL. NAT. Cod. lat. 7899. Fol. 45ᵛ: The *Eunuchus* of Terence

151. ST. GALL, STIFTSBIBL. Cod. 250: Cassiopeia

152. DURHAM, CATHEDRAL. Cod. Hunter 100. Fol. 62ᵛ: Aquarius

153. OXFORD, BODL. LIB. COD. AUCT. F.II.13: Fol. 45ᵛ: The *Eunuchus* of Terence

Figure 5.12 K. Weitzmann, *Illustrations in Roll and Codex*, 2nd ed. Princeton 1970, pl. 44.

Roman consuls kept actors. They are images which attest to a living social practice, but elsewhere and at another time, in a past whose élite imagery upwardly
mobile New Yorkers like Mytileneans might cling to, but whose practices they
could not afford.

Notes

1 For the House of Menander at Pompeii, see Ling 1997, Stefani 2003, and Ling and
   Ling 2005. For Mytilene, the main publication is Charitonidis, Kahil and Ginouvès
   1970. For Antioch, see Dobbins 2000.57–9. The more correct English translation
   in each case should be, for reasons that will become clear, the House of *the*
   Menander.
2 *MNC* 6DM 2–7.
3 The reconstruction was first published and discussed in detail in Csapo 1997b
   (cf. Csapo 1999).
4 *MNC* 6DM 8–11.
5 Tsirvakos 1975.314, pls. 218–19; *MNC* 6DM 4.2–4.3. Further excavation to the
   south was anticipated in 1975 but to my knowledge nothing has been reported.
6 Cf. Charitonidis, Kahil and Ginouvès 1970.105.
7 Charitonidis *et al.* 1970.103; Ellinghaus 1998/9.265.
8 Webster 1971.210; Stefanou 1996.225.
9 Berczelly 1988.121.
10 Webster 1969.ix; Handley 1969.89; Green and Handley 1995.79; much more
   cautious, Green 1994.164–5.
11 Portraits: Richter 1984; Fittschen 1991; Nervegna 2005.85; more recent material in
   Green 2008.116. General reception: Nervegna 2005.
12 *MNC* vol. 1, 85–98. Recent finds make this figure somewhat higher: a new third
   century AD Menander mosaic has been found at Zeugma and one or two new first
   century AD scenes have been found in storerooms of material from Pompeii (see
   below, n. 39).Unpublished so far are two new late second/early third century AD
   mosaics showing the *Theophoroumene* and *Sikyonios* from Kastelli Kissamou in
   Crete: see notice in Markoulaki *et al.* 2004.370–1. I have also heard a rumor of six
   new second century AD Menander mosaics recently discovered at Daphne.
13 Berzcelly 1988; Green 1994.164; Green and Handley 1995.78; Dunbabin 1999.217,
   n. 26.
14 Nervegna 2005.36–82.
15 Barnes 1996 finds no credible attestation for performances of tragedy or comedy
   after 230 AD.
16 Stephanis 1988. *Tragoidoi* are attested until the third century AD while the latest
   komoidos is Syrus (Stephanis 1988, no. 2324), mentioned on a papyrus (*PSI* III 236
   line 30 ff. dated to the late third or early fourth century AD). There is too much
   uncertainty about the date and actual function of the Paulus mentioned as a

komoidos in a fourth century AD epigram (Stephanis 1988, no. 2026): see Nervegna 2005.55.

17   Nervegna 2005.83–116.

18   Stillwell 1941.1–34. Though Dobbins finds a profusion of dining rooms "not unusual in the home of a Roman of high political and social status," the House of Menander has so many that he wonders if it was in fact a dining club (2000.57, 59).

19   Mosaic emblema from Daphne, Princeton 40–435, *MNC* 6HM 4.

20   Marble relief, Vatican 9985 (ex Lateran), *MNC* 3AS 5a. There are copies of the same original in Princeton (*MNC* 3AS 5b) and Berlin (*MNC* 3AS 5c). Bieber 1939.166, caption to fig. 166 (not retained in second edition).

21   Studniczka 1918.29.

22   Friend 1941.

23   Kondoleon 2000.156. Cf. Dunbabin 2003.222, n. 76: "might have served as a private dining room for an intimate group."

24   See Chapter 6, below.

25   Plin. *Ep.* 5.3.2 (reading "Socraticos" with the manuscripts, and not "Sotadicos" with most editors); Plut. *Mor.* 711a–13 f; Athen. 381 f–82a.

26   Cic. *or. dep.* 5 fr. 2.4 (*Pro Q. Gallio*) Schoell.

27   Wiseman 1985.44–5, cf. Wiseman 2000.

28   Parish 1995, Csapo 1997b, Csapo 1999.

29   Kondoleon 2000.156; Huskinson 2003.152, 161.

30   Harrison 2000**b**.142–3.

31   See Chapter 1, pp. 14–22; Csapo forthcoming A.

32   Green 1995b.

33   Marble relief, first century BC, Paris, Louvre 1606 (ex Albani); *MNC* 3AS 4b.

34   Frieze with tragic and comic scenes, late second century BC, House of the Comedians, Delos, *MNC* 3DP 2.

35   Mosaic emblema showing opening scene of Menander's *Synaristosai*, Dioskourides of Samos, late second century BC, Naples 9987, *MNC* 3DM 1; Mosaic emblema with scene from Menander's *Theophoroumene*, Dioskourides of Samos, late second century BC, Naples 9987, *MNC* 3DM 2.

36   Huskinson 2003.159–60; Dunbabin 2004.161–3. Imperial wall paintings and mosaics probably have a relationship to pantomime very much like Attic red figure's relationship to tragedy, representing the myth rather than the performance: see Kondoleon 1994.308–12; Bowersock 2006.31–63.

37   The one likely exception is the possible depiction of the opening scene of the *Oedipus at Colonus* of Sophocles in the House of the Comedians at Delos (Metope VII), *MTS* DP 1 (455) though the blind old man led by the young woman might just as easily be Teresias and his daughter from Euripides' *Phoenissae*.

38   Seeberg 2003.59.

39   In addition to the copies and extracts listed in *MNC* vol. 1, pp. 94–5, note the new mosaic from Kastelli Kissamou (Markoulaki *et al.* 2004.371) and a second and a probable third *Theophoroumene* mosaic from Pompei: Stefani 2000.289, fig. 4 and

Nervegna forthcoming. A new *Theophoroumene* mosaic is also rumored found in Daphne (see n. 12 above).

40 Rumpf 1953.153.

41 Green 1994.111–12, cf. Csapo 1997.169–72.

42 Marble relief, first century AD, Naples 6687, *MNC* 4XS 1. Cameo, *c.*100 BC, Geneva 1974/21133, *MNC* 4XJ 1. Add the terracotta group from Lipari published by Vanaria 2001 to the artifacts listed in *MNC* vol. 1, p. 95 (XZ 41) and see below on the consular diptych of Anastasius.

43 Green 1985b.468.

44 Abadie-Reynal, Darmon, and Manière-Lévêque 2003.

45 See Chapter 1, pp. 16–22.

46 Ling 1995.

47 Ling 1995.249.

48 The classic collections of sources are Reich 1903 and Theocharidis 1940. Mime survives on the public stage at least until the sixth or seventh century AD: Puchner 2002, Roueché 2002. For the survival of mime on the private stage, see below, n. 66. On pantomime, see now Hall and Wyles 2008.

49 Csapo 1997.167; Nervegna 2005.98; see further, Chapter 6, below.

50 On the algebraic and related "performance" papyri, see Nervegna 2007.25–31. She demonstrates that they have nothing to do with performance in the theater.

51 Lib. *ep.* 1066.2 = Norman 1992, no 190.2; Lib. *or.* 64.112 (Foerster 4.497): "When the tribe of tragic poets had been confined [to the schools] … some god, out of pity for the ignorance of the masses, introduced the dance [i.e. pantomime] instead as a way to teach the multitude about the deeds of old, with the result that now even a goldsmith can come off not half badly in an argument with someone from the academy concerning the house of Priam and Laius." On Menander in the schools generally, see Nervegna 2005.117–48.

52 Dunbabin 1996.70.

53 Dunbabin 1996.

54 See Jashemski 1979.38, 101.

55 Jashemski 1979.101 and p. 38, fig. 60. See further *MNC* 5NP 15, 3AS 2f/xz 43, 3AS 3b, 4XS 20a, 4XS 11, 4XS 19, 5XS 8, 5XS 9.

56 Jashemski 1979.23–31, pls. 26, 26 and p. 181.

57 Dunbabin 2003.169–74.

58 See below, Chapter 6.

59 *POxy* 519 fr. a, cf. *POxy* 1050 (= Tedeschi 2003, no. 25, 26; Vandoni 1964, nos. 36, 39). This is presumably provincial upmarket entertainment and a good deal more than the 180 drachmas offered by the *archephodos* of a small town to two pantomimes and their musical accompanists for a five day stint, though in this case there is a further stipulation that they will get thirty loaves of bread, a measure of olives, and two drachmas for a garland: *PFlor* I, 74 (181 AD) = Tedeschi 2003, no. 6; Vandoni 1964, no. 17; cf. Adams 1964.168, 183–4; Stephanis 1988.436, no. 2472.

60 *PCorn* 9 (206 AD) = Tedeschi 2003, no. 11; Vandoni 1964, no. 20. *PGrenf.* II 67 = Tedeschi 2003, no. 14; Vandoni 1964, no. 22). *PGen* I² 73 (= Tedeschi 2003, no. 9;

Vandoni 1964, no. 19) is a contract for 3 entertainers (*paistai*) and an aulete for 28 drachmas a day plus expenses for 7 days with the *prostates* of a *collegium*. For entertainments of private clubs in Egypt see Westermann 1932. The imitation of high-culture, including musical and dramatic performances, is posited for banquets of Roman *collegia* by Horsfall 1996.38.

61   On *kinaidoi*, see Dunbabin 2004.

62   A papyrus from a large Hermopolitan estate of the early fourth century AD includes three separate disbursements of wine to a group of mimes over the course of a year and a half. One can only infer from the volume of other payments in money and kind that the accounts belong to a distinguished family: *StudPal* 20.85 (Rainer E 94 = Wessely 1969.75–7); Wessely 1905.27–8, no. 33 (*eines vornehmen heidnischen Hauses*); Sijpesteijn 1962–3.2 n.7, 7; Maxwell 1993.132–3, no. 27.

63   *PCairoZen* 59417 = Vandoni 1964, no. 63 = Stephanis 1988.306, no. 1703 (comedian); *PColZen* 94.2 = Vandoni 1964, no. 30 (*kinaidos hilaros*); *PColZen*. 94.5 (auletes), cf. *PSI* 416; *PSI* 388 = Vandoni 1964, no. 31 (poets); *PCairoZen* 59603 (Homer lecture). See Orrieux 1985.71; *Hellenika* 35 (1984) 33 no. 21; and Peremans and van't Dack 1950–, VI 17021.

64   Manning 2003.110; Wilcken 1921.385; Turner 1984.143; cf. Orrieux 1985.176.

65   *PRyl* 641; Vandoni 1964, no. 45; Maxwell 1993, no. 26.

66   *POxy* 2480.38–44; Maxwell 1993, no. 25.

67   Hardy 1931.25–38 for the family. Innocent, Bishop of Maronia, calls Strategius *gloriosissimus patricius* (Mansi 1762 col. 818).

68   For Zeugma see the summary in Lightfoot 2001.647: "The well–appointed villas … will have belonged in the main to local merchants and landowners whose prosperity rested as much on the exploitation of the surrounding territory … and of the major trading routes as it did on the spending power of the Roman legionaries."

69   Plin. *ep.* 5.19.

70   Gell. *NA* 2.23, 3.16.3–5. See Chapter 6, pp. 186–8.

71   Nervegna 2005.150 concludes that "'Reading' as such contributed comparatively little in turning Menander into one the best-known Greek authors in antiquity. The extant evidence for the afterlife of Menander's plays on both public and private stages points to actual performance."

72   See, most authoritatively, Dunbabin 1999.303; I have argued the case specifically for Mytilene's House of Menander in Csapo 1997 and Csapo 1999. Against copybooks, but without specifically addressing the theater scenes (except to make an exception of them): Bruneau 1999 and Bruneau 2000.

73   Ling 1991.128–40.

74   Fresco from Pompeii VI.ix.6, first century AD, Bonn E 108, *MNC* 5NP 9. See Csapo 1997.178, Csapo 1999.173. *MNC* vol. 1, pp. 92–3 almost comes to the same conclusion: it is clear that the woman in the fresco carries something in her arms and I believe the absence of the baby is due to careless nineteenth century restoration.

75   A similar position and stance reversal is suspected by *MNC* XZ 44–6 (vol. 1, p. 96) where 4NP 2.3 reverses the archetype represented by 5NP 5a–b.

76 More fully detailed in Csapo 1997 and 1999.166–70. The traditional belief, that this is a different scene, is energetically and naively maintained by Ferrari 2004.130–3, who evidently was unaware of Csapo 1997 until after he completed his analysis (see the confused attempt to shore up his argument in the first footnote).
77 Leyerle 2001.21.
78 Their expressions are notably hedged with considerably more caution. *MNC* vol 1, p. 85: "It is also worth keeping in mind that the changes which were thus gradually brought about in iconographic tradition were not necessarily a matter of 'corruption' alone, but may reflect the copyist's experience of the stage of his own day: bringing costumes, masks, gestures, accessories – as well as, of course, the style – up to date." Green 1994.154: "Despite all that we have just noted, it is an observable phenomenon that the style of masks and costumes continued to develop. Such a process is most unlikely to have occurred without the impetus of performance." Cf. Green 1994.164–5.
79 Delbrück 1929; Grabar 1968.243.
80 Puchner 2002.314.
81 Neiiendam 1992.107.
82 Ivory consular diptych of ca. 500 AD, St. Peterburg Byz 85/11, *MNC* 6DI 2.
83 Ivory consular diptych of Anastasius, 517 AD, St. Petersburg ω 263 (Byz 925/16), *MNC* 6DI 1. Green 1985b; cf. Green 1994.167.
84 As noted in *MNC* 6DI 1 (p. 467).
85 Green 1985.472, more developed in Green 1994.167 from which the quotation.
86 Ivory consular diptych of Anastasius, 517 AD, Cabinet des Médailles et Antiques, Paris. Seeberg 2003.45–6.
87 Seeberg 2003.45–6.
88 Weitzmann 1970.
89 Weitzmann 1970.157.
90 Weitzmann 1970.157–60.

6

The Politics of Privatization
A Short History of the Privatization of Drama from Classical Athens to Early Imperial Rome

Most students of drama, theater history, and dramatic reception ignore theater in the domestic sphere.[1] Take, for example, the scholarship on John Chrysostom and the theater. Chrysostom speaks more of private drama than any ancient author. He constantly rails against the rich turning their houses into theaters, introducing mimes and pantomimes like prostitutes into their homes, or allowing them to perform in the wedding processions of their virgin daughters. Chrysostom has almost as many references to private as to public theater. Yet Theocharidis's classic treatment of Chrysostom's evidence for theater claims that mime was played "in the theater and only exceptionally elsewhere, as for example an intermezzo during the horseraces in the circus."[2] Leyerle's more recent and otherwise very thorough book on Chrysostom and the theater makes only passing mention of private drama.[3] Only students of Senecan tragedy generally take a close interest in private theater: the question of the performance, performability, and venue are central to the study of Senecan drama. This exception is, however, in the general service of the rule: Senecan drama is more often assigned to the private than the public stage, but its performance is nonetheless normally characterized either as mere "recitation" or, more recently, as a "kind of intimate performance in private palaces (with a streamlined apparatus)," characteristics that are then frequently extended to the concept of "private theater" generally, for which Senecan drama serves, by default, as a conceptual model.[4] Ancient private theater, in the final analysis, is commonly conceived at best as marginal and amateurish, and at worst as not really theater at all.

In this chapter I wish to sketch a brief history of the privatization of theater from Classical times to the Early Roman Empire. My purpose is first of all to show that there is a long and changing history before the writing of the Senecan "closet dramas" that threaten to typify it, and secondly to challenge the notion of private theatrical performances as always or normally opposed in character or function to public theater. *Readings*, even dramatic readings and recitations of extracts from tragedy or comedy or possibly whole tragedies, might indeed be delivered to intimate groups by authors, amateurs, or trained lectors in more or less improvised circumstances. The bulk of the evidence, however, indicates that private *performances* of tragedy and comedy normally engaged top-quality actors, elaborate venues, and full productions. Indeed the qualitative similarity between private and public theater has nearly everything to do with a similarity in function.

Discussion of the function of private theater has long been dominated by the assumption that private theater, insofar as it is private, represents a withdrawal from public and political life. Indeed many scholars treat private theater as the culmination of a long depoliticization that is supposed to begin with the putative decline of the polis in the fourth century BC. The 1990s saw significant challenges to the models of decline that have long dominated cultural and particularly theater history,[5] but many related ideas and attitudes live happily on. Take, for example, the treatment of private and public as polar opposites. The fad for structuralism in cultural histories of the 1980s treated them as mutually exclusive categories. One could, for example, flatly deny the possibility of the existence of private theater, either in Greek or in Roman antiquity, on the strength of a good characterization of theater as very public. In the volume *Spettacoli conviviali* (1983), for example, Corbato argued the absence of any link between the Greek theater and the symposium, because "by its very nature the Greek theatrical event was incompatible, in its religious, agonistic, civic and political character, with the requirements of a disinterested, politically disengaged, fundamentally private entertainment."[6] The next essay in the volume, by Brugnoli, argued that because drama in Rome functioned as a mass media event for the public display of power and magnificence by its élite sponsors, it had little place within the private sphere and almost all the textual evidence that seems to imply the contrary is therefore misleading.[7] Both read like a Socratic elenchus, taking the shortcut to a predetermined goal by a series of plausible equations and oppositions, and dispensing with the collection and analysis of concrete evidence.

Scholars with more terrestrial methods sometimes find, however, that far from being polar opposites, public and private can in antiquity be so similar in their means and ends that one cannot properly decide which label to apply. Wallace-Hadrill, for example, demonstrates the inadequacy of modern conceptions of public and private for understanding the Roman house: the higher up the social scale, the more private and public interpenetrate.[8] The opposition is no less problematic in the case of theater. "Public theater" is never as public as the label suggests. Throughout antiquity, individuals paid from their own private pockets at least a large part of the expense of just about all theater, no matter how public we like to think it, and, however much constrained, these private individuals, whether choregoi, agonothetes, monarchs, or aediles, paid for theater on the understanding that the audience would know it to be a gift and receive it accordingly. There is, so far as I know, no evidence for a purely commercial theater in antiquity. There is not even any equivalent for drama of the shortlived gladiatorial shows at Fidenae put on opportunistically when Tiberius suppressed shows in Rome, by an ex-slave who, with Tacitus' disapproval, acted "not from great fortune or political ambition but because he hoped to make a business for filthy profit."[9] Even when theater really is put on for immediate and tangible profit it is always disguised as an act of munificence. At the end of the third century BC the Milesian comic actor Nikophon unexpectedly arrived in the tiny town of Minoa on the island of Amorgos, probably forced to seek shelter on the tiny island by contrary winds and rough seas. An inscription tells us "when he happened upon the harbor he announced that he would perform three dramas over three days."[10] Clearly Nikophon is trying to profit from a bad situation. But the text insists that he proclaimed an intention to "perform for the god" (there were sanctuaries of Dionysus and Apollo in town), and the grateful townspeople subsequently reward him "with a golden crown worth a hundred drachmas" and name him ambassador and benefactor of the people of Minoa. Nikophon no doubt just wanted the money but he could not demean himself and his art by setting up a ticket booth and collecting it directly. He performs, rather, "for Dionysus," but with the clear understanding that the citizens of Minoa will repay the gift with honors and in particular that these honors will include a crown that is easily convertible into hard cash. In the same way all public theater was an object of gift-exchange and as much an act of munificence as private theater. The most important difference is sometimes just the directness of the obligation created by the gift. In the public theater of Hellenistic Athens, for example, it was the city itself that got top credit for the production. Agonothetic monuments tell us that for their very expensive dramatic festivals "the People was choregos," even if it was the agonothete himself who paid the lion's share of the bill – in one recorded case 63,000 drachmas.[11]

I will argue that the difference between public and private theater is not one between political and apolitical, or engaged and aesthetic. The evidence for the performance of drama outside of public theaters shows that private theater to a very large extent supplemented the very political purpose to which public theater was put in the Hellenistic and Roman world, and even served it better precisely because of the more personal bond it created between the sponsor and the viewer.

The Origins of Private Drama in Greece

By the late fifth-century BC Athenian drama (despite Corbato) had already spilled over into the private sphere. It penetrated the élite culture of the schools and the symposium. The parabasis of Aristophanes' *Knights*, for example, tells us that songs of the comic poet Cratinus were the rage at symposia.[12] *Clouds* exploits this novelty in constructing its confrontation between tradition and modernity. After dinner Strepsiades asks Pheidippides to pick up a lyre and sing a song of Simonides or at least recite something from Aeschylus. But Pheidippides rejects the lyre as ridiculously old-fashioned, and Aeschylus as a pompous windbag. To Strespiades' horror, he performs a speech from Euripides' *Aeolus* about a brother screwing his sister.[13] A century later we can see Theophrastus' Self-Centered Man refusing to "sing or recite tragic speeches" or his Late-Life Learner struggling unsuccessfully to memorize tragic speeches in a desperate attempt to attain sympotic respectability.[14]

Despite Strepsiades, however, these passages give no evidence of a revolution, let alone a democratization, in symposium culture. The custom of singing lyric songs was simply extended to include the performance of songs and speeches from the stage. This custom, we are told, saved Athens from destruction. At the symposium where Lysander gathered the principal delegates of the allies to discuss the fate of Athens in 404 BC, the Theban delegate urged razing Athens to the ground, but the Phocean delegate saved the city by singing the parodos of Euripides' *Electra* and reminding the (evidently sentimental) delegates of Athens' greatness.[15]

The entertainments of the Classical Athenian symposium might also include skits and plays of various sorts. What group performances we know of came not from the theater, but from ritual and myth: the famous enactments of the Eleusinian mysteries, for example.[16] These of course required no scripts: they allowed improvisation within a series of well-known actions and events. In the later fifth century more ostentatious symposia might perhaps include mime-like performances. James Davidson suggests that Gnesippus wrote erotic mime skits (*paignia*) specifically for performance at Classical symposia.[17] But few symposia if any are likely to have involved the study of a script. So far as we know, sympotic entertainment normally involved the display of talents and learning that participants had acquired elsewhere. If anything more elaborate was required, then professionals were hired to do the work. Xenophon's *Symposium* is the earliest instance we know of for the importation into an Athenian symposium of professional entertainments more elaborate than a pipe-girl or a dancer.

A new style of symposium entertainment is suggested by a fragment of the early fourth-century BC comic poet Ephippus. The speaker amusingly perverts an oath of the "cross my heart, hope to die" variety: "may I have to learn the dramas of Dionysius by heart … may the great tragedian Theodorus recite speeches to me at a dinner, and may I pass cups to Euripides while regaling him with dinner."[18] Some scholars take this literally as a list of torments the speaker calls upon his own head. But Ephippus' speaker seems rather to condemn himself to high-class sympotic bliss and the reference to Euripides (who died and was buried in Macedon) suggest that Ephippus' speaker models his concept of afterworldly bliss after the conspicuous glamour of the contemporary Macedonian court, which Aristophanes too once likened to the Isles of the Blessed.[19] Archelaus, Philip, and Alexander gathered musicians, poets, actors, mimes, and performers of all sorts.[20] The effect of royal dinner parties upon the popular imagination can be judged from the copious gossip they generated, coming from as early as the time of Euripides and Agathon's residence, and repeated even by the sober Aristotle who was at the court of Amyntas as a boy.[21]

Macedon had an incalcuably great impact upon the history of drama. With consummate skill Archelaus, Philip and Alexander exploited the power of the theater to both public and private ends. Euripides' *Archelaus* was overt propaganda, legitimizing Archelaus' claim to the throne and establishing his claim to Greek heritage.[22] More importantly, the presence at Archelaus' court of the likes of Melanippides, Euripides, Agathon, Timotheus, and Choerilus effectively made Aegae in his day the cultural capital of Greece, and advertised its cultural allegiance to Greece precisely at a time when Macedon's Greekness was most in doubt. In the case of Archelaus our sources mention only poets. Archelaus adopted a style of patronage that was common among Greek tyrants. Polycrates of Samos, Hipparchus of Athens, Hieron and Dionysius of Syracuse also notoriously collected poets in order to add to the glamour of their courts and to secure the friendship of men who had the public ear. Hieron was the first we know of to have extended his patronage to the *dramatic* poets. In this case, we cannot know if tragedians like Aeschylus and Phrynichus might be expected to perform at royal banquets and symposia, as lyric poets presumably did: Aeschylus and Phyrnichus were probably actors as well as poets. But by the time Euripides and Agathon had gone to Macedon the custom of tragic poets also acting in their dramas had long passed. Euripides and Agathon certainly added the sparkle of their wit and epigram (richly attested by ancient anecdotes) to Archelaus' dinner parties but probably did not perform in any professional sense – the speaker in Ephippus' fragment listens to the tragic actor, Theodoros, recite speeches, but passes the cup to Euripides. Archelaus' primary interest in dramatic poets was, however, probably not in the adornment of his private table, but the establishment of an effective line of communication between himself and his subjects. Euripides, at any rate, responded with a propaganda piece for the tyrant: his *Archelaus* was performed at the tyrant's newly created festival of Zeus and the Muses.[23]

It is in the time of Philip the concept of "private theater" first appears in the Greek language.[24] It is also at this time that anything vaguely recognizable as private theater first appears. Philip and Alexander bonded by preference with actors rather than poets. This is partly because they lived in the heyday of the star actor – indeed they contributed largely to the actors' social ascendancy.[25] But there was also some policy in the preference. As the fragment from Ephippus suggests, actors could perform at the symposium in a way that other guests, even poets, could not.[26] It is at the court of Philip that we first hear of an actor performing an extract from drama in a private context (though the same actor performed in Philip's public festival as well).[27] Philip and Alexander entertained guests at dinner with all manner of performances, from magicians, mimes, and dirty dancers to songs performed by the greatest tragedians of the age.[28] The list of entertainments suggests an unprecedented concern for advance planning and a desire to allow their guests a far less active role in the provision of sympotic entertainments than we find in the peer-group symposia of democratic Athens, or even in the pseudo-peer-groups of élite culture heroes collected by Hieron, Dionysius, or Archelaus. But the latter instance makes for an interesting contrast. Philip and Alexander's preference for actors over poets may have a sociological as well as a practical dimension. Unlike Dionysius, Philip and Alexander made no pretense of dining with "peers." Actors had all the glamour of poets, but less of the social pretentions, a good deal less independence, and unlike poets (as the case of Dionysius also suggests) they were far more grateful for the attention (most actors were of humble birth and despised by traditional élites). The record of Philip and Alexander's interactions with actors indicates that the Macedonian monarchs were far less interested in surrounding themselves with peers than with winning the service of very useful retainers. Actors offered the enormous benefit of greater mobility, charm, and speaking skills which made them ideal ambassadors and go-betweens. Most importantly, perhaps, they adapted readily to the more personalized, portable, quick-assembly festival culture developed by Philip and perfected by Alexander. Philip and Alexander were the first, so far as we know, to detach drama from regular religious festivals, and attach it to ad hoc festivals designed to mark their family alliances and personal achievements. Dramatic competions celebrated dynastic weddings, military victories, and funerals.[29] Particularly skillful was Alexander's deployment of stunning theatrical extravaganzas to mark the major victories of his Asian campaign: not only did they help, during his absence, to concentrate the attention of the potentially rebellious Greeks upon his unfailing fortune, wealth, and power, they also helped color these conquests as Panhellenic, not merely Macedonian, triumphs.

Just how Alexander's *ad hoc* festivals were organized at short notice in the most remote corners of the world is likely to remain a mystery. Actors had to be prepared to travel in a matter of weeks from as far away as Magna Graecia to as far away as Susa and Ecbatana. Plutarch tells us that Alexander went to Ecbatana, "dealt with urgent business and once more turned his attention to theaters and festivals, when three thousand scenic artists arrived from Greece."[30] Festivals did not arise with a snap of the royal fingers, despite the way Plutarch puts it, but they did have to follow close upon the impulse of a busy man in a hurry. One is tempted to hypothesize the existence of the actors' unions just to deal with the exigencies, though firm evidence for the unions does not come until some thirty years after Alexander. More probably Alexander himself set up the festival-creating apparatus that the actors' unions were created to imitate (some of them doubtless by the fiat of Alexander's successors, who learned from his successes if not from his mistakes).[31] Military theater (as we will see) became a standard feature of the Hellenistic and, somewhat later, Roman campaigns. Aemilius Paullus later said that a good general organizes festivals and arranges dinners just as easily as he disposes troops.[32]

Alexander's ability to mobilize actors is indeed far more impressive than his ability to mobilize troops. Three thousand independent performers were apparently ready to drop everything at a moment's notice and travel for weeks into the desert to perform in a hostile and barbarian land for troops few of them would consider Greek, let alone sufficiently cultivated to appreciate the subtleties of their art. That such an operation was even possible is ample testimony of Alexander's success in cultivating personal relationships with actors and his ability to forge bonds of loyalty. He did this through generous hospitality and a carefully cultivated reputation for liberality toward actors. The tragedian Athenodorus did not hesitate to throw over an engagement at the Athenian Dionysia and incur a huge fine in order to appear at Alexander's festival at Tyre, correctly anticipating Alexander's willingness to pay the fine.[33] There are many anecdotes about Philip and Alexander's pampering actors with lavish gifts of money and favors: notorious is the story that the comic actor Lykon inserted a request for ten talents in a comedy and that Alexander gave it to him with a smile.[34] Many, ancient and modern, regard such anecdotes as evidence of Alexander's dissipation, if they believe them at all. But even allowing for some exaggeration in the transmission, the anecdotes strike me as evidence of Alexander's shrewd genius for media relations.

In his study of the symposium at Alexander's court, Borza concludes that "Alexander's symposium acquired Greek overtones, characterized mainly by the quality of its entertainment, including dramatic and literary performances and sophistical debates."[35] This is true of Alexander's banquets to the extent that, initially at least, (most of) the entertainments and entertainers were Greek. But it is untrue precisely in the manner that such performances were incorporated into the banquet. The sympotic customs we know from Archaic and Classical Athens were radically reconfigured by the Macedonian monarchs.

Athenian symposia were of compact size and set in rooms that ideally held seven couches and about fourteen guests. In Athens sympotic entertainments generally encouraged interaction among a select peer group: as Schmitt-Pantel puts it "exchange of conversation, of singing, and of different forms of pleasure."[36] Performances were normally short speeches, songs and recitations by the guests themselves, or games and skits in which everyone participated. Even when professional musicians or mimes performed, as in Xenophon's *Symposium*, the emphasis was placed upon the sharing of pleasure among the guests. The Classical Greek symposium was about bonding and required reciprocity. At the Macedonian court, however, social relations were a little more complex. Depending on their momentary purpose, the Macedonian monarchs could assimilate their banquets to a far less egalitarian Persian model.

Royal banquets played an important part in the redistributive economies of the ancient Near East, where tribute was paid in the form of produce sent to the king's table and the kings held ceremonious banquets which "not only gave expressions to the relations between the king and his subjects" but "also contributed to reshaping them."[37] These were conspicous displays of opulence and power. Sargon of Akkad, for example, boasted that he fed 5,400 men daily and Assurnasirpal II left a memorial to a ten-day long entertainment for 69,574 guests.[38] The book of Esther reports that Ahasuerus (Artaxerxes?) in his third year gave a banquet lasting one hundred and eighty days for all the nobles and administrators of the empire and another lasting seven days for all inhabitants of the citadel of Susa.[39] For this banquet no actual numbers of guests are given, but Ctesias and Deinon report that in their day the banquets of the Persian king fed as many as 15,000 men, and Heracleides claims that a thousand beasts a day were slaughtered to provide them with meat.[40] This figure, accepted by most experts, is at least confirmed in scale by Category J of the Persepolis tablets ("Products Delivered to the King") and by a detailed "official list" from the royal palace of the contents of a royal dinner reported by Polyaenus: it includes, to mention only meat courses, 400 sheep, 100 oxen, 30 horses, 400 geese, 300 pigeons, 600 assorted small birds, 300 lambs, 100 goslings and 30 gazelles.[41] The Persepolis tablets mention only quantities of food, not numbers of recipients, but it has been estimated from such quantities as "17,830 liters of flour" (PF 702) that they were intended to feed about 11,886 guests.[42] Most of the guests ate outdoors, others in the palace, but few ever caught sight of their host, who for the most part ate alone and may have had better things to do than spend a large part of every day eating and drinking.[43] Entertainments were provided for these meals by (mainly female) musicians and dancers.[44] When Parmenion seized Damascus after the battle of Issus the inventory he had taken of all the baggage left there by Darius' army included 329 "royal concubine musicians;" their role, according to Heracleides, was to sing and play the lyre during dinner.[45]

The Persian Royal table was thus a very public place, and in other ways too, something more like a theater, or even a legislative assembly, than a symposium.

It served as much of a socio-economic as an alimentary function. The Royal dinner served as "the preeminent location for redistribution" in the form of gifts and precedence: one's place in the social hierarchy was fixed by one's place at the banquet, since dining locations were hierarchically graded, as were the quality and contents of the meals – even the drinking cups ranged from clay to gold in accordance with the dignity of the drinker.[46] The banquet indeed became not only the symbol of the distribution of power and privilege but the forum in which changes in social position were both effected and publically advertised.[47] Above all, banquets were the site of gift-giving in which the king gave tokens of his favor in the site of all – furniture, bowls, goblets, jewelry, or dainties from his table – and accepting them "meant recognition of the overlordship of the Persian king."[48]

Mass banquets seem to have had a certain appeal for Greek kings and tyrants by the early fourth century BC. They appear to have adapted their dining habits a little after the direction of the Persian model. Agathocles' sixty-couch dining hall was one of the wonders of Sicily.[49] But this pales beside the epulary brilliance of Macedon. In what has been identified as Philip's palace at Aegae the main peristyle is a continuous succession of banquet rooms, each capable of holding as many as 30 couches, and providing space in their aggregate for an estimated 278 couches, or well over 500 guests.[50] Literary sources report still larger crowds. On one occasion Alexander is said to have entertained 6,000 officers at dinner.[51] On campaign, according to Ephippus of Olynthus, he regularly dined with 60 or 70 friends: others tell us that the symposium tent he dragged about on campaign held 100 couches.[52] Someone evidently inferred a direct imitation of the content of the Persian king's banquets, since Ephippus records a calculation that determined that, on a per capita basis, Alexander spent as much on his guests as the Persian king.[53] When he celebrated his wedding at Susa, Alexander used his hundred-couch tent for the entertainment of his closest friends, but seated the army, navy, cavalry, ambassadors, and resident Greeks in the adjacent courtyard (which measured four stades, about 800 meters, in perimeter). The guests had to be called to dinner by trumpet. Among other entertainments the diners enjoyed performances of tragedy and comedy.[54] Such arrangements allow no equal exchange and anticipate only very limited bonding between guests.

The bonds formed at banquets like this worked vertically, between guest and host, not horizontally between guests. Royal banquets formed part of a gift economy that "tended to isolate [the recipient] in a one-to-one relationship that connected them to the king."[55] The royal gift economy is, however, a profoundly "unequal exchange," designed to bind the receiver with a duty of loyalty and service, without binding the giver to more than a discretionary undertaking to reward continued loyalty and service.[56] Private theater from the beginning was incorporated into this lopsided gift economy. Private theater was incorporated into the structure of the private royal banquet and shaped by its ethos. It transformed the kind of institutional giving that is familiar from the democratic polis – the giving of public dinners, *hestiasis*, and the sponsoring of drama – from the form of civic liturgies that were mediated by the public sphere and functioned to bind both giver and recipient to the community at large, to the form of a relation of fealty between a lord and his retainer. Private theater eventually even reshaped public theater. David Potter can claim that by the time of the empire "to offer a spectacle was to assert superiority in the symbolic system of exchange that governed social relations within the Greco-Roman city."[57]

Certainly not all Alexander's banquets were so huge as to prevent traditional forms of interaction, including performances by ordinary guests: the smaller ones doubtless maintained an overtly egalitarian form. The larger ones, however, encouraged passive enjoyment of the host's liberality. Entertainment was provided at the host's bidding by star actors or indeed by the host and his family: the ten-year old Alexander is described by Aeschines as performing the kithara and delivering dramatic speeches at the symposia Philip prepared for the entertainment of the Athenian ambassadors in 346 BC; at his last banquet Alexander is said to have "from memory acted out an episode from Euripides' *Andromeda*."[58]

Alexander's successors took note. From him they acquired, on the one hand, the *savoir faire* of winning personal loyalties through lavish banquets and stunning generosity[59] and, on the other, shrewd tricks for manipulating the world's first mass media, to their political advantage. Alexander's successors were careful to promote theater and to cultivate theatrical performers. They established festivals, often in celebration of their victories, sometimes in celebration of themselves. Inscriptions of the Actors' Associations reveal the Ptolemies, Attalids, and Seleucids as their devoted patrons. In return the local actors' associations seem to have assumed responsibility for the organization and maintenance of the royal cult.[60] In Egypt especially, where the identification of the pharaoh with Osiris/Dionysus was well established, the Artists of Dionysus "figured among the most important officials in the kingdom."[61] The public munificence of Ptolemy II, Philadelphus, is amply attested by Callisthenes' eye-witness account of the procession, largely organized by the actors' union, that he gave in the winter of 275/4 BC at the time of the second Ptolemaieia festival honoring his deified father Ptolemy I.[62] His private munificence on this occasion is attested by the same author's account of the resplendent pavilion he constructed to entertain as many as 260 distinguished guests "in the citadel separate from the quarters of the soldiers, actors and tourists."[63] Suggestive of the dinner entertainments provided in the pavilion is the inclusion of six niches on either side that included life-sized figurines of tragic, comic and satyric actors feasting.

That some form of drama regularly entertained Ptolemy's guests is indicated by the fact that he kept mimes and pantomimes, long before we have evidence for their appearance in any public theater.[64] Important ministers imitated the king in their inclusion of theater in private entertainments: the earliest reference to a comic actor on Egyptian papyri is in the accounts of the estate of Apollonius, finance minister of Ptolemy II, along with disbursements to a *kinaidos*, auletes, poets, and even a lecturer on Homer.[65] The value of actors for good media relations can be estimated by the fact that Tlepolemos, in 203 BC, in attempting to establish himself as guardian of Ptolemy V and autocrat of Egypt, is said to have "squandered the royal income" on the Artists of Dionysus – only the officers and soldiers of the palace guard, it seems, had more direct access to his purse.[66] The Ptolemies were so closely linked with the actors' union that some of them virtually joined their ranks, writing and performing for the theater: Ptolemy IV Philopator wrote a tragedy called *Adonis*; Ptolemy XII, known as "the aulete," performed as choraules in private competitions held in the royal palace, and another Ptolemy, probably of the royal family, performed publicly as an actor.[67]

Antiochus II of Syria, rival and son-in-law of Ptolemy Philadelphus, seems to have shared his fondness for pantomimes and mimes, two of whom are said to have been amongst his closest friends.[68] Royal patronage of the arts, from so early a date, was probably responsible for Syria's and Antioch's pre-eminence in both genres. Like the Ptolemies, the Seleucids' passion extended to private performances. In 166 BC Antiochus IV Epiphanes punctuated his victory celebrations at Antioch with a series of private dinners, each with 3,000 to 4,500 guests, including foreign ambassadors and other visiting Greeks. Mimes entertained at dinner and, so, most memorably, did the king himself: Polybius records that he had himself carried in amongst his guests wrapped in a blanket, then, when the music started, he jumped up, danced naked and later performed "along with the mimes." [69] A private performance of Euripides' *Bacchae* attested for a royal betrothal in 53 BC at the neighboring court of Hyrodes of Parthia may seem too good to be true (Crassus' head arrives just in time to be substituted for Pentheus'), but Plutarch at least takes pains to affirm its credibility by pointing out that "they hosted each other at banquets and drinking parties and brought in many Greek entertainments," as Hyrodes "was not ignorant of Greek language and literature," and that his guest Artavasdes of Armenia wrote, among other genres, tragedies.[70]

Alexander's successors appear to have adopted the fashion set by the Macedonian court for the cultivation of dramatic skills, for developing personal relationships with dramatic artists, and for giving dramatic entertainments a central place within the social life of the court, and particularly within the entertainments of large formal banquets.

The Privatization of Drama in Rome

Élite Romans probably learned private theater in the course of their military adventures in the kingdoms of the Hellenistic East. Livy claims that Manlius Vulso's army in 187 BC first brought home spoils won in the war with Antiochus III, father of the party animal (just mentioned above): actors are not specifically named but seem to be implicit in his list of luxury slaves: "harpists, sambuca-players and the other convivial entertainments added to feasts."[71] Polybius put the origin of the Roman taste for "music shows and banquets" a little later in the early 160s BC: "for," he says, "in the course of the war against Perseus and the Macedonians they had quickly acquired the luxurious habits of the Greek in this direction."[72] The same years saw the first direct experiments with Greek festival culture. M. Fulvius Nobilior put on votive games in Rome in 186 BC after his return from campaign in Aetolia to which he invited actors from the Greek East to participate "in order to boost his public profile."[73] In 167 BC during the Macedonian war Lucius Aemilius Paullus sponsored dramatic competitions in the Greek style at Amphipolis; to them came "a multitude of stage-performers of every description."[74] The following year Anicius Gallus sponsored victory games at Rome to celebrate his Illyrian triumph; they were attended by "the most famous actors of Greece."[75]

Theater and the gift economy of which it formed the principal currency were easily adapted to the social and political realities of the Roman Republic. Theater became a staple of the culture of "shows" (*ludi*, including also gladiators and beast-hunts) by which the Roman governing élite won gratitude and influence among the people. In Rome such munificence also served a very specific political end. Because the Roman aediles (and after 22 BC, the praetors) were responsible for organizing *ludi sollemnes*, and because the aedileship was the normal stepping stone to the higher magistracies (the praetorship and the consulship), politically ambitious Roman élites were expected to woo the electorate with lavish games and to make substantial monetary contributions to their success.[76] At this or a later stage in their political career Roman élites also funded one-off festivals, *munera* (literally "gifts"), that marked any convenient occasion, but for which military victories or family funerals provided an especially good pretext. The connection between good shows (gladiatorial games, beast shows and theater) and electoral victory was culturally so obvious that Cicero could defend the consul Murena on a charge of bribing the electorate (*ambitus*) by a simple demonstrating that his client, who put on a good show, had no possible motive for cheating: Murena gave brilliant *ludi* on a silver-plated stage, his rival Sulpicius gave none; Murena's victory was therefore assured (in effect, who needs illegal bribery when the legal form offers certain results?).[77] Games directly connected to future candidacies tended to be potlatches.[78] Scaurus spent many millions of sesterces and went into debt for shows put on during his aedileship in 58 BC.[79] Caelius is said to have spent three patrimonies on shows in preparation for his consular candidacy.[80] Martial would later regard praetorial outlay on games as a good ground for divorce.[81] From the time of the Late Republic a series of laws were passed to limit expenditures on *munera*.[82] Under the Early Empire, the emperor imposed restrictions, we are told, not so much for the purpose of preserving family fortunes as to protect himself from "very wealthy members of the aristocracy who might challenge his domination of spectacle."[83]

The other major opportunity that custom offered the Roman élites for conspicuous public munificence was the funding of public banquets. Gifts of banquets (like gifts of theater) are first attested in the period of the Macedonian Wars (214–167 BC).[84] The funeral games for Publius Licinius in 183 BC included three days of gladiatorial games followed by a banquet for a crowd large enough to fill the forum.[85] In 174 BC T. Flaminius honored his father with four days of funeral games including theater and a public banquet.[86] The first funeral games to be openly incorporated into an electoral campaign, in 129 BC, by Tubero, failed to make the required impression and backfired. Tubero seems to have understood the function of such banquets well enough, but not the required forms of largesse. A man of stoic disposition, he limited the number of guests at the dinner, spread the couches with goatskins, and used cheap crockery; as a consequence (it is said), he failed to win the elections the following year for the praetorship.[87] By the middle of the first century "paying compliments to the people and winning their favor with banquets" was the universally acknowledged path to political advancement.[88] Though public banquets were not always entirely "public" (as Tubero's example shows), Caesar, it seems, really did feed the whole people. The celebration of his combined triumphs in 46 BC ended with a feast for an estimated 198,000 guests.[89] It was not, however, until 45 BC when Caesar celebrated his Spanish triumph in his transtiburtine gardens that "public feasts" of this sort were hosted entirely on private property.[90] Many imitated Caesar in this manoeuver and the populace evidently liked the personal touch, for it unleashed considerable concern among the governing classes about the preservation of the distinction between "public" and "private" – "What difference is there between dragging a banquet into the forum and dragging the forum into your banquet?" asks the elder Seneca.[91] In 67 BC the *lex Capurnia* restricted to members of one's own tribe the number of guests to whom a candidate might provide a private show or dinner.[92] In 44 BC the charter of the Spanish colony of Urso banned the holding of private banquets with more than nine guests per day by candidates for public office, or the friends of candidates for public office.[93] Nero would pass sumptuary laws evidently designed to reduce expenditure on public banquets by banning the use of dining couches and restricting public largesse to the distribution of baskets of food and gifts.[94]

Private entertainments provided more personalized forms of munificence and forged a stronger bond between the doner and the recipient. They also had the added advantage of allowing sponsors to avoid limitations on their political efficacy, like the *lex Villia* which introduced a full year gap between one's aedileship and public games and candidacy for the praetorship, or opportunities to hide from laws like *lex Calpurnia* that attempted to limit such entertainments on private property.[95] The *Commentariolum Petitionis*, a treatise on electioneering ascribed to Quintus Cicero, advises the candidate to "make sure that you and your friends give frequent dinner parties for all groups and especially tribe by tribe."[96] Cicero's speeches show that it was standard practice to give meals to supporters and especially one's own fellow tribesmen at election time.[97] Hospitality to other tribes was included in the definition of bribery (*ambitus*) by the *lex Calpurnia* (mentioned above), so it was regularly stagemanaged through friends, though not without risk, as this was also illegal, but harder to police: Murena's relative Natta arranged a dinner party for the influential century of Knights, before the election.[98]

Private dinners in private spaces were more conducive to the combination of dinner with spectacle (music, dancers, drama – even gladiators could be used to add a splash of color to a private gathering).[99] But we hear of no theatrical entertainments offered to the "whole people" simultaneously with dinner until Flavian times. Such arrangements in Rome would seem to require the spatial arrangements and capacity of the Colosseum or, less suitably, the Circus where Domitian provided dinner and spectacles (including drama and mime) simultaneously to the people at large. Even here, however, the dinner arrangements were necessarily less formal: he provided "picnic baskets" for the entire populace, which they were obliged to eat "on the spot," sitting upright, and tightly packed (despite the fact that Domitian overturned Nero's ban on public dining on couches).[100] From smaller towns in Greece, however, we do hear of public dinner theater from the early first century BC. An inscription from Priene honors one Zosimos who "gave a notable feast to the whole people" and, for the purpose, "hired performers from abroad, including the pantomime Ploutogenes, who was able to beguile by his air, and he exhibited him for three days."[101] The fact that Ploutogenes stayed for three days may suggest serial banquets such as those put on by Antiochus IV for 3,000 to 4,500 guests at a sitting. Priene, albeit a small town of not more than 6,000 people, had only a tiny theater, holding about 700 spectators, and yet, another inscription from first-century BC Priene (plausibly restored) informs us that "during the competitions the agonothete payed from his own and his fellow agonothetes' pockets for a feast in the theater for the citizens, residents, neighbors and slaves."[102] In Acraiphia in Boeotia in

40 AD a list of all the dinners and handouts one Epaminondas gave to the citizens, their wives, slaves and visitors (most often in the gymanasium) informs us that "at the festival he treated in the theater all those watching the drama, including those who had come from the other cities, to such large and lavish cakes that his expenditure was the talk of all the cities in the region."[103] But real theater could only be combined with real dinners to much smaller audiences. As the example of Tubero suggests, the quality of the experience counted for more than the size of the guest-list. Even on a restricted scale the cost of private theater (which always, it seems, included dinner) was prohibitive to all but the wealthiest.

Because of the peculiarities of the Roman constitution, private resources played a larger role (quite literally) in the theaters of the Latin West than in those of the Greek East. Most of the tragedians, comedians, mimes, and panto-mimes known from the Latin West are private property: a large proportion are slaves or freedmen of emperors or of élite Roman families distinguished for their cultural or political ambition. According to Leppin, slaves or freedmen make up more than 75% of the 85 or so performers (including mimes, panto-mimes) in the Latin West whose legal status can be determined.[104] By contrast, the practice is virtually unattested in the Greek East.[105] It was, once again, in the time of the Macedonian wars that we have our first evidence of the private own-ership of actors, consistent with Livy's and Polybius' claims that actors came with the war-booty. The earliest known slave-actor is one Protogenes, evidently a Greek, owned by a Cloulius, perhaps one of the patrician Cloelii, and buried sometime in the later second century BC.[106] The plays of Plautus and Terence (c.205–160 BC) also give a clear indication that at least some of the performers were slaves rented out to the company: in particular, the production notices handed down in the manuscripts of Terence identify the piper Flaccus as a slave of a Claudius, while the actor speaking the prologue to Plautus' *Asinaria* says "May this turn out well for me, for you, for this company, for our masters, and for those who hired us."[107]

Cicero specifically names musically-accomplished slaves as a standard benefit of imperial conquest, at least in the East – not to be expected, he complains, from Britain.[108] From the first century BC we know the names of nine privately owned slave-actors: two comic, two tragic, two pantomimes, and three mimes. All have Greek names and appear to be Greeks serving masters resident in Rome. The comedians were jointly owned and trained by the very wealthy and famous Roman comedian Roscius, largely as an investment.[109] A tragic actor Antipho (owner unknown) was manumitted at a performance reported by Cicero.[110] Two others belong to well-connected and culturally and politically ambitious Roman knights. The mime actress, Volumnia, belonged to the knight Volumnius Eutrapelus, himself an amateur poet, friend of Cassius and Atticus, and Antony's *praefectus fabrum*: Volumnia (alias Cytheris) became Gallus' "Lycoris" and Antony's mistress.[111] The famous pantomime Bathyllus belonged to the knight Maecenas, Augustus' unofficial minister of propaganda and patron of the major Roman poets of his day. The other performers belong directly to the households of the governing class. From ca. 80–40 BC the tombstone of a mime (or perhaps pantomime) actress, Eucharis, announces that she was trained at the expense of her owner Licinia and performed at the entertainments of the noblemen (*ludos nobilium*), which probably means private parties, before she appeared on the public stage. Licinia belonged to the Licinii: whichever of the politically prominent families of this name is indicated, they appear to have specialized in raising musicians and actors.[112] The same Licinia possibly owned a comic actor.[113] Two dramatic slaves, a tragic actor and a mime actress, were owned by Juba, later King of Mauretania, who spent his youth in Rome (the mime inscription was found in Rome).[114] The great pantomime Pylades, main rival of Bathyllus, probably belonged to Augustus.[115]

Despite Livy's claim that "harpists, sambuca players and the other convivial entertainments added to feasts" arrived with the war-booty as early as 187 BC, there is no direct evidence for dramatic performance in a private context in Rome before 107 BC, if we can trust the accuracy of Sallust's portrait of Marius.[116] Plutarch described Marius as a semi-literate boor who could not even sit through the Greek dramas performed at his own games.[117] But Sallust portrays Marius as making a virtue of his boorishness, contrasting his indifference to Greek culture with the luxurious decadence of the Roman nobility who scoff at him for "adorning [his] banquets with little elegance and not owning a single actor or a cook worth more than a farm manager."[118] The interposition of the actor between the banquet and the cook makes it reasonably certain that the actor is conceived as a resource for domestic entertainment. His fellow arriviste Cicero was more diplomatic and consequently even more ambivalent about the prevailing fashion: dramatic performances (*ludi*) at dinner parties were characteristic not only of the extravagant and dissolute, but also of "men of taste and refinement" (*mundi et elegantes*).[119] Indeed, not entertaining with a fully-fledged dramatic performance could win one a reputation for asceticism, as it did Atticus, who provided nothing better than a reader.[120] A little later Augustus could gain a reputation for temperance and simplicity by restricting his dinner-party entertaiments to "musical acts, actors [*histriones* here probably means pantomimes], vulgar showman from the Circus, and storytellers" – more was evidently expected of emperors.[121] Much later the *Historia Augusta* singles out as a sign of Alexander Severus' thrift and old-fashioned virtue the fact that he never had drama performed at his banquets.[122] But despite the Roman historians, sociological, not moral, criteria best describe those who are known to have entertained actors and entertained with actors in the first century BC. The list reads like a *Who's Who* of Rome's most powerful and most ambitious politicians: people like Sulla, Lucullus, Metellus Pius, Verres, Catiline, Gabinius, Antony, and Augustus.[123]

One of the reasons why dinner theater is connected mainly with élites of wealth and ambition is simply one of cost. We have at least some idea of the value of a trained actor in the first centuries BC and AD. Roscius accepted land worth 100,000 sesterces as indemnity for the murder of a young but promising comic actor in which he had only a half interest. Much later the tragic actor Vergilius reportedly sold Nero his half-interest in the tragic actor Glyco for 300,000 sesterces.[124] This is roughly consistent with Pliny's estimate that the manumission of a good pantomime in the mid first century AD might fetch in excess of 700,000 sesterces.[125] One could of course take promising young slaves and have them trained.[126] But this was expensive too. The famous comedian Roscius, for example, trained slaves in return for a half-interest in their profits. On Cicero's admittedly biased estimate the value of the slave was thereby increased from 6,000 to 600,000 sesterces.[127]

There are good reasons why a Roman élite might wish to own rather than hire actors. One is that, as Marius' words (quoted above) imply, the ownership of slave actors was a status symbol. Epictetus lists the ownership of tragedians as no less necessary to the socially ambitious than marble revetment, trains of slaves and freedmen, elegant clothes, plentiful dog-trainers and kitharodes.[128] It is of course for this reason that Petronius makes Trimalchio boast of his purchase of a troupe of comic actors and Homeric mimes, even if he used them only for Atellan farce and carving meat.[129] Many, such as Pliny's Ummidia Quadratilla, made a hobby of collecting and displaying their actors, much as British aristocrats and American ploutocrats used to collect racehorses; but, as the race-horse analogy suggests, hobbies can also be lucrative.[130]

Another reason for buying rather than hiring actors is therefore financial. It was a very good investment. Many actors, retired actors, or slave dealers ran rental agencies.[131] Élite owners also profited by actor-rentals. Ummidia Quadratilla's pantomimes appeared frequently in the theater, as attested by Pliny, and one of her freedmen, Actius Anicetus, is celebrated by some twenty graffito acclamations around the Bay of Naples.[132] For our purposes it is important to note that in Rome private actors were no way inferior to those of the public theater, and indeed were usually the same people.[133] The employment of privately owned actors at public *munera* was so common that Tiberius stopped going to the theater because he could not sustain the expense of freeing actors every time public acclamation demanded it: unlike most emperors, says Dio, he was scrupulous about paying the owners.[134] Marcus Aurelius finally banned manumission *ex adclamatione populi*.[135] Emperors who sponsored many private and public shows with incomparable frequency found it economical to own their own actors. We know the names of actors, often from inscriptions, who belonged to least fourteen different emperors from Augustus to Alexander Severus. The imperial household eventually required a department of theatrical affairs (*scaenica*), run as a business, with an enormous bureaucracy including a *procurator scaenicorum*, a *dispensator scaenicorum*, numerous *magistri* and *scribae*, *locatores*, contractors called *mancipes gregum*, and two corpora of *scaenici graeci* and *scaenici latini*, all of whom were available for private or municipal hire.[136] By 55 BC even the city of Rome maintained public mimes on salary and rented them out for private functions.[137]

Another major capital expenditure in the provision of private theater is the arrangement of a venue suitable for performance. The notion that private drama was generally performed for small and intimate audiences within the traditional Roman triclinium has to be abandoned. The standard triclinium, in Katherine Dunbabin's words: "allows only limited space for entertainers: a little music, recitation, a couple of dancers, but nothing really fancy."[138] Like the Classical Greek *andron* the triclinium was devised for the bonding rituals of the Roman upper classes with their peers "essentially inward-looking, designed to bring diners together in close proximity around the communal table."[139] The reorientation of the function of the banquet towards the display of wealth and power led to a significant transformation of space in the architecture of élite houses. The conspicuous display of hospitality that nurtured private drama required great halls and spacious colonnades. Great halls and spacious colonnades are recommended by Vitruvius for the houses of statesman, precisely because of the number of visitors they were bound to receive.[140] According to Dunbabin, in the Late Republic and Early Empire we begin to see significant alterations in the form of the triclinium in the wealthiest houses from "rooms designed for the traditional small group to a much more monumental and impressive arrangement."[141] She argues that these changes imitate a model first visible in the palace architecture of the Late Hellenistic East. At the first Winter Palace of Herod the Great, for example, a large dining hall, columned on three sides, dominates the palace. The seating implies a "hierarchical arrangement with the ruler reclining in a central position at the end, on the axis of the room" which opens out onto the central courtyard.[142] The new model of dining hall created more space for spectacle, at the cost of traditional intimacy. The central couch often faced an open view of a garden or courtyard, which might easily be turned into a scenic backdrop for spectacles. Eventually the dining hall adopted a still more theatron-like quality, with the adoption of the sigma couch, like that which would have been fitted into the apse at the end of the dining hall at the Palace of the Dux Ripae at Dura Europos (to which a small room containing actors' graffiti was attached).[143] From the sigma couch the faces of all the diners were directed outwards, inhibiting conversation, but facilitating a passive audience reception of the entertainments offered by the host. Those who lacked large dining halls could only provide venues for drama in their courtyards and gardens.[144]

A much smaller expense, though not insignificant, was required for the provision of a stage. The first private stage on record dates to the Late Republic. Sallust tells us that Metellus Pius after his victory in Spain in 74 BC got frequent invitations to dine from the quaestor Gaius Urbinus, and others, who, knowing his tastes: "adorned [their mansions] with tapestries … sprinkled the floor with saffron, and built stages for the presentation of actors."[145] By the time of Nero, Seneca could say (with obvious exaggeration) that "private stages resound thoughout the entire city."[146] Many of these were probably of the relatively modest scale of the stages we find giving onto the peristyle gardens of the House of the Golden Cupids and the House of the Faun in Pompeii.[147] Quintilian worries whether one is in violation of the law prohibiting theatrical displays by Roman citizens if a citizen actor displays his art to the praetor in his garden.[148] Gardens were also a favorite venue even for the more modest entertainment offered by authorial recitations: Juvenal mentions raucous readings of tragedies and *togatae* which break the columns and plane trees of Fronto.[149] But even the wealthy might be more inclined to provide the more economical entertainment of pantomime, which required only a singer and a dancer, and could more easily be accommodated with only a slight expansion of the dimensions of a traditional dining space, such as that recently identified at the Villa Oplontis thought to belong to Nero's second wife, Poppaea.[150]

Many close to the imperial purple went so far as to build actual theaters on their properties. The first we know of is that built by Vedius Pollio on the grounds of his villa at Pausilypum near Naples in the later first century BC. Pollio's theater could seat an estimated 1425–1784 people.[151] He bequeathed it to the emperor Augustus in 15 BC. Even in exile (7–14 AD) at Planasia, Agrippa Postumus felt the need of a theater at his villa, though on a (perhaps cautiously) modest scale, holding a mere 150–200 guests.[152] The imperial palace also certainly had a stage, although I have found no mentioned of it before the time of Caligula.[153] Nero had a private theater in his gardens in Trastevere, big enough, according to the elder Pliny, to satisfy his exhibitionist urges.[154] Domitian had a theater that could seat several hundred attached to his villa at Albanum.[155] Hadrian, who is said to have always put on at his banquets tragedies, comedies, Attellan farce, sambuca players, readers or poets, appears to have had three theaters at his villa at Tivoli, one built in the Greek style (with statues of Tragedy and Comedy at the entrance), and two in the Latin style.[156]

Hadrian's preference for classical drama over mime and pantomime gained him, in his day, much the same reputation for "old-fashioned thrift" that men like Atticus gained for only having readers. It is in the light of this "anti-fashion" that we are probably to read most of the testimony for dinner theater at those cosy and refined aristocratic soirées in the time of Pliny, Plutarch, Aulus Gellius and Athenaeus (very late first and second century AD). As the last example suggests, drama in these élite literary coteries was normally read and not performed, and read either by the guests themselves, or by a slave trained as a lector.[157] Sometimes however comic actors are mentioned in the context of intimate high-society gatherings.[158] Most often "actor" is singular, which suggests a form of recitation. But even when plural comic actors are mentioned the expression is usually "*to listen to* comic actors" (*audire comoedos*).[159] Plutarch mentions tragedy, Old Comedy, New Comedy, pantomime, mime, Platonic dialogue and music as symposium entertainments; his Diogenianus' praise of Menander is most exuberant: "one could more easily regulate the drinking without wine than without Menander."[160] But despite Menander's alleged indispensability, one has to doubt that anything like a stage performance is intended. Menander (like Plato in the same context) is specifically praised in Plutarch's dialogue, not for theatrical, but for textual qualities: linguistic style and good plots, and these mainly for their very undramatic qualities of decorum and sobriety. Full-scale private performances of tragedy and comedy were probably something of a rarity already by the end of the first century AD.

The private recitations and performances of drama that took place at this time are of a very different character from those we know from the Late Republic and early years of the Empire. In the late first and second century AD the intellectual élite among the Roman aristocracy had made a fetish of "old-fashioned" Classical drama.[161] There could be no clearer index than this of the decline in the popular appeal of tragedy and comedy at this time – even despite Hadrian's revival of these genres "in the theater according to the old fashion" (*more antiquo in theatro*).[162] Tragedy and comedy came to be regarded as "noble" genres, and Euripides and Menander distinguished as the "noble" poets, *par excellence*.[163] By this time people could already imagine tragedy and comedy to be eternal and changeless.[164] If they were changeless it was only because the Roman élites made every effort to advance their ossification. Élite men of letters did indeed write new tragedies and comedies, but they wrote with the intention of keeping the genres more dead than alive. Imitation, at any rate, not innovation was the rule. Pliny the Younger, for example, celebrates the life of the poet Vergilius Romanus who "wrote comedies imitating Menander and the comic poets of Menander's day" and these were written not for the stage but "reading to a small group" of fellow paleontologists.[165] A funerary inscription found at Aeclanum has a certain Pomponius Bassulus, who served as duumvir quinquennalis of his city, declare that "I translated a few fine plays of Menander, so as not to squander my leisure time in bestial idleness, and I even took trouble to write new ones" (i.e. new plays *of Menander*, so to speak).[166] This kind of dilettantism was evidently *de rigueur*. Pliny modestly boasts that he wrote a "Greek tragedy" when he was fourteen.[167] Tragedy and comedy were idolized because they were old-fashioned, and read and imitated by men and women who aspired to be just as old-fashioned.

This kind of culture snobbery could only be practiced at school or at home and only among peers. The use of Greek tragedy and comedy as school classics ensured that men with a good education could still understand the now very archaic language and, more importantly, that they had enough respect for the classics to sit through a recitation, even if they could not quite understand it, secure in the knowledge that self-mortification of this kind advertised the very highest degree of cultural refinement.[168] Pliny and his uncle took collusive pride in the fact that they prefered comedy to the normal aristocratic dinner entertainments of "jesters, dirty dancers and fools" (*scurrae cinaedi moriones*); still moreso in the fact that their tastes were shared by only the smallest minority of their class ("how many call for their sandals when the reader or the lyre-player or the comic actor enters!"), indeed, Classical drama had for them less aesthetic than ascetic appeal: it was conceived more as an exercise in self-improvement than as a form of entertainment ("frequently the meal is punctu-ated by comic actors so that pleasure might be spiced by study" – with the clear implication that the pleasure is entirely in the meal and the study entirely in the comedy).[169] For the Plinies, their adulation of the Greek dramatic classics was a matter of household pride. They even named two of their villas "Tragedy" and "Comedy."[170] It would probably be a mistake to suppose that the private recitals and performances praised by Plutarch and practised by Pliny were widespread even among the Roman aristocracy, but it is certainly a mistake to allow such durbars of Trajanic high culture to tint our mental image of upper-class sympo-sia in the Late Republic and Early Empire.

In the first century BC our evidence perhaps allows us to glimpse the coexist-ence of features of both the Classical and the Hellenistic style of dinner party. Unlike Pliny and his friends, the more intimate gatherings of peers in the Late Republic were less interested in sharing the uplifting moral and intellectual qualities of "classical" drama. When it is a matter of intimacy, lateral bonding and sharing between equals, it appears that Republican nobles, like fifth-century Athenians, themselves performed mime skits or paignia and pantomimic dances, usually when the drinking was quite advanced: not drama but mytho-logical skits such as that performed by Quintus Hortensius who played the role of Orpheus for his dinner guests in his own private zoo or by Munatius Plancus, who, at a banquet for Cleopatra, danced the role of Glaucus on all fours naked wearing a fishy tail and with his body painted blue.[171] Cicero had an excellent memory for the potentially compromising party-games of his noble col-leagues.[172] But these modest diversions are a far cry from theater in any strict sense of the word and should not be taken, as they often are, as examples of the manner and style of private theater in Roman society. In the Late Republic and Early Empire private theater existed on a much more formal and ambitious scale. Indeed, apart from the location on private property, it is often only the restriction of the audience to invited guests and the provision of a really good meal that allows us to distinguish it from public theater. The patrons, performers, performance-conditions and purposes of private theater are otherwise usually identical to those of public theater. The Roman political élite cultivated private theater for the very same reason they cultivated public theater. Munificence, public or private, secured loyalty in political campaigns and trials and bought votes at elections. By Dio Chrysostom's day the importance of private theater in an electoral campaign was a cliché: the ambitious politician, he says, provides, in his own house, "a sumptuous banquet daily for at least a hundred people," hiring among others "pipers, mimes, kithara-players, and magicians," and even a star singer or actor, "an Amoibeus or a Polos … for a fee of five talents;" "otherwise," says Dio, "he will get nowhere."[173] It was for the same reason that Murena produced dancers to entertain the tribes when they dined at Natta's house: Cicero makes light of it precisely because the practice was so well-established as to make the connection obvious.[174]

Viewed functionally and contextually drama in Late Republican and Early Imperial Rome, even on the private stage, was far more political than it ever was in the time of the Athenian democracy. Tragedians, comedians and pantomimes were the mass media of the day – as tragedians and comedians were indeed in Athens – but with the difference that the masses were larger and the politics much more openly contested. One would have supposed that in these circumstances actors wielded a good deal of political power. And yet, there is scholarly controversy over the political power of actors. For example, a graffito in Pompeii shows the fan club, *Paridiani*, of the pantomime Paris, known as Paris II, supporting a local candidate for the aedileship.[175] Marie-Hélène Garelli recently denied any political content to these graffiti on the principle that: "such political weight is hardly imaginable for a dancer."[176] This is a surprising claim when one considers that the aedileship is all about bringing theatrical entertainers, like Paris, together with their public. Another Pompeian graffito announces that a candidate will be a "good aedile and a very generous donor of spectacles" (*M. Casellium Marcellum aedilem bonum et munerarium magnum*), and still another shows grateful "viewers of spectacles" (*spectaculi spectantes*) supporting M. Holconius Priscus for the duovirate.[177] In such a context winning the approval of public entertainers would seem no small help. But in a certain sense, Garelli is right. It is not Paris who is said to support C. Cuspius Pansa but the Paridiani (even if Paris' approval can be assumed). The actor was only the public face of a large if loose organization. He did not wield political power; vast networks of patronage wielded power through him.

The astute politician had every reason to cultivate actors. It was not just a fad established by certain eccentric personalities, as Garton suggests in his classic study of Sulla and the theater. Like Alexander and Philip, the senatorial class in Rome needed close connections with artists for a variety of reasons, not least of all to maintain a willing talent pool upon which they could draw when they needed to put on a show. This was especially true in Republican Rome where the production of games were frequent, lavish, and highly competitive. The case of Brutus is instructive. In 44 BC, after the assassination of Caesar, Brutus' personal popularity was so much at issue that he dared not appear in the theater in person. Nevertheless he felt it necessary to put on magnificent games *in absentia*. He personally went to Naples where he is said to have negotiated with most of the Greek artists, but he was constrained to mount a letter campaign to his friends to persuade them to lean on a popular actor, Kanoutios, to participate, "because no Greek could be forced."[178]

What Plutarch means, of course, is that no free man could be forced. This is a very suggestive statement. Whether we think of it Italian style as media ownership or American style as media control, the most compelling reason for Roman élites to wish to own actors may have been political rather than economic.[179] The ownership of an actor was the easiest and most secure means of ensuring that he would be available to perform at your *munera* and parties and – what is at least as important – that he perform in the way that best furthers your cause. The Roman élite's need to control actors was such that even when freed an actor (at least from Hadrianic times) was under certain conditions required by law to perform without charge for his patron, for his patron's friend, or for anyone to whom his patron wished to rent him.[180]

Roman politics were intensely personal and actors with strong personal links could be expected to further a cause more zealously than casual hirelings. Late Republican authors, above all Cicero, amply illustrate the actor's power to mobilize public opinion for any political end. Republican theater was intensely political because it usually formed part of an electoral campaign. It is little wonder, therefore, that Roman audiences should be sensitive to the slightest possible political nuance. Cicero maintained that no passage of comedy capable of being construed as an allusion to current events ever escaped such exploitation by Roman actors or escaped such construal by Roman audiences.[181] His letters and speeches attest to at least eight political disturbances in the Roman theater between 59 and 44 BC, most inspired by actors or mimes.[182] Cicero gives three good examples from the years 59 to 57 BC of just how loose and just how effective such allusions might be.[183] The actor Diphilus delivered, the lines "to our misfortune art thou Great" in such a way as to allude to Pompey ("the Great"), against whom popular sentiment ran so high, says Cicero, that the audience demanded its repetition "a thousand times."[184] At the Ludi Apollinares, the whole company of actors performing Afranius' *Simulans* bent forward looked straight at Clodius, then running for aedile, and loudly in concert intoned the lines "This, Titus, is the sequel, the end of your vicious life!"[185] The famous tragedian, Claudius Aesopus, a close friend of both Marius and Cicero, delivered allusive praise for the exiled Cicero in a performance of tragedies by Accius: he freely interpolated lines into the drama to drive home his point, to thunderous applause, according to Cicero himself, and in the case of one felicitous line, once again "to a thousand encores."[186] In Lebek's view:

> Using the stage for political demonstration was quite common. When performing an old tragedy or comedy, actors felt free to make their material pertinent to contemporary issues. That could be done in various ways, by emphasizing certain lines, by looking at certain persons, or even by adding new passages. The audience had heard some classic passages so often as to take note of any modification, and – particularly in times of crisis – expected appropriate comment from the stage. One cannot escape the impression that, in certain situations, the topicality of the play was planned beforehand. It cannot be proven, but it is quite possible that Aesopus, for the presentations in 57 BC, had deliberately chosen pieces that could be applied to Cicero.[187]

David Potter sees such events as central to the ethos of "engaged viewing" that characterized mass spectacles of Roman society:

> Virtually every aspect of Roman hierarchy was open to challenge – public executions could go awry if the crowd demanded the release of the condemned, gladiators could become heroes, charioteers could become millionaires, and actors might challenge the order of society by the way they chose to utter their lines. To be successful, a spectacle had to offer an opportunity for radical changes of fortune; it had to stir the passions of the viewers.[188]

One might add, that spectacle offered the spectators the feeling that they were in control, when in fact the ultimate control was in the hand of the actor who guided their response. If the allegiance of a good actor was not owned, it had to be bought with courtesies, favors, gifts and honors. Such court was paid to star actors who had captured the public favor that their power was envied by the élite themselves. Laws had to be passed to prevent Roman senators from pursuing careers on the stage or in the circus.[189] Ordinary Roman citizens had to be threatened with a loss of rights if they performed on a public or private stage.[190] Emperors like Gaius and Nero were only the most conspicuous to violate these laws.

Actors and the Military

The distinction between public and private is most obscure in the case of dramatic performances in military contexts and no survey of the politics of the privatization can ignore this topic. The use of drama for the entertainment of troops is first attested for the Macedonian kings, Philip and Alexander, and we may guess that they provided the immediate model for their Hellenistic successors. As we saw in an earlier section of the chapter, Alexander organized dramatic competitions while on campaign and lured actors to entertain his troops with his famed hospitality and prizes. We do have one story of professional stars enlivening military life, set much earlier, in the late fifth century: but only from the fanciful Duris of Samos. Duris, who claimed descent from Alcibiades, adds to the magnificence of Alcibiades' triumphant return to Athens in 408 BC, by having Chrysogonus, the famous aulete, give the tune to his oarsmen and the tragic star Kallippides chant out the rhythm.[191] The story does at least suggest the canon of plausibility with which this early third century BC author of a *Macedonian History* worked (though this particular story came from a *History of Samos*). Alexander's successors, when on campaign, would appear to have made it a regular practice to take actors with them. Plutarch found it strange, at any rate, that in the third century BC the Spartans "alone of all the Greek and royal armies had no accompanying mimes, no conjurers, no dancing girls, not even harpists."[192]

The event that sparked Plutarch's comment was a theatrical performance in 226 BC paid for by the Spartan king Cleomenes, when he chanced to encounter some actors on the road from Messene. The earliest Roman examples of theatrical festivals mounted in the course of a military campaign are by the noted Hellenophiles Paullus and Sulla while on campaign in Greece. I have already mentioned Lucius Aemilius Paullus in 167 BC, who mounted a festival at Amphipolis during the Macedonian war. Much later, Sulla entertained his troops with theater at the celebration of his victory at Chaeronea in 86 BC. Like Paullus, he staged a regular competition, after the Greek manner, with a panel of Greek judges and attracted Greek artists with lavish prizes drawn, doubtless, from his newly won booty.[193] Somewhat serendipitous, by Plutarch's account, were the theatrical performances with which Lucullus regaled his troops after his victory in Armenia in 69 BC.[194] Plutarch tells us the Dionysiac Artists just happened to be present in Tigranocertes to inaugurate Tigranes' new theater and Lucullus had no qualms about regaling his troops with the unwitting gifts of his enemy. Presumably, if the tale is true, Tigranes had prepared the theater and performers in anticipation of his own victory celebration. Antony assembled the Dionysiac Artists to entertain his staff, possibly also his troops at Samos in 32 BC.[195] Like

Sulla, Antony was a notorious playmate of mimes and other entertainers, but he is also the first Roman we know to have regularly taken entertainers in train while on campaign, both for entertaining the troops and for image-building exercises in a little real-life theater. Even in Italy during the civil war, Antony traveled together with his actors as in a Dionysiac procession – Plutarch mentions chariots drawn by lions.[196] At Ephesus, Antony timed his triumphal entrance into the city to coincide with the *Katagogia* (the annual procession for Dionysus).[197] Impersonating the mythical conqueror of Asia, women dressed as bacchants and men dressed as satyrs and pans led the way before him "and the city was full of ivy and thyrsus-wands and harps and panpipes and pipes, and all hailing him as Dionysus."[198] The imperial army later incorporated its own acting troupes, including mimes, tragic and comic actors (some of our latest attested tragic and comic actors come from military contexts), but the professionalization of the army under Augustus radically changed the politics of entertainment in this sphere.[199]

In Republican times, it was not just good military science to keep soldiers entertained. Private munificence directed to the military had a function scarcely different from private munificence directed to tribesmen, knights, or other divisions of the Roman body politic. A well-run military campaign might merge seamlessly with an electoral campaign. It was Lucullus' army, returned for his triumph to Rome in 63 BC, which mobilized to help ensure Murena's election to the consulate. Generosity to soldiers had a measurable political payoff. On the event of Murena's election Cicero remarks: "the military vote has a great deal of influence with the entire Roman people when it comes to electing a consul."[200]

Conclusion

Decadence theory based on class psychology has a long history. It is essentially the model of cultural history that dominated all of antiquity's attempts to comprehend cultural change. It is most explicit in Plato's attempt to explain the impact theater had on acting, music and poetry in his day. He blamed the uneducated tastes of the masses in the theater and regarded the latter as a virtual legislature of mob values (famously branding cultural democracy as a "theatrocracy").[201] But such views long outlived ancient democracy. They are thunderously implicit in the writings of Tacitus and his colleagues. It is no surprise, then, that when Ludwig Friedlaender turned his mind to explaining the great changes in theater in the first centuries BC and AD, he absorbed this class-based decadence theory along with his historical sources. Friedlaender, notably, also lived in an era when traditional aristocratic values were being undermined by emergent democracy (1824–1909).

In the earliest years of the Empire, Friedlaender observed a shift in preference in public theater from tragedy and comedy to mime. He explained it as a symptom of the split between public and private theater: the educated Roman élite invented the private stage to rescue tragedy and comedy from the low farce and sensationalism of mime (to say nothing of spectacles and bloodsports) that the masses demanded for the public theaters.[202] The notion that private theater grew up in response to the aesthetic needs of a sensitive cultural aristocracy repelled by the vulgarity of public theater still dominates the literature in the rare moments when it turns towards explanation of the big contours of theater history. Leppin uses the same class-based model as Friedlaender (though here without explicit mention of private theater) to explain the sudden rise of mime and pantomime under the principate: tragedy and comedy dominated as long as theater was in the hands of the Roman aristocracy, but the emperors catered to the taste of the masses.[203] Goldberg, although criticizing the validity of the "decadence model" as applied to Seneca, nonetheless employs the class-sensibility model in explaining the rise of private theater: "tragedy neither could nor should compete with public spectacles, and the best way to avoid that competition was to change it from a public to a private activity. By becoming private and rhetorical aristocratic poetasters could separate themselves from the world of bluster and vulgarity … Seneca put distance between himself and that world … by using the tools of his education to paint in words the murder and mayhem that mimes and pantomimes of his day could only imitate and the amphitheaters were making real."[204]

But, as we have seen, private theater existed long before this time, and, quite fatally for the theories of these scholars, as we have also seen, it included mime and pantomime, as well as tragedy and comedy, from the beginning. But most problematic is the suggestion that private theater was created as an alternative space and a sort of refuge from the politics and vulgarity of the public theater. Although it did eventually become something like this, before the time of Trajan it was sooner an adjunct to the public theater, and developed, not as a refuge from the realities of public life, but as a space in which the public theater's political function could be pursued even more effectively. If anything the improvisatory freedom of mime and the infinite suggestiveness of pantomime made them far more adaptable to the political purposes of aristocratic sponsors. But it is very clear that the aristocracy did not reluctantly introduce mime or pantomime into the theaters in deference to the wishes of the vulgar mobs and very clear that they did not create private theater as a refuge for "the noble genres" of comedy and tragedy. All four genres owe their survival whether in the private or the public theater to the mutual dependence of the culture of both the élites and the common people on a system by which private and public munificence purchased fidelity and service.

Roman élites probably learned from the Hellenistic courts how to use both public and private theater for self-promotion. Our earliest direct evidence for private theater, at the end of the second century BC, shows that it is already closely integrated into the client-patron system, which itself was developed from Hellenistic models.[205] Except in regard to the number of spectators, private theater might be even more lavish than public. It was put on by the same sponsors. It used the same actors, the same costumes, and the same stage resources. But it was in many ways more effective than public shows. The invitation was more direct and personal. The entertainments were generally more splendid: private theater always formed part of a larger package of entertainments, including dinner. Private theater, produced in the host's own home, provided a better platform for the display of personal status and wealth. For all these reasons it was more effective than public theater in its primary political and economic objective of forging obligations of friendship and service.

Private theater, therefore, was arguably more, not less, political and politically effective than public theater. We should trust the judgement of the Roman Senate in this matter. After the first great theater riots in 14 and 15 AD one of the Senate's first acts was to ban PRIVATE performances of pantomimes and to ban visits by senators to the PRIVATE HOUSES of pantomimes.[206] Public performances continued as before. The Senate readily perceived that political unrest in the theater was sparked by political intrigues and alliances fomented in the so-called private sphere. Apropos of these riots Dio tells us that "Drusus had such close relations with the pantomimes that they even provoked civil discord."[207] William Slater is surely right to argue that these riots were backed and organized by powerful interests, headed by Drusus himself.[208]

I have argued that from the third century BC until the first century AD private drama was very far from being disinterested, politically disengaged, or fundamentally private. On the contrary, whether in Greece or in Rome, private theater might be, and usually was an instrument of undisguised political ambition. Nor is private theater so easily contrasted with public theater as a peer-group bonding ritual might be contrasted to the manipulation of popular opinion through the mass media. It is true that the sponsorship of private theater was largely limited to a very wealthy élite, but this does not imply similar restrictions on the audience. Private performances were sometimes put on for hundreds, thousands, or tens of thousands of guests. Moreover they were, at least until the time of Trajan, mostly directed at larger and more impressionable audiences than those composed by the host's immediate peers. They might be put on for one's tribe, all the tribes, all the citizens, seriatim, or even for the whole army all at once. This was particularly common in the late Republic, when the political ambitions of wealthy and powerful men depended upon the support of the common citizen and soldier. Even in the Empire our sources indicate that this variety of munificence was very much alive, and no less necessary for the success of a provincial civic official than for sustaining the popularity of the emperor himself.[209]

Notes

1   In this chapter, as in the earlier chapters, "theater" normally means the venue for drama and "drama" (unless otherwise qualified) means the classical genres of tragedy, comedy and satyrplay (though the latter does not appear in this discussion). Discussion of mime and pantomime is not, however, avoided, in some cases because terminology does not permit us to decide which genre an actor or a performance belongs too, but also principally because these genres were often performed in the same spaces as the classical genres and so offer parallel evidence. Mime and pantomime however have a very different history, partly because of their much greater adaptability, and it is frequently important to distinguish them from "drama" in the discussion that follows.

2   Theocharidis 1940.115, despite giving quite a lot of evidence for private theater.

3   Leyerle 2001.

4   Among more recent discussions, see Harrison 2000a, Schiesaro 2005 (quoted pp. 278–9), Stroh 2008, Kragelund 2008.

5   Most importantly Le Guen 1995.

6   Corbato 1983.70.

7   Brugnoli 1983.

8   Wallace-Hadrill 1994, esp. pp. 11–12. Cf. D'Arms 1998.

9   The experiment came to an abrupt end. In this case the jerry-built stands collapsed leaving "over 20,000 dead." Tac. *Ann.* 4.62: *ut qui non abundantia pecuniae nec municipali ambitione sed in sordidam mercedem id negotium quaesivisset*; Suet. *Tib.* 40; Dio 58.1a.

10   *IG* XII, 7 226. See Stephanis 1988, 333–4, no. 1871; Lightfoot 2002.218.

11   *IG* II² 834. For agonothetic spending, see Wilson 2000.275–6; Mikalson 1998.56–7. For the cost of the Athenian festival: Wilson 2008.

12   Ar. *Knights* 526–30.

13   Ar. *Clouds* 1353–72. The Greek word is "sings." Dover 1968 *ad loc.* takes exception to the language, since speeches are not sung in comedy but spoken, and so he emends to "perform." Herington 1985.13, 224–5 n. 15 argues that *aeido/aido* and *lego* are interchangeable. For the interpretation see Nagy 1990.107–10; N. Slater 1990.386.

14   Theophr. *Char.* 15.10, 27.2 Diggle. For the significance of the Greek phrase, see Diggle 2004.347–8.

15   Plut. *Lys.* 15.1–3.

16   Murray 1990b makes a strong case that these performances were not parodies.

17   Davidson 2000.

18   Ephippus *PCG* F 16.

19   Ar. *Frogs* 83 with schol. *ad loc.* For Euripides in Macedon, see Chapter 3, pp. 99–100.

20 Archelaus is variously said to have collected Melanippides, Euripides, Agathon, Timotheus, Zeuxis, and Choerilus: Pl. *Rep.* 568a–b; Arist. *Pol.* 1311b30–4; Marsyas *FGrH* 135 F8; Diod. 17.16.3; Satyrus *Life of Euripides* (*POxy* 1176, fr. 39, col 19); Phld. *De Vitiis* col. 13.4; Gellius *NA* 15.20.10; Aelian *VH* 2.21, 13.4; Plut. *Alc.* 192a, *Mor.* 334b and 177b; Athen. 345d; *Vita Eur.* 21–5; [Eur.] *epist.* 5.2 (p. 278 Herch); Schol. Ar. *Frogs* 83; Steph.Byz. 452–3 Meineke = *FGE* anon. 124a (Garulli 2004 guesses that the epigram on Timotheus preserved by Stephanus of Byzantium may have been composed by Lobon). For Alexander and Philip, see Chapter 3, pp. 86–7 and the notes below. We eagerly await Moloney forthcoming.

21 Arist. *Pol.* 1311b 30–4. Cf. Aelian and Plutarch on Agathon in the previous note.

22 In general, see Harder 1985; Revermann 1999–2000; Collard, Cropp and Gibert 2004; Duncan forthcoming.

23 See Chapter 3, pp. 99–100.

24 Athenaeus 350d (= Kallisthenes *FGrH* 124 F 5). The phrase was coined by Stratonicus, for whom see Stefanis 1988.407–9, no. 2310.

25 See Chapter 3 of this book.

26 The practice of enhancing the brilliance of one's symposium by inviting star performers is perhaps anticipated by the Athenian statesmen Themistocles, who "while still young and obscure" invited the kitharist Epicles of Hermione to stay at his house "because he was ambitious that many should seek out his home and come often to see him" (Plut. *Them.* 5.3). We are not told, however, that the kitharist was expected to perform.

27 Diod. 16.92; Suet. *Calig.* 57.4; Joseph *AJ* 19.94; Stob. *Flor.* 34.70.

28 Dem. 2.19; Athen. 1.20a; Diod. 16.92; Athen. 537d. For tragedy and comedy, see further below.

29 Victories: Marsyas *FGrH* 135–6 F 17 (= *PMG* adesp. 840); Dem. *On the False Embassy* 192 f.; Arian 7.14.1; Plut. *Alex.* 29, 72.1, *On Alexander's Luck* 334e. Weddings: Diod. 16.92; Joseph *AJ* 19.94; Suet. *Gaius* 57.9; Chares *FGrH* 125 F 4. Funerals: Arian *Anabasis* 7.14.10. There is no reason to think Hieron mounted an *ad hoc* festival to celebrate his foundation of Aetna; it is far more likely that Aeschylus performed at a regular festival in Syracuse.

30 Plut. *Alex.* 72.1.

31 For the connection between *Alexandrokolakes, Dionysokolakes,* and Artists of Dionysus, see, Le Guen 2001a.1.27; Ceccarelli 2004. For the unions: Le Guen 2001a; Aneziri 2003.

32 Livy 45.32.11; Polyb. 30.14; Plut. *Aem.* 28.9.4–5.

33 Plut. *Alex.* 29.5. See Chapter 3, pp. 86–7.

34 Plut. *Alex.* 29.6; *On Alexander's Luck* 334e.

35 Borza 1995.168.

36 Schmitt-Pantel 1990.19.

37 Briant 1989; Sancisi-Weerdenburg 1995 (quotation); Schmandt-Besserat 2001.

38 Pritchard 1969.268, 560.

39 Esther 1.3–8.

40 Athen. 146c, 145e.

41 Polyaenus *Strat.* 4.3.32. Briant 2002.286–92 evaluates (positively) its credibility. Cf. Lewis 1987; Sancisi-Weerdenburg 1995.295–6.

42 Briant 2002.290.

43 Heracleides *FGrH* 689 F2 (Athen. 145a–f): we may note that according to Heracleides the highest ranking guests were similarly excused from actual attendance (cf. Briant 1989.41). For others attendance was obligatory (Briant 2002.326).

44 Briant 2002.293–4.

45 Athen. 608a, 145c. The custom was readily attributed to Asian monarchs: Athen. 530d, 531a

46 Cf. Ctesias in Athen. 464a, Hdt. 7.119, with Briant 2002.314. For the Persian gift economy, see Sancisi-Weerdenburg 1989.

47 Cf. Xen. *Cyr.* 8.4.5 with Briant 2002.319.

48 See Sancisi-Weerdenburg 1989 (quotation, p. 135).

49 Diod. Sic. 16.83.2.

50 Dunbabin 2003.47.

51 Athen. 17f.

52 Ephippus *FGrH* 126 F 2; Borza 1995.160–1.

53 Ephippus *FGrH* 126 F 2.

54 Chares *FGrH* 125 F 4 (= Athen. 538b–9a; Aelian *VH* 8.6).

55 Briant 2002.324–30 (quotation, p. 325)

56 Briant 2002.316–23.

57 Potter 2006.385.

58 Aesch. 1.168; Nicobule in Athen. 537d–e. Borza (1995.165) wrongly claims that he then forced other guests "to act;" the Greek says "and eagerly guzzling unmixed wine he compelled others to do likewise," i.e. copiously drink unmixed wine. For other royalty performing at their own banquets: Xen. *Anab.* 7.3.21–33 (Seuthes of Thrace); Theopompus *FGrH* 115 F31 (Cotys of Thrace); Diod. Sic. 31.16, Athen. 195 and 439 (Antiochus IV).

59 E.g. Athen. 128c, 148a–b, 466b, 540c.

60 Le Guen 2001a, vol. 1, nos. TE 48, TE 49, TE 60, pp. 277–9, 296, 302–3, vol. 2, 11, 89–90; Le Guen 2007.

61 Le Guen 2001a.1.348.

62 Rice 1983; Coleman 1996; Le Guen 2001a.1.295, 303, and esp. 345–7.

63 Athen. 196a–7c (quotation, 196a) = Callixeinus *FGrH* 627 F 2.

64 Athen. 576f.

65 See Chapter 5, pp. 155–6 and n. 63.

66 Polyb. 16.21.6–9.

67 Schol. Ar. *Thesm.* 1059 = 1 *TrGF* T 119; Le Guen 2001a, TE 61, and p. 300; Stephanis 1988.377–8, nos. 2161–2.

68 Athen. 19c; Stephanis 1988.94, 203, nos. 433 (cf. no. 434), 1112.

69 Polyb, 30.26; Diod. Sic. 31.16.3, Athen. 195f, 439d.

70 Plut. *Crassus* 33.3.

71 Livy 39.6.8.

72 Polyb. 31.25.4: Walbank's translation except for *akroamata*. The *akroamata kai potous* seem to go together here but need not.

73 Livy 39.22.2.
74 Livy 45.32.9. See esp. Edmondson 1999.
75 Livy 45.43; Vell. Pat. 1.9.5; App. 3. 9; Polyb. 30.22.1–12.
76 For the goodwill such games inspired in the electorate, see e.g. Cic. *Fam.* 2.6, 11.16, 11.17.
77 Though Cicero defends Murena here for doing as custom requires, elsewhere (*Fam.* 2.3) we find him writing to Curio saying that "fortune will count for more in gaining you the highest political awards than will shows. Nobody admires the capacity to give shows, which is a function of wealth, not personal ability," a claim rightly dismissed by Beacham as "wishful thinking" (Beacham 1992.240 n. 56).
78 Meier 1980.8 and n. 8; Shatzman 1975.84–8, 164–5.
79 Shatzman 1975, no. 81.
80 Cic. *Cael.* 53, *QF* 3.5.5; Asc. 31c; cf. Cic. *Fam.* 2.6.3.
81 Mart. 10.41.
82 Carcopino 1941.254; Wiedemann 1992.133–8; Futrell 1997.32–3; Potter 2006.391.
83 Carcopino 1941.255; Potter 2006.391.
84 D'Arms 1998.
85 Livy 39.46.2–3.
86 Livy 41.28.11.
87 Cic. *Mur.* 75–6; Val. Max. 7.5.1; Sen. *Ep.* 95.72; D'Arms 1998.35–6.
88 Sall. *Jug.* 4.3; Varro *RR* 3.16.2; Hor. *Epist.* 1.19.37–8.
89 D'Arms 1998.38–40.
90 D'Arms 1998.40–3.
91 Sen. *Controv.* 9.2.9.
92 Cic. *Mur.* 67.
93 *Lex Ursonensis* 132.
94 Suet. *Nero* 16. For such distributions, see W.J. Slater 2000.
95 Shatzman 1975.164.
96 *Comment.Pet.* 41: … *est in conviviis, quae fac ut abs te et ab amicis tuis concelebrentur et passim et tributim.*
97 Cf. Cic. *Planc.* 44–5, 48; *Phil.* 2.116; Shatzman 1975.88–9.
98 Cic. *Vat.* 37, *Sest.* 133, *Mur.* 67, 73 (presumably this is at Natta's own house). Cf. Cic. *Att.* 4.17.4.
99 For gladiators: Nicolaus of Damascus, *FHG* 3.416 (= Athen. 153 f), written between *c.*20 BC–14 AD).
100 Statius *Silv.* 1.6 (l. 73 "plebs scenica"); Suet. *Domitian* 4.5 (*inter spectacula muneris largissimum epulum*); Dio Cassius 67.4.4–5 (τοῖς τε θεωμένοις συχνὰ διὰ τῶν σφαιρίων ἐδίδου, καί ποτε καὶ ἐδείπνισεν αὐτοὺς κατὰ χώραν καθημένους). Public dining on couches: Suet. *Dom.* 7.
101 *IPriene* 113 (=33 McCabe); supplements by Robert 1969–90.1.662–3; translation and discussion by Jones 1991.195.
102 *IPriene* 118, ll. 12–14.
103 *IG* VII 2712, ll. 75–8; cf. Jones 1991.196. Note that even in Classical Athens choregoi regularly treated the theater audiences with free food and wine, even if nothing on

the scale of a complete dinner, and it is likely that *munerarii* did likewise, long before Domitian: Philoch. *FGrH* 328 F 171; Ar. *Wasps* 56–9 (with schol.), *Wealth* 788–801; Athen. 3f; *IG* II² 657, ll. 40–2 with Wilson 2000.275, 383 n. 51; Wilson 2008.118–19.

104 Leppin 1992.40. Leppin includes some musicians in his statistics and does not include some others who should be there, like the exodiarius (mime) Ursus, who is a freedman (unless he is a dancing bear), see *CIL* 6.9798, Maxwell 1993, no. 90; further omissions noted by W. J. Slater 1992.

105 A possible exception is one of our latest attested *tragoidoi*, Elpidephoros, from Dura Europos, ca. 220 AD who may be the slave of the Dux Ripae: see Rostovtzeff *et al.* 1952, no. 945 and p. 36; Stephanis 1988.159, no. 833.

106 *CIL* 1² 1861 + p. 1050 (= Leppin 1992.282–3; Maxwell 1993.117–18, no. 13).

107 See Brown 2002.235–6 (whose translation of Plaut. *Asin.* 2–3 I give with a slight modification); Marshall 2006.83–94.

108 Cic. *Att.* 4.17.6.

109 Cic. *Q. Rosc.*30 f. and passim. They are Panurgus, a *comoedus*, and slave of Fannius Chaerea: Leppin 1992.269; and Eros, whose servile status is likely but not certain: Leppin 1992.235.

110 Cic. *Att.* 4.15; Stephanis 1988.59, no. 225.

111 Cic. *Att.* 10.16.5, *Phil.* 2.58, 77, *Fam.* 9.26.2; Nep. *Att.* 9.4; Leppin 1992.228; Hollis 2007.164, no. 104; Leppin 1992.217.

112 *CIL* 1² 1214 + p. 970, 6.10096 + p. 3492, 1.1009 = *CLE* 55 = *ILS* 5213. See esp. discussion by Wiseman 1985.45; Starks 2008.128 n. 56. For the activity of the *gens Licinia* in the collection of theatrical slaves, see Wiseman 1985.35, Sick 1999.343–5.

113 *AE* 1928 no. 10. The inscription cannot be dated.

114 Leontius: Athen. 343e–f; Stephanis 1534. Ecloga: *CIL* 6.10110 (= *ILS* 5216); Leppin 1992.233; Maxwell 1993, no. 5

115 Leppin 1992.284.

116 Livy 39.6.8, mentioned above.

117 Plut. *Marius* 2.

118 Sallust *Jug.* 85.39: *sordidum me et incultis moribus aiunt, quia parum scite convivium exorno neque histrionem ullum neque pluri preti coquom quam vilicum habeo.*

119 Cic. *Fin.* 2.23.

120 Nepos, *Atticus* 14.1.

121 Suet. *Aug.* 74: *acroamata, histriones, triviales ex Circo ludios … aretalogoi.* Jones 1991.193: "the implication is that this is modest fare: we may suspect that contemporaries of Augustus, not to mention hosts under his immediate successors, would have offered very much more." Cf. Pliny *Ep.* 6.31.13: *ibebamur cotidie cenae: erat modica, si principem cogitares. Interdum acroamata audiebamus, interdum iucundissimis sermonibus nox ducebatur.*

122 *SHA AS* 41.5.

123 Sulla: see Garton 1972.141–67; Lucullus: Plut. *Luc.* 40.1; Metellus Pius: Sallust *Hist.* 2.70; Verres: Cic. *Verr.* 2.4.22; Catiline: Q. Cicero *Comment.Pet.*10; Gabinius, Antony, and Augustus: Suet. *Aug.* 74.

124 Schol. Pers. 5.9.

125 Plin. *HN* 7.128.

126 *BGU* 4.1125 is a contract from Alexandria, 13 BC, between the piper C. Iulius Eros and C. Iulius [Phili?]os, probably a well-known local userer, to teach [Phili?]os' slave, Narkissos, to play a variety of pipes for six months in return for a hundred drachmas. The aim is evidently to make a profit by renting Narkissos out as skilled labour: Bélis and Delattre 1993. Sick remarks that "the names of both the owner and the trainer would seem to derive from the imperial family, and thus they are likely to have been freed imperial slaves or the descendants of such slaves" (1999.338). In addition to Roscius, Cicero mentions another comic actor, Statilius who trained comic actors (*Rosc.* 30). The pantomimes Paris and Pylades may also have trained slaves in their art (Leppin 1992.272–4, 285–6; Fronto *Ver.* 1.1.1).

127 Cic. *Rosc.* 27–8; Sick 1999.339, n. 52.

128 Epict. *Diss.* 4.7.37–8.

129 Petron. 53.13, 59.

130 Plin. 7.24; Sick 1999.

131 Aurelius Plebeius was a mime before becoming a *locator* (*ILS* 5206; Leppin 1992.279; Malavolta 2000; W. J. Slater 2005.319); T. Uttedius Venerianus of Philippi was a Latin mime and later a *promisthota* (*ILS* 5208; Malavolta 2000.544; W. J. Slater 2005.219); M. Sempronius Nikokrates was a poet and kitharist before becoming an impressario (*GVI* 1049, Stephanis 1988.318–19, no. 1781, with W. J. Slater 1992.271). For the term *locator,* which appears also in *ILS* 5195, *CIL* 5, 5889, *CIL* 6, 10092–3 and *CIL* 14, 2299, see Jory 1970.2477; Leppin 1992.177–8; Malavolta 2000. Various papyri of the third century AD detail the dealings of *locatores* in the Faiyum (Vandoni 1964, nos. 19, 22–4 = Tedeschi 2003, nos. 9, 14–16). Pamounis (Stephanis 1988.351, no. 1982), the *locatrix* of *PGen* 73 (= Vandoni 1964, no. 19 = Tedeschi 2003, no. 9), if the reading π[ρ]ο(νοη)τ(ῆς) αὐλητ(ρίδων) is correct, seems to perform with the other *auletrides*. For the term, see Vandoni 1964, nos. 22, 24 (= Tedeschi 2003, 14, 16) and cf. προμηθευτής in *PBrux.* 7.3 (Stephanis 1988.500, no. 2964), προμισθωτής in SEG 30 (1090) 539 and SEG 33 (1983) 466 (who pays for the memorial to his pantomime as does the *locator* in *CIL* 5, 5889).

132 Pliny *Ep.* 7.24.5, 7.24.6, 7.24.8. G. Ummidius Actius Anicetus is commemorated by sixteen graffiti at Pompeii, three in Herculaneum and one at Puteoli: see Franklin 1987.

133 Cf. also Plaut. *Asin.* 2–3 (discussed above); Mart. 6.71.3–6.

134 Suet. *Tib.* 47, Dio 57.11.6: see Leppin 1992.190 and for the general practice, Gourdet 2004.309–11.

135 *Dig.* 40.9,17 pr. See Bollinger 1969.43; Leppin 1992.38.

136 Rostovtzeff *et al.* 1952.39, n. 35; Csapo and Slater 1995.210, 218–20; W. J. Slater 2005.318–19.

137 Cic. *Fam.* 7.1, with W. J. Slater 2002.315–20.

138 Dunbabin 1996.70.

139 Dunbabin 1996.68.

140 Vitr. 6.5.2.

141   Dunbabin 2003.50.
142   Dunbabin 2003.47–50.
143   Rostovtzeff *et al.* 1952.20, 78–9.
144   Dunbabin 2003.144–50.
145   Sallust *Hist.* 2.70 M: *scaenis ad ostentationem histrionum fabricatis.*
146   Sen. *QNat.* 7.32.3. Cf. *ep.* 90.19: *itaque hinc textorum, hinc fabrorum officinae sunt, hinc oderes coquentium, hinc molles corporis motus docentium mollesque cantus et infractos.*
147   See Chapter 5, pp. 154–5.
148   Quint. *Inst.* 3.6.18.
149   Juv. 1.1–13.
150   Zarmakoupi 2007, esp. chs. 4–5, known to me only through Hall 2008.16.
151   Sear 2006.46–7, 129–30.
152   Sear 2006.47, 169.
153   Suet. 54.2.
154   Pliny *HN* 37.2.19; Sear 2006.46. Presumably this is the same as the Horti Agrippinae where the Circus Gaii et Neronis was built: Schmidt 1990.151–2.
155   Sear 2006.46, 119.
156   *SHA Hadr.* 26.4; Sear 2006.46, 140–1.
157   Reading by guests: Plin. *Ep.* 7.17.3; Plut. *Mor.* 712d; Tac. *Dial.* 2.2; Gell. *NA* 2.23.1. Recitations: Plin. *Ep.* 6.21.4; Juv. *Sat.* 1.2–5. Lector: Plin. *Ep.* 1.2–3, 9.17.3; Juv. *Sat.* 1.1–13. See Nervegna 2005.49–51, 102–10.
158   Plin. *Ep.* 1.2–3, 3.1.9, 9.17.3, 9.40.2; Mart. 14.214–15.
159   Plin. *Ep.* 1.2–3, cf. 5.3.2 (*comoedias audio et specto mimos*). Cf. Nervegna 2005.104 n. 88: "It may simply imply that mime shows are more lively than comedy."
160   Plut. *Mor.* 712b–13 f, quotation 712b 2–3.
161   André 1975 has a useful discussion of drama in the second century AD.
162   *SHA Hadrian* 19.6.
163   Gell. *NA* 3.15, 6.5, 17.4, 17.21; Phaedr. 5.1.9; Apul. *Flor.* 16.30.
164   Dio Chrys. *Or.* 57.11.
165   Pliny *Ep.* 6.21.4 = Men. *PCG* T 68.
166   *CIL* 9.1164.
167   Plin. *Ep.*7.4.2.
168   Nervegna 2005.36–148.
169   Plin. *Ep.* 9.17.3 (quotation), 3.1.9 (quotation).
170   Plin. *Ep.* 9.7.3.
171   Varro *re rust.* 3.13.1–5; Vell. Paterc. 2.83.1–2.
172   *Pis.* 22, cf. 19, *Red. sen.* 13, *Dom.* 60, *Planc.* 87, *Cat.* 2.23; *Mur.* 13. Cf. Macr. *Sat.* 3.14.15; Friedlaender 1922.2.137.
173   Dio Chrys. 66.8–11, cf. Jones 1991.195
174   Wiseman 1985.264.
175   *CIL* 4.7919: *C(aium) Cuspium Pansam aed(ilem) o(ro) v(os) f(aciatis) Purpurio cum paridianis* (with Franklin 1987.103–4).

176 Garelli 2007.8, n. 32. Cf. Leppin 1992.192.
177 *CIL* 4.7585 (with Franklin 1980.22).
178 Plut. *Brutus* 21.6. Cf. Cic. *Att.* 15.26 where Cicero expresses himself "extremely anxious for them [the games] to be well attended and to earn all possible popularity."
179 Gourdet 2004.
180 *Dig.* 38.1.25 sec. 1; *Dig.* 38.1.27 (Julian). Cf. *Dig.* 38.1.7 (= Ulpian, *On Sabinus* 28). Gourdet 2004.311–13.
181 Cic. *Sest.* 118–19.
182 Cic. *Att.* 2.19.3 (July 59 BC); *Pro Sest.* 120–3 (59/7 BC); *Att.* 1.15.11 (61 BC); *Fam.* 8.2.1 (June 51 BC); *Att.* 14.2.1 (April 44 BC); *Att.* 14.3.2 (44 BC); *Phil.* 1.36, cf. 231 (July 44 BC). Add Macrob. *Sat.* 2.7.4 (46 BC).
183 Other examples: Suet. *Galba* 13, *Nero* 39.3; Michaut 1911.326; political attacks in Caesar's day: André 1990.169–70.
184 Cic. *Att.* 2.19.3, Val. Max. 6.2.9.
185 Cic. *Sest.* 118.
186 Cic. *Sest.* 120–3 and Schol. Bob. 136fSt.
187 Lebek 1996.42.
188 Potter 2006.385.
189 W. J. Slater 1994.140–3; Suspène 2004.
190 Ducos 1990; Hugoniot 2004.
191 Duris *FGrH* 76 F 70, Plut. *Alc.* 32, Athen. 535d.
192 Plut. *Cleomenes* 12.1–4.
193 Plut. *Sulla* 19.6. Sulla also established contests and sacrifices at Oropos (Amphiaraea) with satyrplay, tragedy, and comedy: Garton 1972.153.
194 Plut. *Lucullus.* 29.3–4, Le Guen 2001a, 1, TL 14.
195 Plut. *Ant.* 56. Le Guen 2001a, 1, TL 15.
196 Plut. *Ant.* 9.3–6, 21.3, 24.1–4; Plut. *Brutus* 45.6–9.
197 Jones 1990.
198 Plut. *Ant.* 24.4. Demetrius Poliorcetes, who portrayed himself as the new Dionysus, similarly timed his triumphal entrances into Athens in 295 BC to coincide with the Dionysia and in 290 to coincide with the Iacchus procession to Eleusis: see Csapo 2008.271–2.
199 We await a comprehensive study of actors and the military by W. J. Slater.
200 Cic. *Pro Murena* 38. Cf. Plut. *Mar.* 7.4; Cic. *Att.* 4.16.6. Meier 1966.193, 198 n. 221, 227 n. 126.
201 See Csapo 2004a and forthcoming B.
202 Friedlaender 1922.2.119 ff.
203 Leppin 1992.148–55. This involves aligning pantomime with the vulgar tastes of the masses, however, which Friedlaender was reluctant to do, since he quite correctly perceived, on the evidence, that pantomime had an equal if not greater appeal to élite sensibilities.
204 Goldberg 2000. 225.
205 See esp. Gruen 1984.158–200, 250–72.

206 Tac. *Ann.* 1.77.13–17: *ex quis maxime insignia, ne domos pantomimorum senator introiret, ne egredientis in publicum equites Romani cingerent aut alibi quam in theatro spectarentur, et spectantium immodestiam exilio multandi potestas praetoribus fieret.*
207 Dio 57.14.10.
208 W. J. Slater 1994.126.
209 See, for example, André 1990; Arnaud 2004.

Bibliography

Abadie-Reynal, C., Darmon, J.-P. and Manière-Lévêque, A.-M. 2003. "La Maison et la Mosaïque des *Synaristôsai* (Les *Femmes au déjeuner* de Ménandre)," in E. Early *et al.* eds., *Zeugma: Interim Reports. JRA* Suppl. 51. Portsmouth, R.I. 79–99.

Adams, B. 1964. *Paramone und verwandte Texte: Studien zum Dienstvertrag im Rechte der Papyri.* Berlin.

Allan, W. 2001. "Euripides in Megale Hellas: Some Aspects of the Early Reception of Tragedy," *G&R* 48: 67–86.

André, J.-M. 1975. "Les 'Ludi Scaenici' et la politique des spectacles au début de l'ère antonine," in Association Guillaume Budé, ed., *Actes du IXe Congrès, Rome, 13–18 avril 1973,* vol. 1. Paris. 468–79.

André, J.-M. 1990. "Die Zuschauerschaft als sozial-politischer Mikrokosmos zur Zeit des Hochprinzipats," in Blänsdorf 1990: 165–73.

Aneziri, S. 2003. *Die Vereine der dionysischen Techniten im Kontext der hellenistischen Gesellschaft. Untersuchungen zur Geschichte, Organisation und Wirkung der hellenistischen Technitenvereine.* Stuttgart.

Anti, C. and Polacco, L. 1969. *Nuove ricerche sui teatri greci acaici.* Padua

Arnaud, P. 2004. "L'empereur, l'histrion et la calque. Un jeu réglé et ses dérèglements," in Hugoniot, Hurlet and Milanezi 2004: 275–306.

Arnott, W. G. 1995. "Menander's Manipulation of Language for the Individualisation of Character," in Martino and Sommerstein 1995: 147–64.

Arnott, W. G. 1996. *Alexis: The Fragments.* Cambridge.

Austin, C. and Olson, D. 2004. *Aristophanes Thesmophoriazusae.* Oxford.

Bacon, H. H. 1961. *Barbarians in Greek Tragedy.* New Haven.

Bain, D. 1984. "Female Speech in Menander," *Antichthon* 18: 24–42.

Bakhtin, M. M. 1981. *The Dialogic Imagination: Four Essays,* edited and translated by M. Holquist. Austin.

Bakola, E. forthcoming. *Cratinus.* Oxford.

Barnes, T. D. 1996. "Christians and the Theater," in Slater 1996: 161–80.

Beacham, R. 1992. *The Roman Theatre and its Audience.* Cambridge, MA.

Beazley, J. D. 1952. "The New York 'Phlyax-Vase,'" *AJA* 56: 193–5.

Bélis, A. and Delattre, D. 1993. "A propos d'un contrat d'apprentissage d'aulète [Alexandrie, an. 17 d'Auguste: 13 a.C.]," in M. Capasso, ed., *Papiri Documentari Greci.* Papyrologica Lupiensia 2. Lecce. 103–62.

Berczelly, L. 1988. "The Date and Significance of the Menander Mosaics at Mytilene," *BICS* 35: 119–26.

Bergmann, B. and Kondoleon, C. eds. 1999. *The Art of Ancient Spectacle*. Washington.

Bernabò Brea, L. 1967. "Studi sul teatro greco di Siracusa," *Paladio* 17: 97–132.

Bernabò Brea, L. 1995. "Ecuba e Taltibio: maschere delle Troiane di Euripide in una tomba liparese del IV sec. a.C.," *SIFC* 13: 3–9.

Bers, V. 1997. *Speech in Speech: Studies in Incorporated Oratio Recta in Attic Drama and Oratory*. Lanham.

Bertino, A. "Sulla fonte di ispirazione della scene di soggeto teatrale sui vasi a figure rosse del IV secolo a.c.," in N. Caffarello, ed., *Achaeologica: Scritti in onore di A. N. Modena*. Florence. 17–28.

Betts, J, Hooker, T., and Green, J. R., eds. 1988. *Studies in Honour of T. B. L. Webster*, vol. 2. Bristol.

Bieber, M. 1939. *The History of the Greek and Roman Theater*. Princeton. (2nd ed. 1961).

Biles, Z. 2007. "Celebrating Poetic Victory: Representations of Epinikia in Classical Athens," *JHS* 127: 19–37.

Biles, Z. forthcoming. "Aeschylus' Afterlife: Reperformance by Decree in 5th C. Athens?" *ICS* 31–2: 206–42.

Blänsdorf, J., ed. 1990. *Theater und Gesellschaft im Imperium romanum*. Tübingen.

Boardman, J. 1990. "Herakles VIII. Herakles' Death and Apotheosis," *LIMC* V: 121–32.

Bollinger, T. 1969. *Theatralis Licentia: Die Publikumsdemonstationen an den öffentlichen Spielen der früheren Kaiserzeit und ihre Bedeutung im politischen Leben*. Winterthur.

Borza, E. N. 1995. *Makedonika*. Claremont, Ca.

Bosher, K. G. 2006. *Theater on the Periphery: A Social and Political History of the Theater in Early Sicily*. Diss. U. Michigan. Ann Arbor.

Bosher, K. G. forthcoming. *Theatre Outside Athens: Drama in Greek Sicily and South Italy*. Cambridge.

Bosworth, A. B. 1980. *A Historical Commentary on Arrian's History of Alexander*, vol. 1. Oxford.

Bowersock, G. W. 2006. *Mosaics as History: The Near East from Late Antiquity to Islam*. Cambridge, Ma.

Braund, D. 2000. "Strattis' *Kallippides:* The Pompous Actor from Scythia?," in Harvey and Wilkins 2000: 151–8.

Bremer, J. M. 1991. "Poets and their Patrons," in H. Hoffmann and A. Harder, eds., *Fragmenta Dramatica: Beiträge zur Interpretation der griechischen Tragikerfragmente und ihrer Wirkungsgeschichte*. Göttingen. 39–60.

Briant, P. 1989. "Table du roi, tribut et redistribution chez les Achéménides," in Briant and Herrenschmidt 1989: 35–44.

Briant, P. 2002. *From Cyrus to Alexander: A History of the Persian Empire*. trans. P. T. Daniels [French original 1996]. Winona Lake, Indiana.

Briant, P. and Herrenschmidt, C. eds. 1989. *Le Tribut dans l'Empire Perse: Actes de la Table ronde de Paris 12–13 Décembre 1986*. Louvain and Paris.

Brommer, F. 1959. *Satyrspiele. Bilder griechischer Vasen*. Berlin.

Brommer, F. 1978/9. "Huckepack," *J. Paul Getty Museum Journal* 6/7: 139–46.

Brommer, F. 1983. "Satyrspielvasen in Malibu," *Greek Vases in the J. Paul Getty Museum* 1: 115–20.

Brown, P. G. M. 2002. "Actors and Actor-Managers at Rome in the Time of Plautus and Terence," in Easterling and Hall 2002: 225–37.

Brugnoli, G. 1983. "Mimi Edaces," in Doglio 1983: 77–90.

Bruneau, P. 1999. "Le répertoire mosaïstique et sa transmission," in D. Mulliez, ed., *Ateliers. La transmission de l'image dans l'Antiquité*. Cahiers de la Maison de la Recherche, Université Charles-de-Gaulle, Lille 3, 21: 45–50.

Bruneau, P. 2000. "Les mosaïstes antiques avaient-ils des cahiers de modèles? (suite et probablement sans fin)," *Ktema* 25: 191–7.

Buhmann, H. 1975. *Der Sieg in Olympia und in den anderen panhellenischen Spielen*. Munich.

Burkert, W. 1966. "Greek Tragedy and Sacrificial Ritual," *GRBS* 7: 87–121.

Butcher, S. H. 1929. *The Poetics of Aristotle*. 4th ed. London.

Calder, W. M. 2006. *Theatrokratia*, ed. R. S. Smith. *Spudasmata* 104. Hildesheim.

Camp, J. 1999. "Excavations in the Athenian Agora 1996 and 1997," *Hesperia* 68: 255–83.

Capps, E. 1900. "Chronological Studies in the Greek Tragic and Comic Poets," *AJA* 21: 38–61.

Capps, E. 1943. "A New Fragment of the List of Victors at the City Dionysia," *Hesperia* 12: 1–11.

Carcopino, J. 1941. *Daily Life in Ancient Rome: The People and the City at the Height of the Empire*. Harmondsworth.

Carey, C. 2004. "Antiphon's Daughter," in D. L. Cairns and R. A. Knox, eds., *Law, Rhetoric, and Comedy in Athens: Essays in Honour of Douglas M. MacDowell*. Swansea. 123–50.

Carpenter, T. H. 1997. *Dionysian Imagery in Fifth-Century Athens*. Oxford.

Carpenter, T. H. 2003. "The Native Market for Red-Figure Vases in Apulia," *MAAR* 48: 1–24.

Carpenter, T. H. 2005. "Images of Satyr Plays in South Italy," in Harrison 2005: 219–37.

Carpenter, T. H. 2009. "Prolegomenon to the Study of Apulian Red-Figure Pottery," *AJA* 113: 27–38.

Ceccarelli, P. 2004. "'Autour de Dionysos.' Remarques sur la dénomination des artistes dionysiaques," in Hugoniot, Hurlet and Milanezi 2004: 109–42.

Ceccarelli, P. and Milanezi, S. 2007. "Dithyramb, Tragedy – and Cyrene," in Wilson 2007b: 187–214.

Chamoux, F. 1998. "Le théâtre grec en Libye," in J. Leclant and J. Jouanna, eds., *Le théâtre grec antique: la tragédie. Actes du 8ème Colloque de la Villa Kérylos à Beaulieu-sur-Mer, les 3 et 4 octobre 1997*. Cahiers de la Villa Kérylos 8. Paris. 128–42.

Chantraine, P. 1974. *Dictionnaire étymologique de la langue grecque*, vol. 3. Paris.

Charitonidis, S., Kahil, L., and Ginouvès, R. 1970. *Les Mosaïques de la Maison du Ménandre à Mytilène*. Antike Kunst Beiheft 6. Bern.

Ciancio Rossetto, P. and Pisani Sartorio, G. eds. 1994. *Teatri greci e romani alle origini del linguaggio rappresentato*. 3 vols. Rome.

Clairmont, C.W. 1993. *Classical Attic Tombstones*, 7 vols. Kilchberg.

Coleman, K. M. 1996. "Ptolemy Philadelphus and the Roman Amphitheater," in W. J. Slater 1996: 49–68.

Collard, C. 2005. "Colloquial Language in Tragedy: A Supplement to the Work of P. T. Stevens," *CQ* 55: 350–86.

Collard, C., Cropp, M. and Gibert, J. 2004. *Euripides: Selected Fragmentary Plays*, vol. 2. Warminster.

Colonna, G. 1976. "Scriba cum rege sedens" in *L'Italie préromaine et la Rome républicaine. Mélanges J. Heurgon*. Rome. 187–95.

Colvin, S. 1999. *Dialect in Aristophanes and the Politics of Language in Ancient Greek Literature*. Oxford.

Corbato, C. 1983. "Symposium e teatro: Dati e problemi," in Doglio 1983: 65–76.

Courtois, C. 1989. *Le bâtiment de scène des théâtres d'Italie et de Sicile: Étude chronologique et typologique*. Archaeologia Transatlantica 8. Providence RI and Louvain-La Neuve.

Craik, E. M., ed. 1990. *"Owls to Athens:" Essays on Classical Subjects Presented to Sir Kenneth Dover*. Oxford.

Crosby, M. 1955. "Five Comic Scenes from Athens," *Hesperia* 24: 76–84.

Cropp, M. 2003. "Hypsiplyle and Athens," in Csapo and Miller 2003: 129–45.

Cropp, M. and Fick, G. 1985. *Resolutions and Chronology in Euripides: The Fragmentary Tragedies. BICS* Supp. 43. London.

Csapo, E. 1986. "A Note on the Würzburg Bell-Crater H5697 ('Telephus Travestitus')," *Phoenix* 40: 379–92.

Csapo, E. 1990. "Hikesia in the Telephus of Aeschylus," *Quaderni Urbinati di Cultura Classica* n.s. 34 (1990) 41–52.

Csapo, E. 1993a. "A Case Study in the Use of Theatre Iconography as Evidence for Ancient Acting," *Antike Kunst* 36 (1993) 41–58.

Csapo E. 1993b. "Deep Ambivalence: Notes on a Greek Cockfight," *Phoenix* 47: 1–28, 115–24.

Csapo, E. 1994. Review/Discussion of 0. Taplin, *Comic Angels and Other Approaches to Greek Drama through Vase-Paintings*, in *Echos du Monde Classique/ Classical Views* 38: 51–8.

Csapo, E. 1997a. "Riding the Phallus for Dionysus: Iconology, Ritual and Gender-Role De/construction," *Phoenix* 51: 253–95.

Csapo, E. 1997b. "Mise-en-scène théâtrale, scène de théâtre artisanale: les mosaïques de Ménandre à Mytilène, leur contexte social et leur tradition iconographique," in B. Le Guen, ed., *De la scène aux gradins*. Pallas 47: 165–82.

Csapo, E. 1999. "Performance and Iconographic Tradition in the Illustrations of Menander," *Syllecta Classica* 10: 154–88.

Csapo, E. 2000. "From Aristophanes to Menander? Genre Transformation in Greek Comedy," in M. Depew and D. Obbink, eds., *Matrices of Genre: Authors, Canons, and Society*. Cambridge Ma. 115–34, 271–6 (notes).

Csapo, E. 2001. "The First Artistic Representations of Theatre: Dramatic Illusion and Dramatic Performance in Attic and South Italian Art," in G. Katz and D. Pietropaolo, eds., *Theatre and the Visual Arts*. Ottawa. 17–38.

Csapo, E. 2002. "Kallippides on the Floor-Sweepings: The Limits of Realism in Classical Acting and Performance Styles," in Easterling and Hall 2002: 127–47.

Csapo, E. 2003. "The Dolphins of Dionysus," in E. Csapo and M.C. Miller, eds., *Poetry, Theory, Praxis*. Oxford. 69–98

Csapo, E. 2004a. "The Politics of the New Music," in P. Murray and P.J. Wilson, eds., *Music and the Muses: The Culture of 'Mousike' in the Classical Athenian City*. Oxford. 207–48.

Csapo, E. 2004b. "The Rise of Acting: Some Social and Economic Conditions behind the Rise of the Acting Profession in the Fifth and Fourth Centuries B.C.," in Hugoniot, Hurlet and Milanezi 2004: 53–76.

Csapo, E. 2005. *Theories of Mythology*. Oxford.

Csapo, E. 2006/7. "The Iconography of the Exarchos," *MeditArch* 19/20: 55–65.

Csapo, E. 2007. "The Men Who Built the Theatres: *Theatropolai, Theatronai,* and *Arkhitektones,*" in Wilson 2007b: 87–115.

Csapo, E. 2008. "Star Choruses: Eleusis, Orphism and New Musical Imagery and Dance," in M. Revermann and P. Wilson, eds., *Performance, Iconography, Reception*. Oxford. 262–90.

Csapo, E. forthcoming A. "The Context of Choregic Dedication" in O. Taplin and R. Wyles, eds., *Pronomos: His Vase and its World*. Oxford.

Csapo, E. forthcoming B. "The Economics, Poetics, Politics, Metaphysics and Ethics of the 'New Music,'" in D. Yatromanolakis, ed. *Politics and Music*.

Csapo, E. and Miller, M. C., eds. 2003. *Poetry, Theory, Praxis: The Social Life of Myth, Word and Image in Ancient Greece*. Oxford.

Csapo, E. and and Miller, M. C., eds. 2007a. *The Origins of Theater in Ancient Greece and Beyond*. Cambridge.

Csapo, E. and Miller, M. C. 2007b. "General Introduction" in Csapo and Miller 2007a: 1–38.

Csapo, E. and Slater, W. J. 1995. *The Context of Ancient Drama*. Ann Arbor.

Dacier, A. 1692. *La Poétique d'Aristote*. Paris (repr. Hildesheim 1976).

Damen, M. 1983. "Actor and Character in Greek Tragedy," *Theatre Journal* 41: 316–40.

D'Arms, J. 1998. "Between Public and Private: the *Epulum Publicum* and Caesar's *horti trans Tiberim,*" in M. Cima and E. La Rocca, eds., *Horti Romani*. Rome. 33–43.

D'Arms, J. 1999. "Performing Culture: Roman Spectacle and the Banquets of the Powerful," in Bergmann and Kondoleon 1999: 301–19.

Davidson, J. 2000. "Gnesippus paigniagraphos: The Comic Poets and the Erotic Mime," in Harvey and Wilkins 2000: 41–64.

Davies, J. K. 1971. *Athenian Propertied Families 600–300 BC*. Oxford.

Dearden, C. W. 1988. "Phlyax Comedy in Magna Graecia: A Reassessment," in Betts, Hooker, and Green 1988: 33–41.

Dearden, C. W. 1990. "Fourth Century Drama in Sicily: Athenian or Sicilian?" in J.-P. Descoeudres, ed. *Greek Colonists and Native Populations*. Oxford. 231–42.

Dearden, C. W. 1999. "Plays for Export," *Phoenix* 53: 139–57.

Delbrück, R. 1929. *Die Consulardiptychen und verwandte Denkmäler*. Berlin.

Del Corno, D. 1975. "Alcuni aspetti del linguaggio di Menandro," *SCO* 24: 13–48.

Del Corno, D. 1979. "Vita cittadina e commedia borghese," in A. Barigazzi *et al.*, eds., *La crisi della polis*. Storia e civiltà dei Greci 5. Milan. 265–98.

Del Corno, D. 1997. "La caratterizzazione dei personaggi di Aristofane attraverso I fatti di lingua e di stile," in Thiercy and Menu 1997: 243–52.

Dentzer, J.-M. 1982. *Le motif du banquet couché dans le Proche-Orient et le monde grec du VIIe au IVe siècle avant J.-C.* BEFAR 246. Rome.

Descoeudres, J., ed. 1990. *Eumousia: Ceramic and Iconographic Studies in Honour of Alexander Cambitoglou.* Mediterranean Archaeology Suppl. 1. Sydney.

Devine, A. M. and Stephens, L. D. 1981. "A New Aspect of the Evolution of the Trimeter in Euripides," *TAPA* 111: 43–64.

Devine, A. M. and Stephens, L. D. 1983. "Semantics, syntax, and phonological organization in Greek: Aspects of the Theory of Metrical Bridges," *CPh* 78: 1–25.

Dickin, M. 1999. *The Distribution of Messenger Roles in Fifth-Century Tragedy.* MA thesis, McMaster.

Dickin, M. 2009. *A Vehicle for Performance: Acting the Messenger in Greek Tragedy.* Lanham, Md.

Diggle, J., ed. 2004. *Theophrastus Characters.* Cambridge.

Dinsmoor, A. N. 1992. "Red-Figured Pottery from Samothrace," *Hesperia* 61: 501–15.

Dobbins, J. J. 2000. "The Houses at Antioch," in C. Kondoleon, ed., *Antioch. The Lost Ancient City.* Princeton. 51–62.

Doglio, F. *et al.* eds. 1983. *Spettacoli conviviali dall'antichità classica alle corti italiane del '400.* Viterbo.

Dover, K. J. 1968. *Aristophanes Clouds.* Oxford.

Dover, K. J. 1987. *Greek and the Greeks: Collected Papers,* vol. 1. Oxford.

Dover, K. J. 1993. *Aristophanes Frogs.* Oxford.

Drougou, S. 1997. "Das antike Theater von Vergina. Bemerkungen zu Gestalt und Funktion des Theaters in der antiken Hauptstadt Makedoniens," *AthMitt* 112: 281–305.

Dubois, L. 1989. *Inscriptions grecques dialectales de Sicile.* Paris and Rome.

Ducos, M. 1990. "La condition des acteurs à Rome: Données juridiques et sociales," in Blänsdorf 1990: 7–18.

Dunbabin, K. M. D. 1996. "Convivial Spaces: Dining and Entertainment in the Roman Villa," *JRA* 9: 66–80.

Dunbabin, K. M. D. 1999. *Mosaics of the Greek and Roman World.* Cambridge.

Dunbabin, K. M. D. 2003. *The Roman Banquet.* Cambridge.

Dunbabin, K. M. D. 2004. "Problems in the Iconography of Roman Mime," in Hugoniot, Hurlet and Milanezi 2004: 161–81.

Duncan, A. 2006. *Performance and Identity in the Classical Greek World.* Cambridge.

Duncan, A. forthcoming. "Nothing to Do with Democracy? Aeschylus and Euripides at the Courts of the Tyrants," in D. Carter, ed. *Why Athens? Rethinking Tragic Politics.* Oxford.

Eagleton, T. 1996. *The Illusions of Postmodernism.* Oxford.

Easterling, P. E. 1993. "The End of an Era? Tragedy in the Early Fourth Century," in Sommerstein *et al.*, 1993: 559–69.

Easterling, P. E. 1994. "Euripides Outside Athens: A Speculative Note," *ICS* 19: 73–80.

Easterling, P. E. and E. Hall, eds. 2002. *Greek and Roman Actors: Aspects of an Ancient Profession.* Cambridge.

Edmondson, J. 1999. "The Cultural Politics of Public Spectacle in Rome and the Greek East, 167–166 BCE," in Bergmann and Kondoleon 1999: 77–95.

Eire, A. L. 1997. "A propos de l'attique familier de la comédie aristophanienne," in Thiercy and Menu 1997: 189–212.

Eliot, C. W. J. 1962. *Coastal Demes of Attika.* Toronto.

Ellinghaus, C. 1998/9. "Das Trikliniumsmosaik im Haus des Menander/Lesbos. Menander und Sokrates laden zum Symposion ein," *Boreas* 21–22: 261–9.

Fantuzzi, M. 1990. "Sulla scenografia dell'ora (e del luogo) nella tragedia greca," *MD* 24: 9–30.

Ferrari, F. 2004. "Papiri e mosaici: tradizione testuale e iconografia in alcune scene di Menandro," in G. Bastianini and A. Casanova, eds., *Menandro: cento anni di papiri. Atti del convegno internazionale di studi Firenze, 12–13 Giugno 2003.* Studi e Testi di papirologia, n.s. 5. Florence. 127–49.

Ferrari, G. 2002. *Figures of Speech: Men and Maidens in Ancient Greece.* Chicago & London.

Ferrari, G. 2003. "Myth and Genre on Athenian Vases," *Classical Antiquity* 22: 37–54.

Feyel, M. 1935. "L'inscription de Phintias-Licata," *REG*: 371–92.

Fitch, J. G., ed. 2008. *Oxford Readings in Classical Studies: Seneca.* Oxford.

Fittschen, K. 1991. "Zur Rekonstruktion griechischer Dichterstatuen. 1.Teil: Die Statue des Menander," *AthMitt* 106: 243–79.

Fotopoulos, D. and Delivorrias, A. 1997. *Greece at the Benaki Museum.* Athens.

Förtsch, R. 1997. "Die Nichtdarstellung des Spektakulären: Griechische Bildkunst und griechisches Drama im 5. und frühen 4. Jh. v. Chr.," *Hephaistos* 15: 47–68.

Fraenkel, E. 1977. *Due seminari romani di Eduard Fraenkel.* Rome.

Franklin, J. L. 1980. *Pompeii: The Electoral Programmata, Campaigns and Politics, A.D. 71–79.* Rome.

Franklin, J. L. 1987. "Pantomimists at Pompeii. Actius Anicetus and his troupe," *AJP* 108: 95–107.

Frederiksen, R. 2002. "The Greek Theatre. A Typical Building in the Urban Centre of the Polis?," in T. E. Nielsen, ed. *Even More Studies in the Ancient Greek Polis.* Stuttgart. 65–124.

Friedlaender, L 1922. *Darstellungen aus der Sittengeschichte Roms.* 10th ed. Aalen.

Friend, A. M. 1941. "Menander and Glykera in the Mosaics of Antioch," in R. Stillwell, ed., *Antioch on the Orontes* III, *The Excavations 1937–1939.* Princeton. 248–51.

Froning, H. 2002. "Masken und Kostüme," in S. Moraw and E. Nölle, eds., *Die Geburt des Theaters in der griechischen Antike.* Mainz. 70–95.

Futrell, A. 1997. *Blood in the Arena: the Spectacle of Roman Power.* Austin.

Garelli(-François), M.-H. 2000. "Des soldats sur la scène comique: espace dramatique et espace civique sous les Sévères dans l'Empire romain," *Pallas* 54: 321–36.

Garelli, M.-H. 2007. *Danser le mythe: La pantomime et sa réception dans la culture antique.* Louvain.

Garland, R. 2004. *Surviving Greek Tragedy.* London.

Garton, C. 1972. *Personal Aspects of the Roman Theatre.* Toronto.

Garulli, V. 2004. *Il peri poeton di Lobone di Argo.* Bologna.

Gebhard, E. 1973. *The Theater at Isthmia.* Chicago and London.

Gebhard, E. 1974. "The Form of the Orchestra in Early Greek Theater," *Hesperia* 43: 402–47.

Gentili, B. 1962. "Nuovo esempio di 'theatron' con gradinata rettilinea a Siracusa," *Dioniso* 15: 122–30.

Ghiron-Bistagne, P. 1974. "Die Krise des Theaters in der griechischen Welt im 4. Jh. v.u.Z." in E. Welskopf, ed., *Hellenische Poleis, Krise, Wandung, Wirkung*, vol. 3. Berlin: 1335–71.

Ghiron-Bistagne, P. 1976. *Recherches sur les acteurs dans la Grèce antique*. Paris.

Ginouvès, R. 1972. *Le théâtron à gradins droits et l'odéon d'Argos*. Paris.

Giuliani, L. 1995. *Tragik, Trauer und Trost: Bildervasen für eine apulische Totenfeier*. Berlin.

Giuliani, L. 2001. "Sleeping Furies: Allegory, Narration and the Impact of Texts in Apulian Vase-Painting," *Scripta Classica Israelica* 20: 17–38.

Giuliani, L. 2003. *Bild und Mythos. Geschichte der Bilderzählung in der griechischen Kunst*. Munich.

Goette, H. R. 1995a. "Griechische Theaterbauten der Klassik—Forschungsstand und Fragestellungen," in Pöhlmann 1995a: 9–48.

Goette, H. R. 1995b. "Beobachtungen im Theater des Amphiareion von Oropos (Studien zur historischen Landeskunde Attikas V)," *AthMitt* 110: 253–60.

Goette, H. R. 2007. "Choregic Monuments and Athenian Democracy," in Wilson 2007b: 122–49.

Goldberg, S. 2000. "Going for Baroque: Seneca and the English," in Harrison 2000a: 209–31.

Golden, M. 1998. *Sport and Society in Ancient Greece*. Cambridge.

Golden, M. 2009. *Greek Sport and Social Status*. Austin.

Goldhill, S. and Osborne, R. eds. 1999. *Performance Culture and Athenian Democracy*. Cambridge.

Gombrich, E. H. 1960. *Art and Illusion: A Study of the Psychology of Pictorial Representation*. London & New York.

Gomme, A. W. and Sandbach, F. W. 1973. *Menander: A Commentary*. Oxford.

Goulaki-Voutira, A. 1999. "Some Notes on Phrynis by Asteas," *Apollo* 15: 13–15.

Gourdet, C. 2004. "Pantomimes et grandes familles sous le Haut-Empire," in Hougoniot, Hurlet and Milanezi 2004: 307–25.

Grabar, O. 1968. *L'art de la fin de l'antiquité et du moyen âge*. Paris.

Grandjean, Y. and Salviat, F. eds. 2000. *Guide de Thasos*. Paris.

Green, J. R. 1985a. "A Representation of the *Birds* of Aristophanes," *Greek Vases in the J. Paul Getty Museum* 2: 95–118.

Green, J. R. 1985b. "Drunk Again: A Study in the Iconography of the Comic Theater," *AJA* 89: 465–72.

Green, J. R. 1991. "On Seeing and Depicting the Theatre in Classical Athens," *GRBS* 32: 15–50.

Green, J. R. 1994. *Theatre in Ancient Greek Society*. London and New York.

Green, J. R. 1995a. "Oral Tragedies? A Question from St. Petersburg," *QUCC* n.s. 51: 77–86.

Green, J. R. 1995b. "Theatrical Motifs in Non-Theatrical Contexts on Vases of the Later Fifth and Fourth Centuries," in Griffiths 1995: 95–121.

Green, J. R. 1995c. "Theatre Production: 1987–1995," *Lustrum* 37: 7–202.

Green, J. R. 1999. "Tragedy and the Spectacle of the Mind: Messenger Speeches, Actors, Narrative and Audience Imagination in Fourth-Century BCE Vase Painting," in Bergmann and Kondoleon 1999: 37–63.

Green, J. R. 2002. "Towards a Reconstruction of Performance Style," in Easterling and Hall 2002: 93–126.

Green, J. R. 2003a. "Smart and Stupid. The Evolution of Some Masks and Characters in Fourth-Century Comedy," in J. Davidson and A. Pomeroy, eds., *Theatres of Action. Papers for Chris Dearden.* Auckland. 118–32.

Green, J. R. 2003b. "Speculations on the Tragic Poet Sthenelus and a Comic Vase in Richmond," in Csapo and Miller 2003.178–84.

Green, J. R. 2006. "The Persistent Phallos: Regional Variability in the Performance Style of Comedy," in J. Davidson, F. Muecke, and P. Wilson, eds., *Drama III: Papers for Kevin Lee. BICS* Suppl. 87. London. 141–62.

Green, J. R. 2007a. "Let's Hear it for the Fat Men: Padded Dancers and the Prehistory of Drama," in Csapo and Miller 2007a.96–107.

Green, J. R. 2007b. Review of Taplin 2007. *BMCR* 2007.10.37.

Green, J. R. 2008. "Theatre Production, 1996–2006," *Lustrum* 50: 7–391.

Green, J. R. forthcoming. *A Catalogue of the James Logie Memorial Collection of Classical Antiquities at the University of Canterbury, Christchurch.* Christchurch, NZ.

Green, J. R. and Handley, E. 1995. *Images of the Greek Theatre.* London.

Gregory, J., ed. 2005. *A Companion to Greek Tragedy.* Oxford.

Griffith, M. 1978. "Aeschylus, Sicily, and Prometheus," in R. Dawe, J. Diggle and P. E. Easterling, eds., *Dionysiaca: Nine Studies in Greek Poetry by Former Pupils, Presented to Denys Page on his Seventieth Birthday.* Cambridge. 105–39.

Griffith, M. 2007. "'Telling the Tale:' A Performance Tradition from Homer to Pantomime," in M. McDonald and J. M. Walton, eds., *The Cambridge Companion to Greek and Roman Theatre.* Cambridge. 13–35.

Griffiths, A., ed. 1995. *Stage Directions: Essays in Honour of Eric Handley,* BICS Suppl. 66. London.

Gruen, E. S. 1984. *The Hellenistic World and the Coming of Rome.* Berkeley.

Hackens, T. 1967. "Le théâtre," *Thorkos* III. Brussels. 75–96.

Haigh, A. E. 1907. *The Attic Theatre,* 3rd ed. Oxford.

Hall, E. 1989. *Inventing the Barbarian: Greek Self-Definition through Tragedy.* Oxford.

Hall, E. 1996. *Aeschylus Persians.* Warminster.

Hall, E. 2002. "The Singing Actors of Antiquity," in Easterling and Hall 2002: 3–38.

Hall, E. 2006. *The Theatrical Cast of Athens: Interactions between Ancient Greek Drama and Society.* Oxford.

Hall, E. 2007. "Greek Tragedy 430–380 BC," in R. Osborne, ed., *Debating the Athenian Cultural Revolution: Art, Literature, Philosophy, and Politics 430–380 BC.* Cambridge. 264–87.

Hall, E. 2008. "Introduction: Pantomime, A Lost Chord of Ancient Culture," in Hall and Wyles 2008: 1–40.

Hall, E. and R. Wyles, eds., 2008. *New Directions in Ancient Pantomime.* Oxford.

Halliwell, S. 1986. *Aristotle's* Poetics. Chapel Hill and London.

Halliwell, S. 1990. "The Sounds of the Voice in Old Comedy," in Craik 1990: 69–79.

Hallof, K. and Stroszeck, J. 2002. "Eine neue Schauspielerstele vom Kerameikos," *AM* 117: 115–31.

Hamilton, R. 1992. *Choes and Anthesteria: Athenian Iconography and Ritual.* Ann Arbor.

Handley, E. 1969. "Notes on the *Theophoroumene* of Menander," *BICS* 16: 88–101.

Handley, E. 1985. "Comedy," *The Cambridge History of Classical Literature* 1. Cambridge. 355–425.

Handley, E. 2000. "Going to Hades: Two Passages of Aristophanes, *Frogs* (786–94, 1–37)," *Acta Ant. Hung.* 40: 151–60.

Handley, E. 2002. "Acting, Action and Words in New Comedy," in Easterling and Hall 2002: 165–88.

Hanink, J. 2008. "Literary Politics and the Euripidean *Vita,*" *PCPS* 54: 115–35.

Harder, A. 1985. *Euripides' Kresphontes and Archelaos.* Leiden.

Hardy, E. R. 1931. *The Large Estates of Byzantine Egypt.* New York.

Harrison, G. W. M., ed. 2000a. *Seneca in Performance.* London.

Harrison, G. W. M. 2000b. "*Semper ego auditor tandem?* Performance and Physical Settting of Seneca's Plays," in Harrison 2000a: 137–49.

Harrison, G. W. M., ed. 2005. *Satyr Drama: Tragedy at Play.* Swansea.

Harvey, D. and Wilkins, J. eds. 2000. *The Rivals of Aristophanes.* London.

Heath, M. 1990. "Aristophanes and his Rivals," *G&R* 37: 143–58.

Hedreen, G. 2007. "Myths of Ritual in Athenian Vase-Paintings of Silens," in Csapo and Miller 2007: 150–95.

Herington, C. J. 1967. "Aeschylus in Sicily," *JHS* 87: 74–85.

Herington, C. J. 1985. *Poetry into Drama: Early Tragedy and the Greek Poetic Tradition.* Berkeley.

Heydemann, H. 1886. "Die Phlyakendarstellungen auf bemalten Vasen," *JdI* 1: 260–313.

Heynen, C. and Krumeich, R. 1999. "10 Sophokles: Unsicheres," in Krumeich, Pechstein and Seidensticker 1999: 393.

Himmelmann, N. 1994. *Realistische Themen in der griechischen Kunst der archaischen und klassischen Zeit.* Berlin & New York.

Hoffmann, A. 2002. *Grabritual und Gesellschaft: Gefäßformen, Bildthemen und Funktionen unteritalisch-rotfiguriger Keramik auf der Nekropole von Tarent.* Leidorf.

Hollis, A. S. 2007. *Fragments of Roman Poetry, c.60 B.C. – A.D. 20.* Oxford.

Hölscher, T. 1973. *Griechische Historienbilder des 5. und 4. Jahrhunderts v. Chr.* Würzburg.

Horsfall, N. 1996. *La cultura della plebs romana.* Cornucopia 2. Barcelona.

Hughes, A. 2003. "Comedy in Paestan Vase Painting," *OJA* 22: 281–301.

Hughes, A. 2006. "The 'Perseus Dance' Vase Revisited," *OJA* 25: 413–33.

Hugoniot, C. 2004. "De l'infamie à la contrainte. Évolution du statut de l'acteur sous l'Empire romain," in Hugoniot, Hurlet and Milanezi 2004: 213–40.

Hugoniot, C., Hurlet, F. and Milanezi, S. eds. 2004. *Le statut de l'acteur dans l'Antiquité grecque et romaine.* Tours.

Huskinson, J. 2003. "Theatre, Performance, and Theatricality in Some Mosaic Pavements from Antioch," *BICS* 46: 131–65.

Hutton, J. 1982. *Aristotle's Poetics*. New York.

Isler, H. P. 2007. *Das Theater: Grabungen 1997 und 1998. Eretria* 18, *Ausgrabungen und Forschungen*. Gollion.

Jashemski, W. F. 1979. *The Gardens of Pompeii*. New Rochelle, N.Y.

Jeffery, L. H. 1990. *The Local Scripts of Archaic Greece,* 2nd ed. rev. by A. Johnston. Oxford.

Jones, C. P. 1990. "Lucian and the Bacchants of Pontus," *EMC* n.s. 9: 53–63.

Jones, C. P. 1991. "Dinner Theater," in Slater 1991: 185–98.

Jordan, D. 2007. "An Opisthographic Lead Tablet from Sicily with a Financial Document and a Curse Concerning *Choregoi,*" in Wilson 2007b: 335–50.

Jory, E. J. 1970. "Associations of Actors in Rome," *Hermes* 98: 224–53.

Jouan, F. 1983. "Réflexions sur le rôle du protagoniste tragique," in *Théâtre et spectacles dans l'antiquité: Actes du Colloque de Strasbourg (5–6 Novembre 1981)*. Travaux du Centre de recherche sur le Proche-Orient et la Grèce antiques 7. Leiden. 63–80.

Kaimio, M. 1999. "The Citizenship of the Theatre Makers," *WürzJbb* 23: 43–61.

Kaltsas, N. 2002. *Sculpture in the National Archaeological Museum, Athens. Catalogue.* Athens.

Kaza-Papageorgiou, K. 1993. "Οδός Ρώμα, πάροδος Ηγησιπύλης (οικόπεδο Αφών N. Λουράντου, Ο.Τ. 272)," *ArchDelt* 48: 67–70.

Kerkhof, R. 2001. *Dorische Posse, Epicharm und attische Komödie*. Munich/ Leipzig.

Keuls, E. 1997. *Painter and Poet in Ancient Greece: Iconography and the Literary Arts.* Stuttgart and Leipzig.

Kondoleon, C. 1991. "Signs of Privilege and Pleasure: Roman Domestic Mosaics," in E. K. Gazda, ed., *Roman Art in the Private Sphere*. Ann Arbor. 105–15.

Kondoleon, C. 1994. *Domestic and Divine: Roman Mosaics in the House of Dionysos.* Ithaca.

Kondoleon, C. 2000. "Mosaic of Menander, Glykera and Comedy," in C. Kondoleon ed., *Antioch. The Lost Ancient City*. Princeton. 156.

Kossatz-Deissmann, A. 1978. *Dramen des Aischylos auf westgriechischen Vasen*. Mainz.

Kossatz-Deissmann, A. 1980. "Telephus travestitus," in H. A. Cahn and E. Simon, eds., *Tainia. Festschrift für Roland Hampe*. Mainz. 281–90.

Kowalzig, B. 2008. "Nothing to Do with Demeter? Something to Do with Sicily! Theatre and Society in the Early Fifth-Century West," in Revermann and Wilson 2008: 128–57.

Kragelund, P. 2008. "Senecan Tragedy: Back on Stage?" in Fitch 2008: 180–94.

Krinzinger, F., and Gassner, V. 1997. "Velia – neue Forschungen auf der Akropolis," *JhÖAI* 66, Beiblatt: 229–51.

Krumeich, R. 1999. "Archäologische Einleitung," in Krumeich, Pechstein and Seidensticker 1999: 41–73.

Krumeich, R., Pechstein, N. and Seidensticker, B. eds. 1999. *Das griechische Satyrspiel.* Darmstadt.

Kurke, L. 1993. "The Economy of *Kudos,*" in C. Dougherty and L. Kurke, eds., *Cultural Poetics in Archaic Greece: Cult, Performance, Politics*. Cambridge. 131–63.

Lambert, S. 2008. "Polis and Theatre in Lykourgan Athens: the Honorific Decrees," in A. P. Matthaiou and I. Polinskaya, eds., Μικρὸς ἱερομνήμων. Μελέτες εἰς μνήμην Michael H. Jameson. Athens. 53–85.

Lauter, H., and Lauter-Bufe, H. 2004. "Thersilion und Theater in Megalopolis. Das Bauensemble im Licht neuer Forschungen," *AA* 2004: 135–76.

Lebek, W. D. 1996. "Moneymaking on the Roman Stage," in Slater 1996: 29–48.

Lefkowitz, M. 1981. *The Lives of the Greek Poets*. London.

Le Guen, B. 1995. "Théâtre et cités à l'époque hellénistique: 'Mort de la cité' – 'Mort du théâtre,'" *REG* 108: 59–90.

Le Guen, B. 2001a. *Les Association de Technites Dionysiaques à l'époque hellénistique.* 2 vols. Nancy.

Le Guen, B. 2001b. "L'activité dramatique dans les îles grecques à l'époque hellénistique," *RÉA* 103: 261–98.

Le Guen, B. 2007. "Kraton, Son of Zotichos: Artists' Associations and Monarchic Power in the Hellenistic Period," in Wilson 2007b: 246–78.

Le Guen, B., ed. forthcoming. *L'Argent de concours*. Vincennes.

Leppin, H. 1992. *Histrionen: Untersuchungen zur sozialen Stellung von Bühnenkünstler im Westen des Römischen Reiches zur Zeit der Republik und des Principats.* Bonn.

Lesky, A. 1983. *Greek Tragic Poetry*, trans. M. Dillon. New Haven and London. Translation of *Die tragische Dichtung der Hellenen*, 3rd ed. 1972.

Lewis, D. M. 1987. "The King's Dinner," *Achaemenid History* 2: 79–87.

Leyerle, B. 2001. *Theatrical Shows and Ascetic Lives: John Chrysostom's Attack on Spiritual Marriage.* Berkeley.

Lightfoot, C. S. 2001. "Trying to Rescue Zeugma," *JRA* 14: 243.

Lightfoot, J. L. 2002 "Nothing to do with the Technitai of Dionysus?" in Easterling and Hall 2002: 209–24.

Lind, H. 1985. "Neues aus Kydathen: Beobachtungen zum Hintergrund der 'Daitales' und 'Ritter' des Aristophanes," *MusHelv* 42: 249–61.

Ling, R. 1991. *Roman Painting*. Cambridge.

Ling, R. 1995. "The Decoration of Roman Triclinia," in O. Murray and M. Tecusan, eds., *In Vino Veritas*. London. 239–51.

Ling, R. 1997. *The Insula of the Menander at Pompeii*. Vol. 1, *The Structures*. New York.

Ling, R. and Ling, L. 2005. *The Insula of the Menander at Pompeii*. Vol. 2, *The Decorations*. Oxford.

Lohmann, H. 1998. "Zur baugeschichtlichen Entwicklung des antiken Theaters: Ein Überblick," in G. Binder, ed., *Das antike Theater: Aspekte seiner Geschichte, Rezeption und Aktualität*. Trier. 191–249.

Lucas, D. W. 1968. *Aristotle Poetics*. Oxford.

Luppe, W. 1969. "Zu einer Choregeninschrift aus AIΞONAI (*IG* II/III² 3091," *APF* 19: 147–51.

Luppe, W. 1973. "Nochmals zur Choregeninschrift *IG* II/III² 3091," *APF* 22–3: 211–12.

McClure, L. K. 1995. "Female Speech and Characterization in Euripides," in Martino and Sommerstein 1995: 35–60.

McClure, L. K. 1999. *Spoken Like a Woman: Speech and Gender in Athenian Drama*. Princeton.

Maffre, J.-J. 2000. "Comédie et iconographie: les grands problèmes," in *Actes du colloque Le théâtre grec antique: la comédie, Cahiers de la Villa "Kérylos"* 10: 269–315.

Makres, A. 1994. *The Institution of the* Choregia *in Classical Athens*. Diss. Oxford.

Malavolta, M. 2000. "*Manceps Gregum*. Letture antiche e recenti di C.I.L. XIV 2299 (= I.L.S. 5206)," in G. Paci, ed., *EPIGRAPHAI: miscellanea epigrafica in onore di Lidio Gasperini*. Rome. Vol. 1: 541–7.

Manganaro, G. 1990. "*Metoikismos-Metaphora* di Poleis in Sicilia: Il caso dei Geloi di Phintias e la relativa documentazione epigrafica," *Annali della Scuola Normale Superiore di Pisa* 20: 391–408.

Manning, J.G. 2003. *Land and Power in Ptolemaic Egypt*. Cambridge.

Mansi, J. D., ed. 1762. *Sacrorum Conciliorum Nova et Amplissima Collectio*, vol. 8. Florence.

Markoulaki, S., Christoudoulakos, I., and Frangonikolaki, C. 2004. "Η αρχαία Κίσαμος και η πολεοδομική οργάνωση" in A. Ausilio, ed., *Creta romana e protobizantina: atti del congresso internazionale, Iraklion 23–30 settembre 2000*. Athens. Vol. 2: 355–80.

Marshall, C. W. 1997. "Comic Technique and the Fourth Actor," *CQ* 47: 77–84.

Marshall, C. W. 2001. "A Gander at the Goose Play," *Theatre Journal* 55: 51–71.

Marshall, C. W. 2006. *The Stagecraft and Performance of Roman Comedy*. Cambridge.

Marshall, C. W. and van Willigenburg, S. 2004. "Judging Athenian Dramatic Competitions," *JHS* 124: 90–107.

Martino, F. de and Sommerstein, A. H., eds., 1995. *Lo spettacolo della voce*. Bari.

Matthaiou, A. P. 1990/1. "Σῶν," *Horos* 8–9: 179–82.

Maxwell, R. L. 1993. *The Documentary Evidence for Ancient Mime*. Diss. Toronto.

Meier, C. 1980. *Res publica amissa*. 2nd ed. Wiesbaden.

Merkelbach, R. and Stauber, J. 2002. *Steinepigramme aus dem griechischen Osten* IV: *Die Südküste Kleinasiens, Syrien und Palästina*. Munich and Leipzig.

Mertens, D. 2004. "Siracusa e l'architettura del potere. Un schizzo," *Sicilia Antiqua* 1: 29–34.

Michaut, G. 1911. *Historie de la comédie romaine*. Paris.

Micheli, M. E. 1998. "Rilievi con maschere, attori, poeti. Temi di genere e/o ispirazione poetica?" *BdA* 83: 1–32.

Mikalson, J. 1998. *Religion in Hellenistic Athens*. Berkeley.

Miller, M. C. 2004 [2006]. "In Strange Company: Persians in Early Attic Theatre Imagery," *MeditArch* 17: 165–72.

Miller, M. C. forthcoming. "I am Eurymedon: Tensions and Ambiguities in Athenian War Imagery" in D. Pritchard, ed. *Democracy and War*. Cambridge.

Mingazzini, P. 1965/6. "Pitture vascolari e frontespizi di drammi teatrali," *RPAA* 38: 69–77.

Mittens, K. 1988. *Teatri greci e teatri ispirati all'architettura greca in Sicilia e nell'Italia meridionale, c. 350–50 a.C. Un Catalogo*. AnalRomInstDan Suppl. 13. Rome.

Mittens, K. 1993. "Theatre Architecture in Central Italy: Reception and Resistence," in P. G. Bilde, *et al.* eds., *Aspects of Hellenism in Italy: Towards a Cultural Unity?* Acta Hyperborea 5. Copenhagen. 91–106.

Mitsos, M. 1965. "Χορηγικὴ ἐπιγραφὴ ἐκ Βαρκίζης," *AE:* 163–7.

Moloney, E. forthcoming. *Theatre for a New Age: Macedonia and Ancient Greek Drama.*

Moore, M. B. 1997. *The Athenian Agora,* vol. 30: *Attic Red-Figure and White-Ground Pottery.* Princeton.

Morenilla-Talens, C. 1989. "Die Charakterisierung der Ausländer durch lautliche Ausdrucksmittel in den *Persern* des Aischylos sowie den *Acharnen* und *Vögeln* des Aristophanes," *IF* 94: 158–76.

Moret, J.-M. 1975. *L'Ilioupersis dans la céramique italiote.* Geneva.

Moretti, J.-Ch. 1991. "L'Architecture des théâtres en Grèce (1980–1989)," *Topoi* 1: 7–38.

Moretti, J.-Ch. 1992. "Les entrées en scène dans le théâtre grec: l'apport de l'archéologie," *Pallas* 38: 79–107.

Moretti, J.-Ch. 1993. "Les débuts de l'architecture théâtrale en Sicile et en Italie méridionale," *Topoi* 3: 72–100.

Moretti, J.-Ch. 2000. "Le théâtre du sanctuaire de Dionysos Eleuthérius à Athènes, au Ve s. av. J.-C.," *REG* 113: 275–98.

Murray, O., ed. 1990a. *Sympotica: A Symposium on the* Symposion. Oxford.

Murray, O. 1990b. "The Affair of the Mysteries: Democracy and the Drinking Group," in Murray 1990a: 149–61.

Nagy, G. 1990. *Pindar's Homer.* Baltimore.

Neiiendam, K. 1992. *The Art of Acting in Antiquity.* Copenhagen.

Nervegna, S. 2005. *The Ancient Reception of Menander.* Diss. Toronto.

Nervegna, S. 2007. "Staging Scenes or Plays? Theatrical Revivals of 'Old' Greek Drama in Antiquity," *ZPE* 162: 14–42.

Nervegna, S. forthcoming. "Menander's *Theophorumene* between Greece and Rome," *AJP* 131.

Nicholls, R. V. 1995. "The Stele-Goddess Workshop: Terracottas from Well U 13:1 in the Athenian Agora," *Hesperia* 64: 405–92.

Nielsen, I. 2002. *Cultic Theatres and Ritual Drama: A Study in Regional Development and Religious Interchange between East and West in Antiquity.* Aarhus.

Norman, A. F. 1992. *Libanius: Autobiography and Selected Letters.* Cambridge.

Nünlist, R. 2002. "Speech in Speech in Menander," in Willi 2002b: 219–60.

Ober, J. and Hedrick, C., eds. 1996. *Demokratia: A Conversation on Democracies Ancient and Modern.* Princeton.

Olson, D. 1998. *Aristophanes Peace.* Oxford.

Olson, D. 2000. "We Didn't Know Whether to Laugh or Cry: The Case of Karkinos," in Harvey and Wilkins 2000: 65–74.

Olson, D. 2002. *Aristophanes Acharnians.* Oxford.

Orrieux, C. 1985. *Zénon de Caunos, parépidémos, et le destin grec.* Paris.

Panofka, T. 1849. "Komödienscenen auf Thongefäßen," *Archäologische Zeitung* 7: 18–21, 34–44.

Parker, R. 1994. "Athenian Religion Abroad," in R. Osborne and S. Hornblower, eds., *Ritual, Finance, Politics: Athenian Democratic Accounts Presented to David Lewis.* Oxford. 339–46,

Parker, R. 2005. *Polytheism and Society at Athens.* Oxford.

Parrish, D. 1995. "The Architectural Design and Interior Décor of Apartment I in Insula 2 at Ephesus," in R. Ling, ed., *Fifth International Colloquium on Ancient Mosaics 2. JRA* Suppl. 9. Ann Arbor. 143–58.

Pavlovskis, Z. 1977. "The Voice of the Actor in Greek Tragedy," *CW* 71: 113–32.

Peremans, W. and van't Dack, E. 1950–. *Prosopographia Ptolemaica.* Louvain.

Petrovic, A. 2003. "Die Sprache des Wachters in der *Antigone* des Sophokles am Beispiel seines ersten Auftritts," *MH* 60: 193–209.

Petzl, G. 2004. "Seviteurs d'Arès – Serviteurs des Muses: sur la coexistence de deux mondes séparés," in S. Follet, ed., *L'hellénisme d'époque romaine: Nouveaux documents, nouvelles approaches, 1er s. a.C. –IIe s. p.C. Actes du colloque international à la mémoire de Louis Robert, Paris, 7–8 juillet 2000.* Paris. 287–95.

Pickard-Cambridge, A. 1927. *Dithyramb, Tragedy and Comedy.* Oxford.

Pickard-Cambridge, A. 1968. *The Dramatic Festivals of Athens.* 2nd ed. rev. by J. Gould and D.M. Lewis. Reissued with supplement, 1988. Oxford. [First edition 1953].

Pingiatoglou, S. 1992. "Eine Komödiendarstellung auf einer Choenkanne des Benaki-Museums," in H. Froning *et al.*, eds., *Kotinos: Festschrift für Erika Simon.* Mainz. 292–300.

Piqueux, A. 2006. "Quelques réflexions à propos du cratère en cloche d'Astéas 'Phrynis et Pyronidès'," *Apollo* 22: 3–10.

Plepelits, K. 1970. *Die Fragmente der Demen des Eupolis.* Vienna.

Pöhlmann, E., ed. 1995a. *Studien zur Bühnendichtung und zum Theaterbau der Antike.* Frankfurt.

Pöhlmann, E. 1995b. "Aristophanes auf der Bühne des 5. Jh," in Pöhlmann 1995a: 136–40.

Pöhlmann, E. 1998. Review of Taplin 1993. *Gnomon* 70: 385–90.

Polacco, L. 1986. "In Macedonia, sulle tracce di Euripide," *Dioniso:* 56: 17–30.

Polacco, L. and Anti, C. 1981. *Il teatro antico di Siracusa,* I. Rimini.

Poli-Palladini, L. 2001. "Some Reflections on Aeschylus' *Aetnae(ae)*," *RhM* 144: 287–325.

Potter, D. S. 2006. "Spectacle," in D. S. Potter, ed., *A Companion to the Roman Empire.* Oxford. 385–408.

Potts, L. J. 1962. *Aristotle on the Art of Fiction.* Cambridge.

Preiser, C. 2000. *Euripides: Telephos.* Spudasmata 78. Hildesheim, Zurich & New York.

Pritchard, J. B. 1969. *Ancient Near Eastern Texts Relating to the Old Testament.* 3rd ed. Princeton.

Puchner, W. 2002. "Acting in Byzantine Theatre: Evidence and Problems," in Easterling and Hall 2002: 304–24.

Raaflaub, K. 1983. "Democracy, Oligarchy, and the Concept of the 'Free Citizen' in Late Fifth-Century Athens," *Political Theory* 11: 517–44.

Raaflaub, K. 1984. "Zur Freiheitsbegriff der Griechen," in C. E. Welskopf, ed., *Soziale Typenbegriffe im alten Griechenland und ihr Fortleben in den Sprachen der Welt,* vol. 4. Berlin. 180–405.

Reger, G. 1994. "The Date and Historical Significance of IG XII v 714 of Andros," *Hesperia* 63: 309–21.

Reich, H. 1903. *Der Mimus: ein Litterar-Entwicklungsgeschichtlicher Versuch.* Berlin.

Reilly, J. 1994. "Standards, Maypoles, and Sacred Trees?," *AA* 499–505.

Revermann, M. 1999–2000. "Euripides, Tragedy and Macedon: Some Conditions of Reception," *ICS* 24–25: 451–67.

Revermann, M. 2006a. *Comic Business*. Oxford.

Revermann, M. 2006b. "The Competence of Theatre Audiences in Fifth- and Fourth-Century Athens," *JHS* 126: 99–124.

Revermann, M. and Wilson, P., eds. 2008. *Performance, Iconography, Reception: Studies in Honour of Oliver Taplin*. Oxford.

Rhodes, P. J. 2006. *A History of the Classical Greek World*. Oxford.

Rice, E. E. 1983. *The Grand Procession of Ptolemy Philadelphus*. Oxford.

Richter, G. M. 1984. *The Portraits of the Greeks*. Abridged & Revised by R. R. R. Smith. Oxford.

Ringer, M. 1998. *Electra and the Empty Urn: Metatheater and Role Playing in Sophocles*. Chapell Hill and London.

Robinson, E. G. D. 2004 [2006]. "Reception of Comic Theatre amongst the Indigenous South Italians," *Mediterranean Archaeology* 17: 193–212.

Roselli, D. K. 2005. "Vegetable Hawking Mom and Fortunate Son: Euripides, Tragic Style and Reception,' *Phoenix* 59: 1–49.

Roselli, D. K. 2007. Gender, Class and Ideology: The Social Function of Virgin Sacrifice in Euripides' Children of Herakles," *ClAnt* 26: 81–168.

Roselli, D. K. forthcoming. *Spectators as Producers: The Theater Audience of Classical Athens*. Austin.

Rossi, L. E. 1989. "Livelli di lingua, gestualità, rapporti di spazio e situazione drammatica sulla scena attica," in L. De Finis, ed., *Scena e spettacolo nell'antichità. Atti del convegno internazionale di studio (Trento 28–30 Marz. 1988)*. Florence. 63–78.

Rostovtzeff, M. I., Bellinger, A. R., Brown, F. E. and Welles, C. B. 1944. *The Excavations at Dura-Europos: Preliminary Report of the Ninth Season of Work 1935–1936, Part I, The Agora and Bazaar*. New Haven.

Rostovtzeff, M. I., Bellinger, A. R., Brown, F. E. and Welles, C. B. 1952. *The Excavations at Dura-Europos: Preliminary Report of the Ninth Season of Work 1935–1936, Part III, The Palace of the Dux Ripae and the Dolichenum*. New Haven.

Rothwell, K. 2007. *Nature, Culture,and the Origins of Greek Comedy*. Cambridge.

Roueché, C. 2002. "Images of Performance: New Evidence from Ephesus," in Easterling and Hall 2002: 254–81.

Rumpf, A. 1953. *Malerei und Zeichnung der klassischen Antike*. Handbuch der Archäologie 4. Munich.

Rumpf, A. 1961. "Attische Feste – Attische Vasen," *BJb* 161: 208–14.

Rusten, J. S. 2006. "Who 'Invented' Comedy: The Ancient Candidates for the Origins of Comedy and the Visual Evidence," *AJP* 127: 37–66.

Rusten, J. S. forthcoming. "A Forgotten Witness to Comic Art: The Phanagoria Chous (Hermitage State Museum 1869.47 Φα)," *Hesperia*.

Samiou, C. and Anthanasiades, G. 1987. "Αρχαιολογικές και αναστηλοτικές εργασίες στο θέατρο των Φιλιππών," *AErgoMak* 1: 353–62.

Sancisi-Weerdenburg, H. 1989. "Gifts in the Persian Empire," in Briant and Herrenschmidt 1989: 129–46.

Sancisi-Weerdenburg, H. 1995. "Persian Food Stereotypes and Political Identity," in J. Wilkins, D. Harvey and M. Dobson, eds., *Food in Antiquity*. Exeter. 286–302.

Sandbach, F. H. 1970. "Menander's Manipulation of Language for Dramatic Purposes," in E. Turner, ed., *Ménandre*. Entretiens sur l'antiquité classique 16. Geneva. 113–43.

Sande S. 1992. "Il giovane di Mozia – un attore?," *ActaIN* 8: 35–51.

Schauenburg, K. 2000. *Studien zur unteritalischen Vasenmalerei* II. Kiel.

Schauenburg, K. 2003. *Studien zur unteritalischen Vasenmalerei* VI. Kiel.

Schauenburg, K. 2005. *Studien zur unteritalischen Vasenmalerei* VII–VIII. Kiel.

Schiesaro, A. 2005. "Roman Tragedy," in R. W. Bushnell, ed., *A Companion to Tragedy*. Oxford. 269–86.

Schmandt-Besserat, D. 2001. "Feasting in the Ancient Near East," in M. Dietler and B. Hayden, eds., *Feasts: Archaeological and Ethnographic Perspectives on Food, Politics and Power*. London. 391–403.

Schmidt, M. 1967. "Dionysien," *Antike Kunst* 10: 70–81.

Schmidt, M. 1998. "Komische Teufel und andere Gesellen auf der griechischen Komödienbühne," *Antike Kunst* 41: 17–32.

Schmidt, P. L. 1990. "Nero und das Theater," in Blänsdorf 1990: 149–63.

Schmitt-Pantel, F. 1990. "Sacrificial Meal and *Symposion*: Two Models of Civic Institutions in the Archaic City," in Murray 1990a: 14–33.

Scholl, A. 2000. "Die älteste Satyrmaske des griechischen Theaters? Zur Kopie eines frühklassischen Reliefs in Kopenhagen," *Antike Kunst* 43: 44–52.

Scodel, R. 2001. "The Poet's Career, the Rise of Tragedy, and Athenian Cultural Hegemony," in D. Papenfuss and V. M. Strocka, eds., *Gab es das Griechische Wunder?* Mainz. 215–28.

Scullion, S. 2003. "Euripides and Macedon, or the Silence of the *Frogs*," *CQ* 53: 389–400.

Seaford, R. 1984. *Euripides Cyclops*. Oxford.

Sear, F. 2006. *Roman Theatres: An Architectural Study*. Oxford.

Seeberg, A. 2003. "Tragedy and Archaeology, Forty Years After," *BICS* 46: 43–75.

Segal, C. 1985. "Choral Lyric in the Fifth Century," in P. E. Easterling and B. M. W. Knox, eds., *The Cambridge History of Classical Literature*, Vol. 1, *Greek Literature*. Cambridge. 222–44.

Seidensticker, B. 1999. "Philologisch-literarische Einleitung," in Krumeich, Pechstein and Seidensticker 1999: 1–40.

Shapiro, H. A. 1987. "Kalos-Inscriptions with Patronymic," *ZPE* 68: 107–18.

Shapiro, H. A. 1992. "*Mousikoi Agones*: Music and Poetry at the Panathenaia," in J. Neils, ed., *Goddess and Polis: The Panathenaic Festival in Ancient Athens*. Princeton. 53–76.

Shatzman, L. 1975. *Senatorial Wealth and Roman Politics*. Brussels.

Shear, J. L. 2001. *Polis and Panathenaia: The History and Development of Athena's Festival*. Diss. Pennsylvania.

Shear, J. L. 2003a. "Atarbos' Base and the Panathenaia," *JHS* 123: 164–80.

Shear, J. L. 2003b. "Prizes from Athens: The List of Panathenaic Prizes and the Sacred Oil," *ZPE* 142: 87–105.

Sick, D. H. 1999. "Ummidia Quadratilla: Cagey Businesswoman or Lazy Pantomime Watcher," *ClAnt* 18: 330–48.

Sifakis, G. M. 1995. "The One-Actor Rule in Greek Tragedy," in Griffiths 1995: 13–24.

Simon, E. 1983. *Festivals of Attica*. Madison.

Simon, E. 2002. "Ein neuer signierter Kelchkrater des Asteas," *NumAntCl* 31: 115–27.

Simon, E. 2004. "The Paestan Painter Asteas," in C. Marconi, ed. *Greek Vases: Images, Contexts and Controversies, Proceedings of the Conference sponsored by The Center for the Ancient Mediterranean at Columbia University, 23–24 March 2002*. Leiden. 113–22.

Sijpesteijn, P. J. 1962/3. "Aurelia Charite und ihre Familie," *JÖBG* 11–12: 1–8.

Slater, N. W. 1990. "The Idea of the Actor," in Winkler and Zeitlin 1990: 385–95.

Slater, N. W. 2002. *Spectator Politics: Metatheater and Performance in Aristophanes*, Philadelphia.

Slater, W. J. 1984. "*Nemean One*: The Victor's Return in Poetry and Politics," in D.E. Gerber, ed., *Greek Poetry and Philosophy: Studies in Honour of Leonard Woodbury*. Chico. Ca. 1–18.

Slater, W. J., ed. 1991. *Dining in a Classical Context*. Ann Arbor.

Slater, W. J. 1992. Review of Leppin 1992, *BMCR* 03.04.05.

Slater, W. J. 1994. "Pantomime Riots," *ClAnt* 13: 120–44.

Slater, W. J., ed. 1996. *Roman Theater and Society*. Ann Arbor.

Slater, W. J. 2000. "Handouts at Dinner," *Phoenix* 54: 107–22.

Slater, W. J. 2002. "Mime Problems: Cicero *ad Fam.* 7.1 and Martial 9.38," *Phoenix* 56: 315–29.

Slater, W. J. 2005. "Mimes and Mancipes," *Phoenix* 59: 316–23.

Small, J. P. 2003. *The Parallel World of Classical Art and Text*. Cambridge.

Small, J. P. 2005. "Pictures of Tragedy?" in Gregory 2005: 103–18.

Smallwood, V. and Woodford, S. 2003. *Corpus Vasorum Antiquorum. Great Britain. Fasc. 20, The British Museum. Fasc. 10, Fragments from Sir William Hamilton's Second Collection of Vases recovered from the Wreck of HMS Colossus*. London.

Sommerstein, A. H. 1989. *Aeschylus Eumenides*. Cambridge.

Sommerstein, A. H. 1995. "The Language of Athenian Women," in Martino and Sommerstein 1995: 61–85.

Sommerstein, A. H., Halliwell, S., Henderson, J. and Zimmermann, B., eds. 1993. *Tragedy, Comedy and the Polis: Papers from the Greek Drama Conference (Nottingham 18–20 July 1990)*. Bari.

Sparkes, B. A. 1975. "Illustrating Aristophanes," *JHS* 95: 122–35.

Stanford, W. B. 1937–8. "Traces of Sicilian Influence in Aeschylus," *Proceedings of the Royal Irish Academy* 64 C: 229–40.

Starks, J. H. 2008. "Pantomime Actresses in Latin Inscriptions," in Hall and Wyles 2008: 157–68.

Starr, C. 1991. *A History of the Ancient World*. 4th ed. Oxford.

Stefani, G. 2000. "Mosaici sconosciuti dall'Area Vesuviana," in F. Guidobaldi & A. Paribeni eds., *Atti del VI Colloquio dell'Associazione Italiana per lo Studio e la Conservazione del Mosaico*. Ravenna. 279–90.

Stefani, G., ed. 2003. *Menander: La Casa del Menandro di Pompei*. Milan.

Stefanou, D. 1996. "Die Menander-Mosaiken von Mytilene: Ein paganes Glaubens-bekenntnis? Bemerkungen zur Deutung der Trikliniumsmosaiken im 'Haus des Menander' in Mytilene/ Lesbos duch L. Berczelly," *Boreas* 19: 221–7.

Steinhart, M. 2004. *Die Kunst der Nachahmung*. Mainz.

Steinhauer, G. 2001. *Το Αρχαιολογικό Μουσείο Πειραιώς*. Athens.

Stephanis, I. E. 1988. Διονυσιακοὶ Τεχνῖται. Herakleion.

Stevens, P. T. 1937. "Colloquial Expressions in Euripides," *CQ* 31: 182–91.

Stevens, P. T. 1945. "Colloquial Expressions in Aeschylus and Sophocles," *CQ* 39: 95–105.

Stevens, P. T. 1976. *Colloquial Expressions in Euripides*. Wiesbaden.

Stillwell, R., ed. 1941. *Antioch-On-The-Orontes III*. Princeton.

Storey, I. C. 2003. *Eupolis Poet of Old Comedy*. Oxford.

Storey, I. C. 2005. "But Comedy has Satyrs Too," in Harrison 2005: 201–18.

Stroh, W. 2008. "Staging Seneca: The Production of Troas as a Philological Experiment," in Fitch 2008: 195–220.

Stucchi, S. 1975. *Architettura cirenaica*. Rome.

Studniczka, F. von, 1918. "Das Bildnis Menanders," *Neue Jahrbücher für das klassische Altertum* 41: 1–31 [reprinted in K. Fittschen, ed. 1988, *Griechische Porträts*. Darmstadt. 185–219].

Summa, D. 2004. "Una dedica coregica inedita," *ZPE* 150: 147–8.

Summa, D. 2006. "Attori e choreghi in Attica: Iscrizioni dal teatro di Thorikos," *ZPE* 157: 77–86.

Suspène, A. 2004. "Les ordres supérieurs sur la scène et dans l'arène de la fin de la République aux Flaviens: le sens politique d'une passion pour les spectacles," in Hugoniot, Hurlet and Milanezi 2004: 327–52.

Sutton, D. F. 1987. "The Theatrical Families of Athens," *AJP* 108: 9–26.

Taillardat, J. 1962. *Les Images d'Aristophane*. Paris.

Taplin, O. 1977. *The Stagecraft of Aeschylus*. Oxford.

Taplin, O. 1987. "Phallology, Phlyakes, Iconography and Aristophanes," *PCPS* 33: 92–104.

Taplin, O. 1993. *Comic Angels and other Approaches to Greek Drama through Vase-Paintings*. Oxford.

Taplin, O. 1997. "The Pictorial Record," in P. E. Easterling, ed., *The Cambridge Companion to Greek Tragedy*. Cambridge. 69–90.

Taplin, O. 1999. "Spreading the Word through Performance," in Goldhill and Osborne 1999: 33–57.

Taplin, O. 2006. "Aeschylus' *Persai* – the Entry of Tragedy into the Celebratory Culture of the 470s?," in F. Cairns and V. Liapis, eds., *Dionysalexandros, Essays for A. Garvie*. Swansea. 1–10.

Taplin, O. 2007. "A New Pair of Pairs," in J. Elsner, H. Foley, S. Goldhill, E. Hall, C. Kraus, eds., *Visualizing the Tragic: Essays for Froma Zeitlin*. Oxford. 177–96.

Taplin, O. and Wyles, R. eds., forthcoming. *Pronomos, his Vase and its World*. Oxford.

Tedeschi, G. 2003. "Lo spettacolo in età imperiale e tardo antica nella documentazione epigrafica e papirologica," *Papirologica Lupensia* 1: 87–187.

Telò, M. 2007. *Eupolidis Demi*. Florence.

Telò, M., and Porciani, L. 2002. "Un'alternativa per la datazione dei *Demi* di Eupoli," *QUCC* 72: 23–40.

Theocharidis, G. C. 1940. *Beiträge zur Geschichte des byzantinischen Profantheaters im IV. und V. Jahrhundert, hauptsächlich auf Grund der Predigten des Johannes Chrysostomos, Partriarchen von Konstantinopel.* Thessaloniki.

Thiercy, P. and Menu, M. eds., 1997. *Aristophane: La langue, la scène, la cité.* Bari.

Thompson, H. A. 1950. "Excavations in the Athenian Agora, 1949," *Hesperia* 19: 313–37.

Thuillier, J. P. 1985. *Les jeux athlétiques dans la civilisation étrusque.* Rome.

Todisco, L., ed. 2002. *Teatro e Spettacolo in Magna Grecia e in Sicilia.* Milan.

Todisco, L., ed. 2003. *La ceramica figurata a soggetto tragico in Magna Grecia e in Sicilia,* Archaeologica 140. Rome.

Todisco, L. 2006. *Pittura e ceramica figurata tra Grecia, Magna Grecia e Sicilia.* Bari.

Travlos, J. 1988. *Bildlexikon zur Topographie des antiken Attika.* Tübingen.

Trendall, A. D. 1988. "Masks on Apulian Red-Figured Vases," in Betts, Hooker, and Green 1988: 137–154.

Trendall, A. D. 1990. "Two Bell-Kraters in Melbourne by the Tarporley Painter," in Descoeudres 1990: 211–15.

Trendall, A. D. 1991. "Farce and Tragedy in South Italian Vase-Painting," in T. Rasmussen and N. Spivey, eds., *Looking at Greek Vases.* Cambridge. 151–82.

Tsirvakos, E. 1975. "Ἀρχαιότητες καὶ Μνημεῖα Νησῶν Αἰγαίου," *ADelt* 30 B2: 314.

Turner, E. 1984. "Ptolemaic Egypt," *CAH* 7.1, *The Hellenistic World.* Cambridge. 118–74.

Tzachou-Alexandri, O. 1999. "The Original Plan of the Greek Theater Reconsidered: The Theater of Euonymon of Attica," in R. F. Docter and E. M. Moormann, eds., *Proceedings of the XVth International Congress of Classical Archaeology, Amsterdam, July 12–17, 1998.* Amsterdam. 420–3.

Vanaria, M. G. 2001. "Il gruppo fittile dello scavo XXXIId," in L. Bernabò Brea, M. Cavalier and F. Villard, *Meligunìs-Lipára XI.2. Gli scavi nella necropoli greca e romana di Lipari nell'area del terreno vescovile.* Palermo. 759–61.

Vandlik, K. 2002. "Phrynis," *Bulletin du Musée Hongrois des Beaux-Arts* 97: 21–32.

Vandoni, M. 1964. *Feste pubbliche e private nei documenti greci.* Milan.

van Straten, F. T. 1995. *Hiera Kala.* Leiden.

Vatin, C. 2004. *Ariane et Dionysos.* Paris.

Vetta, M. 1995. "La voce degi attori nel teatro attico," in Martino and Sommerstein 1995: 61–78.

Vierneisel, K., and Scholl, A. 2002. "Reliefdenkmäler dramatischer Choregen im klassischen Athen – Das Münchner Maskenrelief für Artemis und Dionysos," *MüJb* 53: 7–55.

Voutiras, E. 1991/2. "Παίδων Χορός," *Egnatia* 3: 39–55.

Wallace, R. W. 1997. "Poet, public, and 'theatrocracy:' audience performance in classical Athens," in L. Edmunds and R. W. Wallace, eds., *Poet, Public and Performance in Ancient Greece.* Baltimore and London: 97–111.

Wallace-Hadrill, A. 1994. *Houses and Society in Pompeii and Herculaneum.* Princeton.

Webster, T. B. L. 1948. "South Italian Vases and Attic Drama," *CQ* 42: 15–27.

Webster, T. B. L. 1956. *Greek Theatre Production*. London.

Webster, T. B. L. 1969. *Monuments Illustrating New Comedy*. 2nd ed. *BICS* Suppl. 24. London.

Webster, T. B. L. 1970. *Sophocles Philoctetes*. Cambridge.

Webster, T. B. L. 1971. Review of Charitonidis *et al.* 1970, *JHS* 91: 210–1.

Weitzmann, K. 1970. *Illustrations in Roll and Codex: A Study of the Origin and Method of Text Illustration*. 2nd ed. Princeton.

Welsh, D. 1983. "IG II/2 2343, Philonides and Aristophanes' Banqueters," *CQ* 33: 51–5.

Wessely, C. 1905. "Ein Altersindizium in Philogelos," *SBWien* 149.5.

Wessely, C. 1969. *Studien zur Palaeographie und Papyruskunde* vol. 20, *Catalogus Papyrorum Raineri. Series Graeca. Pars 1*. Amsterdam.

West, M. L. 1990. "Colloquialism and Naïve Style in Aeschylus," in Craik 1990: 3–12.

Westermann, W. L. 1932. "Entertainments in the Villages of Greco-Roman Egypt," *JEA* 18: 16–27.

Whitehead, D. 1986. *The Demes of Attica 508/7 – ca. 250 BC*. Princeton.

Wiedemann, T. E. J. 1992. *Emperors and Gladiators*. London.

Wiegand, A. 1997. *Das Theater von Solunt*. Mainz.

Wilcken, U. 1921. "Alexander der Grosse und die hellenistische Wirtschaft," *Schmollers Jahrbuch* 45: 349–420.

Wiles, D. 1997. *Tragedy in Athens: Performance Space and Theatrical Meaning*. Cambridge.

Willi, A. 2002a. "Languages on Stage: Aristophanic Language, Cultural History, and Athenian Identity," in Willi 2002b: 111–50.

Willi, A., ed. 2002b. *The Language of Greek Comedy*. Oxford.

Willi, A. 2003. *The Languages of Aristophanes: Aspects of Linguistic Variation in Classical Attic Greek*. Oxford.

Williams, R. 1976. *Keywords: A Vocabulary of Culture and Society*. London.

Williams, R. 1977. "Lecture on Realism," *Screen* 18: 61–74.

Wilson, N. G. 1999. "Travelling Actors in the Fifth Century?" *CQ* 49: 625.

Wilson, P. 1996. "The Use of Tragedy and the Tragic in the Fourth Century," in M.S. Silk, ed., *Tragedy and the Tragic: Greek Theatre and Beyond*. Oxford. 310–31.

Wilson, P. 1997. "Amymon of Sikyon: A First Victory in Athens and a First Tragic Khoregic Dedication in the City? (*SEG* 23.103b)," *ZPE* 118: 174–8.

Wilson, P. 2000. *The Athenian Institution of the Khoregia*. Cambridge.

Wilson, P. 2007a. "*Nike's* Cosmetics: Dramatic Victory, the End of Comedy and Beyond," in C. Kraus, *et al.*, eds., *Visualizing the Tragic: Drama, Myth and Ritual in Greek Art and Literature*. Oxford. 257–87.

Wilson, P., ed. 2007b. *The Greek Theatre and Festivals*. Oxford.

Wilson, P. 2007c. "Sicilian Choruses," in Wilson 2007b: 351–77.

Wilson, P. 2007d. "Choruses for Sale in Thorikos? A Speculative Note on *SEG* 34, 107," *ZPE* 161: 125–34.

Wilson, P. 2008. "Costing the Dionysia," in Revermann and Wilson 2008: 88–127.

Wilson, P. forthcoming. "Pronomos, the Man and the Music," in Taplin and Wyles, eds., forthcoming.

Wilson, P. and Csapo, E. 2009. "The End of the Khoregia in Athens: A Forgotten Document," in M.C. Martinelli, ed. *La Musa Dimenticata: Aspetti dell'esperienza musicale greca in età ellenistica*. Seminari e Convegni 18. Pisa. 47–74.

Winkler, J. J. and Zeitlin, F. I., eds. 1989. *Nothing to do with Dionysos?* Princeton.

Wiseman, T. P. 1985. *Catullus and his World.* Cambridge

Wiseman, T. P. 2000. "Liber: myth, drama and ideology in Republican Rome," in C. Bruun, ed., *The Roman Middle Republic: Politics, religion and historiography c. 400–133 BC.* [=Act Instituti Romani Finlandiae 23], Rome. 265–99.

Wood, E. M. 1996. "Demos versus 'We the People:' Freedom and Democracy, Ancient and Modern," in Ober and Hedrick 1996: 121–37.

Zacharia, K. 2003. "Sophocles and the West: The Evidence of the Fragments," in A. H. Sommerstein, ed., *Shards from Kolonos: Studies in Sophoclean Fragments.* Bari. 57–76.

Zangrando, V. 1997. "A proposito della dimensione colloquiale nella litteratura greca," *SFIC* 15: 188–207.

Zarmakoupi, M. 2007. *Villae Expolitae: Aspects of the Architecture and Culture of Roman Country Houses on the Bay of Naples.* DPhil. Diss. Oxford.

Zwierlein, O. 1966. *Die Rezitationsdramas Senecas.* Meisenheim am Glan.

Index

Page numbers followed by n refer to notes on that page.

Achaeus 92–3, 101
acting 31, 47, 55, 69–70, 74–6, 88,
    117–35
  illusionism in 47, 73
  mimicry 126–9
  realism in 69, 117–35
  see also actors; realism
actor(s) 10, 12, 14, 21, 22, 31, 86–9, 94,
    98, 101, 103–7, 117–20, 121, 125,
    126–9, 144, 148, 149, 156, 158,
    169, 172–8, 179, 182–5, 187,
    189–91, 192–5
  cost of 155, 183–5
  cultivation of 172–8, 190–1, 192, 195
  depictions of 10, 12, 14–15, 19, 21, 22,
    23–9, 30–1, 42–70, 73, 75, 148,
    149, 153
  fines for non-appearance 86–7, 174
  gifts to 86–7, 170, 174, 191
  income of 87, 106, 128–9, 185, 189
  latest 144, 154, 158
  manumission of 182, 184, 190
  ownership of 156, 182–5, 190–1
  organizations of 106–7, 126, 174;
    see also actor(s), trade unions of;
    fan clubs; theatrical families
  political power of 87, 173, 178,
    189–91, 194–5
  prize 21, 87, 89n, 105, 126
  professionalization of 83–107

  rental of 184–5, 190
  selection of 89
  star system 84, 87, 89, 104–5, 129,
    146, 173, 177, 189, 192; see also
    fan clubs
  trade unions of 107, 174, 177–8, 192
  training of 88, 126, 156, 182, 183–4
  traveling 103–4, 172–4, 192–3
  war booty 179
  see also Aeschines; Archias;
    Aristodemos; Athenodorus;
    Claudius Aesopus; Diphilus;
    Kallippides; Kanoutios;
    Kleandros; Lykon; Mynniskos;
    Neoptolemos; Nikostratos;
    Parmenon; Polos; Roscius;
    Satyros; Theodoros
adoration 14–22, 148
  see also choregic dedication(s),
    imagery; monoposiast; votive(s)
aedile 169, 179–81, 189, 191
Aegean islands 86, 94, 100–1, 102, 104,
    122, 149, 151, 156, 170, 192
  see also Mytilene
Aemilius Paullus 174, 179, 192
Aeschines 87, 94, 177
Aeschylus 6, 39–40, 45, 67, 75, 85,
    88, 96–7, 117, 120–4, 129–31,
    171, 172
Agathocles 176

Agathon 16n, 99–100, 127, 172
Agesilaus 104–5, 120
agonothete 169, 170, 181
Alcibiades 131, 192
Alexander 86, 87, 103, 172–8, 190, 192
Alexander Severus 183
Alexis 86, 98, 131n
Amyntas 99, 172
Anastasius 159–60
    see also diptychs
Anicius Gallus 179
Anthesteria (at Athens) 23–4, 31, 55
    see also choes
Antioch 140, 144–5, 148, 153–4, 156,
        158, 168, 178
Antiochus II 178
Antiochus III the Great 179
Antiochus IV Epiphanes 178
Antony 182–4, 192–3
Apollonius 155, 178
Archelaus 99, 172, 173
Archias 86, 98
Ariphron 93
aristocracy 11n, 83, 119, 122, 134–5,
        168–96
    see also democracy; oligarchy; tyranny
Aristodemos 86, 87, 94, 98
Aristophanes 2, 12, 16, 38, 39, 55–61, 66,
        67, 76, 88, 90–1, 93, 99, 105, 119,
        120–4, 127–31, 133–4, 170–1, 172
Aristotle 40, 88, 91, 93, 98, 99, 117–19,
        124–5, 128, 133, 172
art see acting; actor(s), depictions of;
        choregic dedication(s), imagery;
        copy tradition; costume;
        figurines; funerary art; masks;
        mosaic; painting; realism; reliefs;
        sculpture; vasepainting
Artavasdes II 178
Asia Minor 86, 101, 102, 170, 181, 193
Asteas 61–4
Athenaeus 147, 187
Athenodorus 87, 174
Atticus 182, 183, 186

audience 26–7, 47, 83, 106, 119,
        120–3, 169, 181–2, 185, 186,
        189–91, 195
    see also theatron
Augustus 183, 184, 185, 186, 193
aulete see piper(s)

Black Sea 8, 24, 100, 101
bribery (ambitus) 179, 181
    see also lex Calpurnia

Caesar 180, 190
Caligula 186, 191
cameo 151–3
canonization 39–40, 67, 150
Capodarso Painter 67–70
Carcinus 40, 88
Central Greece (excluding Attica) 86,
        99–100, 102, 104, 130, 171, 179,
        181–2, 192
choes (sing. chous) 14, 15, 23–8, 31, 75
choregic dedication(s) 13–23, 29, 30–1,
        43–4, 90–5, 105, 148
    imagery 13–23, 43–4, 75–6, 148, 153;
        see also adoration; monoposiast;
        victory, imagery
    chariots 17, 27–8, 193
    Eros (and related figures) 20, 21,
        23, 43–4
    garlands 15, 23, 26, 43–4
    ribbons 23, 26, 43, 148
    tripods 16, 19, 23
    see also votive(s)
choregos 13, 16–17, 19, 20, 21, 24, 28,
        30, 75–6, 90–5, 97, 101, 105,
        106–7, 148, 169, 177
    joint-choregoi (synchoregoi) 90–1, 93
chorodidaskalos see chorus trainer
chorus 2, 5, 6–23, 27, 30–1, 42, 43–4, 47,
        52, 65, 70, 73, 74–6, 88, 89, 91, 97,
        100, 105, 106–7, 120, 127, 130,
        148, 153
    see also dithyramb; genre scenes;
        satyrplay

chorus trainer (didaskalos, director or chorodidaskalos) 13, 19–21, 30, 88, 90–5, 105, 106
Cicero 147, 179, 181, 182, 183, 184, 188, 189, 190–1, 193
circular chorus see dithyramb
class see social class
classicism 39, 67, 144, 149–53, 183, 187–8
    see also copy tradition
Claudius Aesopus 191
clubs 144n, 155
    see also fan clubs
comedy passim, see Aristophanes; Cratinus; Deinolochus; Ecphantides; Ephippus; Epicharmus; Eupolis; Menander; Nicostratos; Phormis; Plautus; Strattis; Terence
    Megarian 39, 85, 99
Constantinople 158
consul 158, 163, 179, 180, 193
copy tradition (in plastic arts) 143, 145, 149–53, 156–61
costume 5, 6–8, 9–11, 14–15, 17, 19–22, 24–9, 41, 47, 49–51, 53–8, 59–61, 61–2, 65, 66, 68–9, 71, 98, 123, 125, 131–3, 144, 146, 148, 156, 158–62, 188, 193
    see also masks
Cratinus 39, 92, 171
Cyprus 101, 102
Cyrene 101, 102, 130

dancers 154–6, 171, 173, 181, 185, 188, 192
    see also mime(s); pantomime(s)
Daphne see Antioch
Demetrius of Phaleron 135
democracy 2n, 83, 114, 119–24, 129, 130n, 134, 171, 173, 174–5, 177, 189, 193
    see also aristocracy; oligarchy; tyranny
Demosthenes 87, 94, 103

Deinolochus 97
Dicaeogenes 93
didaskalos see chorus trainer; poets
dinner parties see symposium
Dio Cassius 195
Dio Chrysostom 189
Dionysia (at Athens)
    City 13, 28–9, 31, 40, 74, 83, 86–95, 97, 104, 105, 126, 174
    pompe 24
    prizes 13, 16, 21, 23, 40, 61, 84, 105
    Rural 89–95, 105–6
Dionysius 86, 171, 172, 173
Dionysus 5, 11–12, 14–16, 19–22, 23, 26, 28–9, 42–4, 53, 60–1, 70, 84, 120–3, 148, 153, 170, 177, 193
    god of mysteries and afterlife 22–3, 44, 60, 148; see also funerary art
    god of theater 14–16, 19–22, 30, 84, 132n, 148, 170
    sanctuary of 14, 16, 19, 22, 95, 148–9, 170
    Theater of (Athens) 83, 88
    see also Anthesteria; Dionysia; ritual
Dioskourides 9
    see also mosaic
Diphilus 190–1
diptychs 158–61
dithyramb 11–12, 13, 16, 23, 27, 43, 90, 93, 94, 95, 100, 101
Domitian 181, 186
Dura Europos 182n, 185
Duris 192

Ecphantides 92, 99
education see schools
Egypt 102, 130, 155–6, 177–8
    see also Ptolemy
Ephippus 171–3
Epicharmus 39–40, 75, 97
Epicurus 147
epinikia 16–17, 148
Eumenides Painter 45
Eupolis 28, 38, 39, 62–4, 73, 99

Euripides 3–5, 39, 55–6, 65, 66, 67, 85,
    88, 91, 93, 97–8, 99–100, 101,
    119, 120–5, 128–34, 143, 147,
    153, 171–2, 177, 178, 187

fan clubs 184, 189
    see also clubs
Fasti 91, 105, 106
festivals 13, 21, 31, 40, 47, 55, 62, 86, 87,
    97, 100, 101, 103, 105–7, 172,
    173, 177
    occasional 86, 87, 100, 173, 179;
        see also munera
    see also Anthesteria; Dionysia; Lenaea
figurines 29, 31, 53, 72, 74, 101–2, 105,
    151, 153, 177
Flaminius 180
Fulvius Nobilior 179
funerary art 22–3, 44, 148
    see also Dionysus, god of mysteries
        and afterlife

Gaius see Caligula
Gellius 156, 187
genre scenes 2, 17–22, 42–3, 96
gift economy 107, 169–70, 176–96
gladiators 150, 170, 179, 180, 181, 191
Glykera 144–6
Greece see Aegean islands; Central
        Greece; Ionian islands; Macedon;
        North Aegean; Peloponnese

Hadrian 154, 186, 187, 190
Hellenization 38–40, 173, 179, 182–4
Heracles 17, 21, 27, 48, 59–61, 74, 121
Herculaneum 149
Hermes 15–17
Herod the Great 185
Hieron 82n, 96, 172, 173
Homer 2, 94, 118–19, 143, 153, 155, 178
Hyrodes II (Orodes) 178

idealism 124–6, 134
Ionian islands 103

Italy 38–76, 86, 96–9, 102, 104, 173,
    190, 193
    see also Herculaneum; Pompeii; Rome;
        Sicily; Taranto; vasepainting,
        West Greek

John Chrysostom 168
Juba 183
judges 16, 26, 97, 99, 105

Kallippides 96, 104–5, 117–20, 121,
    133–4, 192
Kanoutios 190
Kleandros 101, 103–4

lector (reader) 156, 168, 183, 186–7
Lenaea (at Athens) 86, 88, 90, 91, 92, 98,
    105, 126n
Leningrad Painter 5–6
lex Calpurnia 180–1
Libanius 154
literacy 15
Lucullus 184, 192–3
Lykon 86, 87, 174
Lycurgus 23–4, 86
Lysander 171

Macedon 86, 99, 102, 146, 172–6,
    179–82, 192
    see also Alexander; Amyntas;
        Archelaus; Philip
Maecenas 183
magicians 173, 189, 192
Manlius Vulso 179
Marcus Aurelius 184
Marius 183–4, 191
masks 5, 6, 7, 11, 14, 17, 19, 20, 23, 27,
    28, 29, 42–4, 47, 49–51, 52, 54, 57,
    59, 61–2, 66, 68–9, 74, 95, 98, 99,
    106, 126, 131–3, 140, 141, 144,
    146, 148, 149, 154, 158–60
    see also choregic dedication(s);
        costume
Mausolus 86

McDaniel Painter 49–51, 52
Menander 9, 127–9, 131–4, 140–61, 187
mime(s) 26, 146–7, 149–50, 155–6,
        158, 168, 171, 172, 173, 175, 178,
        181, 182–5, 186–7, 188–9, 190,
        192–3, 194
    philosophical 147
mimesis 2, 118–19
    see also acting; art; costume; mask;
        music; painting; sculpture; realism
monoposiast 14–15, 19–22, 43–4, 148
    see also choregic dedication(s),
        imagery; votive(s)
mosaic 9, 133, 143–58
munera 179–80, 184, 189, 190
munificence see gift economy
Murena 179, 181, 189, 193
music 5, 14–15, 16, 26, 52, 61–3, 89, 104,
        106, 130, 154, 158, 175, 179, 181,
        183, 185, 186, 187, 192–3
    see also New Music; piper(s); Phrynis;
        Pronomos
Mynniskos 101, 117–18, 121
myth 1–5, 17, 20–2, 26, 30, 41, 44–5, 52,
        69, 73, 96, 97, 119, 123, 171, 188
mythicization of narrative 1–31, 42–5,
        52, 70–6
    see also realism
Mytilene 61, 101, 133, 140–63

Neoptolemos 86, 87
Nero 180, 181, 184, 186, 191
New Music 61–3, 85, 104, 130
Nikostratos (actor) 104, 119n
Nikostratos (poet) 93
North Aegean 86, 102

oligarchy 122–3
    see also aristocracy; democracy;
        tyranny
orchestra 7, 26, 46–7, 52, 82

Painter of the Perseus Dance 25–7,
        47, 73

painting 151, 153
    free standing 14, 22, 23, 72, 90, 151
    fresco 147, 148
    scene painting
    see also choregic dedication(s);
        vasepainting
Pan Painter 15–16, 27
pantomime(s) 26, 146–7, 149–50, 155,
        168, 177, 181, 182–4, 186, 187,
        188, 189, 194–5
Parmenon 127
Peloponnese 89, 100, 102, 104, 120, 192
performance realism see realism;
        mythicization of narrative
Persia 173, 175–6
Philip 86, 87, 172–7, 190, 192
Phormis 39, 97
Phrynichus 6, 40, 97, 172
Phrynis 61–3
pinakes see choregic dedication(s);
        painting; reliefs
Pindar 27
piper(s) 5, 6, 8–9, 10, 11–12, 13, 19, 21,
        24, 30, 75, 88–9, 94, 95, 100, 105,
        106, 155, 171, 182, 189, 192, 193
    selection of 88
    see also Pronomos
Plato 16n, 95, 98–9, 119, 128, 140–1,
        147, 157, 187
Plautus 53, 131n, 182
Pliny (Elder) 125, 186, 187
Pliny (Younger) 146, 156, 184, 187–8
Plutarch 23, 86, 96, 97, 131, 147, 173,
        178, 183, 187, 188, 190, 192
poets 17, 21, 22–3, 43, 47, 75, 84, 85–6,
        88–9, 90–3, 105, 106–7, 120–6,
        143, 148, 149, 155, 168, 172–3,
        178, 187, 191
    depictions of 20–1, 22–3, 26, 43–4, 47,
        61, 74–5
    non-Athenian origins 85–6, 98
    payment for 84, 100, 105, 155
    see also Aeschylus; Achaeus; Agathon;
        Ariphron; Aristophanes; Cratinus;

poets (*Cont'd*)
    Deinolochus; Dicaeogenes;
    Dionysius; Ecphantides;
    Ephippus; Epicharmus; Eupolis;
    Euripides; Menander; Nikostratos;
    Phormis; Phrynichus; Pindar;
    Plautus; Ptolemy IV; Simonides;
    Sophocles; Strattis; Terence;
    theatrical families; Timotheus
Polos 86, 87, 189
Pompeii 140, 143n, 149, 151, 153–4, 157,
    184, 186, 189
Pompey 190–1
praetor 179–81, 186
privatization of drama 144–63, 168–96
Pronomos 12, 20–21
Pronomos Painter 19–22, 30, 42, 43–4,
    72, 74, 106, 148
Ptolemy I Soter 177
Ptolemy II Philadelphus 155, 177–8
Ptolemy IV Philopator 178
Ptolemy V Epiphanes 178
Ptolemy XII Auletes 178
Pyronides 62–4

reader *see* lector
realism 1–31, 40–76, 117–35
    acting 69, 117–35
    plastic arts 1–31, 40–76
    see also actor(s), depictions of; acting;
        genre scenes; idealism
reliefs 13–15, 17, 19, 20, 22, 74, 90, 106,
    147, 148, 149, 151
ritual 5–6, 11–12, 17, 23–4, 27, 45, 57,
    100, 132n, 171, 185, 193, 195
    see also epinikia
Rome 53, 146, 158, 163, 169, 170,
    179–96
Roscius 182, 184

satyr(s) 5–6, 11, 20, 29, 42, 44, 72, 130,
    148, 153, 193
    see also satyrplay
Satyros 86

satyrplay 5–6, 10–11, 17, 19–22, 31, 42,
    72, 73, 75, 92, 105, 106, 130, 149,
    153, 177
    see also satyr(s)
scene specificity 47–8, 66
Schiller Painter 53–8, 60, 64, 85
schools 143, 153, 154, 170, 188
sculpture 22, 23, 29, 72, 90, 147, 148, 154
    see also choregic dedications; reliefs
Seneca (Elder) 180, 186
Seneca (Younger) 168, 194
Sicily 39–41, 67–8, 75–6, 85, 86, 96–9,
    102, 103, 173, 176
    see also vasepainting, West Greek
Simonides 27, 96, 171
social class 30–1, 75–6, 88–9, 91,
    104–7, 118–35, 153–6, 161–3,
    169–96
Socrates 147
Sophocles 39, 67, 69–70, 88, 90–1, 92–3,
    96, 119, 120, 121, 124–5, 128–31,
    143, 153
Spain 102, 180, 186
sport 2, 17, 27, 84, 150, 161–3
stage 26, 46–7, 51–2, 67–8, 73, 98, 146,
    148, 149, 154, 186–7
Strattis 105
Sulla 183, 190, 192–3
symposium 2, 16, 20, 23, 31, 43, 75,
    146–9, 169, 170–7, 187–8
    see also monoposiast; victory,
        celebration
synchoregoi see choregos, joint-choregoi

Tacitus 170, 193
Taranto (Tarentum) 41–61, 98
Tarporley Painter 40–52, 53, 66, 67, 72,
    73, 75
Technitai *see* actor(s), trade unions of
Telephanes 94
Telephus 3–5, 55–8, 65, 66, 92, 119
Terence 53, 161–3, 182
theater
    in art 1–31, 38–76, 148

buildings 85, 86, 89, 95–102, 141, 181,
    186, 192; *see also orchestra*; stage;
    theatron
demise of 143–4, 147–63, 170, 187
finance 83, 89, 155, 170, 177; *see also*
    actor(s); choregos; theatrical
    families
geographical spread of 41, 45, 48–52,
    58, 66–7, 83–107, 129
see also privatization of drama
theater realism in art *see* realism
theatrical families 88
theatron 47
    see also audience; theater
Theodoros 87, 94, 106, 128, 171–2
Tiberius 170, 184
Tigranes 192
Timotheus 40, 92–3, 172
Totenmahl *see* monoposiast
tragedy *passim*, *see* Achaeus; Aeschylus;
    Agathon; Carcinus; Dicaeogenes;
    Dionysius; Euripides;
    Phrynichus; Ptolemy IV;
    Nikostratos; Sophocles
Trajan 146, 188, 194, 195
Tubero 180, 182
tyranny 119n, 83, 100, 114, 172
    see also Agathocles; Archelaus;
    aristocracy; democracy; Dionysius;
    Hieron; Mausolus; oligarchy

Ummidia Quadratilla 184

vasepainting 1–31, 38–76, 96, 101, 148
    Attic 1–31, 40–52, 65, 66, 70–6, 105,
        106, 148
    Boeotian 100
    West Greek 1, 3, 4, 26, 38–76, 85, 148
        Apulian 41–61, 67, 98
        Campanian 42
        Lucanian 41, 98
        Paestan 42, 43, 45, 61–4
        Sicilian 42, 67–70, 97–8
    see also Asteas; Capodarso Painter;
        genre scenes; Leningrad Painter;
        McDaniel Painter; Painter
        of the Perseus Dance; Pan
        Painter; Pronomos Painter;
        Schiller Painter; Tarporley
        Painter
victory
    celebration 13, 16, 17, 44, 148–9, 153,
        179, 180, 192; *see also epinikia*
    imagery 13–23, 27–8, 43–4, 75, 148–9,
        153, 193; *see also* choregic
        dedications, imagery
    personified 17, 23, 27–8, 43–4
votive(s) 30
    see also choregic dedications

wild beasts 150, 158, 179, 188

Xenophon 94, 100, 105, 171, 175

Zeugma 143n, 153, 156